# Urban Sprawl

Edited by Gregory D. Squires

# Urban Sprawl

## CAUSES, CONSEQUENCES & POLICY RESPONSES

THE URBAN INSTITUTE PRESS
Washington, D.C.

**THE URBAN INSTITUTE PRESS**
2100 M Street, N.W.
Washington, DC 20037

Library of Congress Cataloging in Publication Data

Urban sprawl : causes, consequences, and policy responses / edited by Gregory D. Squires.
    p. cm.
Includes bibliographical references and index.
    ISBN 0-87766-709-8 (pbk. : alk. paper)
    1. Cities and towns—United States—Growth. 2. Urban Policy—United States—Case studies. I. Squires, Gregory D.
    HT384.U5 U77 2002

                                                                2002002535

ISBN 0-87766-709-8 (paper, alk. paper)

Printed in the United States of America

# Contents

# Acknowledgments

This book reflects the collaborative efforts of many individuals and organizations. I would like to thank the Annie E. Casey Foundation for the financial support it provided for this project. In addition, my sincere appreciation goes to the sociology departments at the University of Wisconsin-Milwaukee and George Washington University for the encouragement they have provided me over the years.

This book, of course, is the product of the knowledge and hard work of the contributors. I want to thank each of them for their enthusiasm and cooperation throughout this effort. And all of us want to express our appreciation to the many individuals and organizations around the country striving to improve the lives of low-income and working families and make our communities better places for all of us.

# Urban Sprawl and the Uneven Development of Metropolitan America

Gregory D. Squires

"If you people can't afford to live in our town, then you'll just have to leave."
Bill Haines, Mayor of Mt. Laurel, New Jersey, 1970
(Kirp, Dwyer, and Rosenthal 1995, 2)

"Urban sprawl is public enemy No. 1."
Suburban Milwaukee resident (Lorenzen 2000, 13A)

One fall afternoon in 1999, two soccer moms played cat-and-mouse games during the homebound rush hour on the increasingly congested Interstate 65 outside of Birmingham, Alabama. After tailgating, lane changing, and brake slamming over four miles of expressway, they came to a red light. Gena Foster jumped out of her sport-utility vehicle and approached Shirley Henson in her Toyota 4Runner. Henson grabbed her .38 caliber revolver, lowered her window, and shot Foster to death. In recent years, traffic has doubled on this stretch of highway, which remains just two lanes each way, as the pace of sprawl outgrows Shelby County's ability to expand the local infrastructure. Heightened "road rage" is just one of the costs.

Nationwide, the American Automobile Association's Foundation for Traffic Safety reported an increase of road rage incidents of nearly 60 percent between 1991 and 1996 resulting in 28,000 deaths annually during these years. Increasing traffic congestion and the accompanying stress that are associated with urban and suburban sprawl reflect the social costs of the nation's emerging patterns of metropolitan development

(Putnam 2000: 142–143; Sipress 1999). The social impact of uneven spatial development in urban America, however, is not a new story.

Uneven development has long been the preeminent feature of urban and metropolitan growth in the United States. In recent years, the word "sprawl" has crept into the vocabulary of scholars, public officials, and community organization leaders who are wrestling with diverse challenges posed by urban life (Galster et al. 2000). Anthony Downs, long one of the nation's most distinguished students of the city, concluded, "Suburban sprawl has been the dominant form of metropolitan-area growth in the United States for the past 50 years" (Downs 1998, 8).

The patterns of growth noted by Downs are intricately interwoven with the range of problems long associated with cities. This book examines the multifaceted causes and consequences of sprawl and uneven development generally as well as the debates over a range of proposed policy responses. It explores the many social costs attributed to sprawl as well as the benefits that some attribute to this form of development. In addition, it examines what has been learned from various efforts to counter emerging patterns of uneven development and mitigate the accompanying costs. The overriding focus of these debates remains the uneven development of the cities and suburbs that form the nation's metropolitan communities.

## Structural, Spatial, and Social Development of Metropolitan Communities

Sprawl can be defined as a pattern of urban and metropolitan growth that reflects low-density, automobile-dependent, exclusionary new development on the fringe of settled areas often surrounding a deteriorating city. Among the traits of metropolitan growth frequently associated with sprawl are unlimited outward extension of development; low-density housing and commercial development; leapfrog development, "edge cities," and more recently "edgeless cities"; fragmentation of land use planning among multiple municipalities; reliance on private automobiles for transportation; large fiscal disparities among municipalities; segregation of types of land use; race and class-based exclusionary housing and employment; congestion and environmental damage; and a declining sense of community among area residents (Downs 1999; Garreau 1991; Katz and Bradley 1999; Lang 2000; Rusk 1999). However, these spatial patterns of development are rooted in a context of substantial economic restructuring. Moreover, these spatial and structural changes exacerbate a number of social problems that have long plagued urban communities. Each of these trajectories of change, in turn, feeds back and nurtures the other.

During the past five decades, two major forms of economic restructuring have changed the face of urban communities. The loss of thousands of manufacturing jobs coupled with the growth of service positions—including high-paid producer service industries (e.g., accounting, finance, law, management, information processing) and low-wage personal services jobs (e.g., hotel and restaurant workers)—have fueled the uneven development of metropolitan areas. If the 1970s represented the decade of deindustrialization, the basic pattern persisted through the 1980s and 1990s. Between 1988 and 1998, manufacturing employment dropped from 19.3 million to 18.8 million, while those employed in services and retail trade grew from 50.5 million to 66.5 million (Bluestone and Harrison 2000, 228). Increasing globalization of the economy, whereby production is decentralized while control and administration are centralized, has furthered these trends. The growing significance of finance, information, and communication industries has exacerbated these geopolitical dimensions of economic activity (Bluestone and Harrison 1982, 2000; Harrison and Bluestone 1988; Wilson 1987, 1996, 1999; Sassen 1994). These economic shifts have stimulated the development of downtown office space, convention centers, and cultural facilities where relatively well-off professionals work and play, and the suburban communities where they tend to live. So downtown and outlying suburban development has proceeded while many urban neighborhoods and inner-ring suburbs have deteriorated.

These structural and spatial developments have, in turn, nurtured growing inequalities of income and wealth. Between the early 1970s and mid-1990s, median household income declined by 2 percent from $33,006 to $32,264. While it rose slightly in the late 1990s, it remains below the 1989 median in terms of purchasing power. Those in the bottom fifth saw their share of income drop between 1977 and 1999 from 5.7 percent to 4.2 percent while the share going to the top fifth grew from 44.2 percent to 50.4 percent. More significantly, the buying power of household income for those in the bottom 60 percent—the majority of households—declined, with the steepest declines experienced by those in the bottom fifth. Meanwhile, those in the top 1 percent experienced a 120 percent increase in their household income, from $234,700 to $515,600. During the mid-1970s, CEOs at major corporations earned 41 times the income of typical factory workers. By 1996, this ratio reached 209. The share of total wealth held by the top 1 percent grew from 33 percent in 1962 to 39 percent in 1997. Such inequalities are the highest in the industrial world (Blau 1999, 12–17; Wolff 1994, 8–10; Marshall 2000, 3–7; Johnston 1999, 14). Moreover, despite many advances in civil rights, black median family income dropped from 58.7 percent of the non-Hispanic white median in 1972 to 57.0 percent in 1998. The decline for Hispanic families was even steeper, from 70.0 percent to 57.4 percent (U.S. Census Bureau 1999, B-8, B-9). The economic expansion of the 1990s began to trickle down to those in the lower economic rungs in the last two or three years of the decade, but this has not altered the fundamental patterns that have emerged over the past quarter century (Teixeira and Rogers 2000, 57–61).

These developments feed back on each other. Households with lower incomes and the greatest economic need find housing in suburban communities, where jobs are growing fastest, increasingly difficult to afford. As jobs become more distant, it is also more difficult to participate in informal networks through which job placements are often made. This is most evident for racial minorities and particularly African Americans. As jobs and particularly those that pay a living wage become harder to find, poverty, and the concentration of poverty, increase in urban areas. Tax revenues and public services decline. As physical conditions deteriorate and resources leave the community, so-called "underclass behaviors" that are at variance with what are traditionally viewed as mainstream or middle-class norms increase. These communities become less attractive to private capital. These cycles are mutually reinforcing. Uneven economic, spatial, and social development are all interrelated pieces of the metropolitan puzzle (Jargowsky 1996; Wilson 1987, 1996; Massey and Denton 1993).

It is important to note that these developments are not inevitable, and they do not flow naturally from free market forces. Markets are real and people do make choices. However, markets operate within, and individual choices are constrained by, public policy and private sector decisionmaking. Tax policies have long favored new development in outlying communities and overseas over reinvestment in older urban facilities and communities. Demands for tax breaks from state and local governments and concessions from unions, along with the proliferation of contingent work forces, have intensified various trajectories of economic inequality. Many employers have replaced full-time workers with part-time and temporary workers, consultants, subcontractors, and other contingent workers. Two-tiered wage plans have been implemented, offering far lower wages to new entrants into the workforce than veterans performing the same tasks receive. Moreover, while the minimum wage was recently increased, corporate pressure continues to keep its value below what it was 20 years ago. Urban renewal programs destroyed many city neighborhoods in favor of downtown business development. Federally subsidized highways and mortgage loans fueled suburban development and expedited inner city decline. Exclusionary zoning laws by most suburban municipalities, racial steering by real estate agents, and redlining by financial institutions created and continue to reinforce segregated housing patterns (Orfield 1997; Holland 1986; Goldsmith and Blakely 1992; Jackson 1985; Rusk 1999; Squires 1994; Harrison and Bluestone 1988; Marshall 2000; Luria and Rogers 1999).

This confluence of intersecting forces of uneven development has framed the evolution of urban and metropolitan communities in recent decades. It is also the context within which prevailing debates over urban and suburban sprawl have emerged.

## Sprawling Patterns of Development

For decades, cities have been expanding upward and outward. Technological innovations like structural steel and elevators made high-rise buildings possible, fueling a proliferation of skylines and concentrated settlements across urban communities. Air-conditioning opened up the South to development (Contosta 1998). More dramatic has been the outward expansion of cities and metropolitan areas. The sheer numbers of people accounted for part of this growth, but the number of square miles of land that has been developed has proceeded at a far greater pace than the increase in population. Transportation technologies, including the emergence of trains and automobiles, played an important role. But the outward expansion has been driven by a number of political, economic, and social forces and has been closely associated with emerging inequalities in the distribution of wealth produced in those communities and nationwide.

Between 1950 and 1990, metropolitan areas expanded from 208,000 square miles housing 84 million people to 585,000 square miles housing 193 million. Population in these communities grew by 128 percent while the land area on which they resided grew 181 percent. Population density declined from 407 to 330 persons per square mile. Urban communities have been consuming land at a rate that is approximately 50 percent greater than the population growth (Rusk 1999, 68). In the 1990s, land consumption proceeded at twice the rate of the population increase (U.S. Department of Housing and Urban Development 2000, 40). At the same time the number of political jurisdictions within metropolitan areas increased from 193 to approximately 9,600 cities, towns, villages, townships, and counties (Rusk 1999, 67). In 1960, the nation's population was roughly one-third urban, one-third rural, and one-third suburban. By 1990, suburbanites were close to half the population (Schneider 1992, 33) and in 1992, for the first time, they accounted for a majority of the nation's voters (Dreier 2000, 7). In addition, while in recent years several downtown areas have experienced a population increase and project more in the near future (The Brookings Institution Center on Urban and Metropolitan Policy and the Fannie Mae Foundation 1998), the overwhelming continuing pattern is the exodus of households from central cities to the suburbs. In 1996 alone, 2.7 million people left a city for a suburb while just 800,000 made the opposite move (Katz and Bradley 1999, 27). Between 1970 and 2000, the suburban share of the total metropolitan population increased consistently from 55.1 percent to 62.2 percent (U.S. Department of Housing and Urban Development 2000, 63). This pattern accelerated in the 1990s relative to the previous decade. Between 1990 and 2000, the suburban population grew by 17.7 percent compared with 8.0 percent for central cities (U.S. Census Bureau 2001; Lewis Mumford Center 2001).

More significant than these demographic shifts is the growing inequality associated with the spatial developments. In 1960, per capita income in cities was 105 percent of their surrounding suburbs. By 1990, that ratio fell to 84 percent (Cisneros 1993, 25). Poverty rates rose by more than half in the nation's cities, increasing from 12.6 percent in 1970 to just over 20 percent in 1995, while rising slightly in the suburbs from 7 percent to just under 9 percent (U.S. Department of Housing and Urban Development 1997, 32, Exhibit 8). Cities tended to gain lower-income residents and lose upper-income residents, while the share of families in each income group remained virtually unchanged in the suburbs. Between 1969 and 1998, the share of families in central cities with low incomes grew from 21.9 percent to 25.5 percent while the share with high incomes declined from 18.3 percent to 16.6 percent. In the suburbs, low-income residents accounted for 14.8 percent of the total in 1969 and 14.9 percent in 1998, while high-income families accounted for 26.2 percent and 25.8 percent during these years (U.S. Department of Housing and Urban Development 2000, 22). Middle-income residents declined in central cities from 59.9 percent to 57.6 percent, while the share of middle-income residents remained virtually the same in the suburbs (U.S. Department of Housing and Urban Development 1997, 38). These income disparities reflect shifts in the number and types of jobs by region. Manufacturing and professional service jobs shifted toward suburban and downtown areas generally benefiting suburban over urban residents (Ginzberg 1993). Even during the mid-1990s, at the heart of one of the longest economic expansions in the nation's history, job growth was greater in suburban than in urban communities. A study of 92 large metropolitan areas found that 75 percent of cities lost private-sector employment market share to their suburbs (Brennan and Hill 1999, 1). Between 1992 and 1997, the share of metropolitan area jobs located in the suburbs increased from 55 percent to 57 percent, with the rate of job growth reaching 17.8 percent in the suburbs compared with 8.5 percent in cities (U.S. Department of Housing and Urban Development 2000, X, 10). While cities have made a slight comeback relative to their suburban ring on some economic measures, development patterns of recent decades have overwhelmingly favored suburban communities, and it would be premature to conclude that this basic trend has been reversed (U.S. Department of Housing and Urban Development 2000, iv).

Perhaps even more noteworthy are four concomitant trends. First, disparities between central cities along with their inner-ring suburbs and the newer outer-ring suburbs (the "favored quarter") in many metropolitan areas are growing (Orfield 1997). Second, in most metropolitan areas, incomes in central cities and suburbs have tended to move in the same direction. During the 1980s, when incomes of central cities increased, the incomes of suburban residents increased as well, but at a higher rate. When incomes of central city residents declined, so did that of neighboring suburbanites, though not to the same extent (Cisneros 1993, 23, 24; Luria and Rogers 1999, 10–11). Third, poverty has become much more concentrated. Between 1970 and 1990, the number of census tracts in which the poverty rate was 40 percent or greater and the number of people living in such tracts doubled (Jargowsky 1996, 30). Fourth, racial segregation persists as a central feature of metropolitan housing markets, particularly in those communities with large African-American populations. The 2000 census shows that a substantial number of racial minorities moved to the suburbs during the 1990s. In the nation's 100 largest cities, non-Hispanic whites constitute a majority of the population in just 52 cities, down from 70 in 1990. However, racial minorities, and particularly African Americans, remain highly segregated from white households and neighborhoods (Lewis Mumford Center 2001; Schmitt 2001). Unlike the case for other racial minorities, education and income do not affect the extent to which African Americans are segregated from whites in the nation's dual housing markets (Massey and Denton 1993; Denton 1999).

Overall, the basic pattern of urban development during the post–World War II years has been one of outward expansion. People, resources, and wealth have consistently shifted away from city centers. Moreover, this expansion has been associated with various trajectories of inequality and uneven development.

## Causes of Sprawl and Uneven Development

Families choose to live in those communities that offer the most attractive bundle of goods the families can afford. The quality of local schools, crime rates, access to retail shops, availability of parks and playgrounds, fire and police protection, and transportation networks are among the amenities most families consider. Similarly, businesses locate where it is most profitable for them to do so. Safety and transportation issues are a concern to businesses as well. Access to markets and raw materials are often considerations. In his influential essay, Charles Tiebout (1956) argued that metropolitan areas are best served by competition among local governments to provide the most attractive bundle of goods that households and businesses will select by voting with their feet. This perspective continues to shape much land use planning and scholarly debate on metropolitan development (Hayward 1998). However, these competitive processes do not exist, and individual choices are not made, in the laissez-faire environment envisioned by such rational choice proponents. Public policy decisions at all levels of government and decisions by many private businesses, particularly large corporate entities, sharply curtail the choices for many and nurture the uneven development of cities and metropolitan areas.

A critical feature of land use planning in the United States is the deference state governments have long provided to local jurisdictions. Ease of municipal incorporation coupled with a fiscal system that finances most local services from the local tax base has led to the balkanization of many metropolitan areas and pervasive exclusionary practices among outlying suburban authorities (Altshuler et al. 1999).

In his discussion of "the sprawl machine," David Rusk (1999, 82–100) describes the major forces that have nurtured this pattern of development. Subsidies for homeownership and the automobile have been particularly critical. The advent of the long-term, 30-year mortgage, coupled with federally subsidized mortgage insurance in the 1930s that permitted routine down payments of 20 percent and often 10 percent and even less, made homeownership available to many households that otherwise could never contemplate owning their own home (Jackson 1985). The creation of government-sponsored enterprises such as Fannie Mae, Freddie Mac, and Ginnie Mae provided far greater access to mortgage credit, particularly in newer suburban communities. Federal tax laws that enable homeowners to deduct the interest on their mortgage loans and property taxes on their homes further subsidize homeownership and encourage those who can afford to buy to purchase even larger, more expensive homes. This multibillion dollar tax break, more than half of which goes to households with incomes above $100,000, far exceeds any assistance going to renters or low-income households generally (Goldsmith 1999, 4; Harney 2002). In 1997, the foregone taxes were more than four times HUD's direct spending on housing subsidies, a benefit more likely to accrue to low-income families (Pastor et al. 2000, 175). In 2000, this deduction provided $74 billion in benefits, with the wealthiest 1 percent of taxpayers receiving 21 percent of the benefit compared with a benefit of less than 2 percent for the bottom half of all taxpayers. HUD's total annual subsidies for low- and moderate-income housing reaches approximately $16 billion (Fox 2001). Federally subsidized highways, cheap fuel provided by keeping taxes on gasoline far below the rate of other industrialized countries, and the far greater pressure on mass transit systems than highways to pay for themselves all assist outlying auto-dependent suburban development, often at the expense of urban communities.

The exclusionary nature of these policies has sometimes been indirect, but at other times it has been quite explicit. The Federal Housing Administration (FHA), which insured mortgage loans almost exclusively in suburban communities from its inception in the 1930s through the early 1960s, "warned of inharmonious racial groups" and observed in its early underwriting manuals that "if a neighborhood is to retain stability, it is necessary that properties shall continue to be occupied by the same social and racial classes. A change in social or racial occupancy generally contributes to instability and a decline in values" (U.S. Federal Housing Administration 1938, par. 937). Until the 1948 Supreme Court case of *Shelley v. Kramer*, racially restrictive covenants were enforceable by the court system. Exclusionary zoning ordinances (e.g., minimum lot sizes, maximum density requirements, and limitations on multifamily housing) persist in most suburban communities today. While the stated objective generally is to preserve the character of the local community, racial segregation is often the effect. Moreover, this is not always an unintended effect. When the mayor of Mt. Laurel, New Jersey, told those people who could not afford the cost of housing in his community that they would simply have to leave, there was little doubt in anybody's mind that he was referring to people of color.

Government, however, is not acting alone. Various arms of the private housing industry have shaped and perpetuated dispersed and racially segregated housing markets. Racial steering by real estate agents, red-lining by mortgage lenders and property insurers, and discriminatory appraisal practices all serve to favor development in outlying, predominantly white communities while acting to limit housing choice and undercut property values in low-income urban communities, particularly those with high concentrations of minority populations (Fix and Turner 1999; Turner and Skidmore 1999; Squires 1997).

Dispersal of business activity also reflects both public policy and private decisionmaking, again with adverse racial affects and in ways that exacerbate inequality generally. When businesses relocate or expand in outlying suburban areas and avoid more central urban locations, they often do so, again, because of the amenities and profit-making potential those locations offer. Undeveloped "greenfield" sites outside of central cities are often cheaper to develop than "brownfield" sites within cities that had previously been used for other purposes. Reducing the cost of labor has been another objective. Dispersal has also long been a strategy used by some businesses to discourage organizing efforts and to allow management to exert greater control over labor (Gordon 1978). However, these decisions are not simply responses to signals emitted by a free market. Public policy decisions that result in increasing subsidization of roads, sewer systems, and other infrastructure requirements of newer, outlying communities coupled with the deterioration of the urban infrastructure, at least in part because of inadequate public investment, help local businesses make such decisions.

In efforts to compete with neighboring jurisdictions and to attract capital from outside the region altogether, local jurisdictions often offer tax abatements, below-market-rate loans, training grants, and other sub-sidies. There is much debate over the impact of such development strate-gies, particularly in terms of whether they result in increased economic activity, tax revenues, and jobs, or simply a rearrangement of where that economic activity, which would have taken place anyway, occurs (Barnekov, Boyle, and Rich 1989; LeRoy 1997; Ellen and Schwartz 2000). While some communities may gain, at least in the short run, there is evi-dence that such competition often hurts central cities while benefiting already-prospering surrounding suburban municipalities. One recent study of the Twin Cities area, for example, found that the suburb of Anoka—located 15 miles northwest of Minneapolis—attracted 29 firms and 1,600 jobs with a tax incentive. All the relocations occurred within the metropolitan area, with 15 of the firms moving from Minneapolis or one of its inner-ring suburbs. The net effect of these subsidized relocations was to move jobs away from the region's minority and low-income population (LeRoy, Hinkley, and Tallman 2000). The city of Minneapolis and its inner-ring suburbs were clearly hurt by this move. While Anoka benefited, it is unclear if this repre-sented a net gain for the region, or whether the outlying suburbs needed such subsidies to grow. As one local observer stated, "Subsidiz-ing economic development in the suburbs is like paying teenagers to think about sex" (Wray 1999).

## Costs of Sprawl, Benefits of Sprawl

A number of costs have been attributed to sprawl and uneven develop-ment. In addition, several benefits have been noted as well. In fact, some of the apparent liabilities of sprawl have been pointed to as evidence of its contribution to the welfare of metropolitan areas.

Perhaps the most concrete costs associated with sprawl are various envi-ronmental problems that are exacerbated by this pattern of development. The outward expansion of metropolitan areas, particularly given the automobile-dependent lifestyle it nurtures, increases air pollution and a range of diseases including asthma, lung cancer, and heart problems. Water quality erodes as development increases pollution that poisons rivers, lakes, and other bodies of water. Consumption patterns stimulate greater use of energy, despoil forests, damage the stratospheric ozone layer, and possibly contribute to global warming. Farm and forestland itself is consumed as residential and commercial development proceeds outward (Goldsmith 1999, 19). In chapter 2, "The Environmental Impacts of Sprawl," David Cieslewicz examines the range of environmental impacts and their uneven consequences for metropolitan areas and their surrounding regions.

Fiscal disparities among communities are intensified, which augment several trajectories of inequality. Outlying wealthy communities have a larger tax base and fewer social service needs to finance. Disparities in the quality of public services grow. Equal educational opportunity has become a mirage in part because of the reliance on local property taxes to fund public schools. As industry seeks out those outlying communities, the relocation of jobs exacerbates urban/suburban economic disparities. The growing concentration of poverty and hypersegregation of urban communities are both causes and effects of these trends. In turn, these developments are associated with crime rates, drug use, racial tensions, and other social costs that are higher than might otherwise be the case (Altshuler et al. 1999; Massey and Denton 1993; Wilson 1987, 1996; Jargowsky 1996; Duany, Plater-Zyberk, and Speck 2000). In chapter 3, "Sprawl, Concentration of Poverty, and Urban Inequality," Paul Jargowsky examines the increasing inequality and concentration of poverty in metropolitan areas. In chapter 4, "Sprawl, Fragmentation, and the Persistence of Racial Inequality," john powell shows how that concentration is "racialized" and explores the impact of sprawl on the opportunity structure confronting racial minorities generally.

Discussions of sprawl and associated costs often focus on transportation and land use. Sprawl often leads to inefficient land use practices. Sprawling development requires large infrastructure investments for roads, sewer systems, schools, and other public services. At the same time, infrastructure within central areas goes unused and, in some cases, deteriorates due to inadequate public investment. Traffic congestion results in more people spending more time in their automobiles (Downs 1998, 9; Duany et al. 2000, 85–99; Sierra Club 2000). In addition, it contributes to the increasing occurrence of road rage leading to conflicts— and increasingly killings—among drivers, as noted earlier in the shooting death of a young mother in a Birmingham, Alabama, suburb (Sipress 1999). An emerging issue that has not been systematically explored is the impact of such development on families. In chapter 5, "Transportation, Land Use, and the Impacts of Sprawl on Poor Children and Families," Amy Helling reveals how the quality of life for many households, particularly those in disadvantaged circumstances, is limited by common planning practices and the sprawling patterns of development they nurture.

Sense of community and connectedness to place are often undermined by these patterns of development and not just for those at the lower end of the socioeconomic spectrum. While there are obvious benefits to mobility, freedom itself and the capacity to fully actualize one's individuality can be harmed by the absence of a place and community in which one's life is embedded (Bellah et al. 1985; Langdon 1994; Leach 1999; Moe and Wilkie 1997; Duany et al. 2000). Sprawl undercuts civic engagement due to the time spent commuting, the increasing segregation and homogeneity of neighborhoods, and the growing separation of home and work, all of which nurture physical and social fragmentation (Putnam 2000). Spatial and socioeconomic polarization are intricately integrated phenomena. Former Labor Secretary Robert Reich wrote about "the secession of the successful" in describing how the wealthiest fifth of U.S. families were basically removing themselves from the public lives of their communities, and the severe costs of that secession (Reich 1991). Wealthy families increasingly move into gated communities (Blakely and Snyder 1997) where they are protected by private security guards. They seek out their recreation at private clubs. They send their children to private schools. In doing so, their support for public services, including public schools, wanes, and those institutions, along with the people served by them, suffer.

Even many of the apparent winners in the process of sprawl and uneven development, however, are starting to experience severe costs. Families of inner-ring suburbs who thought they had escaped the woes of the city now find that they incur some of the same costs as development spins further outward. Many suburban employers cannot find the workers they need, in part because of the unaffordability of suburban housing. The cost of housing has increased much faster than incomes for decades, but even during the recent economic expansion, between 1997 and 1999, rents and house prices grew by more than twice the rate of inflation (U.S. Department of Housing and Urban Development 2000, viii). Some employers have taken extraordinary measures to assist selected employees. For example, the Milwaukee suburb of Elm Grove, where the median housing value is approximately $250,000 compared with $120,000 for the metropolitan area, subsidizes a second mortgage of $65,000 for three years for its village manager so that person can afford to live in the village. This incentive is worth almost $4,000 to the incumbent. Since the funds are taken from an account that pays 5 percent interest, which is the rate of the loan, all the village loses is some liquidity, according to Village Manager Andrea Steen Crawford (2000). According to Michele Frisby of the International City Management Association, more lucrative incentive programs are increasingly common in communities where the cost of housing is well above the metropolitan area average (Ortiz 1999). Many employers find they have to offer higher salaries, pay more for relocation expenses, buy an employee's former home, and subsidize various costs associated with homeownership to attract executives (Dreier, Schwartz, and Greiner 1988). Many communities would also like schoolteachers, police officers, firefighters, and other municipal employees to live in town. Moreover, some private firms would like their factory workers and office staff to have a similar opportunity. However, this is becoming increasingly difficult to accomplish (Squires et al. 1999).

Urban and suburban sprawl do provide benefits for at least some residents. Such development provides a low-density lifestyle with ease of commuting and access to shopping for those who live and work in selected suburban areas. It provides greater separation from the problems of poverty, racial conflict, and other issues generally associated with city life. Clearly, many families prefer single-family homes on large lots in communities that are distant from urban centers (Danielsen, Lang, and Fulton 1999, 521–522; Downs 1998, 8; Gordon and Richardson 2000, 6, 14–15). Arguing that the share of land consumed by development is quite small relative to the total amount of land in the United States (about 3.4 percent), further sprawl is advocated as a key to creating opportunities for racial minorities and immigrants who are just starting to enjoy the American dream and to encourage economic growth generally (Easterbrook 1999, 543). If there are costs associated with sprawl, from this perspective they are well worth the price. For example, traffic congestion may be a problem for some. But, it is argued, this reflects the increasing opportunities for women and racial minorities to get good jobs, buy decent cars, and get to work in the same comfort that others have long enjoyed (Hayward 1998, 12).

No doubt many families have indeed enjoyed the lifestyle afforded them by current patterns of uneven spatial and socioeconomic development. However, the costs are mounting and communities are starting to respond. In 1998, more than 240 initiatives were placed on local and state ballots seeking to limit the adverse effects of sprawl. In 1999, 1,000 land use measures were introduced in state legislatures and 200 were enacted into law (Rinard 2000). That same year President Bill Clinton and Vice President Al Gore issued a "Building Livable Communities" proposal calling for several federal actions to ameliorate sprawl (Office of the Vice President 1999). Many of these initiatives call for regional planning to stem the growth of outward development and encourage development in central locations through brownfield redevelopment, in-fill housing, and new business expansion that utilizes existing infrastructure. If most of these proposals focused on preserving open space and reducing traffic for middle-class residents enjoying their suburban lifestyle, it is also the case that affordable housing, access to jobs, and related equity issues have drawn increasing attention. Over the past few decades, public policy has therefore been somewhat contradictory; some actions fueled sprawl while others were designed to limit this pattern of development. Hank Savitch discusses the contradictions that have emerged from the intersections of federal, state, and local policy in chapter 6, "Encourage, Then Cope: Washington and the Sprawl Machine."

## Responses to Sprawl and Uneven Development

Contradictory forces, both public and private, have historically shaped urban and metropolitan development. In recent years, many communities have responded to the phenomena of sprawl and uneven development with a range of so-called "smart growth" proposals that embody many common themes and practices. In general, such proposals call for more metropolitan or regional planning that makes more efficient use of existing resources and provides a more equitable distribution of the costs and benefits of uneven development. Among the objectives of many proposals are

1. more effective reuse of existing land and infrastructure resources,
2. restrictions on development in outlying suburban and exurban areas,
3. development of a range of transportation modes and less reliance on the automobile,
4. concentration of residential and commercial development in central locations and along the lines of mass transit arteries,
5. creation of areawide revenue sharing and regional investment pools,
6. more affordable housing construction and distribution of such housing throughout metropolitan areas,

7. more vigorous enforcement of fair housing laws, and
8. increased public and private investment in central cities to achieve more balanced development throughout the region.

Some communities now have several years of experience with anti-sprawl policy initiatives. Others have more recently launched ambitious planning efforts. While the jury is still out on many of these initiatives, some of the results are in.

Atlanta, for example, is often referred to as the poster child for urban sprawl. In 1999, the governor of Georgia was given substantial zoning and land use planning authority allowing him to override local controls in order to stem sprawl and encourage development within the city. In chapter 7, "Suburban Expansion in Atlanta: 'The City without Limits' Faces Some," Charles Jaret examines events leading up to these developments in Atlanta and what has transpired in these early efforts.

In 1979, Portland, Oregon, created an urban growth boundary around the metropolitan area that encourages investment in the downtown and central city areas while discouraging development beyond that boundary. There has been considerable debate over the impact of this policy, whether it has achieved the intended effects, and whether there have been unintended negative consequences. In chapter 8, "Planning a Sustainable City: The Promise and Performance of Portland's Urban Growth Boundary," Carl Abbott examines Portland's history and concludes that overall it is achieving the original goals.

In recent years a legislative coalition in the Minneapolis-St. Paul area has created and expanded the authority of the Metropolitan Council to address several land use planning issues. One of the most controversial policy initiatives in that community has been a successful push for regional tax base revenue sharing, which has substantially reduced per capita property tax disparities in the region. In chapter 9, "Politics and Regionalism," Myron Orfield examines the historical contours of regional reform efforts and how initial opposition to tax base sharing in the Twin Cities was overcome by the creation of a coalition that included the cities of Minneapolis and St. Paul and older inner-ring suburbs experiencing fiscal and social distress.

Chicago has experienced many of the same trends that have affected the Twin Cities and many other metropolitan areas. In chapter 10, "Less Sprawl, Greater Equity? The Potential for Revenue Sharing in the Chicago Region," Wim Wiewel, Joe Persky, and Kimberly Schaffer examine the potential benefits that might accrue to Chicago residents from some form of tax base revenue sharing.

In 1997, the state of Maryland enacted one of the most comprehensive, statewide smart growth legislative programs providing incentives for in-fill development while denying similar subsidies for projects outside of the target area. In chapter 11, "Maryland's 'Smart Growth': Using Incentives to Combat Sprawl," Jim Cohen explores what will be required for this initiative to have a positive impact on urban development.

These policy initiatives and the regional planning perspective generally have their detractors. As indicated above, some observers find sprawl to be a sign of progress that should be encouraged rather than a problem to be ameliorated. From this perspective, efforts to limit sprawl are self-serving tactics to preserve a lifestyle for those who have already achieved it while pulling up the ladder behind them and denying it to others (Easterbrook 1999). It is argued that there are unintended consequences, such as the rising prices of housing in Portland, which make homeownership more difficult for low-income residents (Hayward 1998; Gordon and Richardson 2000). To the extent that there are problems, market-based solutions would be more effective from this perspective. For example, if traffic congestion is a problem, then perhaps the solution is more tolls for those who use the roads and highways (Fischel 1999). In the 12th and final chapter, "Equity and the Future Politics of Growth," Jeff Henig examines the competing claims and potential steps that might be responsive to the problems of sprawl, focusing on the equity issues associated with uneven development.

## The Uneven Future of Metropolitan Development

In 1999, the Fannie Mae Foundation surveyed 149 urban experts—members of the Society for American City and Regional Planning History—to compile a list of the top 10 influences on the American metropolis over the past 50 years and the 10 most likely influences for the next 50 years (Fishman 1999, 2000). Almost every item on each list constitutes a critical piece of the current debate over urban sprawl and what, if anything, should be done.

The top 10 influences of the past 50 years were

1. the 1956 Interstate Highway Act and dominance of the automobile,
2. FHA mortgage financing and subdivision regulation,

3. deindustrialization of central cities,
4. urban renewal,
5. Levittown and the mass-produced suburban tract home,
6. racial segregation and job discrimination in cities and suburbs,
7. enclosed shopping malls,
8. sunbelt-style sprawl,
9. air-conditioning, and
10. the urban riots of the 1960s.

All of these influences have been identified as engines fueling the dynamics of sprawl and uneven development. Potential future consequences of such development, and potential solutions to the associated costs were also noted in the 10 most likely future influences:

1. growing disparities of wealth
2. suburban political majority
3. aging of the baby boomers
4. perpetual "underclass" in central cities and inner-ring suburbs
5. "smart growth" environmental and planning initiatives to limit sprawl
6. Internet
7. deterioration of "first-ring" post-1945 suburbs
8. shrinking household size
9. expanded superhighway system of "outer beltways" to serve new, edge cities
10. racial integration as part of the increasing diversity in cities and suburbs

Clearly, sprawl has been the dominant pattern of urban and metropolitan development over recent decades and one that is likely to persist into the near future. However, it is not simply a spatial phenomenon. Sprawl is a pattern that is both a cause and consequence of economic restructuring and emerging social inequalities. These three trajectories of change—spatial, structural, and social—are parts of the same complex process of uneven development shaping urban and metropolitan development. This complex process presents many challenges for policymakers, business leaders, community groups, and citizens alike. It is a challenge that may well be the central social policy question for the early years of the 21st century if not longer.

# REFERENCES

Altshuler, Alan, William Morrill, Harold Wolman, and Faith Mitchell, eds. 1999. *Governance and Opportunity in Metropolitan America.* Washington, D.C.: National Academy Press.

Barnekov, Timothy, Robin Boyle, and Daniel Rich. 1989. *Privatism and Urban Policy in Britain and the United States.* New York: Oxford University Press.

Bellah, Robert N., Richard Madsen, William M. Sullivan, Ann Swidler, and Steven M. Tipton. 1985. *Habits of the Heart: Individualism and Commitment in American Life.* Berkeley: University of California Press.

Blakely, Edward J., and Mary Gail Snyder. 1997. *Fortress America: Gated Communities in the United States.* Washington, D.C.: The Brookings Institution.

Blau, Joel. 1999. *Illusions of Prosperity: America's Working Families in an Age of Economic Insecurity.* New York: Oxford University Press.

Bluestone, Barry, and Bennett Harrison. 1982. *The Deindustrialization of America: Plant Closings, Community Abandonment, and the Dismantling of Basic Industry.* New York: Basic Books.

———. 2000. *Growing Prosperity: The Battle for Growth with Equity in the 21st Century.* Boston: Houghton Mifflin Company.

Brennan, John, and Edward W. Hill. 1999. "Where Are The Jobs? Cities, Suburbs, and the Competition for Employment." Washington, D.C.: The Brookings Institution, Center on Urban and Metropolitan Policy (November).

The Brookings Institution Center on Urban and Metropolitan Policy and the Fannie Mae Foundation. 1998. "A Rise in Downtown Living." Washington, D.C.: The Brookings Institution Center on Urban and Metropolitan Policy and the Fannie Mae Foundation (November).

Cisneros, Henry G. 1993. "Interwoven Destinies: Cities and the Nation." In *Interwoven Destinies: Cities and the Nation,* edited by Henry G. Cisneros. New York: W. W. Norton & Company.

Contosta, David R. 1998. "Architecture." In *Encyclopedia of Urban America: The Cities and Suburbs,* edited by Neil Larry Shumsky. Santa Barbara: ABC-CLIO, Inc.

Danielsen, Karen A., Robert E. Lang, and William Fulton. 1999. "Retracting Suburbia: Smart Growth and the Future of Housing." *Housing Policy Debate* 10 (3): 513–40.

Denton, Nancy A. 1999. "Half Empty or Half Full: Segregation and Segregated Neighborhoods 30 Years After the Fair Housing Act." *Cityscape: A Journal of Policy Development and Research* 4 (3): 107–22.

Downs, Anthony. 1998. "The Big Picture: How America's Cities Are Growing." *Brookings Review* 16 (4): 8–11.

———. 1999. "Some Realities about Sprawl and Urban Decline." *Housing Policy Debate* 10 (4): 955–74.

Dreier, Peter. 2000. "Sprawl's Invisible Hand." *The Nation* (February 21): 6–7.

Dreier, Peter, David C. Schwartz, and Ann Greiner. 1988. "What Every Business Can Do About Housing." *Harvard Business Review* (September–October): 52–61.

Duany, Andres, Elizabeth Plater-Zyberk, and Jeff Speck. 2000. *Suburban Nation: The Rise of Sprawl and the Decline of the American Dream.* New York: North Point Press.

Easterbrook, Gregg. 1999. "Comment on Karen A. Danielsen, Robert E. Lang, and William Fulton's 'Retracting Suburbia: Smart Growth and the Future of Housing.'" *Housing Policy Debate* 10 (3): 541–47.

Ellen, Ingrid Gould, and Amy Ellen Schwartz. 2000. "No Easy Answers: Cautionary Notes for Competitive Cities." *Brookings Review* 18 (3): 44–47.

Fischel, William A. 1999. "Sprawl and the Federal Government." *Cato Policy Report* XXI (5): 1, 10–12.

Fishman, Robert. 1999. "The American Metropolis at Century's End: Past and Future Influences." *Housing Facts & Findings* 1 (4): 1, 6–15.

———. 2000. "The American Metropolis at Century's End: Past and Future Influences." *Housing Policy Debate* 11 (1): 199–213.

Fix, Michael, and Margery Austin Turner, eds. 1999. *A National Report Card on Discrimination in America: The Role of Testing.* Washington, D.C.: The Urban Institute.

Fox, John O. 2001. "Many Unhappy Returns: They're Cutting Taxes, What They Ought to Cut Is the Code." *Washington Post,* 27 May, B-2.

Galster, George, Royce Hanson, Hal Wolman, Stephen Coleman, and Jason Freihage. 2000. "Wrestling Sprawl to the Ground: Defining and Measuring an Elusive Concept." Paper presented at the annual meeting of the Urban Affairs Association, Los Angeles, Calif., May 5.

Garreau, Joel. 1991. *Edge City: Life on the New Frontier.* New York: Anchor.

Ginzberg, Eli. 1993. "The Changing Urban Scene: 1960–1990 and Beyond." In *Interwoven Destinies: Cities and the Nation,* edited by Henry G. Cisneros. New York: W. W. Norton & Company.

Goldsmith, William W. 1999. "Resisting the Reality of Race: Land Use and Social Justice in the Metropolis." Cambridge, Mass.: Lincoln Institute of Land Policy.

Goldsmith, William W., and Edward J. Blakely. 1992. *Separate Societies: Poverty and Inequality in U.S. Cities.* Philadelphia: Temple University Press.

Gordon, David M. 1978. "Capitalist Development and the History of American Cities." In *Marxism and the Metropolis: New Perspectives in Urban Political Economy,* edited by William K. Tabb and Larry Sawers. New York: Oxford University Press.

Gordon, Peter, and Harry W. Richardson. 2000. "Critiquing Sprawl's Critics." *Cato Policy Analysis* 365.

Harney, Kenneth R. 2002. "Tax Benefits Tilted to Aid Homeowners." *Washington Post,* 9 February, H-1.

Harrison, Bennett, and Barry Bluestone. 1988. *The Great U-Turn: Corporate Restructuring and the Polarizing of America.* New York: Basic Books.

Hayward, Steven. 1998. "Legends of the Sprawl." *Policy Review* 91 (September–October): 26–32.

Holland, Stuart. 1986. Personal communication with Gregory D. Squires, November 5.

Jackson, Kenneth. 1985. *Crabgrass Frontier: The Suburbanization of the United States.* New York: Oxford University Press.

Jargowsky, Paul A. 1996. *Poverty and Place: Ghettos, Barrios, and the American City.* New York: Russell Sage Foundation.

Johnston, David Cay. 1999. "Gap between Rich and Poor Found Substantially Wider." *New York Times,* 5 September.

Katz, Bruce, and Jennifer Bradley. 1999. "Divided We Sprawl." *The Atlantic Monthly* 284 (6): 26–42.

Kirp, David, John P. Dwyer, and Larry A. Rosenthal. 1995. *Our Town: Race, Housing and the Soul of Suburbia.* New Brunswick: Rutgers University Press.

Lang, Robert E. 2000. "Office Sprawl: The Evolving Geography of Business." Center on Urban and Metropolitan Policy, The Brookings Institution Survey Series (October).

Langdon, Philip. 1994. *A Better Place to Live: Reshaping the American Suburb.* Amherst: The University of Massachusetts Press.

Leach, William. 1999. *Country of Exiles: The Destruction of Place in American Life.* New York: Pantheon Books.

LeRoy, Greg. 1997. *No More Candy Store: States and Cities Making Job Subsidies Accountable.* Chicago: Federation for Industrial Retention and Renewal, and Washington, D.C.: Grassroots Policy Project.

LeRoy, Greg, Sara Hinkley, and Katie Tallman. 2000. *Another Way Sprawl Happens: Economic Development Subsidies in a Twin Cities Suburb.* Washington, D.C.: Institute on Taxation and Economic Policy.

Lewis Mumford Center. 2001. "Metropolitan Racial and Ethnic Change—Census 2000." http://www.albany.edu/mumford/census/. (Accessed April 24.)

Lorenzen, John. 2000. "Urban Sprawl Is Region's Worst Enemy." *Milwaukee Journal Sentinel,* 19 January, 13A.

Luria, Daniel D., and Joel Rogers. 1999. *Metro Futures: Economic Solutions for Cities and Their Suburbs.* Boston: Beacon Press.

Marshall, Ray, ed. 2000. *Back to Shared Prosperity: The Growing Inequality of Wealth and Income in America.* Armonk, N.Y.: M. E. Sharpe.

Massey, Douglas S., and Nancy A. Denton. 1993. *American Apartheid: Segregation and the Making of the Underclass.* Cambridge, Mass.: Harvard University Press.

Moe, Richard, and Carter Wilkie. 1997. *Changing Places: Rebuilding Community in the Age of Sprawl.* New York: Henry Holt and Company.

Office of the Vice President. 1999. "Clinton-Gore Livability Agenda: Building Livable Communities for the 21st Century." Washington D.C.: The White House (January 11).

Orfield, Myron. 1997. *Metropolitics: A Regional Agenda for Community and Stability.* Washington, D.C.: Brookings Institution Press, and Cambridge, Mass.: Lincoln Institute of Land Policy.

Ortiz, Vikki. 1999. "Delafield to Help New Employee Buy Home." *Milwaukee Journal Sentinel,* 10 December, B1.

Pastor, Jr., Manuel, Peter Dreier, J. Eugene Grigsby III, and Marta Lopez-Garza. 2000. *Regions That Work: How Cities and Suburbs Can Grow Together.* Minneapolis: University of Minnesota Press.

Putnam, Robert D. 2000. *Bowling Alone: The Collapse and Revival of American Community.* New York: Simon and Schuster.

Reich, Robert B. 1991. *The Work of Nations.* New York: Vintage Books.

Rinard, Amy. 2000. "Economy Fuels Sprawl's Rise on Capitol Agenda." *Milwaukee Journal Sentinel,* 30 January, A1, 10.

Rusk, David. 1999. *Inside Game Outside Game: Winning Strategies for Saving Urban America.* Washington, D.C.: Brookings Institution Press.

Sassen, Saskia. 1994. *Cities in a World Economy.* Thousand Oaks, Calif.: Pine Forge Press.

Schmitt, Eric. 2001. "Whites in Minority in Largest Cities, The Census Shows." *New York Times,* 30 April, A1.

Schneider, William. 1992. "The Suburban Century Begins." *The Atlantic Monthly* 270 (1): 33–44.

Sierra Club. 2000. *Sprawl Costs Us All: How Your Taxes Fuel Suburban Sprawl.* San Francisco: Sierra Club.

Sipress, Allan. 1999. "Road Rage Death Wasn't All That Surprising." *Milwaukee Journal Sentinel,* 18 November, A19, 24.

Squires, Gregory D. 1994. *Capital and Communities in Black and White: The Intersections of Race, Class, and Uneven Development.* Albany: SUNY Press.

———, ed. 1997. *Insurance Redlining: Disinvestment, Reinvestment, and the Evolving Role of Financial Institutions.* Washington, D.C.: The Urban Institute Press.

Squires, Gregory D., Sally O'Connor, Michael Grover, and James Walrath. 1999. "Housing Affordability in the Milwaukee Metropolitan Area: A Matter of Income, Race, and Policy." *Journal of Affordable Housing and Community Development Law* 9 (1): 34–73.

Steen Crawford, Andrea. 2000. Personal interview with Gregory D. Squires, March 3.

Teixeira, Ruy, and Joel Rogers. 2000. *Why the White Working Class Still Matters: America's Forgotten Majority.* New York: Basic Books.

Tiebout, Charles. 1956. "A Pure Theory of Local Expenditures." *Journal of Political Economy* 64: 416–24.

Turner, Margery, and Felicity Skidmore, eds. 1999. *Mortgage Lending Discrimination: A Review of Existing Evidence.* Washington, D.C.: The Urban Institute.

U.S. Census Bureau. 1999. *Money Income in the United States.* Washington, D.C.: Superintendent of Documents.

———. 2001. "Population Estimates of Metropolitan Areas, Metropolitan Areas inside Central Cities, Metropolitan Areas outside Central Cities, and Nonmetropolitan Areas by State for July 1, 1999 and April 1, 1990 Population Estimates Base." http://www.census.gov/population/estimates/metro-city/ma99-06.txt. (Accessed April 26, 2001.)

U.S. Department of Housing and Urban Development. 1997. *The State of the Cities.* Washington, D.C.: U.S. Department of Housing and Urban Development.

———. 2000. *The State of the Cities 2000.* Washington, D.C.: U.S. Department of Housing and Urban Development.

U.S. Federal Housing Administration. 1938. *Underwriting Manual.* Washington, D.C.: U.S. Government Printing Office.

Wilson, William J. 1987. *The Truly Disadvantaged: The Inner City, the Underclass, and Public Policy.* Chicago: University of Chicago Press.

———. 1996. *When Work Disappears: The World of the New Urban Poor.* New York: Alfred A. Knopf.

———. 1999. *The Bridge over the Racial Divide: Rising Inequality and Coalition Politics.* Berkeley: University of California Press.

Wolff, Edward N. 1994. *Top Heavy: A Study of the Increasing Inequality of Wealth in America.* New York: The Twentieth Century Fund.

Wray, Lyle. 1999. *St. Paul Pioneer Press,* 28 February. Cited in Greg LeRoy, Sara Hinkley, and Katie Tallman. *Another Way Sprawl Happens: Economic Development Subsidies in a Twin Cities Suburb* (Washington, D.C.: Institute on Taxation and Economic Policy, 2000), 44.

# 2

# The Environmental Impacts of Sprawl

David J. Cieslewicz

The next time you sit down to a breakfast plate brimming with pancakes and you reach for the pure maple syrup, think about sprawl. Hard to perceive, but there is a connection. When you admire the work of Frank Lloyd Wright, when you curse the sport-utility vehicle bearing down on you, when you wonder what to do about the dandelions in your lawn, when you think about the *Exxon Valdez*, and when you see a deer carcass on the side of the road, contemplate sprawl. There is a connection between sprawl and all of these things.

The problems of land use are not just problems for land. Land use is the key factor behind the remaining water and air quality issues we face. Air and water pollution originate from two kinds of sources. "Point" sources come from a limited number of easily identifiable places— often the end of a pipe discharging into a waterway or a smokestack spewing emissions into the air. "Nonpoint" sources are usually harder to find and control because small amounts of pollutants seep into the air and water from such sources as farm fields, lawns, construction sites, parking lots, roads, and the tailpipes of millions of vehicles. Pollution from point sources of air and water pollution has been dramatically reduced. The remaining problems are, to a greater extent than ever before, issues of nonpoint sources and these nonpoint sources are strongly related to land use. Auto and truck travel are a leading source of air pollution despite cleaner running engines; we are giving back some of our clean air

23

benefits by driving more and we are driving more because of development patterns that demand it. Runoff from construction site erosion, chemicals used on sprawling suburban lawns, and gasoline and oil residue from parking lots and roads are leading causes of water pollution.

This chapter explores the role sprawl plays in energy consumption, climate change, land use, air and water pollution, and biological diversity. To a large extent, to determine the environmental impacts of sprawl we need to simply follow the cars.

### Energy: The Valdez Sailed for Us

Auto and truck travel has exploded in the United States since World War II. That explosion is the key force behind the energy consumption, air quality impacts, and climate changes brought about by sprawl. It has also greatly contributed to the decline in water quality and biological diversity that we have experienced in recent decades. Auto travel has increased far beyond what simple population increases would predict. Vehicle miles traveled in the United States increased 140 percent between 1950 and 1990, while population rose 40 percent during the same period.

The United States, with not quite 5 percent of the world's population, consumes one-third of its transportation energy (Benfield et al. 1999, 50; OTA 1994b). The environmental implications of this came crashing into our living rooms on March 24, 1989, when the *Exxon Valdez* rammed a reef in Alaska's pristine Prince William Sound. Before it was over, 240,000 barrels of oil had spilled, the shoreline was covered in heavy crude, and images of dying wildlife filled national news casts (Yergin 1991, 785). Thousands of enraged Americans drove to rallies to denounce Exxon.

But simply blaming the callous corporate giant is too easy. Certainly, there is historical impetus in the oil industry to constantly expand markets and Exxon was found guilty of negligence. Still, it is right to ask why the giant tanker was in Prince William Sound that morning at all. To a large extent, American consumers put it there because American land use patterns demand more oil consumption every year.

### Land: Broadacre Nightmare

In the early 1930s Frank Lloyd Wright predicted—and heartily endorsed— almost every major change in the American landscape that would take place over the next six decades. He understood how cars, which he loved with unbridled passion, would change our sense of space. He predicted—and applauded—the decline of cities, the advent of rural subdivisions and super highways, and even the coming of "Stop 'n Go." (Wright actually designed a convenience store–gas station in Minnesota.) His mistake was to believe that all of this would be wonderful, healthful, aesthetically pleasing, and morally and culturally uplifting. Wright's idea of Utopia was "Broadacre City," where every family would have at least one acre of property (Wright 1932).

Unfortunately, Frank Lloyd Wright's vision of the future was all too clear and his prescriptions were followed all too carefully. The most ubiquitous form of modern American congestion is the suburban freeway. This congestion exists because we faithfully applied Wright's prescription for what to do about congestion in the city. We built Wright's dream of broad highways and broad-acre cities and his dream became our nightmare.

Certainly, we should expect that with a growing population some land will be consumed for development. The problem is that we are consuming far more land than simple population growth would predict. For example, between 1970 and 1990, the population of the Milwaukee metropolitan area increased by 3 percent while the amount of land it consumed for development went up 38 percent. That pattern is repeated in every major metropolitan area in America whether it is rapidly growing or shrinking. Over that same period in Los Angeles, the population expanded by 45 percent while land area growth increased by 300 percent. Cleveland *lost* 11 percent of its population, but picked up 33 percent in land consumed for development (Benfield et al. 1999, 7; Diamond and Noonan 1996).

It is sometimes argued that land consumption is not a problem, simply because there is so much of it. Frank Lloyd Wright himself made this argument, claiming that there were 57 acres for every person in America. That was in 1932, however, when there were 130 million Americans. In 1999, with 275 million Americans, there were 26 acres per person in the continental United States. That figure counts every acre of prime farmland as well as Yellowstone and Yosemite national parks, deserts and mountains, and every acre of protected park, habitat area, and green space in the nation.

The view that the American landscape is so vast that it does not demand any constraint on development does not take into account the need for agricultural and recreational land and the need for open space in order to maintain natural systems, biological diversity, and even the American myth of "wilderness." Ironically, one of the key tenets of American folklore—the room to roam and to be independent—is being obliterated by that same desire to live apart. As more of us move out into the "wide open spaces," they become less wide open.

The simple *consumption* of more land is not the only problem. The *way* in which land is developed is also an issue. Virtually every new development since World War II has been designed for ease of auto travel. By strictly dividing land into vast large-lot, single-family-home subdivisions connected to ever larger shopping malls and business "parks" by wide highways and streets, we have made driving mandatory in virtually every new development built in America in the last half of the 20th century. In fact, this development pattern means even short trips demand auto travel. One in four automobile trips is less than one mile in length (Benfield, et al. 1999, 42; Oge 1995).

Americans drive much more than Europeans, but the reason is not just related to the greater spaces of the American countryside. In the United States, the pattern of development itself leads to more driving for even short distances. Both in the United States and in Europe, about 90 percent of all trips are less than 10 miles. Yet per capita vehicle miles driven in Europe are about 40 percent of those driven in the United States. The key difference is not so much that Americans have farther to go, but that they drive more frequently; Europeans tend to substitute walking, biking, or mass transit for these short trips (Nivola 1999, 18). Compact European development patterns make this possible.

In addition to the amount and the manner in which land is developed in America, another important factor is the locations where most development is taking place. There is an unfortunate coincidence between sprawling suburban areas and some of our best farmland. Many cities grew up precisely because of their proximity to good farmland. They were the interface between farmers and their markets. In addition, land that is good for farming is very often also good for development. Deep, well-drained soils and modest slopes are attractive for both farming and development (Buttel et al. 1994, 1).

According to the American Farmland Trust, counties with high levels of both prime farmland and development pressure account for 79 percent of our nation's fruit, 69 percent of our vegetables, 52 percent of our dairy products, and over one-fourth of our meats and grains. The Trust calculates that we are losing prime farmland at the rate of 46 acres *per hour*

(Benfield et al. 1999, 65). As farms are pushed from these more productive soils by the sprawling suburbs being spun out from cities, agriculture
demands more chemical inputs to increase its production per acre.

## Climate: Sprawl and Maple Syrup

On a bright March morning a Wisconsin farmer tramps into his wood-
lot and drives a bit about an inch and a half into a mature maple tree. He
withdraws the bit and inserts a spile (a small spout), hangs a bucket to
catch the sap, and moves on to the next tree. After he has tapped about
15 trees, the farmer returns to the first to see how the sap is running, but
barely a drop has oozed from the tree. The time-honored ritual of maple
syrup production in Wisconsin is over.

This imaginary scene of a syrup-dry future may come to pass if global
warming continues at its present pace. Maple syrup depends on cold
because sugar maple trees need sustained winter temperatures below
40 degrees Fahrenheit to survive. A report by the Office of Technology
Assessment (1994a) predicts that, because of global warming, maple
syrup production will end in the entire continental United States except
for the very northern tip of Maine. Under this scenario, Wisconsin's climate and the species of plants and animals dependent on it will shift to
one not unlike present-day Kansas. Cool northern forests will give way
to dry prairie and oak savanna.

Already, scientists at Aldo Leopold's farm in south central Wisconsin,
repeating observations he made over 50 years ago, are finding that spring
is arriving about one week earlier now than it did then. For some species,
the season has advanced even more rapidly. When Leopold walked his
farm in the 1930s, Canada geese returned each year around March 22.
For the last 20 years, the average return date has been February 28
(Lavendel 1999).

There is no question that the earth's climate is getting warmer. The
earth's mean surface air temperature has increased 0.5 to 1.1 degrees
Fahrenheit in the last 100 years, and the National Oceanic and Atmospheric Administration reports that the 20th century was the warmest in
history (Warrick 1998). While there has been disagreement in the scien-
tific community about the causes of that warming, a strong consensus is
rapidly developing toward the point of view that most of this warming is
human caused. The Intergovernmental Panel on Climate Change (IPCC),
an organization of thousands of scientists from 120 nations that assesses
the peer-reviewed climate change literature, has reached this conclusion.

The primary culprit is carbon dioxide, which is produced when fossil fuels are burned for industry and for transportation. Carbon dioxide ($CO_2$) traps solar heat at the earth's surface. Levels of carbon dioxide in the atmosphere have increased from 280 particles per million (ppm) in 1850 to 370 ppm today and they are expected to double over the next century (Fauber and Vandenbrook 2000).

Transportation accounts for one-third of all the greenhouse gases produced in the United States and the contribution from the transportation sector is growing faster than the others. The average car burns 550 gallons of gasoline per year and produces 8,800 pounds of carbon dioxide. Light trucks (sport-utility vehicles and minivans) burn about twice as much gas and produce twice as much carbon dioxide. Light truck sales now account for about half of all vehicle sales. Indeed, the greenhouse gas emissions produced by cars and light trucks are projected to leap by 55 percent over the next 10 years if current trends in increased travel and vehicle preference continue (Benfield et al. 1999, 48–51; Office of Air Quality Planning 1998; Oge 1995; Office of Mobile Sources 1993; National Vehicle and Fuel Emissions Laboratory 1995).

The U.S. responsibility for the greenhouse gases suspected in global warming is far out of proportion to other nations. Of all of the mobile sources of greenhouse gases in the world, the United States, with not even 5 percent of the world's population, contributes 34 percent of the pollutants (Benfield et al. 1999, 50–52; IPCC 1995). This is due in part to U.S. land use patterns. Even New York City has a population density only one-third that of Frankfurt and one-fifth that of Tokyo (Nivola 1999; 4). In addition, suburban Denver residents, in turn, now consume gas at a rate 12 times greater than the citizens of Manhattan (Benfield et al. 1999, 60) because of the spread-out development pattern there.

So the chain is very real. Sprawling land use patterns in the United States require more driving. This leads to the production of more greenhouse gases that fuel global warming, which in turn leads to changes in our very landscape and even to the culture that is shaped by it.

## Air: Squandering the Gains

Air quality in the United States has improved in the last three decades, but this improvement has been in spite of and not because of our land use patterns. Lead in our air is down 97 percent since 1977, carbon monoxide is down 61 percent, and smog has been reduced by 30 percent. (Improvements are notably absent for carbon dioxide, the leading greenhouse gas.) These gains are largely due to government-mandated improvements in vehicle emissions and from improvements in point sources such as utilities and industry (Benfield et al. 1999, 48; Oge 1995). These gains would have been even greater, however, if we had held increases in vehicle miles traveled to the rate of increase in the driving population.

Today's cars produce 70 percent less nitrogen oxides and 80 to 90 percent less hydrocarbons than 1960s models. While each car was becoming cleaner, however, the number of cars and the number of vehicle miles driven was skyrocketing. Between 1969 and 1990, the U.S. population increased by 21 percent, but the number of miles driven per capita went up 72 percent (Benfield et al. 1999, 51). As a result, the U.S. Department of Energy predicts that U.S. carbon emissions will grow at an average rate of 1 percent per year, with transportation sources growing 20 percent faster than the average. The U.S. Environmental Protection Agency (EPA) has found that total hydrocarbon emissions could reverse their decline and start to edge up again in the next several years because of increased driving. *Total* nitrogen oxide emissions from vehicles are already at higher levels then they were 20 years ago, even with the much cleaner burning engines in each vehicle. Ozone and particulate pollution are also both projected to rise (Benfield et al. 1999, 58; Office of Mobile Sources 1993).

We are starting to give back air quality gains because sprawling development patterns demand more driving. Table 2.1 compares the land and air impacts of development at densities of one lot per five acres (a typical rural subdivision in Wisconsin), one lot per one acre (Frank Lloyd Wright's "broadacre city"), eight lots per acre (a typical suburban neighborhood built in the early part of the 20th century), and 50 units per acre (a dense urban development by Wisconsin standards, but trivial compared with New York City). The table projects the impacts if all 400,000 new housing units projected to be built in Wisconsin over the next 20 years were built at each density. It demonstrates that development at the density of even the relatively leafy suburban neighborhoods of 80 to 100 years ago would have half the air quality impact and only 2.5 percent of the land consumption of the five-acre-lot scenario. One important aspect of these early suburbs was that they were often referred to as "streetcar suburbs," meaning that they were built at densities that were

Table 2.1 *Projected Environmental Impact of 400,000 New Housing Units*

| Density (acres per unit) | Land Used (in thousands of acres) | VMT (in thousands) | Fuel Used[a] (in thousands of gallons per year) | Emissions (in thousands of pounds per year) | | | | Impact on Land Consumption[b] (%) | Impact on Air Quality[b] (%) |
|---|---|---|---|---|---|---|---|---|---|
| | | | | $CO_1$ | NOx | $CO_2$ | VOCs | | |
| 5 | 2,000 | 12,000,000 | 413,793 | 422,068 | 29,379 | 6,620,689 | 56,275 | 100.0 | 100.0 |
| 1 | 400 | 11,000,000 | 379,310 | 386,896 | 26,931 | 6,068,965 | 51,586 | 20.0 | 92.0 |
| 0.125 | 50 | 6,000,000 | 206,896 | 211,034 | 14,689 | 3,310,344 | 28,137 | 2.5 | 50.0 |
| 0.02 | 8 | 3,200,000 | 110,344 | 112,551 | 7,834 | 1,765,517 | 15,006 | 0.4 | 27.0 |

*Source:* Extrapolated from projections of VMT based on housing density in research done by John Holtzclaw (1994) and from pollution figures cited by Benfield et al. (1999).

*Notes:* VMT = vehicle miles traveled per year; $CO_1$ = carbon monoxide; NOx = nitrogen oxide; $CO_2$ = carbon dioxide; and VOC = volatile organic compound.

[a] Fuel consumption assumes 29 miles per gallon, the equivalent of a Ford Taurus.

[b] Impact is expressed as a percentage of the land and air impacts at 1 unit per 5 acres.

low compared with the central cities but high enough to support the streetcars, which served as their primary link to downtown areas (Goddard 1994, 68).

Air pollution has implications for human health. Carbon monoxide is linked to reduced work capacity and manual dexterity, poor learning ability, and difficulty in performing complex tasks. Nitrogen oxides and volatile organic compounds are precursors to ozone, which poses health risks to the elderly, the young, and to persons with respiratory problems. It damages lung tissue, aggravates asthma, and induces choking, coughing, and stinging eyes (Benfield et al. 1999, 56–58; Office of Air and Radiation 1995; Office of Mobile Sources 1993). Even healthy people are advised to refrain from strenuous outdoor exercise during times of high ground level concentrations of ozone.

Ozone is also a problem for plant life. For example, studies suggest that white pines in southeast Wisconsin, a "severe non-attainment area" under the Federal Clean Air Act are experiencing signs of stress related to pollution. The air quality problem here is the result of high levels of ground level ozone, which are caused in large part by automobile use that is demanded by the sprawling Milwaukee and Chicago suburbs—a typical situation for most major metropolitan areas in the United States. Ozone damages vegetation by attacking the coating of a leaf, decreasing its productive qualities. According to a University of Wisconsin Extension study: "Ozone can also damage the guard cells, which control the opening and closing of stomates. This reduces the ability of the guard cells to close the stomates and keep air pollutants from entering a plant through the surfaces of its leaves. When atmospheric pollutants enter leaves and damage plant tissues, plants can lose nutrients that are vital to their growth and maintenance"(Morton, Johnson, and May 1997, 1). The study notes that exposure to ozone concentrations of 16 ppm or greater over a short period of time can visibly injure most plant species. Every summer, ozone levels in southeast Wisconsin exceed this level. Indeed, a study in Maryland found that ozone damage to crops amounted to a $40-million-per-year problem (Benfield et al. 1999, 56; Office of Mobile Sources 1993).

Some hope that new technological advances will make up for the dramatic increases in vehicle miles driven. For example, in late 1999, Honda introduced the Insight, a small car that features an electric motor combined with a three-cylinder gasoline engine. The gas engine can be smaller and lighter because the electric motor supplies additional power when needed. Meanwhile, the electric batteries never need recharging because the motor acts as a generator when the car is decelerating. Honda combined this technology with the latest in lightweight construction to achieve EPA mileage ratings of 61 miles per gallon in the city and 70 miles per gallon on the highway. The Insight meets California's ultra low emission vehicle standard, which is driving the industry toward greater fuel efficiency. Still, even Honda only claims improvements for emissions that cause smog, but not greenhouse gases (Honda 2000).

Moreover, fuel efficiency that brings lower operating costs is likely to simply result in still more driving. One expert, the Brookings Institute's Pietro Nivola, asserts that only higher gas prices will result in less energy consumption (Gilbert 2000).

## Water: Missing the Point

Much like air pollution, great progress has been made in the United States over the last three decades in cleaning up "point sources" of water pollution. Point sources are pollutants that come from a single source, often the end of a pipe discharging into a waterway. Examples include municipal sewerage treatment plants and industries like paper making. The remaining water quality problems we face largely originate from "nonpoint" sources or places like farm fields, lawns, roads, parking lots, and construction sites. Nonpoint or runoff pollution is now the leading cause of water pollution in America, impacting 40 percent of the nation's surveyed waterways (Benfield et al. 1999, 80; Arnold and Gibbons 1996).

Studies indicate that negative impacts result when impervious surfaces like roads, parking lots, and rooftops exceed 10 percent of the area inside a watershed. The problem is amplified if the makeup of the impervious surface is more transportation related (roads, parking lots, and driveways) than it is rooftops. This is because transportation-related surfaces often contain oil, grit, and road salt and are usually interconnected, allowing pollutants to accumulate and flow down into streams and lakes.

The attempt to solve the problem of water pollution caused by transportation-related hard surfaces through the use of large lot sizes only makes the ultimate problem even worse. In fact, large-lot developments have been estimated to deliver up to three times more sediment than traditional, dense urban developments (Benfield et al. 1999, 84; South Carolina Coastal Conservation League 1995). The better solution is probably to direct more intense development to already highly developed watersheds and away from those that are sparsely developed. A watershed that has a high percentage of impermeable surfaces is not likely to be further degraded by more development, but one that is hovering around 10 percent impermeable surface can be saved if development that would have happened there is instead redirected to an already degraded watershed.

There is at least one positive water *quantity* impact of sprawl: if development occurs on private septic systems, then groundwater levels remain relatively stable. In some large municipal water systems, water is drawn from high-capacity wells, used, and then sent to municipal sewerage treatment plants where it is treated and discharged to a river or stream flowing out of the watershed. As a result, groundwater is drawn down, which can reduce springs, stream flows, and surface water levels. This, in turn, can harm species like trout, which depend on cool, rapidly moving streams. Sprawling rural developments on private septic systems return the effluent to the same groundwater table and watershed. As a result, they provide a closed system and therefore there is no net loss of groundwater or reduction in surface water flow rates and levels (Hall 1998).

These closed systems are far from perfect, however. Because they do not treat nitrates, private septic systems, when they are concentrated in close proximity, contribute to significant increases in nitrate levels in drinking water. Moreover, their land use impacts can be substantial. For example, the proposed introduction of new system types in Wisconsin is predicted to increase development pressure on nine million acres (25 percent of the Wisconsin landscape) because thin soils and steep slopes, which restrict the use of conventional systems, are not barriers to the new technology (Wisconsin Department of Commerce 1997, 81).

## Biodiversity: Deer and Development

The diversity of plant and animal species on earth is declining at a rapid rate as habitat is destroyed and as certain species become overrun by a few dominant species. Very often these species are not native to the area and so they lack natural predators. Sprawl plays a role in the loss of biological diversity.

One prominent example of the link between sprawl and the loss of biodiversity is the explosion in white-tailed deer populations. Hunted to near extirpation in the Northeast and Midwest by 1900, populations have risen steadily since then. Today, deer populations often go beyond those found prior to European settlement (Nelson 1997, 107–108).

Such numbers have led to a common sight along American highways: white-tailed deer lying dead at the side of the road. In Wisconsin, deer accounted for 1 in 20 vehicle accidents in 1978, but 1 in 6 by 1995. The common response is to place the blame on the size of the deer population, but a closer examination suggests that the problem is related to suburban sprawl in several ways.

Two elements contribute to car-deer accidents. One, of course, is rising human and deer populations. A factor often ignored, however, is the presence of more cars on rural highways. Following a pattern that has become typical across the United States, the amount of vehicle miles driven on rural Wisconsin highways has nearly doubled since 1983, owing to sprawling development patterns. An analysis done by 1000 Friends of Wisconsin found that the number of rural miles driven explains nearly three times as many of the car-deer accidents as does herd size.

In addition to mixing more cars with more deer, suburban sprawl contributes to the size of the herd in at least three ways. First, as rural subdivisions and estates replace farms, and as new roads are built to accommodate that growth, more "edge habitat," or places where wooded areas meet fields or lawns, is created. Deer thrive in edge habitat. In thick forest, food is scarce because branches are too high for deer to reach while the forest floor is dark and relatively little vegetation grows there. Open fields are good for foraging but they do not provide cover. But a patchwork of subdivisions and farm fields is perfect for deer because refuges are mixed with forage opportunities. Second, as land ownership becomes more fragmented, hunting opportunities decrease. While farmers usually welcome and even encourage deer hunting to reduce crop damage from browsing, new rural residents of sprawling subdivisions and widely scattered single homes usually shut down their land to hunting due to safety concerns or opposition to hunting. Third, because rush hours correspond roughly with dawn and dusk during large parts of the year, more cars are on the highways at the times of the day when deer are most active (Cieslewicz and Hanson 1999; Waller and Alverson 1997).

The rising deer population is not just a problem for suburban commuters. It is also a problem for biological diversity because deer have a voracious appetite for trees, shrubs, and herbaceous plants. Deer have been described as a "keystone species" because heavy browsing by dense deer populations reduce not just the diversity of plants, but also the diversity of mammals that depend on them. Studies indicate that some bird species disappear in areas of high deer concentrations (Waller and Alverson 1997).

Another example of the role sprawl plays in the reduction of biodiversity is the loss of habitat for neotropical migrant songbirds. These birds, such as warblers, winter in Central America and pass through the Midwest on their way to and from Canada. An important stopover point is the Baraboo Hills, a block of relatively untouched deciduous forest in south central Wisconsin, not far from Aldo Leopold's farm. As suburban sprawl creeps up from Madison, about 30 miles south, the relatively untouched forest is becoming fragmented with homes, roads, and power lines. This fragmentation creates points of entry for non-native species of plants like buckthorn and honeysuckle, which choke off native plants and trees. In addition, they help introduce predators like house cats, which account for an alarming number of songbird kills. Perhaps 39 million birds are killed by cats in Wisconsin each year (Coleman et al. 1997).

Finally, our problems circle back on themselves. As mentioned at the start of this chapter, to take the measure of environmental problems caused by sprawl, we need to follow the cars. The dramatic increase in driving caused by our sprawling, auto-dependent development patterns force the exploration for oil into increasingly environmentally sensitive areas. The attack on biological diversity in Prince William Sound caused by the *Valdez* can be traced back to our need for gasoline to power the vehicles that we must drive to get around the places we have built thousands of miles away. The *Valdez* sailed for us.

## The Environmentally Good City

Cities are the antidote to the problems of sprawl. Their benefits are described in Milwaukee Mayor John Norquist's book, *The Wealth of Cities*, where he writes:

> Cities are, on balance, good for the environment. New Yorkers pollute far less, on average, than their suburban neighbors. More gasoline is needed to support the auto-dependent lifestyle; more electricity must be generated to heat and cool the large, stand-alone homes; more resources must be used to provide roads, pipes,

and utility lines to the scattered sites; more energy must be consumed to supply water and return sewage from homes farther and farther away from municipal plants; more trucks must use more gas to move products farther and farther; more chemicals are applied to control the weeds on larger and larger lawns and more water to keep those lawns green; and, most important, more land must be cleared and leveled to accommodate the same amount of living. (Norquist 1998, 139)

The policy answers to sprawl are numerous and complex, but few of them are possible in a practical political sense until we resolve the fundamental confusion that predominates popular discussion—and even discussion among sophisticated environmental activists—about sprawl, cities, and the environment. Polls show that Americans oppose two things—sprawl and greater density. A recent survey by the Pew Center for Civic Journalism found that sprawl came out at the top of an open-ended question about the most important issues facing Americans in their own communities (Greenberg 2000). A survey of Wisconsin residents found, however, that while 34 percent believed that most development should take place in Wisconsin's largest cities, only 6 percent wanted to live there themselves. Meanwhile, a national survey found that 77 percent of Americans would oppose building even single-family homes at higher densities in their neighborhoods (Gould 2000; National Association of Home Builders 1999).

In other words, we oppose only the affliction and the cure. We will not solve the problems of sprawl until we resolve this contradiction and we learn to embrace city life—living in places of real, compact urban form with all of their advantages as well as disadvantages—as the most positive environmental choice an individual can make.

REFERENCES

Arnold, Chester, L., Jr., and C. James Gibbons. 1996. "Impervious Surface Coverage: The Emergence of a Key Environmental Indicator." *Journal of the American Planning Association* 62: (2): 243–58.

Benfield, F. Kaid, Matthew D. Raimi, and Donald D. T. Chen. 1999. *Once There Were Greenfields.* Washington, D.C.: Natural Resources Defense Council and Surface Transportation Policy Project.

Buttel, Frederick H., Douglas Jackson-Smith, and Spencer D. Wood. 1994. *Agricultural Change and Urban Development: The Case of Dane County.* Madison, Wis.: Agricultural Technology and Family Farm Institute.

Cieslewicz, David, and Jason Hanson. 1999. *Deer and Development: How Sprawl Impacts the Deer Herd, Hunters, Auto Safety and Your Pocket Book.* Madison, Wis.: 1000 Friends of Wisconsin.

Coleman, John S., Stanley A. Temple, and Scott R. Craven. 1997. *Cats and Wildlife: A Conservation Dilemma.* Madison, Wis.: Cooperative Extension Publications.

Diamond, Henry, and Patrick Noonan. 1996. *Land Use in America.* Washington, D.C.: Island Press.

Fauber, John, and Tom Vandenbrook. 2000. "A Change in the Seasons." *Milwaukee Journal Sentinel,* 28 May.

Gilbert, Craig. 2000. "Candidate's Energy Plans Elicit Doubt." *Milwaukee Journal Sentinel,* 16 July.

Goddard, Stephen B. 1994. *Getting There: The Epic Struggle between Road and Rail in the American Century.* New York: HarperCollins.

Gould, Whitney. 2000. "Growing Smarter: The Struggle with Sprawl." *Milwaukee Journal Sentinel,* 30 January.

Greenberg, Brigitte. 2000. "Americans Most Concerned with Local Issues, Poll Shows." *Associated Press,* 15 February.

Hall, Dee J. 1998. "Dane County Water Levels Are Dropping." *Wisconsin State Journal,* 11 January.

Holtzclaw, John. 1994. *Using Residential Patterns and Transit to Decrease Auto Dependence and Costs.* San Francisco, Calif.: Natural Resources Defense Council.

Honda. 2000. "Honda Insight Takes Automotive Efficiency to a New Level." http://www.honda.ca/athondaca/press_releases/hondaauto_insight_2.asp. March 27.

International Panel on Climate Change (IPCC). 1995. "Summary for Policymakers of the Contribution of Working Group I to the IPCC Second Assessment Report." Geneva, Switzerland: IPCC.

Lavendel, Brian. 1999. "Weather Out of Whack." *Isthmus,* 8 January.

Morton, A., J. Johnson, and T. May. 1997. "Direct Damage of Air Pollution to Forest Vegetation." Madison, Wis.: University of Wisconsin Extension.

National Association of Home Builders (NAHB). 1999. *Consumer Survey on Growth Issues.* Washington, D.C.: NAHB.

National Vehicle and Fuel Emissions Laboratory. 1995. *Annual Emissions and Fuel Consumption for an Average Vehicle.* Washington, D.C.: U.S. Environmental Protection Agency.

Nelson, Richard. 1997. *Heart and Blood: Living with Deer in America.* New York: Random House.

Nivola, Pietro S. 1999. *Laws of the Landscape.* Washington, D.C.: Brookings Institution Press.

Norquist, John. 1998. *The Wealth of Cities.* Reading, Mass.: Addison-Wesley.

Office of Air and Radiation. 1995. *Air Quality Trends—1994: Six Principle Pollutants.* Washington, D.C.: U.S. Environmental Protection Agency.

Office of Air Quality Planning and Standards. 1998. *National Air Quality and Emissions Trends Report.* Washington, D.C.: U.S. Environmental Protection Agency.

Office of Mobile Sources. 1993. *Automobiles and Ozone.* Washington D.C.: U.S. Environmental Protection Agency.

Office of Technology Assessment. 1994a. "Climate Treaties and Models: Issues in the International Management of Climate Change." Washington, D.C.: U.S. Government Printing Office.

———. 1994b. *Saving Energy in U.S. Transportation.* Washington, D.C.: U.S. Government Printing Office.

Oge, Margo. 1995. "Automotive Emissions: Progress and Challenges." Presentation to
    Automotive Management Briefing Session, Traverse City, Mich., August 9.
South Carolina Coastal Conservation League. 1995. *Getting a Rein on Runoff: How Sprawl
    and the Traditional Town Compare.* Land Development Bulletin Number 7.
    Charleston, S.C.: South Carolina Coastal Conservation League.
Waller, Donald M., and William S. Alverson. 1997. "The White-Tailed Deer: A Keystone
    Herbivore." *Wildlife Society Bulletin* 25 (2): 217–26.
Warrick, Joby. 1998. "Earth at Its Warmest in Past 12 Centuries." *Washington Post*,
    8 December.
Wisconsin Department of Commerce. 1997. *Draft Environmental Impact Statement
    Related to Private Onsite Wastewater Treatment Systems and Sanitation.* Madison,
    Wis.: Wisconsin Department of Commerce (June 23).
Wright, Frank Lloyd. 1932. *The Vanishing City.* New York: Stratford Press.
Yergin, Daniel. 1991. *The Prize.* New York: Touchstone.

# 3

# Sprawl, Concentration of Poverty, and Urban Inequality

Paul A. Jargowsky

Two trends dominated the evolution of metropolitan areas in the second half of the 20th century. First, at least until the recent economic boom, the majority of the central cities of major U.S. metropolitan areas were in a decades-long period of decline relative to the suburbs.[1] Second, metropolitan areas simultaneously experienced rapid development in their outer suburban rings. These two central facts, in themselves, are uncontroversial. Nevertheless, there is a lively debate about the causes of these trends and about their social and economic significance. Some argue that the recent suburban explosion is simply a manifestation of growth, rising incomes, and a general preference for suburban living. Others argue that growth is out of control and results from foolish government policies and perverse incentives to local governments, developers, and homeowners.

Disagreement also persists about the causal ordering of these two central facts. Did the decline of the central cities inspire suburban sprawl by giving the middle class ample reason to flee the frightening poverty and social disorder of the inner city? Or did suburban sprawl erode the tax base and siphon off middle-class families and institutions, thereby destabilizing central-city neighborhoods and causing their decline? The ultimate significance of the pattern of suburban growth and central-city decline for poverty and inequality is poorly understood and subsequently underweighted in policy debates about metropolitan development.

The driving forces behind suburban sprawl deliver new developments, which are both disproportionately aimed at the highest tier of the income distribution and geographically distant from the urban core. In its wake, this development process leads to concentrations of poverty that are both physically and socially isolated from the mainstream of society and the bulk of educational resources and employment opportunities. These spatial disparities increase poverty in the short run and reduce equality of opportunity, therefore contributing to inequality in the long run. The low density, environmental impact, and aesthetic aspects of new suburban neighborhoods are important facets of the sprawl debate, but such issues are not central to the concern over sprawl's role in poverty and inequality.

The goal of this chapter is to demonstrate and explore sprawl's equity dimension. It begins with an examination of the decline of central cities relative to suburbs, as well as the surge in the concentration of poverty at the urban core. The following section develops the links between suburban development patterns and the fortunes of the central city. The final section addresses the implications of the bifurcated pattern of metropolitan development for poverty, inequality, and equality of opportunity.

## Central-City Decline

The nation's major cities have always served the function of integrating low-income persons into the national economy. Waves of immigrants from Europe, Asia, Latin America, and elsewhere have passed through the inner-city neighborhoods of many large urban areas. While most people associate cities like New York, San Francisco, Los Angeles, and Miami with immigration, in fact almost every major city has or at least once had neighborhoods associated with ethnic immigration. Moreover, large cities, especially in the North, attracted waves of the rural poor—white and black—as the nation shifted from an agricultural to an industrial economy. Thus, while urban areas have always been characterized by concentrations of poor persons and poor neighborhoods, they also have served the function of helping the poor to assimilate into a new country and a new economy (Hicks 1994).

Following World War II, a number of factors converged to change the nature of the relationship between urban centers and poverty. First, the proliferation of the automobile reduced workers' reliance on proximity to employment centers and public transportation systems. Second, the GI Bill and economic prosperity made it realistic for nonagricultural middle-class persons to aspire to own detached single-family homes, surrounded by grass and trees.[2] Third, a heightening of racial tensions in the wake of the northward migration of southern blacks, culminating in the race riots of the 1960s, led many whites to flee as far as they could from the burgeoning and seemingly insoluble concentration of social problems at the urban core. A related point is that school desegregation made it harder to avoid contact with minority groups and economically disadvantaged persons merely by living in a middle-class or higher-income neighborhood; families believed they had to relocate outside the central-city school district altogether to avoid the threats, real or perceived, that school integration posed to their children. Fourth, as discussed elsewhere in this volume, a myriad of public policies provided additional incentives and subsidies that encouraged suburbanization.

The cumulative effect of these developments was a sea change in the role of cities in the American class system. Historically, movements of poor persons into the urban core—seeking a port of entry into the American mainstream—led to the concentration of urban poverty. By 1970, however, a different dynamic began to develop. The white middle class, followed by the black middle class, began to leave the inner city for suburban destinations. Selective migration of the nonpoor out of the central city replaced selective migration of the poor into the central city as a key mechanism leading to increases in the concentration of poverty (Jargowsky and Bane 1991; Wilson 1987). A number of cities, particularly in Texas and California, continue to have significant streams of poor people migrating in from abroad (Frey 1993). Only in these cities are the populations of central-city residential neighborhoods growing. For most metropolitan areas, however, the primary trend has been deconcentration. As Berry and Gillard (1977, 1) noted, "counter-urbanization has replaced urbanization as the dominant force shaping the nation's settlement patterns."

Some central cities were able to use expansion and annexation to partly retain dominion over their population and tax base, but many were constrained by existing suburbs that locked their boundaries in place. As a result, central cities have declined relative to suburbs in both population and economic status. The population of the central cities of the 100 largest metropolitan areas grew by 9.2 percent between 1970 and 1998, while the suburbs of those metropolitan areas grew by 59 percent (calculated from Exhibit 1–8, U.S. Department of Housing and Urban Development [HUD] 2000, 23).[3] Central cities lag in job growth generally and high-tech job growth in particular (HUD 2000, 5, 40). Central cities have much higher poverty rates than suburbs. In 1999, for example, the poverty rate of central cities was 16.4, compared with 8.3 percent in suburban areas (U.S. Census Bureau 2000).

Even in the 1990s, when metropolitan economies were strong and many downtowns were booming, the central cities continued to lag the suburbs in population growth. The 2000 Census showed that the population of central cities rose 9.7 percent over the 1990s, compared with 22.4 percent for the suburbs. The suburbs' share of the U.S. population rose from 46.2 percent in 1990 to 50 percent in 2000, for the first time reaching half the total U.S. population. Over the same period, the central-city share of the U.S. population actually fell, from 31.3 percent to 30.3 percent. As a share of the metropolitan population, the central cities declined even faster, from 40.4 percent in 1990 to 37.7 percent in 2000.

The most visible manifestation of this trend has been the rapid expansion of high-poverty ghettos and barrios at the center of large metropolitan areas and the decline of middle-class residential areas within the confines of the central city. The poor, especially the minority poor, are increasingly isolated in depopulated urban wastelands. Such neighborhoods often exhibit severe signs of economic distress, including vacant and dilapidated housing units, high levels of unemployment, high rates of single parenthood, problems with gangs and violence, and widespread drug and alcohol abuse. The elevated levels of social problems in these neighborhoods should not be misinterpreted to imply that all or even most neighborhood residents share such characteristics, an error known as the "ecological fallacy" (Robinson 1950; Myers 1954). However, it is true that all residents of neighborhoods with disproportionate levels of social problems are exposed to and must cope with the social environments that result.

Nationally, the number of poor persons residing in high-poverty neighborhoods very nearly doubled between 1970 and 1990, rising from 1.9 million to 3.7 million.[4] The *concentration of poverty*, defined as the percentage of all poor persons living in poor neighborhoods, increased from 12.4 to 17.9 percent. Furthermore, poverty concentration is much higher for minority groups. For example, 33.5 percent of the black poor and 22.1 percent of the Hispanic poor lived in high-poverty neighborhoods in 1990, compared with 6.3 percent of the white poor.

Some metropolitan areas experienced huge increases in the concentration of poverty among both blacks and Hispanics. For example, in Detroit, a relatively low 11.3 percent of blacks lived in high-poverty areas in 1970; by 1990, the figure nearly quintupled, rising to 53.9 percent. Thus, by 1990, more than half the black poor in Detroit had to contend with both low family income and severely disadvantaged neighborhood context as well. Other cities experienced devastating increases in the concentration of poverty among blacks, including New York (27 percent), Chicago (21.4 percent), and Pittsburgh (21.7 percent). There were also a number of cities with huge increases in the Hispanic concentration of poverty, including New York (18.8 percent), Philadelphia (48.4 percent), and Detroit (33.8 percent). The vast majority of cities had increases in either black or Hispanic concentration of poverty or both. The exceptions are places like Boston, Phoenix, and Washington, D.C.—cities that experienced strong economic growth between 1970 and 1990. If the spatial context of daily living has an effect on the subjective experience of poverty, then what it means to be poor has changed for the worse in recent decades. In the vast majority of cities, the poor were increasingly isolated from the mainstream of society in high-poverty ghettos and barrios.

Poverty is concentrated in the United States for a number of different reasons. Historically, the single most important factor has been racial residential segregation. African Americans have poverty rates more than three times as high as non-Hispanic whites. At the same time, the vast majority of blacks live in a relatively small number of highly segregated neighborhoods (Massey and Denton 1993). In this way, historic segregation by race has had the effect of concentrating poverty (Massey 1990; Massey and Eggers 1990). If the black population were evenly dispersed among the much larger white population, there would be virtually no concentration of poverty by the measures used above, because the poverty of blacks would be "diluted" by the larger number and lower poverty rate of the majority group.

On the other hand, racial concentration reached its peak in 1970, the base year for the comparisons made earlier. The cause of the *increases* in concentrated poverty between 1970 and 1990 cannot be racial segregation, which declined by small to moderate amounts across the vast majority of metropolitan areas during this period (Farley and Frey 1994; Harrison and Weinberg 1992).[5] If anything, the declines in racial segregation between 1970 and 1990, other things equal, would have led to lower levels of concentration of poverty.

The state of the local economy has a profound effect on poverty concentration. As the economy declines, the overall poverty level rises. However, it is not necessarily true that an increasing metropolitan *poverty rate* will lead to a higher *concentration of poverty*. In fact, the opposite could occur. Suppose that the high-poverty area contains the nonworking poor, and that the newly unemployed poor created by an economic downturn reside in other neighborhoods scattered throughout the city. In that case, the concentration of poverty could actually fall as poverty itself rises. But in fact what happens is that, as the overall poverty level rises, the effect is felt disproportionately in the high-poverty areas and the "borderline" neighborhoods in the immediate vicinity of the existing poverty concentrations. These neighborhoods are borderline in two senses: they physically border the existing high-poverty areas, and they tend to have poverty rates in the 30 to 40 percent range. In a downturn, these neighborhoods see their poverty rates rise above the 40 percent level, and so there is an expansion of the high-poverty zone and all of the residents of the larger area are numbered among the concentrated poor.

Despite the importance of the labor market in explaining the concentration of poverty, the economy is not the only factor that affects the concentration of poverty. On average, across all metropolitan areas, there was a substantial increase in the concentration of poverty between 1970 and 1990. Yet, again on average, the economies of these metropolitan areas actually improved, which should have led to decreases in the concentration of poverty, other things equal. Obviously, other things were not equal.

As noted above, inner-city neighborhoods are also embedded in metropolitan housing markets in which the dominant trend is deconcentration. Suburbs at the far edge of metropolitan areas are developed and typically cater to higher-income families. As this group moves from the inner-ring suburbs, middle-class families take their places, moving themselves from central-city residential neighborhoods. This process of selective out-migration systematically reduces the income level of the residents left behind in the neighborhoods near the center of the metropolitan area. As a result, more neighborhoods have sufficiently high poverty rates to be considered high-poverty neighborhoods.

Figure 3.1 shows the expansion of high-poverty area in the Detroit metropolitan area, while Figure 3.2 shows the expansion of the high-poverty zones in the Houston metropolitan area.[6] Consistent with the discussion above, the physical size of the high-poverty neighborhoods in these two cities expanded dramatically. A far greater proportion of

(*text continues on page 47*)

Figure 3.1  *The Expansion of Detroit's Ghetto (Census Tracts by Poverty Rate, 1980 and 1990)*

20–40% in poverty

40% or more in poverty

1990

1980

Detroit

Oakland

Macomb

Wayne

*Source:* U.S. Census Summary File 3A for 1980 and 1990, tabulations by the author.

Figure 3.2  *The Expansion of Houston's Ghettos and Barrios (Census Tracts by Poverty Rate, 1980 and 1990)*

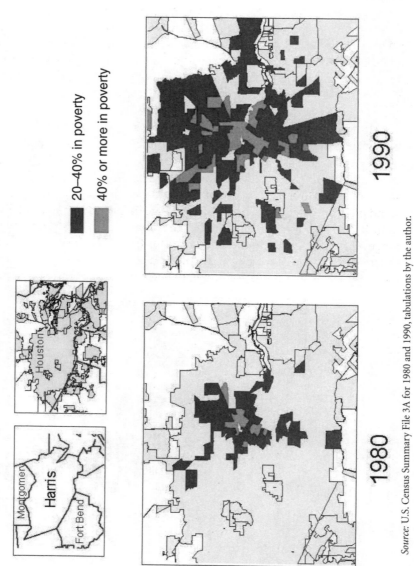

20–40% in poverty

40% or more in poverty

1990

1980

*Source:* U.S. Census Summary File 3A for 1980 and 1990, tabulations by the author.

the land area of both of these central cities consisted of high-poverty neighborhoods by 1990. In the case of Detroit, this occurred through a combination of increasing poverty and out-migration of nonpoor persons, resulting in a higher poverty rate in the "borderline" census tracts. In Houston, poverty actually declined in the 1980s, so the increase in the number of high-poverty tracts was driven mostly by newly arriving Mexican immigrants and the out-migration of the nonpoor from those neighborhoods. Thus, cities in very different economic trajectories both experienced a large expansion of their blighted area.

Further evidence on this point is provided by table 3.1, which compares the growth of high-poverty neighborhoods by several different measures between 1980 and 1990. The first measure is the percentage change in the square kilometers of the high-poverty area and thus represents the change in the geographic extent of the high-poverty census tracts. The second measure given is the percentage change in the total population living in high-poverty neighborhoods. The final measure is percentage change in the number of high-poverty census tracts. In most of the metropolitan areas listed, the physical size of the high-poverty neighborhoods grew faster than the population living in such areas. In other words, the

Table 3.1 *Percentage Change in the Size of High-Poverty Areas within Select Major Metropolitan Regions, 1980–1990*

| Metropolitan Area | Size as measured by: | | |
|---|---|---|---|
| | Geographic Area[a] | Population | Number of Census Tracts |
| New York | 51 | −4 | −11 |
| Los Angeles | 107 | 123 | 40 |
| Chicago | 108 | 7 | 35 |
| Philadelphia | 48 | −9 | 1 |
| Detroit | 307 | 248 | 192 |
| Dallas-Ft. Worth | 51 | 135 | 100 |
| Washington, D.C. | 52 | −43 | 0 |
| San Francisco | 136 | 37 | 8 |
| Houston | 232 | 243 | 292 |
| Boston | 39 | 36 | 25 |
| Minneapolis-St. Paul | 563 | 224 | 200 |

Source: Author's tabulations from 1980 and 1990 Census data.

Note: All figures represent net changes.

[a] Calculated from 1980 and 1990 Census tract boundaries by J. D. Kim, University of Texas at Dallas.

ghettos and barrios of these cities were larger, but less dense in 1990 than they were in 1980. Even places where the total population of high-poverty areas *declined* between 1980 and 1990 (such as New York and Washington, D.C.) experienced large *increases* (51 and 52 percent, respectively) in the size of their high-poverty zones.

There were a few exceptions—places where the population grew faster than the size of the impoverished area. These are Los Angeles, Dallas-Ft. Worth, and Houston. Each of these areas was experiencing substantial immigration of Mexicans. Nevertheless, these cities did follow the pattern of a large increase in the geographic extent of the high-poverty area.

Racial segregation and the labor market both have important effects on the concentration of poverty, but neither of these variables can explain the rapid rise in the concentration of poverty between 1970 and 1990. Segregation was declining and the economy was improving over this period. Instead, the long-term trend toward increases in the concentration of poverty has to do with a spatial restructuring of metropolitan areas that leads to a hollowing out of the central cities and larger areas of urban blight. This process seems to move on in good times and bad, working quietly in the background to undermine the central city and increase economic segregation.

Over the past 90 years, many central cities have been experiencing a renaissance. When the income and poverty data for the 2000 Census are released, we may well see declines in the concentration of poverty in the areas with the strongest economic growth. It is certainly what would be expected given the analysis presented above: a strong economy differentially benefits central cities just as much as a weak one differentially hurts. Assuming, however, that the current economic peak cannot be maintained indefinitely, it is fair to ask how much of the current boom in the central city will survive the next recession. To answer this question, we have to look more closely at the connections between central-city decline and urban sprawl, which has continued and even accelerated during the current economic boom.

## Urban Sprawl and Central-City Decline

Arguably, the United States is unique among western industrial nations in the extent of concentration of poverty. This claim is difficult to verify empirically, because neither the poverty rate nor the census tracts that serve as proxies for neighborhoods can be replicated in any consistent way across nations. Nevertheless, it seems clear that most European cities are not nearly as segregated by race and class as is common in the United States (Musterd and Ostendorf 1998; van der Wusten and Musterd 1998).[7] The United States is also unique in that "affluent and middle-class Americans live in suburban areas that are far from their work places" (Jackson 1985, 6). While the previous section examined the concentration of poverty, this section addresses the issue of suburban sprawl and argues that these two types of American exceptionalism are not unrelated.

There are many different and sometimes contradictory conceptions of the term "sprawl" extant in the literature. The current ambiguity regarding the meaning of sprawl is reminiscent of the discussion of the underclass in the mid-1980s. The latter term was brought to the fore by a series of widely read research papers by William Julius Wilson, culminating in the publication of *The Truly Disadvantaged* (1987). In Wilson's conception, the term "underclass" referred to persons residing in neighborhoods so socially isolated and economically disadvantaged that they became enveloped in a "tangle of pathology." However, the term was also adopted by social conservatives as a way to refer to persons caught up in a permissive cultural climate, and who therefore acted irresponsibly and caused their own poverty (Magnet 1993). Liberals and urban advocates used the term as a loose synonym for the urban poor, one which placed an emphasis on their relationship to the larger class structure of American society. Further difficulties ensued when researchers attempted to operationalize the term for measurement purposes (Ricketts and Sawhill 1988; Abramson and Tobin 1994). Researchers, policymakers, and advocates adopted a trendy term and elided its meaning in convenient directions, ultimately destroying its usefulness.

The debate about sprawl has some of the same characteristics, and faces a similar danger. However, to understand the implications of sprawl for poverty and inequality, it is necessary to assign some concrete meaning to the term. Gregory Squires, in chapter 1, offered the following definition:

> Sprawl can be defined as a pattern of urban and metropolitan growth that reflects low-density, automobile-dependent, exclusionary new development on the fringe of settled areas often surrounding a deteriorating city (2).

According to this definition, sprawl is not a fixed set of characteristics of a region's housing stock, but rather a characterization of the area's growth over time. The definition identifies several different characteristics that comprise sprawl, which have differing potential effects on poverty and inequality.

The first characteristic of sprawl is low density. Density refers both to the average number of persons per acre in new developments, but also to the discontinuous nature of the developments themselves. Transportation planners and environmentalists are particularly concerned with this aspect of sprawl. Low-density residential areas are inherently difficult to serve with public transportation in a cost-effective manner, resulting in nearly total reliance on individual automobiles for transportation. The resulting air pollution, traffic congestion, and land consumed by highway construction are negative externalities, the cost of which is not factored into either the developers 'or homebuyers' economic calculus. On the other hand, waves of suburban movers have shown a marked preference for lower density, indicating that there are benefits as well.

There is no question that the density of cities has been declining for decades, for a variety of reasons. For one thing, changes in transportation and communication have made lower density possible. For another, increasing real incomes have resulted in greater demand for space, both larger housing units and greater spacing between units. Thus, as far as sprawl is concerned, the question is not whether densities are declining but whether they are declining more rapidly than can be explained by the underlying economics.

Squires' definition also stresses that sprawl is rapid growth at the periphery of a city or metropolitan area. In its provocatively titled report "Sprawl: The Dark Side of the American Dream," the Sierra Club defined sprawl as "low-density development beyond the edge of service and employment" (Sierra Club 1998). On the other hand, growth at the periphery of existing developed areas is exactly what one would expect. Sprawl, in the sense of peripheral development, is certainly not a new phenomenon. By this definition, all cities and metropolitan areas have been sprawling throughout history. One can map the developed areas of London or Chicago or any major city over many decades or centuries and, except for the occasional catastrophe, cities expand over time, with the fastest rate of growth in housing stock taking place in the fringe of the developed area. Between 1810 and 1820, the suburbs of New York grew faster than the central city, though at that time, well before New York's great consolidation, the "suburbs" included places like Brooklyn that we now consider the central city. Areas outside Philadelphia County grew faster than the county in that decade as well. The growth in Boston's suburbs first outpaced the growth of the city itself in the 1830s; Cleveland and St. Louis experienced the same phenomenon in the 1840s (Jackson 1985, 316).

The term "sprawl," as it is generally used, is loaded with pejorative connotations that go beyond Squires' definition. Sprawl is said to be unplanned and illogical development. It is criticized for being ugly, dehumanizing, and socially isolating. Popular books have denounced sprawl for producing "jive-plastic commuter tract-home wastelands" that are a "wasteful, toxic, agoraphobic-inducing spectacle" (Kunstler 1993, 10). Movies such as *Blue Velvet* and *American Beauty* play up the idea that the conformity and monotony of suburban neighborhoods socially isolate people, generating perversity and hypocrisy in equal and complementary degrees. There are perhaps a dozen other ways to think about the meaning of sprawl that have been bandied about in the literature (Galster et al. 2000).

There is no necessary connection between urban sprawl, in the senses defined above, and poverty, inequality, or the concentration of poverty. If the new suburbs developed with a complete menu of housing types, from gated communities to low- and moderate-income housing, segregation by income could actually decline as the city expanded. Rapid peripheral growth could, after all, be a source of jobs and reduce poverty and inequality. Low-density development could in theory provide a higher quality of life for low-income persons than dense, dangerous neighborhoods in central-city housing projects. A "jive-plastic" tract home in a suburban wasteland might well be preferable to a "jive-concrete" housing project in the center of an urban wasteland.

Sprawl is related to poverty and inequality mainly because sprawl creates a greater degree of separation between the income classes. From the perspective of urban inequality, the key element of Squires' definition is that the new growth is "exclusionary." That is, if new development— whether planned or unplanned, ugly or beautiful, high density or low density—accentuates segregation of the rich and middle class from the poor, then and only then does it contribute to the concentration of poverty. Sprawl produces vast areas of concentrated wealth in the favored sectors of the city, while leaving the poor geographically and socially isolated in the central city. While other aspects of sprawl have impacts on the poor as well, such as environmental degradation and low density, it is the pronounced tendency toward economic segregation that is the most likely to have dynamic effects on income distribution.

The key question, therefore, is the relevance of sprawl to economic segregation and the concentration of poverty. Figure 3.3 shows the temporal pattern of housing construction for Minneapolis-St. Paul. The outer black boundary indicates the extent of the metropolitan areas as defined by the Census Bureau. The inner black boundaries are the city boundaries of the central cities of the metropolitan area. The balance of the area can be thought of as the suburbs. The boundaries of individual suburban places and towns, as well as census tract boundaries, have been omitted to avoid unduly cluttering the map. In looking at the map, however, it is important to keep in mind that the procedure used by the Census Bureau to create metropolitan area definitions operates at the county level. Thus, whole counties are either added or excluded. Thus, the non–central-city areas include some largely vacant and unincorporated land.

The shadings indicate the median year in which homes were built in the census tracts. Neighborhoods in the central cities of the metropolitan area were largely constructed prior to 1949. Undoubtedly, there are newer units in all these neighborhoods, a product of infill development or new construction on the site of razed units. In addition, older units may have been substantially renovated one or more times since their construction. Nevertheless, at least half the housing units in these neighborhoods were originally constructed prior to 1950.

At the fringes of the central cities and in the immediately contiguous suburbs, there is a ring of neighborhoods in which the median year built is between 1950 and 1959. There are also a number of small "islands" of construction during this period at noncontiguous locations. These were small towns that were essentially separate communities rather than suburbs of Minneapolis and St. Paul. Later, these were absorbed into the suburbs as the metropolitan area expanded. Further rings of suburbs were constructed in the 1960s, 1970s, and 1980s. These data are from the 1990 Census, so in the last category of neighborhoods the median housing unit was constructed within 10 years of the census date. These are basically new neighborhoods. Consistent with the notion that suburban sprawl is occurring at the periphery of the metropolitan area, the new neighborhoods form a ring at the far edge of the developed part of the metropolitan area.

Figure 3.3  *The Pattern of Suburban Development in Minneapolis (Median Year Built, by Census Tract)*

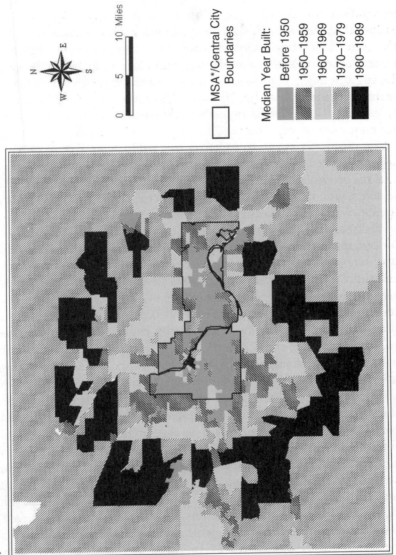

Median Year Built:
Before 1950
1950–1959
1960–1969
1970–1979
1980–1989

MSA*/Central City Boundaries

N
W    E
S

0    5    10 Miles

*Source:* U.S. Census Summary File 3A for 1990, tabulations by the author.

* MSA = metropolitan statistical area.

Minneapolis-St. Paul is a very graphic illustration of the pattern of sequential rings of suburban development. Figures 3.4 and 3.5 show the median year built zones for Detroit and Houston, respectively. There are far fewer neighborhoods in the Detroit metropolitan area that were built primarily in the 1980s. Nevertheless, all three metropolitan areas, despite their regional and economic differences, exhibit a striking "bull's eye" pattern of concentric rings of development. As noted above, it is not surprising that as the population of an area grows, new development takes place at the periphery. John Dillinger, when asked why he robbed banks, reportedly replied, "because that's where the money is." Newer suburbs are build in concentric rings because that's where the land is.

For this pattern to be troublesome from the point of view of poverty and inequality, there must be an interaction between this new growth and the household income of residents. If new suburbs were built, replete with new schools, parks, and other amenities, and the benefits of these new places were equally accessible across the economic spectrum, sprawl would not perpetuate poverty and reduce access to opportunity. Indeed, the housing stock of newer suburbs could in principle be a force for racial and economic integration as long as it was more spatially accessible than the existing pattern of housing stock in the metropolitan area, not a tough criterion to meet.

Ultimately, whether sprawl is involved in the concentration of poverty is an empirical question and depends on the regulatory environment and characteristics of the housing market that generates the new development. In fact, as suburban development occurs in the United States, it is linked very closely to the income distribution. The political and economic forces that shape suburban development are described in detail elsewhere in this book. From the point of view of urban poverty, the key issue is how the resulting pattern of economic development interacts with the income distribution.

Table 3.2 shows the mean, standard deviation, and coefficient of variation of neighborhood mean household income associated with the decade of development across all U.S. metropolitan areas. That is, for all U.S. metropolitan areas, metropolitan neighborhoods are categorized by decade according to the five categories of median year built illustrated in figure 3.3: 1949 and earlier, 1950s, 1960s, 1970s, and 1980s. Each of these neighborhoods has a mean household income. The far right column shows values for metropolitan areas generally; that is, it includes all neighborhoods (census tracts), regardless of whether they are in a central

(*text continues on page 57*)

Figure 3.4 *The Pattern of Suburban Development in Detroit (Median Year Built, by Census Tract)*

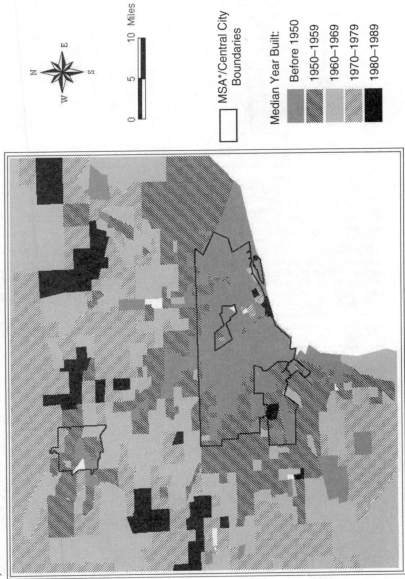

*Source:* U.S. Census Summary File 3A for 1990, tabulations by the author.

* MSA = metropolitan statistical area.

Figure 3.5  *The Pattern of Suburban Development in Houston (Median Year Built, by Census Tract)*

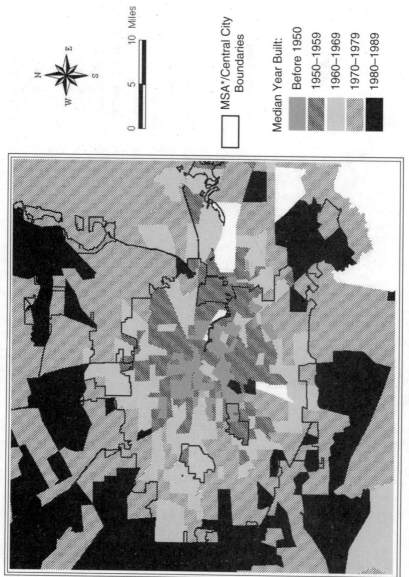

Median Year Built:

Before 1950

1950–1959

1960–1969

1970–1979

1980–1989

MSA*/Central City Boundaries

N
W    E
S

0    5    10  Miles

*Source:* U.S. Census Summary File 3A for 1990, tabulations by the author.

* MSA = metropolitan statistical area.

Table 3.2  *Household Income Characteristics by Decade of Neighborhood Development and Type of Area, 1990*

| Median Year Built | Central City | Suburbs | All |
|---|---|---|---|
| | Mean Household Income ($) | | |
| 1949 and earlier | 32,500 | 42,501 | 35,370 |
| 1950–1959 | 34,336 | 44,854 | 40,240 |
| 1960–1969 | 37,215 | 44,784 | 42,291 |
| 1970–1979 | 38,829 | 43,915 | 42,626 |
| 1980–1989 | 44,873 | 50,549 | 49,037 |
| | Standard Deviation of Neighborhood Mean Incomes ($) | | |
| 1949 and earlier | 17,174 | 24,267 | 19,994 |
| 1950–1959 | 18,441 | 21,921 | 21,123 |
| 1960–1969 | 19,097 | 20,194 | 20,156 |
| 1970–1979 | 16,400 | 16,734 | 16,796 |
| 1980–1989 | 16,609 | 17,229 | 17,250 |
| | Coefficient of Variation | | |
| 1949 and earlier | 0.53 | 0.57 | 0.57 |
| 1950–1959 | 0.54 | 0.49 | 0.52 |
| 1960–1969 | 0.51 | 0.45 | 0.48 |
| 1970–1979 | 0.42 | 0.38 | 0.39 |
| 1980–1989 | 0.37 | 0.34 | 0.35 |

*Source:* Tabulations by the author and J. D. Kim, from 1990 Census STF 3C.

*Notes:* Data are compiled by Census tracts, which serve as proxies for neighborhoods. Tracts that are partially in central cities and suburbs have the parts counted separately in their respective categories, except that the median year built is determined once at the full-tract level.

city or suburban locale.[8] Neighborhoods with a median year built of 1949 or earlier, on average across the nation, had a mean income of approximately $35,000, compared with $49,000 for neighborhoods in which the median year built is in the 1980s.[9] Neighborhoods whose median housing unit was built in the intervening years, 1950 to 1979, had intermediate mean household incomes in the range of $40,000 to $43,000. There is a monotonic relationship between the decade of construction of the neighborhood's median housing unit and the mean income of the households that occupy those units. Remember, as in Figures 3.3 to 3.5, that these year-built categories tend to be at the fringes of the metropolitan area, so that to a large extent the year-built categories represent specific geographic zones.

Table 3.2 also shows the mean incomes for neighborhoods categorized by central city or suburban location.[10] Controlling for median year built, central city neighborhoods have consistently lower mean incomes than the comparable cohort of suburban neighborhoods. The general pattern of correlation between the age of the median house and the mean income of the neighborhood is maintained both within central cities and within suburbs.

In addition to building housing units to attract higher income families, fringe suburbs use zoning and other devices to limit access to lower-income families. The stock aerial photograph, symbolic of suburban conformity, shows mile after mile of virtually identical households. While nobody expects that the poor will live in the same neighborhoods as the rich, the aspect of suburban development that increases economic segregation is that entire sectors of the metropolitan area are devoted exclusively to one type of housing.

One way to evaluate the extent of such segregation is to look at the standard deviation of neighborhood mean incomes by cohort of year built, as shown in the second panel of table 3.2. The standard deviation of household income seems to follow an inverted "U" pattern, first rising, then falling as we move from older to newer neighborhoods. As expected, the lowest values are found in the newest neighborhoods. Disaggregating the central cities and suburbs reveals the pattern even more clearly. Within the suburbs, the standard deviation of the neighborhood mean incomes generally decreases as the median year built increases. Thus, the mean increases and the variance decreases the more recently the suburb was built. Within central cities, there is much less of a difference between neighborhoods by median year built, and no clear direction in the relationship.

The differences in the variability of neighborhood mean incomes by median year built are even larger than the standard deviations imply. Generally, when distributions have different means, it is appropriate to normalize the standard deviation by the mean. This quotient is referred to as the coefficient of variation (CV), and is shown in the bottom panel of table 3.2. The "U" pattern disappears once the mean is controlled. There is a consistent pattern of less variability in neighborhood mean incomes as measured by the CV in central cities, in suburbs, and overall. In the suburbs, the CV is 40 percent lower in the newest neighborhoods compared with the oldest. Clearly, whether measured by the standard deviation directly or by the CV, the newer suburban neighborhoods are more homogeneous than the older cohorts of neighborhoods.

The newer neighborhoods are also more homogeneous in terms of race and ethnicity. Looking across all metropolitan areas in 1990, the oldest neighborhoods were about 60 percent non-Hispanic white and therefore about 40 percent minority. As the neighborhood vintage becomes more recent, the non-Hispanic white proportion increases. The most recent neighborhoods—those in which the median housing unit was constructed in the 1980s—were 80 percent non-Hispanic white. However, when disaggregating by central city versus suburb, it turns out that all suburban neighborhoods, regardless of era of construction, are about 80 percent non-Hispanic white. Clearly, racial segregation in the suburbs is not a new pattern, and the older suburbs were constructed at a time when racial discrimination in housing was even stronger than it is today. Within central cities, the non-Hispanic white percentage varies from just about half in the older neighborhoods to 75 percent in the newest neighborhoods.

Suburbanization has been going on since cities were invented. At first, suburbanization was limited by the transportation capacities of the foot and the horse. Once the transportation infrastructure made longer commutes possible, suburbs began to appear along streetcar lines (Warner 1962). The automobile and the construction of modern, high-speed roads opened up the suburbs even further. Suburbanization has always been about two different things. In the first place, people move to the suburbs to translate their economic success into desirable neighborhood amenities, such as single-family homes, yards, and good schools (Gans 1967, 31–41). Second, as Park (1926) argued long ago, urban environments are shaped by the attempts of successful and mobile groups of persons to translate social distances between themselves and lower status groups into physical distances that protect them from the real and perceived threats posed by the lower status groups.

Suburbanization has, therefore, always involved both the "pull" of desirable suburban characteristics and the "push" of undesirable central-city characteristics. This dual nature of suburbanization did not start with the riots of the 1960s, with the dramatic increases in crime in the central city in the 1970s, or with the emergence of the particular set of development patterns now called sprawl. To argue, that sprawl is related to central-city decline is not to argue that sprawl is what causes central-city decline. It clearly does play a role, but it is just as valid to argue that central-city decline is what causes sprawl. The "pull" of the suburbs is enhanced by the construction of large modern homes in ethnically and economically homogenous suburbs, perhaps with walls and a private security force. The "push" of central cities is exacerbated as higher-income families leave, the fiscal condition of the central cities worsens, and the quality of public services, particularly education, declines.

The process is a spiral, and the relative balance of push and pull clearly varies over time. At the time of the riots, push clearly predominated. In the late 1990s, as families moved from one distant suburb to an even more distant suburb, the pull of the amenities offered by the latest housing developments was probably relatively more important. It is pointless to argue about which of the two factors is the driving force in a fundamentally circular process of sprawl and decay.

Arguing that sprawl and central-city decline are related does not imply that developers who construct housing units demanded by the market, or the families who choose suburban units with a wonderful complement of amenities, are evil people. Both groups are making decisions based on the incentives and the rules of the game as they exist in our metropolitan areas. Those incentives result from a complex set of tax rules, zoning rules, development subsidies, and governmental institutions that are detailed elsewhere in this volume. These policy rules and mechanisms reflect both local preferences and the political power of development interests. They fundamentally shape the current pattern of development.

Sam Bass Warner argued that the decline of the central cities and the suburban explosion are part of a "chronic urban disease" that feeds on "a healthy body of everyday behavior and aspirations" (1972, 154). From the point of view of current suburbanites, the term "disease" may seem a bizarre description of a process that results in highly desirable housing developments. But the result of the process is the spatial separation of racial and income classes, the implications of which are addressed in the next section. The social, economic, and political costs of this development pattern, which accumulate slowly over many decades, need to be weighed and evaluated. If such costs are onerous, then a change in the rules and policies within which the development process occurs may well be justified.

## The Social Significance of Poverty Concentration

William Julius Wilson (1987) called attention to the connection between the increasing spatial isolation of the poor and the "tangle of pathology" extant in the modern ghetto: high levels of drug and alcohol abuse, low levels of attachment to the mainstream labor force, out-of-wedlock childbearing, gang violence, and other troubling manifestations of self-destructive behaviors. Although these social conditions had not escaped the notice of journalists or Hollywood movie producers, the academic community had been reluctant to address such issues in the aftermath of the furor over the "Moynihan Report." Daniel Patrick Moynihan (1965) called attention to the rise of out-of-wedlock childbearing among blacks in the inner city and was vehemently attacked for "blaming the victim."

Wilson's work was notable for connecting the social conditions of the inner city to quantitative assessments of the concentration of poverty. Wilson showed that there was a significant increase in the degree of spatial isolation of the black poor in Chicago and an expansion in the geographic size of the high-poverty neighborhoods in that city. He linked the changing social conditions to a combination of decreases in real opportunity, brought about by deindustrialization and the suburbanization of employment, and the social isolation of the poor. In other words, the black poor were increasingly spatially and thus socially isolated from both the white community and even the black middle class.

Figure 3.6 shows a series of linkages and interactions through which urban sprawl and the spatial isolation of the poor affect poverty and inequality in the short run, and equality of opportunity in the long run. Volumes could be and have been written about each of the arrows in the diagram. The previous section presented evidence that the current development process affects the neighborhood environment by concentrating poverty. The following discussion is not meant to provide an exhaustive discussion of the remaining links, but rather to highlight how the current patterns of metropolitan development, including sprawl and the concentration of poverty, help to generate poverty and worsen inequality.

## The Labor Market/Housing Link

Ultimately, whether an individual is poor is determined by how much income that individual and the members of that individual's family can command in the labor market. While that is primarily determined by the individual's skills and attributes in combination with the characteristics of the labor market, it is also affected by the pattern of racial and economic segregation in a number of ways.

In the first place, most new jobs are being produced in the suburbs (Kasarda 1985, 1988). While a solid core of jobs remain in the downtown

Figure 3.6  *The Interrelationships of Poverty and Inequality*

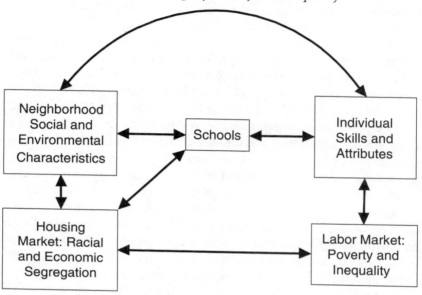

business district, the suburbs are home to new office parks and mini-downtowns at the intersection of major thoroughfares. Moreover, as new suburbs are constructed at greater and greater distances from the urban core, many jobs connected to this prosperous residential base—in grocery stores, restaurants, and dry cleaning establishments, in addition to yard work, swimming pool maintenance, domestic help, and other services—must move in tandem. At the same time, the analogous jobs in the central city wither as the households remaining in the central-city neighborhoods consist increasingly of poor households with less spending power.

The divergence between the centralized pattern of residence for the poor, particularly the minority poor, and the increasingly distant location of the new job base produces a spatial mismatch. The spatial mismatch hypothesis as first proposed by Kain (1968) concerned blacks trapped in the inner city by racial discrimination in housing markets, leading to a segregated and centralized pattern of black neighborhoods. The existence of constraints on movement is a central part of the spatial mismatch story. Without constraints, households would simply shift their residence pattern to match the location of employment opportunities, much the same way regional migrations and worldwide immigrant flows have done throughout history.

While the racial constraints on mobility have arguably been relaxed, they still hold considerable force. In addition, the phenomenon of sprawl has strengthened the barriers to movement based on economic status, which differentially impacts minority groups. Through the mechanisms described in the previous section and elsewhere in the this volume, explicit legal discrimination against low- and moderate-income households prevents them from moving to the areas with the fastest growth in the employment. Low-income blacks and Hispanics face both types of constraints, but as the size and homogeneity of the outer suburbs grow, it would be a mistake to underestimate the extent to which poor whites are also constrained from making optimal relocation decisions.

Given constraints on housing mobility, there are at least four reasons why the spatial mismatch between the inner-city poor and suburban jobs may matter (Ihlanfeldt and Sjoquist 2000, 116–117). In the first place, it may be difficult for the poor to get jobs because of the lack of public transportation or the difficulty and expense of reverse commuting by car. Long commuting time and high commuting costs both reduce the effective wage rate, especially if the base pay rate is low to begin with. Second, information about jobs may not reach into inner-city neighborhoods that have few social, political, or economic ties to the suburbs. Third, employers in the suburbs may exercise more racial discrimination in hiring because they operate in the virtually all-white environment of the suburbs. Even if the employer would not mind hiring minority workers, the employer may wish to indulge customers who are not comfortable dealing with minorities or poor whites from the central city. Fourth, the central-city workers may fear they will be treated unfairly in the largely white suburban labor market. This may be based on past experience in terms of wages, working conditions, and promotions, reducing the incentives to seek out suburban jobs and endure long commutes.

## The Neighborhood/Individual Link

"Poor neighborhoods are poverty machines," writes David Rusk (1999, 123), the former mayor of Albuquerque, succinctly capturing the popular view that disadvantaged neighborhoods diminish the life chances of their residents. The view is widely held and deeply believed. People who "escape the projects" are viewed as minor miracles, and their success is viewed as somehow more virtuous, or at least less probable, than someone raised at the local country club. Because people believe that distressed neighborhoods affect outcomes, especially for children, people with high aspirations for themselves or their children will move out, even if it requires a substantial financial sacrifice.

Neighborhood effects on individual outcomes, in a general sense, could be due to race, space, or class, as well as interactions among these dimensions. Effects related to the racial composition of a neighborhood are commonly called "segregation effects." For example, segregation by race yields black neighborhoods that are more cut off from information about jobs, both because the jobs may be located in white neighborhoods or because the information about job openings does not easily cross the racial divide. The previous section discussed effects due to the physical location of a neighborhood relative to sources of opportunity—the "spatial mismatch." Commonly, however, people use the term "neighborhood effects" to refer to hypothesized effects of the wealth and/or poverty of a neighborhood's residents—or closely related variables, such as family structure or joblessness—on the outcomes for specific individuals within the neighborhood, other things being equal.

The class composition of a neighborhood might influence individuals, even after controlling for their own economic status, through a number of different mechanisms. A concentration of poor neighbors might lead people, especially teens, to emulate negative behaviors, resulting in worse outcomes even after controlling for the influence of a person's immediate family and personal characteristics. This is the so-called "contagion" or "epidemic" model (Crane 1991). Alternatively, or perhaps simultaneously, high-poverty neighborhoods could lack role models and adults who, working through neighborhood institutions like churches and community groups, act as "social buffers" against the effects of deprivation (Wilson 1987). Poor neighborhoods might be underserved by institutions, public and private, that would be available to assist a poor person living in a better-off neighborhood (Jencks and Mayer 1990). While the empirical evidence on neighborhood effects is mixed, more recent studies and common sense argue that neighborhoods can make a big difference in residents' quality of life, their ability to compete effectively in the labor market, and their success in raising children.

The dangers of an isolated and impoverished neighborhood environment may be particularly strong for adolescents, whose search for personal identity makes them more vulnerable to negative influences than adults regardless of their neighborhood and family situation. Elijah Anderson (1991) notes that even in so-called "underclass" neighborhoods, teens are exposed to and lured by multiple visions of how to behave:

> The stable "decent" family with its belief in upward mobility and options for the future provides one. The street culture, which revolves around violence, drugs, sex, having babies out of wedlock, and other problem behavior, provides the other. . . . Virtually all teenagers are at risk and vulnerable to the alluring street culture, and most will dally with the experience; ultimately, many successfully resist. Those who are not well supervised and raised with optimism toward the future may linger in the street culture and may eventually succumb to its standards (397).

It is an exaggeration to say that high-poverty areas create a rigid underclass locked in a self-perpetuating culture of poverty. Children can and do navigate the temptations of the street and succeed in life. But every day in a child's life there is a chance that he or she can make a bad choice or take a risk that turns out badly. The concentration of poverty increases the number and allure of the negative possibilities and increases the probability that ghetto and barrio youth will fall into a downward spiral.

## The Special Role of the Connection to Schools

When poor families are clustered geographically, and a grid of school districts and school attendance zones is also imposed geographically, poor children will also be clustered in school. Schools in poor neighborhoods have greater needs and a lower tax base than suburban schools. It is harder to hire and retain high-quality teachers in the inner city when pay and working conditions are better in suburban districts. In some cases, teachers who continually deal with children from troubled families develop low expectations for students (Farkas 1996; MacLeod 1995). Given the importance of human capital in the modern economy, lower-quality education for the children of the poor will, at the least, perpetuate poverty and is likely to contribute to widening income inequality over time (Levy 1995). Farkas (1996) makes a similar argument concerning what he calls "cultural capital"—the skills, habits, and styles that help to determine a child's ability to succeed in the mainstream economy. Schools also play a role in parents' decisions about where to live, creating a feedback loop between school quality and neighborhood quality.

## The Political Dimension

In his classic work, *Suburbia* (1959), Robert Wood called attention to the fragmentation of governance within metropolitan areas:

> This superimposition of provincial government on cosmopolitan people provides a strange pattern of incongruity. Within a single economic and social complex . . . hundreds and hundreds of local governments jostle one another about. Counties overlie school districts, which overlie municipalities, which overlie sanitary and water districts, which sometimes overlie townships and villages. . . . By ordinary standards of effective, responsible public services, the mosaic of suburban principalities creates governmental havoc (9–10).

If governmental fragmentation is so debilitating, surely governments would consolidate and merge in response to public demand. "Yet," Wood continues, "with extraordinarily few exceptions the ranks of suburban governments hold fast" (11). Indeed, despite occasional city/county consolidations, suburban fragmentation has continued unabated in the decades since Wood wrote these words.

The incredible staying power of fragmented government stems from the fact that there are some important things it does very well. First of all, highly differentiated local governments provide a wide array of choices. Individuals can choose the local jurisdiction that provides the optimal package of housing and public amenities given the housing cost and tax burden (Tiebout 1956). In particular, wealthier families can indulge a taste for placing physical distance between themselves and lower socioeconomic groups (Park 1926). The ability of whites to flee to newer suburbs also may help to maintain racial segregation, as middle-income blacks move into resegregating inner-ring suburbs.[11]

At the same time that spatial separation of income groups compounds poverty and contributes to the growth of inequality, it also reduces public support for policies that might address this cycle. Wealthier segments of society no longer share a common local government with other income groups, and they have little contact with the poor. Stereotypes and distrust are likely to grow, and the capacity to undertake large-scale changes in public policy is likely to diminish. While there is no clear empirical evidence on the point, it is certainly plausible that economically and politically polarized metropolitan areas will find it more difficult to make sustained investments in neighborhoods, education, transportation, and other areas. Rather than making such investments in the future, many wealthier people are simply retreating into suburban enclaves and voting for legislators who promise to lower their taxes. The walls around many new suburban developments probably have little or no effect on crime, but they are a potent symbol of the process that is unfolding in our nation.

## Conclusion

Sprawl and central city decline are part of one unified process of metropolitan change, played out in the context of population growth, higher incomes, fixed political boundaries, and local autonomy. This process generates metropolitan areas in which the poor—especially the minority poor—live at a great remove from the areas of fastest job growth, and leaves the poor socially isolated as well. The poor are harmed directly for a number of reasons. They are less likely to learn about suburban job opportunities and to have the skills necessary to be realistic candidates for them. Even if they have the requisite skills, find out about suburban jobs, and are able to navigate inefficient public transportation systems to go out to apply for them, as virtual foreigners in the suburbs they face a higher degree of discrimination in hiring and promotion. The concentration of the poor leads to a concentration of social problems. Residents may be harmed directly, by falling victim to violent crime, or indirectly, by being drawn into counterproductive activities.

Neighborhoods, then, have a myriad of direct and indirect effects on poverty, and on the distribution of intellectual and social capital that determines, at least in part, the degree of inequality in our society. Sprawl, at least as it currently operates, is clearly part of a larger process that leads to more spatial, racial, social, and economic distance between urban and suburban neighborhoods. These multiple dimensions of difference between lower-income, central-city neighborhoods and affluent exurban neighborhoods contribute directly to poverty in the short run by reducing the capacity of the inner-city poor to find out about, obtain, and remain in jobs in the high-growth sectors of the metropolitan area. These differences also hinder the development of human and cultural capital in the next generation, setting the stage for greater poverty and inequality for generations to come. Finally, the political aspect of sprawl weakens the collective capacity to respond to the challenges of poverty and inequality. For all of these reasons, the public debate about sprawl needs to move beyond the ugliness of strip malls, traffic jams in the suburbs, and disappearing farmland. Instead, the country needs to come to terms with the ways in which sprawl slowly but steadily increases inequality and reduces social and economic mobility.

## NOTES

Research for this chapter was supported in part by the Century Foundation. This chapter also draws heavily on prior research funded by the Russell Sage Foundation. The author would like to thank Brian Berry, Xavier de Souza Briggs, Marie Chevrier, Don Hicks, John Kain, Gregory Squires, and an anonymous reviewer for helpful comments and suggestions. Jeong-Dai Kim performed invaluable research assistance. Comments and questions are welcome. Contact the author at jargo@utdallas.edu or by mail: School of Social Sciences (GR 31), Univ. of Texas at Dallas, 2601 N. Floyd Rd., Richardson, TX 75080.

    1. Metropolitan areas, in concept, include one or more major central cities and the nearby suburbs that are closely tied to those cities' spheres of influence. In practice, the Census Bureau defines metropolitan areas by a complex set of criteria regarding population size, density, commuting patterns, and other factors.

    2. Increasing the level of home ownership had been a goal of federal policy since the Hoover Commission of the 1930s (Jackson 1985, 193–94), in part to stave off the communist menace.

    3. Here the term "suburbs" is being used broadly to refer to all parts of metropolitan areas outside the central cities, as defined by the Census Bureau.

    4. As of this writing, the 2000 Census data for income and poverty have not been released, and so the concentration of poverty figures for 2000 are not yet available. Census tracts serve as proxies for neighborhoods (White 1987). High-poverty neighborhoods are defined as census tracts with poverty rates of 40 percent or higher. The figures reported here track 239 U.S. metropolitan areas, including all major metropolitan areas and 91.6 percent of the entire metropolitan population in 1990 (Jargowsky 1997, Table A.1). The remaining areas had not yet been designated as metropolitan areas as of 1970. Such areas were generally not divided into census tracts, and so for these areas it is impossible to identify the trend in concentration of poverty.

    5. Massey and Eggers (1990) argue that an *interaction* between the level of racial segregation and increases in poverty acts to concentrate poverty. While this interaction effect could operate even in the context of moderate declines in racial segregation, their model testing this hypothesis is misspecified (Jargowsky 1997, 42–43). Further analyses testing for an effect of this type of interaction on the concentration of poverty found no evidence for it (Jargowsky 1997, 181–83).

    6. Since the poor neighborhoods tend to be a relatively small area at the center of the much larger expanse of the metropolitan area, both maps have smaller key maps showing county and city boundaries to provide a sense of the location of the high-poverty area within the larger area.

    7. Obviously, European nations are far from classless societies. Class distinctions are maintained more through culture and expectations than through spatial separation. The point is that there is less racial and class segregation in their residence patterns.

8. Census tracts are not nested within city, place, and town boundaries. Thus, it is possible for a given census tract to be partly in a central city and partly in suburb.

9. All means and standard deviations are weighted by the number of households in the tract. To be clear, the number of housing units is not identical to the number of households because some units are vacant. Vacant units are included in the median-year-built calculation, but obviously not included in the mean-household-income calculation.

10. As noted earlier, some census tracts span the central city and the suburbs. For such tracts, the median year built is determined for the whole tract, and this median is mapped on to both parts of the tract. The households in the part of the tract in the central city are included in the central city mean for the given age cohort, and the part not in the central city is included in the suburban group for that cohort.

11. Actually, whites don't have to actively flee. All that is required is a decline in the rate of replacement by whites of housing units that experience normal turnover.

# REFERENCES

Abramson, Alan J., and Mitchell S. Tobin. 1994. "The Changing Geography of Metropolitan Opportunity: The Segregation of the Poor in U.S. Metropolitan Areas, 1970 to 1990." In *Fannie Mae Annual Housing Conference, 1994*. Washington, D.C.: Fannie Mae Office of Housing Policy Research.

Anderson, Elijah. 1991. "Neighborhood Influences on Inner-City Teenage Pregnancy." In *The Urban Underclass*, edited by Christopher Jencks and Paul E. Peterson (375–98). Washington, D.C.: Brookings Institution.

Berry, Brian J. L., and Quentin Gillard. 1977. *The Changing Shape of Metropolitan America: Commuting Patterns, Urban Fields, and Decentralization Processes, 1960–1970*. Cambridge, Mass.: Ballinger.

Crane, Jon. 1991. "Effects of Neighborhood on Dropping Out of School and Teenage Childbearing." In *The Urban Underclass*, edited by Christopher Jencks and Paul E. Peterson (299–320). Washington, D.C.: Brookings Institution.

Farkas, George. 1996. *Human Capital or Cultural Capital? Ethnicity and Poverty Groups in an Urban School District*. Hawthorne, N.Y.: Aldine de Gruyter.

Farley, Reynolds, and William H. Frey. 1994. "Changes in the Segregation of Whites and Blacks during the 1980s: Small Steps toward a More Integrated Society." *American Sociological Review* 59(1):23–45.

Frey, William H. 1993. "People in Places: Demographic Trends in Urban America." In *Rediscovering Urban America: Perspectives on the 1980s*, edited by Jack Sommer and Donald A. Hicks. Washington, D.C.: Office of Housing Policy Research, U.S. Department of Housing and Urban Development.

Galster, George, Royce Hanson, Hal Wolman, Stephen Coleman, and Jason Freihage. 2000. "Wrestling Sprawl to the Ground: Defining and Measuring an Elusive Concept." *Housing Policy Debate* 12(4):681–717.

Gans, Herbert. 1967. *The Levittowners: How People Live and Politic in Suburbia*. New York: Pantheon Books.

Harrison, Roderick J., and Daniel H. Weinberg. 1992. "Changes in Racial and Ethnic Residential Segregation, 1980–1990." Paper prepared for the American Statistical Association meetings, Boston, Mass., July 29.

Hicks, Donald A. 1994. "Revitalizing Our Cities or Restoring Ties to Them? Redirecting the Debate." University of Michigan *Journal of Law Reform* 27(3–4): 813–75.

Ihlanfeldt, Keith R., and David L. Sjoquist. 2000. "The Geographic Mismatch between Jobs and Housing." In *The Atlanta Paradox*, edited by David L. Sjoquist (116–27). New York: Russell Sage Foundation.

Jackson, Kenneth T. 1985. *Crabgrass Frontier: The Suburbanization of the United States.* New York: Oxford University Press.

Jargowsky, Paul A. 1997. *Poverty and Place: Ghettos, Barrios, and the American City.* New York: Russell Sage Foundation.

Jargowsky, Paul A., and Mary Jo Bane. 1991. "Ghetto Poverty in the United States: 1970 to 1980." In *The Urban Underclass*, edited by Christopher Jencks and Paul E. Peterson (235–73). Washington, D.C.: Brookings Institution.

Jencks, Christopher, and Susan E. Mayer. 1990. "The Social Consequences of Growing Up in a Poor Neighborhood." In *Inner-City Poverty in America*, edited by Laurence E. Lynn, Jr. and Michael G. H. McGeary (111–86). Washington, D.C.: National Academy Press.

Kain, John F. 1968. "Housing Segregation, Negro Employment, and Metropolitan Decentralization." *Quarterly Journal of Economics* 82(2):175–97.

Kasarda, John. 1985. "Urban Change and Minority Opportunities." In *The New Urban Reality*, edited by Paul E. Peterson. Washington, D.C.: Brookings Institution.

———. 1988. "Jobs, Migration, and Emerging Urban Mismatches." In *Urban Change and Poverty*, edited by Michael G. H. McGeary and Laurence E. Lynn, Jr. (148–98). Washington, D.C.: National Academy Press.

Kunstler, James Howard. 1993. *The Geography of Nowhere: The Rise and Decline of America's Man-Made Landscape.* New York: Simon and Schuster.

Levy, Frank. 1995. "The Future Path and Consequences of the U.S. Earnings/Education Gap." *Economic Policy Review* 1(1):35–41.

MacLeod, Jay. 1995. *Ain't No Makin' It: Aspirations and Attainment in a Low-Income Neighborhood.* Boulder, Colo.: Westview Press.

Magnet, Myron. 1993. *The Dream and the Nightmare: The Sixties' Legacy to the Underclass.* New York: Morrow.

Massey, Douglas S. 1990. "American Apartheid: Segregation and the Making of the Underclass." *American Journal of Sociology* 96(2):329–57.

Massey, Douglas S., and Nancy A. Denton. 1993. *American Apartheid: Segregation and the Making of the Underclass.* Cambridge, Mass.: Harvard University Press.

Massey, Douglas S., and Mitchell L. Eggers. 1990. "The Ecology of Inequality: Minorities and the Concentration of Poverty, 1970–1980." *American Journal of Sociology* 95(5):1153–88.

Moynihan, Daniel P. 1965. *The Negro Family: The Case for National Action.* Washington, D.C.: U.S. Department of Labor, Office for Family Planning and Research.

Musterd, Sako, and Wim Ostendorf. 1998. "Segregation, Polarisation and Social Exclusion in Metropolitan Areas." In *Urban Segregation and the Welfare State: Inequality and Exclusion in Western Cities*, edited by Sako Musterd and Wim Ostendorf (1–14). New York: Routledge.

Myers, Jerome K. 1954. "Note on the Homogenity of Census Tracts: A Methodological Problem in Urban Ecological Research." *Social Forces* 32:364–66.

Park, Robert E. 1926. "The Urban Community as a Spatial Pattern and a Moral Order." In *The Urban Community*, edited by Ernest W. Burgess (3–18). Chicago: University of Chicago Press.

Ricketts, Erol R., and Isabel V. Sawhill. 1988. "Defining and Measuring the Underclass." *Journal of Policy Analysis and Management* 7(2):316–25.

Robinson, W. S. 1950. "Ecological Correlations and the Behavior of Individuals." *American Sociological Review* 15(3):351–57.

Rusk, David. 1999. *Inside Game, Outside Game: Winning Strategies for Saving Urban America.* New York: Brookings Institution Press.

Sierra Club. 1998. "Sprawl: The Dark Side of the American Dream." http://www.sierraclub.org/sprawl/report98/report.asp. (Accessed December 2001.)

Tiebout, Charles M. 1956. "A Pure Theory of Local Expenditures." *Journal of Political Economy* 64:416–24.

U.S. Census Bureau. Poverty and Health Statistics Branch/HHES Division. 2000. "Table 8. Poverty of People, by Residence: 1959 to 1999" (March Current Population Survey, Historical Poverty Tables). Revised September 26, 2000. http://www.census.gov/hhes/poverty/histpov/hstpov8.html.

U.S. Department of Housing and Urban Development. 2000. *The State of the Cities 2000.* Washington, D.C.: Government Printing Office.

van der Wusten, Herman, and Sako Musterd. 1998. "Welfare State Effects on Inequality and Segregation." In *Urban Segregation and the Welfare State: Inequality and Exclusion in Western Cities*, edited by Sako Musterd and Wim Ostendorf (238–47). New York: Routledge.

Warner, Sam Bass. 1962. *Streetcar Suburbs.* Cambridge, Mass.: Harvard University Press.

———. 1972. *The Urban Wilderness: A History of the American City.* New York: Harper and Row.

White, Michael J. 1987. "American Neighborhoods and Residential Differentiation." In *The Population of the United States in the 1980s*, edited by National Committee for Research on the 1980 Census. New York: Russell Sage Foundation.

Wilson, William Julius. 1987. *The Truly Disadvantaged: The Inner-City, the Underclass and Public Policy.* Chicago: University of Chicago Press.

Wood, Robert C. 1959. *Suburbia: Its People and Their Politics.* Boston, Mass.: Houghton Mifflin.

# 4

# Sprawl, Fragmentation, and the Persistence of Racial Inequality

## Limiting Civil Rights by Fragmenting Space

john powell

In the last few years, scholars have given a growing amount of attention to sprawl and to some of the social implications of sprawl. They have seldom discussed the central importance of racial inequity, the attendant consequences of "racialized" concentrated poverty, and, more recently, gentrification. Although there are a wide variety of negative consequences to urban sprawl, and many factors that have contributed to the rapid spread of sprawl, we cannot develop an adequate understanding of sprawl without examining the central role of race. The focus of this chapter is to reach a better understanding of how urban sprawl, racial inequity, concentrated poverty, and gentrification are all bound up together.

This chapter will begin with an exploration of the history of urban sprawl in the United States, and the central role that race has played in urban sprawl. Following this will be a discussion of how these sprawl patterns have directly affected the segregation of racial minorities into situations of racialized concentrated poverty. The last and critical part of the chapter will deal with gentrification, and the relationship between gentrification and concentrated poverty. This connection may seem counterintuitive, because scholars often present gentrification and concentrated poverty as opposing phenomena. Gentrification and concentrated poverty are closely related, however, in that they both tend to isolate low-income people and racial minorities from opportunity. Concentrated poverty has traditionally pulled opportunities away from communities, whereas gentrification operates in the opposite direction, by displacing and pushing communities away from opportunities. The dynamics of gentrification differ between rich, poor, and middle-class cities. These differences, and the reasons why concerns about gentrification should be thought of differently in each of these city types will be discussed. The chapter will end with a discussion of current debates about gentrification and concentrated poverty, and personal suggestions for strategies in addressing the problem and framing the discussion.

## A Framework for Discussing 20th Century Sprawl

Before discussing the history of American sprawl, it is important to establish a framework that highlights the important differences between earlier sprawl and the sprawl that has occurred largely since World War II. Some of these differences will be explored, including some of the causes. First, however, some of the key distinctions will be set out in broad terms to help clarify what could otherwise be a confusing attempt to crystallize the role of race from the 1930s to the present.

The outward expansion of population from the urban center to outlying suburbs is one facet of sprawl, and has long been part of American urbanization. However, the sprawl that has occurred largely since World War II is qualitatively and quantitatively distinct from earlier types of outward spread. Although the movement of populations from the core of the city had already begun in many urban areas by the middle of the 19th century, this movement directly involved only a small part of the population and did not undermine the viability of the city. Indeed, the outward movement of people from the urban core to the suburbs was how most cities grew during the 19th century, and in the early part of the 20th century these outlying areas were then annexed and incorporated into the city. Given the cost involved, most of the people who participated in this early form of sprawl were either rich or upper-middle class. Hence, this early sprawl did not involve broad sections of the population, nor did it undermine the vitality of the cities. In addition, the federal government barely played any role in the early expansion of metropolitan areas.

During the early portion of the 20th century, the nature of sprawl began to change. Independent governmental jurisdictions, with independent functions and fiscal capacities, arose outside the central cities.

Through discriminatory housing policies that subsidized a mass movement of white Americans to these separate municipalities, the federal government nurtured these jurisdictions' growth. Over time, a powerful system of institutionally racist policies subsidized and encouraged the movement of opportunity structures out of the central city into these developing suburbs. This movement isolated central-city residents, including African Americans and other racial minorities, from needed jobs and resources. Under strong influence from the federal government, the new local governmental structures fragmented metropolitan areas and led to the geographic and municipal sorting of people. This movement of whites to the suburbs coincided with the large-scale migration of African Americans from the rural South to cities in the North and West. The rise of suburban jurisdictions and the concurrent migrations of white and African Americans forever racialized urban space. These historical events provide some perspective on the current state of racialized concentrated poverty and the politics surrounding gentrification. With this in mind, let us turn to the history of sprawl in the United States.

## The History of Racialized Urban Sprawl

The 20th century saw a complete restructuring of the American landscape and lifestyle as the country has become predominantly suburbanized. This suburbanization, particularly following World War II, has been fundamentally different from other types of urban expansion due to the size and scope of expansion, the integral importance of government policies, and the creation of politically fragmented metropolitan areas. Two patterns or processes have primarily fueled this dramatic reconfiguration of the American landscape. The first has been the improvement in transportation technology; the second has been a series of government tax and mortgage policies that have consistently favored growth on the suburban periphery over the central city. While both patterns have influenced race and class, the second pattern of government subsidy has been more explicitly racial. This second process has been both pro-white and anti–racial minority, with a particular institutional and personal hostility toward African Americans. The migration of white Americans, as well as businesses and employment opportunities, to the suburbs has severely racialized urban space and opportunity structures as it has established a racial divide between central cities and the suburbs. This process has been central in creating the wealth whites enjoy today and the lack of wealth and opportunity in the black community (Oliver and Shapiro 1995).

The suburbanization of America occurred within the context of two great internal migrations: the migration of millions of African Americans from the rural South to the urban North and South, and the concurrent migration of millions of white Americans from the central cities to the suburbs. The migration of African Americans generally occurred in two waves. The first wave took place in the decades on either side of World War I. Between 1910 and 1920, 525,000 African Americans made the trip north; an additional 877,000 came during the 1920s (Denton and Massey 1993, 29). The second wave, which began during World War II, was much larger: In the 1950s, 1.5 million African Americans migrated north, and in the 1960s, 1.4 million migrated in the same direction (Denton and Massey 1993, 45). We can likewise place the white migration from the center of urban areas to the periphery in two waves that occurred at the same time as the above-mentioned African-American shifts, with the more massive and important starting in the 1950s. A study of 168 metropolitan areas found that in 1950, 60 percent of America's metropolitan population lived in central cities (Rusk 1993, 5). Today, suburbs represent not only a majority of the metropolitan area, but also a majority of the overall American population.

The massive private, commercial, and industrial transition to suburbia, and particularly its racially exclusionary component, has not naturally occurred. Benign technological and market forces have not driven the transition, nor has the simple exercise of private choice. Rather, a wide variety of formal governmental policies has driven and subsidized the suburbanization process. Further, local policies and practices, along with widespread racial discrimination and white violence, have supported these government policies. Federal government policies, many of which still exist today, have encouraged development at the periphery of urban areas, instigated racially discriminatory practices, and accommodated discrimination and intentional residential segregation. By so doing, they have significantly aided the spatial racialization of America. Formal government real estate, mortgage, and tax policies racialized urban space by favoring development in white areas at the urban periphery and formally entrenching segregationist real estate practices. Exclusionary practices in the 1920s and 1930s occurred at the intrajurisdictional and often at the neighborhood level, with cities continuing to be the center of the region, and controlling most of the regional population and resources. The local control began to rapidly change when, during the late 1930s, the federal government became involved in housing policies as it formalized, institutionalized, and nationalized racially exclusionary patterns that had informally existed for years.

The primary means by which the government supported segregated, single-residence communities was through the home appraisal standards the Home Owners Loan Corporation (HOLC) and the Federal Housing Authority (FHA) created and used for mortgage loans and insurance. The HOLC/FHA system incorporated a number of different factors for evaluating homes and neighborhoods, such as "relative economic stability" and "protection from adverse influences" (Jackson 1985, 207). The underwriting manual explicitly reflected the racial bias inherent in the program by requiring the housing agencies to investigate areas "to determine whether incompatible racial or social groups are present, for the purpose of making a prediction regarding the probability of the location being invaded by those [non-white] groups" (Schill and Wachter 1995, 143). HOLC and FHA created four categories for neighborhood value and appeal that placed the highest value on homogeneous white neighborhoods. The agencies placed neighborhoods where racial minorities lived in the lowest category, regardless of the quality of housing stock. Often, the presence of a single racial minority household placed an entire neighborhood in this low, undesirable category. Because the color that denoted this low category on FHA maps was red, the practice of denying mortgages in racially undesirable neighborhoods became known as "redlining." Federal appraisal standards therefore discouraged investment in the central cities, especially in neighborhoods populated by racial minorities. Furthermore, the federal programs provided greater funding for the building of new homes than for the restoration of older housing stock and encouraged single-family rather than multifamily development. Because a large number of private lenders adopted these standards, and HOLC often made its maps available to firms to easily identify "risky" lending zones, these racially biased mortgage practices became systematized across the country. The systemization of these federal programs created a pattern of lending practices that encouraged investment in new white suburban neighborhoods to the detriment of older, racial minority city neighborhoods (Jackson 1985, 195–218).

Low-income racial minorities felt the effects of these federal practices most strongly after World War II. The combination of depression and war had created a 16-year lull in house building. Pent-up demand following the war, combined with encouraging federal real estate policies, created a housing boom in the 1950s. Immediately after the war, the government built massive subdivisions to house the middle-class parents of the baby-boom generation, and whites moved to the suburbs as never before. The subsidized "white flight" was the birth of modern sprawl. Federal tax and mortgage policies, which HOLC and FHA created, facilitated the housing boom. In 1944, the Veterans Administration (VA), which was created in part to ensure that returning veterans could buy their own homes, expanded those federal policies. Before these federal programs, prospective homebuyers frequently had to pay 40 or 50 percent of the cost of a home as a down payment and retire the remainder of the debt within five years (Jackson 1985, 138–56). The federally insured mortgage policies dramatically changed the housing market by allowing mortgages to cover 90 percent of the cost of a house and by extending the mortgage payments period up to 30 years. This represented a complete transformation of the housing market, the impact of which is difficult to gauge now that such long-term mortgages are the norms. As a result, white people were strongly encouraged to buy homes in the suburbs on long-term, federally insured mortgages. The monthly payments were so radically low that it was cheaper to buy a new house than to rent (Jackson 1985, 231–33). Even for those whites that did not have any personal racial animus, it become economically more rational to move to the white suburbs. The federal government did not just reflect the existing racial animus, it both institutionalized and inculcated it. In some instances, if a white owner wanted an insured mortgage and did not have a racially restrictive covenant in the deed of his/her house, FHA would require putting the racially restrictive covenant in the deed before insuring the mortgage (Rusk 1999, 86). African Americans and other racial minorities were not included in this housing boom. Thus, FHA and VA lending practices continued to exclude central-city neighborhoods, and the real estate business institutionalized racial discrimination.

A comprehensive study of real estate policies conducted in the 1950s by Rose Helper revealed that 80 percent of real estate agents in Chicago refused to sell homes located in white neighborhoods to racial minorities, and 70 percent refused to rent to racial minorities in these neighborhoods (Denton and Massey 1993, 50). Levittown, Long Island, which came to epitomize the urban sprawl explosion of the 1950s, is another good example. The developer of Levittown publicly refused to sell homes to African Americans and, in 1960, not one of Levittown's 82,000 residents was black (Jackson 1985, 241). The trend was nationwide. The Kerner Commission, established by President Lyndon Johnson to study the causes of racial tension following the 1968 riots, found that between 1950 and 1966, 98 percent of African-American population growth occurred in metropolitan areas, primarily in central cities, while between 1960 and 1966, 78 percent of white population growth occurred in suburban areas (Boger 1993, 1299). The suburb/city racial divide is also present in terms of homeownership. In 1989, roughly 69.4 percent of white American households owned a home, compared with only 43 percent of African-American households (powell 1996, 92). As noted previously, the exclusion of African Americans from suburban housing occurred at the same time as large numbers of African Americans were migrating into northern metropolitan areas. Because of this exclusion, African Americans were forced to settle in concentrated, segregated communities in the central city. This trend continued throughout the postwar years, and African Americans found themselves increasingly isolated in dilapidated central cities. The trend was due to the combination of racial discrimination in real estate that prevented African Americans from leaving their neighborhoods and biased, federally influenced mortgage practices that prevented money from entering central cities.

Besides lending and mortgage practices, other federal policies have hastened suburban development and encouraged racial segregation. The most notable is perhaps the large federal commitment to road building. As those who would assert that suburbanization is a naturally occurring phenomenon, the successive revolution in transportation *enabled* outward expansion of American urban areas. However, the development and use of transportation technology did not occur in a haphazard or disinterested manner. Rather, the federal government built and funded transportation in a manner that served the needs of suburbanizing middle-class whites, to the detriment of racial minorities, who largely lived in central cities. The federal government, at the behest of suburbanizing whites, facilitated, subsidized, and hastened residential, commercial, and industrial flight to the suburbs through the massive expenditure of funds for highway construction. It has spent over $652 billion for highway construction, as well as additional billions for infrastructure and maintenance for suburban areas (Rusk 1999, 91; Judd and Swanstrom 1994, 180–81, 207–209, 392). Highway construction has made suburban living both affordable and convenient, and has allowed middle-class whites the freedom to live at greater distances from their workplaces. The development of highways, along with government tax policies, has made it advantageous for businesses to relocate to the suburbs rather than improving existing plants in urban areas, thereby removing the employment and production base of many central cities.

In addition to providing opportunities for white flight from central cities, the federal construction of highways without comparable funding for public transportation has severely limited the ability of racial minorities to reach now-distant job sites. Job opportunities now require a car, which is often beyond the means of central-city residents. For instance, in Philadelphia and Boston, roughly 50 percent of African-American central-city households do not have access to a car, while the number is 69.3 percent in New York City (Kasarda 1985, 56). Often, as in Detroit, highways take commuters from the white suburbs to downtown skyscrapers without providing any exits into African-American central cities, emphasizing that the federal government built the transportation system to serve the exclusive needs of suburban residents. In addition, the construction of highways is not a benign presence to which African-American inner-city residents simply do not have access. The federal government, with the construction of overpasses, has destroyed or severely devalued urban neighborhoods and used highways as physical barriers to separate racially identifiable neighborhoods. For instance, New York City built some overpasses so low as to prevent buses, and the central-city residents who depend on them for transportation, from passing beneath them (powell 1996, 95–96).

Exclusionary government policies have been key to the growth of racially segregated suburbs. Yet, it is crucial to emphasize the role of local racial discrimination, exclusion, and white violence in ensuring that African Americans have been kept out of suburban areas and consequently consolidated into concentrated, segregated areas. Racial exclusion and discrimination on a local level has been one of the major features of suburban development. In the past, municipalities in new subdivisions or incorporated suburbs drafted explicitly racially discriminatory ordinances and deed covenants (Jackson 1985, 155; Denton and Massey 1993, 36).

In cases where formal exclusions did not exist, informal real estate practices often resulted in the exclusion of African Americans from suburban or predominantly white areas. Most real estate agents simply refused to sell homes to African-American families, but when the influx of African Americans became so great that their expansion into adjacent neighborhoods became unavoidable, many real estate agents engaged in techniques such as "blockbusting." Blockbusting was a way to control the expansion of African-American areas by scaring whites into believing in an imminent "invasion" of African-American people, and having the whites flee their neighborhood. By moving African Americans into neighborhoods as white people fled, blockbusting created total neighborhood turnover. Thus, African Americans attempting to escape racial segregation found themselves not in an integrated community, but rather in a newly formed, carefully controlled addition to other segregated African-American neighborhoods (Denton and Massey 1993, 37–38).

In addition, white violence has been a major tool of racial exclusion, and it is important to emphasize the role of racist violence and terrorism in maintaining segregated sprawl patterns. Violence against African Americans in northern metropolitan areas increased dramatically following their first major migration north. A series of communal race riots in which whites attacked, beat, shot, and lynched African Americans broke out in cities like New York, East St. Louis, and Chicago, reaching their peak just after World War I. African Americans were prevented by whites' use of force from moving into white neighborhoods. In Chicago, for instance, whites bombed 58 African-American homes between 1917 and 1921. Besides the bombings, mob violence, rock throwing, gunshots, and cross burnings were standard responses by whites to new African-American residents. Although such overt violence peaked in the 1920s, it has remained a sporadic feature of urban racial dynamics (Denton and Massey 1993, 35). For instance, Martin Luther King Jr. met one of the most violent and enraged white crowds of his civil rights career in the Chicago suburb of Cicero, Illinois.

Racialized localism, which local racial discrimination and violence exemplify, has been strengthened through the most important and unprecedented feature of urban sprawl following World War II—the creation of fragmented metropolitan areas in which the central cities are divided from the surrounding suburbs by municipal and jurisdictional boundaries. These boundaries also served as racial dividers between white suburbs and cities that racial minorities populated. Formerly large cities expanded by means of annexation, meaning they simply absorbed new developments on the metropolitan periphery into the city. However, as cities became associated with low-income people and racial minorities, who were considered dangerous, border areas separated themselves from the city by forming their own governments and refusing to allow the city to absorb them. The result was a tremendous increase in local governments, tax jurisdictions, school districts, and municipal boundaries, so that metropolitan areas became patchworks of small jurisdictions (Jackson 1985, 138–56). The fragmentation of the government transformed spatial and power arrangement in the metropolitan areas. While in 1950, 193 city governments administered 60 percent of America's metropolitan residents, by 1990, 70 percent of the residents of the same metropolitan regions fell under the governance of 9,600 suburban cities, towns, villages, townships, and counties (Rusk 1999, 67). By 1972, the New York City area had over 1,400 local governments (Jackson 1985, 277). Today, even a smaller metropolitan area like Minneapolis/St. Paul has 187 local governments, each with its own land use powers (Orfield 1997, Map 1-1). Although it is rarely mentioned, the more fragmented a metropolitan area is, the more racially and economically segregated it is (Weiher 1991).

It is important to note that this fragmented sprawl occurred during the same period that African Americans and other racial minorities were pressing the government for inclusion and an end to the formal Jim Crow clauses. The response to these demands for civil rights was ambivalent. As the country moved to end formal Jim Crow laws, it embraced de facto Jim Crow practices by inscribing segregation in the geography. For example, courts and policymakers began to distinguish between intrajurisdictional and interjurisdictional segregation. Intrajurisdictional segregation referred to segregation within a single jurisdiction, whereas interjurisdictional described segregation across jurisdictional lines. Courts effectively placed a constitutional stamp on racialized localism by limiting a remedy to only intrajurisdictional segregation and denying relief to interjurisdictional segregation except in very limited circumstances. This practice functionally undermined many of the civil rights efforts of the 1950s and 1960s (Ford 1994). The re-sorting of whites, not just to new neighborhoods, but also to new municipalities, explains the persistent racial segregation in housing markets and metropolitan school districts. While segregation existed before World War II, it was on a neighborhood level; residents, even in segregated neighborhoods, still captured cities' resources. The segregation after the war allowed municipalities to shield their resources from the excluded racial minorities. Thus, despite the efforts of the civil rights movement, in a jurisdictional sense we are more racially segregated today than in 1950 (Rusk 1999, 67–71).

The fragmentation of metropolitan politics and policies has solidified the boundaries of racial space. The imposition of artificial local divisions has freed white suburban residents and municipalities from sharing the responsibility for problems associated with urban concentrated poverty, even though white flight and urban abandonment is a chief cause of city resource depletion and poverty.

The postwar expansion and solidification of segregated communities of color reached its peak in the late 1960s and the 1970s as many middle-class whites left central cities in the wake of riots that took place in the late 1960s. At the same time, federally subsidized "urban renewal" programs worked in concert with white flight to concentrate people of color and isolate them from opportunities that had been moved to the suburbs. These urban renewal projects resulted in the demolition of large numbers of low-income buildings. In the process, the federal programs destroyed many stable racial minority communities and replaced them with large, densely populated public housing projects. These projects, initially intended to be temporary residences, ultimately became long-term housing for low-income racial minorities (Jackson 1985, 224–30).

Postwar urban sprawl and fragmentation patterns created a racially charged boundary between the city and the suburbs. In 1990, only 33 percent of white metropolitan residents lived in central cities, whereas 67.8 percent of African-American metropolitan residents lived in central cities (powell 1996, 84). Where the different policies had previously racialized space on a neighborhood scale, they now racialized it along municipal lines between the city and the suburbs. The ramifications of this concentration of racial minorities and low-income people in central cities is that those areas with the most need for social services are the least equipped to provide them. Suburban municipalities have been largely shielded from the effects of public deprivation and the costs of confronting them. In essence, the racialization of space has subsidized the growth and affluence of white suburban America at the expense of center-city racial minorities (powell 1996, 84). In addition, the racialized suburbanization and fragmentation of metropolitan areas have isolated racial minorities' communities from opportunities that are now located in the suburbs. As a result, despite many legal victories, African Americans and other racial minorities are still without full access to opportunities such as housing, desegregated schools, and jobs.

Before ending this section on the history of fragmented racialized space, it is important to highlight that these practices and policies continue to define our present racially segregated metropolitan geographic. Although the federal government stopped its explicit underwriting policies in 1950, it has failed to take action to dismantle racialized fragmentation. A number of experts have demonstrated that once racialized fragmented space is created, it reproduces itself even in the absence of a racial animus (Ford 1994; Boger 1993; Denton and Massey 1993). Government policies and practices have not only produced racialized fragmented space, but have racialized the accumulation of wealth. We have had a public policy of investing in whites and white communities and disinvesting in African Americans and African-American communities (Conley 1999, 25–54). Wealth segregation, like the segregated geographic, reproduces itself without present racist policies unless the nature and rules of the game change. In order to overcome the continuing effects of fragmented racialized space, there would need to be a deliberate policy to disestablish the federal practices presently in effect that the more explicit policies set in motion (Roisman 1995; Boger 1993). The historical importance of the role the government has had in institutionalizing and expanding fragmented metropolitan areas to the detriment of African Americans and the central cities cannot be overstated. Yet, there is a persistent effort to explain segregation in the landscape and in wealth in terms of cultural factors and the personal choices of African Americans and whites. However, even a casual look at the formation and dynamics of metropolitan space makes it clear that this interjurisdictional segregation cannot be explained by personal preferences, natural processes, or even the difference in socioeconomic status of blacks and whites (Roisman 1995, 487–88; Conley 1999, 25–54).

Many of the concerns we face today, including continued segregation, an urban underclass, the limited effect of our civil rights goals, and concentrated poverty are directly related to this fragmented racialized space (Roisman 1995; Denton and Massey 1993; Ford 1994). The continued widespread discrimination in the housing market enhances the continuation of this fragmented space. As will be discussed below, this discrimination is most destructive when it is interjurisdictional. Indeed, the fragmentation of space along interjurisdictional lines is the most important impediment to substantively achieving civil rights (powell 1999b). This interjurisdictional segregation is how we have isolated minorities from participating in both the creation and the benefit of opportunity structures—participation that is critical for full citizenship.

The government, however, has done more than just passively accept these massive opportunity-denying structures for blacks and opportunity-enhancing structures for whites. In many ways, the government has continued to consolidate and maintain this racial fragmentation and segregation by often adopting a confused doctrine that both naturalizes and constitutionalizes localism (Ford 1994). There is nothing natural about how this fragmentation of space came into being or the timing of the adoption of legal barriers to protect it. Frequently, in the context of education and housing segregation, courts make it difficult to challenge interjurisdictional segregation by placing the fragmentation beyond the scope of a court's remedy. At the same time the U.S. Supreme Court announced the end of formal Jim Crow, it supported the inscription of Jim Crow into the geographic land scale. The Court's message to white Americans continues to be, "You are not your black brothers' and sisters' keepers; in fact, they are not your brothers and sisters." The government, instead of implementing public policies to disestablish these structures, encouraged us to adopt individual responsibility. Yet, while individual responsibility may be appropriate in some contexts, racially fragmented space could not have been put together without public policy and public money, nor can it be taken apart without these resources. This continues to be the reality and challenge that we confront today.

## Racialized Concentrated Poverty and Urban Sprawl

One of the benefits of the civil rights movement was the marginal opening of the housing market to middle-class blacks and other racial minorities. The housing options available to middle-class blacks are still more limited than are those for middle-class or low-income whites. However, since 1970, middle-class African Americans have often left the central cities in search of opportunity structures. During this same period, the United States has experienced an explosion in racialized concentrated poverty. Indeed, some have argued that it is the movement of middle-class African Americans that has caused concentrated poverty (Wilson 1997, 19). While having an impact on concentrated poverty, the movement of middle-class African Americans clearly is not the cause of concentrated poverty. Instead, the overall structure of our segregated housing market caused this concentrated poverty and created the dynamics of sprawl over the last 50 years.

Concentrated poverty is defined as an area in which 40 percent or more of its residents have incomes below the federally defined poverty level (the 1990 federal poverty level was $12,700 for a family of four). Further, concentrated poverty is a highly racialized phenomenon. It describes the living conditions of about 5 percent of all metropolitan residents, but over 30 percent of all minority metropolitan residents. Between 1970 and 1990, the number of concentrated poverty census tracts in the United States more than doubled, and the number of people living in such tracts nearly doubled, while the overall population increased by only 22 percent. By 1990, of the nearly eight million Americans living in concentrated poverty, over one-half were African American and one-quarter were Hispanic (Institute on Race and Poverty 1999, 5).

The most debilitating effect of concentrated poverty is the denial of access to economic, educational, and social opportunity structures. Racial minorities have not only been segregated from whites, but also segregated from opportunity. Employment, one of the most important of these opportunities, has moved along with middle-class whites to the periphery of metropolitan areas. In 1970, only 25 percent of the nation's offices were located in the suburbs. More recent information indicates that over 60 percent are now located in the suburbs (Pierce 1993, 28). The total proportion of metropolitan manufacturing jobs located in central cities fell from 63.3 percent in 1950 to 46.2 percent in 1980, and continued to fall throughout the 1980s and 1990s (Jargowsky 1997, 122–23). Thus, the move to the suburbs, as well as the movement of jobs overseas, has deprived many cities of their working-class employment base. For instance, in the 20-year period from 1967 to 1987, Philadelphia lost 64 percent of its manufacturing jobs, while Chicago lost 60 percent, New York City lost 58 percent, and Detroit lost 51 percent. In absolute numbers, these percentages represent the loss of 160,000 jobs in Philadelphia, 326,000 in Chicago, 520,000 in New York, and 108,000 in Detroit (Wilson 1997, 29–30), for a total of more than one million jobs. Nationwide, the loss of these jobs from the cities to the suburbs occurred at the same time the number of people living in concentrated poverty nearly doubled and has been a direct cause of intense inner-city poverty. Cities tend to capture high-end professionals like lawyers and computer analysts on the one hand, and low-end service workers like hotel and restaurant employees, on the other. Minority residents have generally been forced to seek low-paying service and unskilled jobs or be unemployed. Because of a lack of transportation and limited housing options, many city residents cannot gain access to employment opportunities that have moved to the suburbs. In addition, racial discrimination in employment, housing, and educational opportunities has operated to concentrate and isolate racial minority communities in the central cities from economic opportunities now located in the suburbs.

In his book, *When Work Disappears*, William Julius Wilson documents the social ramifications of intense, concentrated joblessness. According to Wilson, in the nation's 100 central cities in 1990, the ratio of employed to jobless people in nonconcentrated poverty census tracts was three times greater than in concentrated poverty tracts (Wilson 1997, 19). Wilson's work indicates that the concentration of unemployment has social ramifications beyond the economic consequences. He argues that joblessness affects all levels of social organization, including the prevalence and strength of social networks, the extent of collective supervision and personal responsibility residents assume in addressing problems, and participation in formal or voluntary organizations (Wilson 1997, 20–21).

The intense concentration of poverty also profoundly affects education and places powerful impediments on minority children living in high-poverty areas. When low-income children are concentrated into segregated schools, they must confront both their own poverty and the effects of concentrated poverty on the school system. The importance of the intense concentration of poverty is indicated by a number of recent studies showing that low-income students attending low-poverty schools perform on average better than middle-income students attending high-poverty schools. The disparity in performance is even more exaggerated where the low-income student is from a middle-class neighborhood and the middle-class student is from a high-poverty neighborhood (Brenzel and Kantor 1993, 384). The concentration of poverty results in higher dropout and teenage pregnancy rates, lack of parental involvement, inability to pay for books or other supplies, and a lack of adult role models with educational experience.

Children living in poverty also suffer more from family instability (Denton and Massey 1993, 153). Low-income families in urban areas tend to move more frequently; African-American and Hispanic families in these districts often change residences three or more times a year, forcing children to attend many different schools. Children in poor families are more likely to arrive at school hungry and ill prepared for learning (Institute on Race and Poverty 1999, 22–23). Drug and alcohol abuse and crime also affect poverty-stricken schools much more than they affect more affluent schools in other districts. Concentrated poverty, resulting in a large proportion of the students in a school being poor, exacerbates and compounds the effects of these poverty-related problems in such a way that they become systemic. Teachers and staff in these districts must spend more time and resources dealing with family and health crises, security, and children not adequately prepared for learning (Orfield 1997, 18).

Intensely concentrated poverty not only clusters, but also actually increases violent crime. The likelihood for violent crime is clear from the fact that while violent crime declined for the nation as whole, rates of violent crime dramatically increased in the segregated African-American communities. In 1995, African-American teenagers were 11 times more likely to be shot to death than were their white peers. Whereas young African-American males were killed at a rate of 45 per 100,000 in 1960, by 1990 they were killed at a rate of 140 per 100,000, compared with a rate of about 20 per 100,000 for young white males (Massey 1995, 1205). A number of studies have shown a direct link between racial segregation, concentrated poverty, and violent crime. A study Ruth Peterson and Lauren Krivo conducted found that black-white segregation was by far the most important factor in determining disproportionate murder rates (Massey 1995, 1209). Given that crime is usually associated with poverty, it is not difficult to understand that concentrating poverty into a small area also concentrates crime in that area, or that concentrating a particular group of people economically and geographically, as racial minorities have been in America, generates higher crime rates in areas where those groups live.

The most pernicious effect of the high crime rates produced by concentrated poverty is that middle-class whites benefit directly from having crime contained in racially segregated communities, rather than spread evenly throughout society. Because crime is often concentrated away from white neighborhoods, many white Americans view high crime as endemic to racial minority communities, rather than as a product of economic and residential isolation. As a result, the products of segregation paradoxically raise the perceived costs of desegregation for whites, while imposing ever-higher penalties for African Americans and other racial minority communities (Massey 1995, 1227). The effects of polarizing crime between white and racial minority neighborhoods increase dramatically when racial minorities are segregated across municipal lines. Like other social problems that result from concentrated poverty, when crime is isolated on the "minority" side of the municipal boundary, suburban whites are spared from having to share the fiscal or social burdens of having to contend with crime. White communities and municipalities are actually subsidized through the isolation of crime in central cities.

In addition to employment and education, racial minorities are removed from other important opportunities, such as adequate housing, health care, and childcare. The social context of concentrated poverty is marked by crime, increased rates of teen pregnancy, and drug and alcohol abuse. The context created has the tendency to perpetuate multigenerational poverty. Lacking role models with strong educational or employment backgrounds, inner-city students see their opportunities limited and feel that they cannot escape their circle. They tend to lose their sense of "destiny control" and develop a feeling of powerlessness. Aside from these important sociological factors, the creation of multigenerational poverty due to limited access to opportunity has clear economic terms. For instance, the exclusion of African Americans and other racial minority communities from homeownership investment opportunities has severely limited their ability to accumulate wealth. Homeownership and home equity are the major ways in which people accumulate wealth in America. Because families borrow against their homes for college tuition and new business capital, the racial gap in homeownership exacerbates and further entrenches economic disparities and perpetuates racial poverty. African Americans experience cumulative disadvantages while whites experience cumulative advantages, including the ability to reap the benefits of government homeownership tax benefits (powell 1996, 86–89).

Concentrated poverty is best understood in terms of cumulative causation rather than in terms of a single indicator (Galster 1998). The sorting process that generates concentrated poverty creates a web of opportunity-denying structures that limit the capacity of low-income minorities. Concentrated poverty can also be understood as a tax that the more powerful middle and upper classes impose on the residents of impacted communities by extracting opportunities away from low-income communities while refusing to share the regional responsibility or risk.

Racial segregation, concentrated poverty, and lack of opportunity are not local issues or the products of a "culture of poverty" but directly result from political fragmentation and urban sprawl. The displacement of opportunities from central cities toward the suburbs and the confinement of racial minorities to segregated inner-city areas have been intrinsic components throughout the history of suburbanization. The irony of racially segregated sprawl patterns is that municipalities with the greatest need for social services are the least able to provide them, due to a lack of tax base. The policies have therefore placed higher tax burdens on those least able to pay, while they have spared affluent suburbs from having to confront the costs of poverty, which are concentrated on the other side of the city/suburb boundary. The result of this polarization of economic resources has been a fragmented regional competition for tax base, in which many cities have tried to attract middle-class commercial and residential interests to reenter the central city. Poor cities in the midst of these fragmented regions often suffer from an infrastructural deficit, meaning they do not have the taxing capacity to efficiently or effectively service their aging infrastructure.

## Gentrification and Concentrated Poverty

Much of the current discussion of housing and urban sprawl centers around gentrification, which is often presented as a foil for, or as the antithesis of, concentrated poverty. This opposition between concentrated poverty and gentrification, however, is wrong. Gentrification and concentrated poverty are actually closely related in that they are both processes that tend to isolate racial minorities from opportunity structures. It is useful to view these processes through a variety of analytical lenses to understand how they interact with each other in different ways. Two examples of such lenses differentiate between gentrification in rich, poor, and middle-class cities, and gentrification on a neighborhood, city, and regional scale.

The term "gentrification" is emotionally and politically charged and, as a result, it is often misused or imprecisely used. In general, and especially for the purposes of this chapter, *gentrification is the process of neighborhood, citywide, or regional change that results in the large-scale displacement of lower-income residents by higher-income residents. These neighborhoods are not in transition to become mixed income, multiracial communities; instead, they are in transition to become middle- and upper-middle class communities.* Although many people use the term "gentrification" interchangeably with "urban revitalization" to describe any commercial or residential improvements in urban neighborhoods, or to simply refer to the physical renovation or upgrading of housing stocks

(Kennedy and Leonard 2001, 4), these are misapplications of the term. There is often a physical component to gentrification that involves the upgrading of housing stocks, but the primary meaning of the word lies in the displacement of lower-income residents by higher-income residents, such that the character of the neighborhood or city is changed. The policies that support gentrification have the effect and sometimes the intent of driving the low-income resident out. Such displacement is cause for concern when it is involuntary and displaces the "original" residents who would prefer to stay in their neighborhood. Because of the dynamics of gentrification, there are increased evictions, rapidly rising rents, and/or increases in property taxes that the older residents cannot afford.

There is often a clear racial component to gentrification, as higher-income white households replace lower-income racial minority households, sometimes in the very same neighborhoods that experienced white flight or traumatic urban renewal in the 1950s and 1960s (Kennedy and Leonard 2001, 4). Gentrification, which results in this type of racial displacement, undermines the quest for racial equality in the housing market and the formation of stable mixed-income neighborhoods. It is another instance in the long history of urban sprawl patterns that have served the needs of high-income, predominantly white residents at the expense of lower-income racial minority communities.

While housing advocates who attack concentrated poverty may fail to consider and address the destructive force of gentrification, in today's hot housing market, advocates are more likely to challenge gentrification. For this reason, this discussion will focus on the problems associated with concentrating on gentrification and ignoring concentrated poverty, although a similar analysis would apply to focusing on concentrated poverty and ignoring gentrification. In the current climate, many housing advocates, especially in rich and middle-class cities, view gentrification as the issue threatening their constituency the most. They often see the public focus on concentration of poverty as a justification for gentrifying impacted areas and dispersing low-income racial minorities. The fear for racial displacement is not unfounded. Many city policymakers are interested in building or solidifying a middle-class housing base and pushing low-income people out of their jurisdictional boundaries. These policymakers understand some of the implications of concentrated poverty. Low-income residents do not generate much in the way of taxes and have high needs. In most instances, low-income residents lack political power to effectively oppose these displacement policies.

While advocates focused on gentrification are right to be concerned about the dispersal or pushing out of low-income people, they often fail to address the problems of concentrated poverty.

Indeed, gentrification and concentrated poverty are simply two varieties of the same destructive social phenomenon that isolates low-income racial minorities from opportunity structures. Concentrated poverty usually isolates low-income people at the core of the region while gentrification generally isolates low-income people from new opportunities created in the center of the region. Too often, those who would challenge gentrification see the anticoncentrated poverty folks as their foe, while those who challenge concentrated poverty attack antigentrification folks as their foe. The animosity between the two camps is a serious mistake. Both gentrification and concentrated poverty isolate low-income people from opportunity structures through the sorting of housing. They are opportunity-denying practices. The response must be to pursue opportunity-based housing strategies on a level consistent with both the need for housing and the distribution of opportunity regionwide.

The forces that drive gentrification are analogous to pressure differentials that produce weather patterns resulting in air rushes from areas of high to low pressure. In gentrification, money and resources move from high-income areas to low-income areas. Similarly, the polarization of resources in a metropolitan region create a large differential in cost and value, such that when pressure is created through sudden job or population growth, resources flood rapidly into lower-income areas, destabilizing neighborhoods and displacing former residents. Gentrification is usually harmful for racial minority communities living in concentrated poverty because it tends to move or push low-income people away from emerging opportunities. Although gentrification creates marked changes in formerly dilapidated neighborhoods, such as improvements in housing stock and land values, it does not necessarily do anything to eliminate concentrated poverty. Rather, because gentrification necessarily implies the displacement of lower-income residents by higher-income residents, "original" residents—often racial minority residents—frequently cannot afford to stay in their neighborhoods any longer and do not benefit from the changes and improvements that take place. As a result, gentrification merely produces a reconfiguration of concentrated poverty by moving it from one place to another. The implications of concentrated poverty remain the same, whether it is located in the center or at the periphery of a metropolitan area.

In many ways, gentrification can be more harmful to racial minority communities than concentrated poverty, as families under gentrification are detached from community institutions, such as schools, churches, and childcare arrangements, as well as long-standing social networks of families and friends (Kennedy and Leonard 2001, 8). In addition, gentrification entails a form of exclusionary displacement, in that changes in a neighborhood, city, or region prevent *future* low-income households from moving into the area and benefiting from improved opportunities. In addition, the housing programs frequently relocate displaced families in other concentrated poverty areas.

Although any involuntary displacement is harmful, there are gradations to the impact of gentrification and displacement, depending on whether the displacement is happening on a neighborhood, city, or regional scale. Neighborhood scale or intrajurisdictional gentrification involves the displacement of people into other neighborhoods within the same city. Even if there is gentrification in some neighborhoods in a low-income or middle-class city, this does not entail gentrification on a citywide level. Indeed, a city can be in the process of becoming poorer notwithstanding modest gentrification at a neighborhood level. This does not mean that under such circumstances gentrification is not harmful. However, it is different from gentrification on a larger scale. Gentrification on a city scale, or interjurisdictional gentrification, is much more damaging in that it moves low-income people not only to other neighborhoods, but also to other *cities*, which are often underequipped to provide needed social services. This sort of gentrification is another product of the fractured nature of metropolitan areas and can create the same polarization in resources and opportunity as is found between wealthy suburbs and poverty-stricken inner cities, only in reverse. Regional gentrification is the most damaging, because it means that low-income people are unable to find housing anywhere in the region and are forced to either double up in overcrowded housing or seek opportunity and housing by migrating to other areas.

## Causes of Gentrification

Gentrification is caused by a complex array of regional, citywide, and neighborhood-based factors, and its causes differ from region to region and neighborhood to neighborhood. The larger forces that combine to create gentrification may be market driven or initiated unknowingly by regional or city actions. Many of the causes of gentrification are regional in scope and often difficult to pinpoint, yet they tend to adversely affect racial minority communities. Therefore, it is important to understand how larger forces impact gentrification and concentrated poverty. It is also important to examine and question why those larger forces tend to have such adverse effects for racial minorities living in concentrated poverty. The most important reason for understanding the causes of concentrated poverty and gentrification, therefore, is to fashion an effective remedy.

The most often noted cause for gentrification is a rapid growth in regional population or jobs. Such growth does not need to center in the heart of downtown; job growth along a city's periphery can also spur gentrification. For example, between 1995 and 1997, 286,675 new jobs were created in the San Francisco Bay area. Most of these jobs were located in the Silicon Valley area, which is 45 miles south of the city of San Francisco. Yet, this growth in regional jobs appears to be the primary force behind gentrification in affordable neighborhoods in San Francisco, like the Mission District, which was historically a Hispanic neighborhood. Job growth has also occurred in other cities like Atlanta and Washington, D.C., where new higher-income households are just as likely to reverse-commute to jobs in the suburbs as they are to work downtown (Kennedy and Leonard 2001, 9).

Housing market dynamics also play a crucial role in producing gentrification. These dynamics include a number of factors, including constrained supply, relative affordability, lucrative investment potential, and large rent gaps. The most important of these factors is constrained supply. Most of the other factors become relevant in the presence of a tight housing market. Again, San Francisco provides a good example. As mentioned above, between 1995 and 1997, the Bay area produced nearly 300,000 new jobs, but built only 31,000 new homes. In 1998, the city gained 10,000 new jobs, but built only 874 new units (Smith 1999, 18–20). Basic supply and demand tends to drive the price of housing up in a tight market, but it also forces higher-income people to seek homes in areas where they formerly would not have lived, such as areas that racial minorities populate.

Although the importance of a constrained housing supply is crucial in producing gentrification, the existence of potentially valuable housing stock is also important. Buyers are much more likely to purchase homes in low-cost areas if housing stock provides for potential renovation and lucrative investment. As stated earlier, home equity is one of the most important sources of wealth in America; many investors seek out neighborhoods with gentrification potential that will dramatically increase the value of aging housing stock. Similarly, where real estate interests have systematically devalued a rental area, a rental gap often emerges, such that there is a great difference between the potential value of a property before and after renovation (Kennedy and Leonard 2001, 10). Ironically, the systematic devaluation of housing in the central cities due to widespread, racially discriminatory "redlining" practices is now one of the major forces driving gentrification.

City policies can also positively or negatively affect gentrification. Some examples of policies that accelerate gentrification are tax incentives offered for middle-class homebuyers, a reduced number of affordable units, demolition of existing low-income housing, and, of course, exclusionary zoning. Examples of policies that slow gentrification include rent control, subsidies for low-income tenants, construction of mixed-income housing, and inclusionary zoning. In addition, a myriad of other factors can contribute to an area's gentrification appeal, including its proximity to transportation, job sites, shopping centers, or other amenities, such as theaters, museums, or waterfronts (Kennedy and Leonard 2001, 11).

## Gentrification in Rich, Poor, and Middle-Class Cities

The dynamics of gentrification, and the likelihood that it will occur at all, differ significantly in rich, poor, and middle-class cities. A tight, expensive housing or rental market located near a smaller, concentrated area of low-income housing is much more likely to create gentrification pressures than a large, poverty-stricken area that contains a great deal of empty space and vacant homes. A more detailed discussion of the characteristics of rich, poor, and middle-class cities, and an illumination of some recent trends in the three types of cities, will clarify how issues of housing and gentrification differ among the three.

Rich, poor, and middle-class cities should be considered in relation to the region surrounding them. For our purposes, rich cities can be thought of as having a median per capita income and fiscal capacity close to or greater than the regional average, or at about 90 percent of the regional average or higher. Middle-class cities have a median per capita income and fiscal capacity that is roughly 60 to 90 percent of the regional average, and poor cities have a per capita income and fiscal capacity of less than 60 percent of the regional average. Consider a comparison among seven metropolitan regions: Seattle, San Francisco, Boston, Chicago, Minneapolis-St. Paul, Cleveland, and Detroit. Seattle and San Francisco represent rich cities, Chicago and Minneapolis-St. Paul are middle-class cities, and Cleveland and Detroit represent poor cities. Boston wavers between being a rich and a middle-class city.

Rich cities such as San Francisco, Seattle, and the in-between city of Boston often have a growing or stable population base, and generally have poverty rates close to or less than the regional average. Property values in rich cities are generally also comparable to the regional average. The situation is different in poor cities such as Detroit or Cleveland, which have a much larger proportion of high-poverty census tracts compared with the surrounding region, and suffer from property values that are much lower than the surrounding suburbs. The difference between rich and poor cities can also be seen in terms of race. A much higher percentage of racial minorities tend to populate poor cities, and particularly racial minorities who live in concentrated poverty, than the surrounding region. While rich cities also tend to have a higher racial minority population than the surrounding suburbs, the difference between the city and the region is generally much lower than in poor cities. Middle-class cities tend to be somewhere in between these two extremes.

Figures 4.1 through 4.5 show these trends and differences. Figure 4.1 depicts the percentage of people who live in poverty in both the regions and the cities for the seven metropolitan areas. Detroit and Cleveland, both poor cities, have poverty rates close to three times that of the regional average. This 3-to-1 city-to-region poverty ratio drops to 2 to 1 for the middle-class cities, and for the two rich cities, it is even less. Figure 4.2, which depicts single-family property values for the seven cities, complements and reflects figure 4.1. For Detroit and Cleveland, the median family property values are one-third to one-half the regional average, while values in Seattle and San Francisco are very close to, or equal to, the regional average. Thus, poor cities contain far more than their share of regional poverty, and a much lower proportion of regional wealth, as reflected in property value. As a result, the areas with the

Figure 4.1   *Population at or below the Poverty Level in Seven Metropolitan Areas, 1990 and 1997 (percent)*

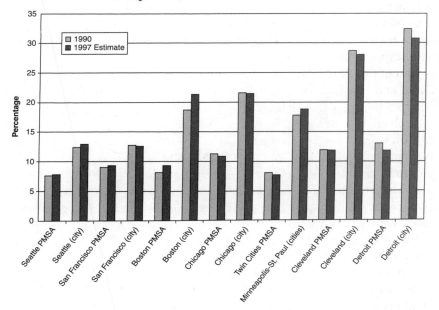

*Sources:* U.S. Department of Housing and Urban Development (1990); U.S. Census (1997). PMSA = primary metropolitan statistical area.[1]

greatest needs are the same areas that have the fewest resources available to pay for those needs.

Figures 4.3 and 4.4 indicate the racial dynamics of rich, poor, and middle-class cities, as well as the racial dynamics of concentrated poverty in these cities. Figure 4.3 depicts the percentage of racial minorities in the region and the city. All of the cities have higher racial minority populations than the surrounding regions, but in the poor cities of Detroit and Cleveland, the difference in racial minority population is much starker than it is in the other cities. The Detroit metropolitan region is predominantly white, with a racial minority percentage of about 25 percent. The city of Detroit, on the other hand, has a majority of people of color; the city is almost 80 percent African American. A similar but somewhat less marked city/region differential appears in Cleveland. The racial minority population in the city of San Francisco is over 50 percent, although this percentage is only 10 to 15 percent higher

Figure 4.2  *Single-Family Property Values in Seven Metropolitan Areas, 1990*

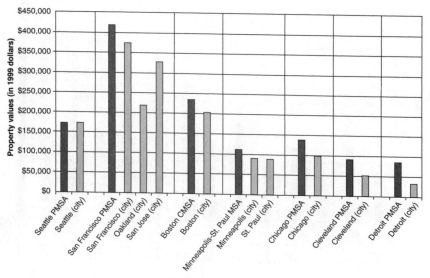

*Source:* U.S. Department of Housing and Urban Development (1990).
MSA = metropolitan statistical area.[2]
PMSA = primary metropolitan statistical area.
CMSA = consolidated metropolitan statistical area.[3]

than the regional ratio. In Seattle, this difference is even smaller. Boston, Chicago, and Minneapolis-St. Paul fall somewhere in between, although the older, larger cities of Boston and Chicago have a larger minority population and city/region imbalance than the somewhat newer, and much whiter, Minneapolis-St. Paul.

Figures 4.4, 4.5, and 4.6, respectively, depict the percentage of low-income African Americans, Hispanics, and whites living in concentrated poverty in these regions (Jargowsky 1997, 20). Clearly, in poor and middle-class cities, African Americans are much more likely to live in concentrated poverty, and the total proportion of African-American people living in concentrated poverty has increased dramatically since 1970. In Chicago, the percentage of African Americans living in concentrated poverty doubled from 1970 to 1990, and in Detroit, the percentage increased *fivefold*. In the rich cities, on the other hand, the percentage of African Americans living in concentrated poverty declined or increased

Figure 4.3  *Racial Ethnic Groups in Seven Metropolitan Areas,*
*2000 (percent)*

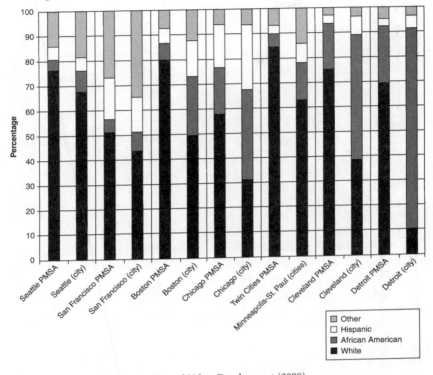

*Source:* U.S. Department of Housing and Urban Development (2000).
PMSA = primary metropolitan statistical area.

only slightly, as in Boston and San Francisco, or remained fairly constant, as in Seattle.

These figures sketch a picture of rich, poor, and middle-class cities.
They show that rich cities benefit from relatively high tax bases and relatively low poverty rates, while poor cities, populated primarily with
racial minorities, suffer from disproportionately low land values and tax
bases, and from very high poverty rates. Throughout the postwar period,
poor cities have also been plagued by massive depopulation—as middle-
class whites have moved out—and by deindustrialization and the migration of jobs and opportunity away from the city. This trend in the movement of job opportunities continued into the 1990s, although rich cities

Figure 4.4  *Black Poor in Tracts with over 40 Percent Poverty in Seven Metropolitan Areas (percent)*

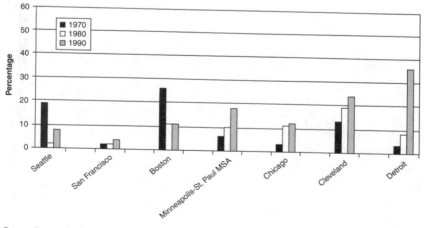

*Source:* Jargowsky (1997).

have not suffered as much from the removal of jobs. Figure 4.7 shows the percentage change in jobs from 1991 and 1997 in the seven cities (U.S. Census). Although regionwide job growth was strong in every area examined, the middle-class and poor cities saw a significant drop in jobs, emphasizing the departure of employment opportunities toward the

Figure 4.5  *Hispanic Poor in Tracts with over 40 Percent Poverty in Seven Metropolitan Areas (percent)*

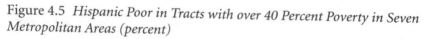

*Source:* Jargowsky (1997).
MSA = metropolitan statistical area.

Figure 4.6  *White Poor in Tracts with over 40 Percent Poverty in Seven Metropolitan Areas (percent)*

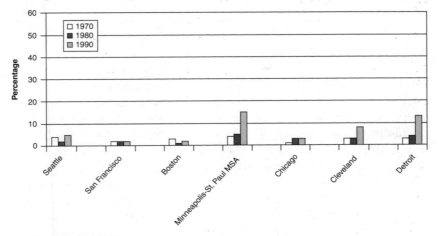

*Source:* Jargowsky (1997).
MSA = metropolitan statistical area.

Figure 4.7  *Change in Jobs in Seven Central Cities and Their Regions, 1991 to 1997 (percent)*

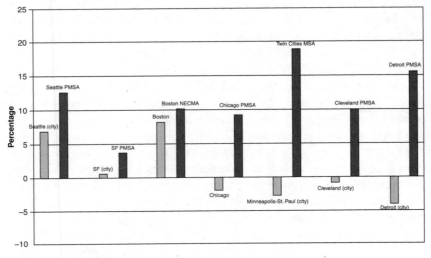

*Source:* Jargowsky (1997).
MSA = metropolitan statistical area.
PMSA = primary metropolitan statistical area.
NECMA = New England county metropolitan area.

suburbs. Such job loss has not been a problem in rich cities, as indicated by the fact that job opportunities continued to grow in Seattle, San Francisco, and Boston.

## Poor Cities and Gentrification

Due to the massive outflow of residents and jobs from poor cities and the concurrent centralization of poor people into public housing, these cities have experienced high levels of depopulation, demolition, and building abandonment over the past few decades. As a result, these cities have a high volume of vacant lots and homes. Detroit, which once had a population of almost two million people, now has a population of approximately one million (Vergara 1997, 26–28). The amount of open space found in the heart of cities such as Detroit, Cleveland, and Chicago is startling. The area around 12th Street in Detroit, for instance, was once the most densely populated neighborhood in the city. By 1993, after fires and abandonment, the area was covered with tall grass, and raccoons, turtledoves, and pheasants populated the area (Vergara 1997, 26–28).

The presence of so much vacant land allows poor cities to revitalize without the same fear of gentrification. Cleveland is a good example of revitalization efforts and dynamics in a poor city. Cleveland was once a major corporate headquarters and manufacturing town with a thriving population of one million. Beginning in 1950, however, white middle-class residents began to leave the city for the surrounding suburbs, and by 1970, the city's population had declined to half a million people, mostly composed of lower-income racial minorities. Throughout the past few decades, the housing stock in Cleveland has declined, and even the city's relatively strong communities had thousands of empty lots. In recent years, Cleveland has experienced some modest economic revitalization, but has not seen the kind of gentrification pressures that a number of middle-class and rich cities have. The few neighborhoods that have seen an inflow of higher-income residents have not seen any displacement, because new middle-class residents have primarily moved into new housing that was built on previously vacant land. Because there has not been displacement, the new residents have helped to revitalize the neighborhood, and they have seen this as an improvement (Kennedy and Leonard 2001, 43–44). This sort of revitalization and stable growth are badly needed in poor cities such as Cleveland and Detroit, since they still have a large number of concentrated poverty census tracts.

Despite the desperate need and potential for revitalization in cities like Detroit and Cleveland, residents and racial minority communities often strongly oppose strategies that seek to bring middle class resources into the city. While the presence of an urban middle class could actually lower the concentration of poverty and provide service jobs for minority community members, city residents misunderstand such efforts to build middle-class communities as efforts to gentrify their neighborhoods. This fear persists even though the revitalization strategies entail in-fill development, which would not result in any widespread extrajurisdictional gentrification.

There are a number of reasons for these fears of gentrification. First, people fear that the middle-income residents attracted by revitalization programs will ultimately displace racial minority residents from their neighborhoods. Second, many poor cities still have unmet low-income housing needs, and residents may feel that concentrating on the development of middle-class housing will divert resources away from those who most need them. Third, the benefits (especially to current residents) of attracting middle-class residents or housing have not been made clear. Fourth, because these programs are often, justifiably, viewed in racial terms, they appear as political ploys that pander to white suburbanites at the expense of racial minority communities (powell 1999a, 11).

In addition, inner-city racial minority communities are often wary of regional approaches to address the issues of sprawl and concentrated poverty. Regionalism suggests the need to overcome fragmented municipal approaches through cross-jurisdictional cooperation that will address issues affecting the entire region. Inner-city racial minority communities have resisted regional strategies for fear of losing cultural control and identity and sacrificing political power within their communities. As history has shown, these fears are often well founded. The redrawing of political boundaries has often been used to disempower racial minorities, and the needs of well-to-do whites have traditionally taken precedence over the needs of low-income racial minorities (powell 1999a, 11). While the fears of minority communities are well founded, resource-depleted inner-city communities have much to gain by developing mixed-income housing and adopting federated regionalism, which would preserve local political power while allowing communities to benefit from the sharing of regional resources. Unlike the unstable mixed-income neighborhoods that result from gentrification, revitalization strategies relying on in-fill or partial/small-scale gentrification that may relocate a small number of residents to a different neighborhood create more stable mixed-income communities (powell 1999a, 12). Therefore, residents of poor cities should not necessarily view these revitalization efforts as gentrification.

## Rich Cities and Gentrification

The large-scale abandonment and job loss found in poor cities are not seen in rich cities. Thus, it seems that these cities do not have serious problems with concentrated poverty. However, this appearance can be deceptive in that rich cities often experience a reconfiguration, rather than an absence, of concentrated poverty. In San Francisco, for instance, the number of high-poverty tracts has remained fairly small and constant (12 to 13 since 1970), while other American cities have experienced a large increase in high-poverty tracts during the same period (Jargowsky 1997, 222–54).

However, a closer examination reveals that city policies have displaced lower-income people and people of moderate means through gentrification, or have simply kept them out of the city because of housing costs. These low-income people are often forced to move into nearby poor cities or suburbs. In the San Francisco Bay area, the city of San Francisco contains approximately 20 percent of the region's concentrated poverty census tracts. The remaining 80 percent are located in nearby cities, such as Oakland and San Jose (U.S. Department of Housing and Urban Development, 1990). Thus, areas of concentrated poverty and limited access to opportunity exist near the city, but are in other jurisdictions. In this way, just as suburbs benefit from the concentration of poverty in central cities, rich cities like San Francisco and Seattle are in effect subsidized by not having to share their resources with low-income residents that have been displaced to other municipalities.

Gentrification is thus cause for major concern in regions where rich cities like San Francisco and Seattle are located. As noted previously, the implications and effects of concentrated poverty are the same whether it is located at the center or the periphery of a metropolitan region. In the case of cities like San Francisco, not only are people forced out of their homes and away from opportunity, but also they are often pushed out of the city into areas with fewer social resources to address their needs. This forced displacement out of not only a neighborhood but out of the city is called extrajurisdictional or complete gentrification. Like white flight, it creates a racial boundary along the municipal borders between city and suburb.

The balance between revitalization and displacement is much more delicate in middle-class cities such as Minneapolis-St. Paul. Although gentrification is much more likely to occur in such middle-class cities than in poor cities, these cities are still losing population and still tend to contain a disproportionate amount of regional low-income housing. Middle-class in-fill projects are still valuable to low-income neighborhoods that contain many vacant lots. Therefore, although middle-class cities must try to maintain a middle-class or mixed-income presence, they must also watch carefully to ensure that gentrification and displacement do not occur on a large scale. If the goal of a middle-class city is to remain a middle-class city, it must keep a substantial middle-class while providing housing opportunity for low-income residents.

## Current Strategies and Debates

Gentrification is a particularly pertinent and emotionally charged topic because it is often raised in connection with two pressing and inter-related issues facing American urban areas: the need to dismantle and eliminate concentrated poverty, and the need to ensure an adequate supply of affordable housing. Scholars and policymakers often frame the debate as a mutually exclusive competition between the need to create mixed-income developments and the need to maintain an adequate supply of affordable housing. Because many of the plans to dismantle densely populated, high-poverty public housing projects in favor of mixed-income neighborhoods decrease the amount of affordable housing, many people oppose such revitalization efforts on the grounds that these efforts result in a net loss of housing stock for low-income people. However, criticism should not be directed at efforts to create stable, mixed-income communities. That is, the problem is not whether or not revitalization needs to take place. It is clearly needed, especially in poor cities and even most middle-class cities. The object of criticism should be the fact that current government policies do not provide for an adequate supply of affordable housing in other areas to make up for any potential loss of units as a result of revitalization.

Many communities where multifamily public housing units were built are in a sea of concentrated poverty. The neighborhoods need to address this concentration of poverty. However, reducing the overall number of affordable units is not the way to achieve this. Low-income housing, even in concentrated neighborhoods, is certainly better than no housing. However, opportunity-based housing is better still. Any discussion of gentrification, revitalization, or concentrated poverty must be understood in the context of the nationwide affordable housing crisis. As the number of people living in poverty has increased dramatically since 1970, so has the need for decent affordable housing. The nation has experienced a net loss of units relative to its low-income population, and federal cutbacks in the production of housing have added to an increasingly acute affordable housing shortage. In 1970, there were one million more affordable apartments nationwide than families who needed them (National Housing Law Project 1996). Today, the country is about five million units short due to widespread demolition and the explosion of the low-income population. Of the approximately 15 million households that qualified for federal housing assistance in 1996, only about 4.5 million received assistance. Waiting lists for housing assistance in many cities span several years, and potential applicants often must wait years just to get on the waiting lists (DeParle 1996, 52).

In the context of such a massive shortage, low-income communities and housing activists are skeptical of any revitalization program that threatens a further reduction in the supply of affordable housing. Many current strategies, such as the program that resulted from the *Gautreaux* lawsuit in Chicago and the federal HOPE VI (Home Ownership and Opportunity for People Everywhere) program, emphasize the demolition of concentrated, dilapidated public housing, the deconcentration of poor communities of color, and the creation of stable, mixed-income housing. However, due to policy changes and poor planning, these programs have resulted in a large net loss of housing units, given that the programs do not replace demolished units. What has occurred, therefore, is the creation of mixed-income developments at the expense of low-income residents, who these programs displaced and left without housing. That is, these programs have demolished large housing projects and replaced only a small portion of the units on site in the midst of other, more expensive units. At the same time, the housing programs have not created affordable low-income housing in other neighborhoods. Therefore, what was billed as a revitalization and poverty deconcentration program appears to more accurately represent gentrification. As a result, the term "mixed-income housing" has become associated with the term "gentrification," along with its connotations of racially charged displacement.

## Gautreaux v. Chicago Housing Authority

The debate surrounding the *Gautreaux* lawsuit, and the way the lawsuit has interacted with other housing efforts in Chicago, highlights the complex nature of the issues and the inadequacy of present efforts to alleviate concentrated poverty and provide decent affordable housing. Thirty years ago, in *Gautreaux v. Chicago Housing Authority* (CHA), a group of public housing residents filed suit against CHA, alleging that CHA's site selection and tenant assignment plans were racially discriminatory in that it illegally concentrated low-income racial minorities into small, densely populated areas. In 1971, the Supreme Court entered a judgment against CHA, finding that it had intentionally maintained patterns of racial segregation in family public housing. The *Gautreaux* ruling included a comprehensive new plan for site selection and family assignment to remedy the discrimination. The focus of the suit was a requirement that for every unit of public housing constructed in a "limited" area, defined as an area with a 30 percent or more African-American population, three units had to be built in a "general" area, defined as an area with a 70 percent or greater white population.

The U.S. Department of Housing and Urban Development (HUD) was implicated in a companion case to the *Gautreaux* suit for knowingly acquiescing in CHA's discriminatory practices, and likewise the Court ordered HUD to take remedial action. Following the Supreme Court's ruling, HUD was required to create and fund a demonstration program that would use Section 8 rental subsidies to help *Gautreaux* families move to low-poverty neighborhoods throughout the Chicago metropolitan area. Through this program, about 7,100 families moved to low-poverty areas, and the Court dismissed HUD from the case in 1997, finding that the housing agency had fulfilled its obligation (Stasell and Wilen 2000, 123–125).

The programs resulting from the *Gautreaux* ruling appear to be model programs to achieve the deconcentration of poverty, and the HUD-sponsored movement of thousands of families to middle and high-income neighborhoods is an example of a successful relocation program. Over the years, however, a number of factors have undermined the strength of the *Gautreaux* ruling itself. The rate of housing to be built in limited and general areas was changed from 3-to-1 ratio to 1 to 1, meaning that for each unit built in a limited area, only one had to be built in a general area. In addition, a third category of neighborhoods was created, designated as "revitalizing" neighborhoods, which were and still are defined as neighborhoods with large minority populations that are undergoing redevelopment. Because they were expected to become integrated areas in a short time, such neighborhoods did not have to be matched on a one-to-one basis with units built in "general" areas. This practice is still taking place. The neighborhoods with such infamous Chicago housing projects such as Henry Horner, Cabrini-Greene, and ABLA (Addams, Brooks, Loomis, and Abbott public housing developments) have been given "revitalizing" designations, allowing developers to construct units on the site of large public housing projects without matching them to scattered developments in other parts of the metropolitan area (Stasell and Wilen 2000, 125–27).

Courts consider 10 factors in determining whether or not an area is "revitalizing," including the area's accessibility to shopping, attractive features, transportation, the quality of the housing stock, and whether the area is undergoing visible redevelopment (Stasell and Wilen 2000, 126). It is interesting to note that of these 10 factors, 7 match factors that Maureen Kennedy and Paul Leonard cite as indicative of gentrification having occurred or occurring in the near future (Kennedy and Leonard 2001, 7). This has added to the confusion surrounding the terms "revitalization" and "gentrification," and it is understandable, then, for low-income residents in Chicago to equate revitalization with gentrification.

Aside from court-generated setbacks to the program, mismanagement on the part of CHA and racial discrimination have hindered the progress of low-income housing in Chicago. CHA and the City of Chicago have stalled and avoided the construction of scattered-site, low-income housing units in white areas. While the *Gautreaux* suit involved 40,000 families, no low-income housing was built between 1969 and 1974, and as of October 1999, the programs had constructed fewer than 3,000 scattered-site units. The agency and the City of Chicago built only 131 of these units in predominantly white neighborhoods. Although the court receiver who was assigned the task of improving public housing after CHA was deemed unable to do so claims that high land prices hinder the construction of units in white areas, doubtless strong local opposition and "not in my back yard" attitudes have affected their reluctance (Stasell and Wilen

2000, 126). The collusion of forces that has frustrated attempts to deconcentrate poverty in Chicago and undermined the strength of the *Gautreaux* program is not unique to Chicago, but has affected other programs
across the country. For instance, a similar suit was brought against the
Minneapolis Housing Authority (MHA) in the early 1990s. Just as in the
*Gautreaux* case, the court found that MHA had illegally concentrated
low-income racial minorities into public housing, and ruled that a number of public housing projects would have to be demolished and replaced
with scattered-site housing. The case, and subsequent affordable housing
demolition, fell in the middle of a major affordable housing crisis. Due to
a lack of resources and neighborhood unwillingness to absorb public
housing, the city has been unable to procure or build nearly enough units
to make up for those lost through demolition.

*Gautreaux* continues to affect the development of public housing in
Chicago, although the elements that have been added to the ruling—
especially the "revitalization" designation—have often complicated and
undermined attempts to improve Chicago's housing situation. In order
to cut building costs, developers have requested that the courts designate
as "revitalizing" areas those slated for demolition or improvement, such
as the Henry Horner projects. This designation, which courts have
granted, allows city developers to build units in these areas without matching these developments with further low-income developments in other
areas in the Chicago region. Since one goal of redeveloping public housing projects is to build stable, mixed-income neighborhoods rather than
simply rebuilding the original projects, the number of units designated
for low-income people built on the site of the old projects is lower than
the number of homes that previously existed there. However, because
those same areas are designated as "revitalizing," the city is not required
to build additional housing in other areas to replace them. The result has
been a net loss in affordable housing as developers construct market-
value housing on the former sites of public housing without a concurrent construction of additional low-income housing.

Although many of the problems facing public housing residents in
Chicago, including poor management by the CHA, may be unique to
Chicago, the root of the problem of inadequate opportunity-based public housing lies elsewhere. Indeed, the current housing crisis is national in
scope, affecting cities throughout the United States. The federal government greatly exacerbated these problems with policies it took or failed to
take. Congress repealed the one-for-one replacement requirement, which

formerly required that housing programs and agencies had to replace every public housing unit they demolished. Therefore, HUD or local housing authorities can demolish public housing units without replacing them, dramatically increasing the pace at which affordable housing is lost. In addition, Congress changed the HOPE VI program, which was originally intended to revitalize distressed public housing along the lines of the original *Gautreaux* plan, to primarily emphasize demolition. Finally, Congress enacted a "vouchering out" law, which requires the demolition of public housing projects and the issuance of Section 8 vouchers. With a Section 8 voucher, a resident may find housing through a private landlord and use the voucher as rental assistance. Governments sometimes administer such vouchers where it is deemed more cost-effective than building additional public housing. Because there is no relocation guidance offered to residents, they often wind up moving into areas of concentrated poverty or have a very difficult time finding housing of any kind.

## "Gentrification" versus Affordable Housing

How does the complicated debate about public and affordable housing, exemplified by the events in Chicago, Minneapolis, and the HOPE VI program, relate to issues of urban sprawl, concentrated poverty, and gentrification? Clearly, the present crisis in affordable housing is a direct result of historical, regionally driven, racializing urban sprawl patterns. However, the failure of city and federal efforts to deal with concentrated poverty, and the resulting net loss of affordable housing, are often attributed to "gentrification" rather than the racially discriminatory legacy of urban sprawl. Instead of the regional factors that drive concentrated poverty and gentrification, the criticism of some housing advocates has turned toward the term "mixed-income," which is viewed suspiciously by those who see it as a euphemism for gentrification. As a result, the issue is sometimes framed as a choice between gentrification, which is taken to mean any revitalization or mixed-income efforts, and the supply of affordable housing and the maintenance of minority political control. This can create opposition to efforts to redevelop housing projects and place families in lower-poverty neighborhoods where they could have access to better schools, jobs, and services.

These fears are also often framed using a rhetoric of choice, the argument being that gentrification limits the degree of choice people have over where they live, when in fact people should be given the choice to live wherever they want—including their old neighborhood. Although choice in housing is important to consider relative to the choices available to others, the argument that all people should have unlimited choice in housing, or in just about anything, has some dangerous implications. The discourse of unlimited choice, which both sides employ in debates on concentrated poverty and gentrification, is dangerous because it reduces issues of public concern to private matters. That is, the choices people make about their housing necessarily impact and circumscribe choices that others make. As with all things, the choices people make about housing have powerful public and political ramifications; to argue that all people should be given unlimited choice simplifies the reality by suggesting that people can make private choices about housing without also affecting issues of public concern.

Logically, of course, we all know that people are constrained in their housing options, often by economics, but also simply by the fact that if more than one person chooses to live in a given house, the person who buys that house has necessarily frustrated the other person's choice. It is important, therefore, to acknowledge that there will always be constraints on the choices people have about housing. Having said this, it is clear that some constraints placed on choices are not legitimate, while others are. For example, to constrain one group's choices because of race or gender raises serious questions of fairness. It is fairness or justice that informs us about how we should think about the constraints put on our choices. What justice requires and permits should constrain choices we have. This clearly requires the expansion of choices for low-income racial minority tenants. The goal of the government is not, as is often argued, to effectuate each individual's unlimited choice, but rather to try to ensure that the constraints that the government will necessarily place on housing choices are defined by what justice permits and requires.

The debate that pits affordable housing against "gentrification" can be found in a recent article by Wendy Stasell and William Wilen, who note that it is debatable whether mixed-income housing benefits very low income African Americans. Stasell and Wilen quote John Calmore, who says, "Regardless of whether the integrating group is white or non-white, the benefit accruing to the latter is virtually nonexistent" (Stasell and Wilen 2000, 141). Stasell and Wilen, Calmore, and others question whether mixed-income or integration efforts actually provide economic and sociological benefits to low-income racial minorities, or whether they actually "destroy non-white political power, sense of community, culture, and neighborhood based support systems" (Stasell and Wilen 2000, 142). Again, the underlying fear is that low-income racial minority residents will not be able to benefit from improvements in their neighborhood if they are forced out of the revitalization process. It is important to note how this reframes the issue away from concentrated poverty toward the policy of reducing the overall number of housing units available to low-income residents. Despite the fact that the housing market remains highly segregated, these arguments suggest that integration is at the heart of the affordable housing crisis. The argument seems to equate concentration of poverty with the increased production of affordable housing and mixed income with both gentrification and integration and the lack of affordable housing. This is clearly not accurate. While the cost associated with land in poor neighborhoods may make it cheaper to build on that land, the other cost associated with building on such sites may outrun such savings.

Our housing policies for the most part have not concerned themselves with concentrated poverty, and yet there is still a lack of affordable housing. By far the most important constraint on affordable housing is the lack of resources made available for this purpose. Another constraint is the ability of cities and communities to effectively oppose or opt out of low-income housing being placed in their locale, especially if it will house racial minorities. These constraints not only limit both the siting and production of affordable housing but also add to concentrated poverty. It is certainly true that the current policies under HOPE VI, which encourage the destruction of public housing without any concurrent replacement elsewhere, reduce this housing stock. But this approach does not entail mixed-income housing or integration. As stated above, a neighborhood that is gentrifying is probably not moving toward integration. In addition, one has to wonder why mixed-income housing has worked so much better for low-income whites than for low-income African Americans.

Given the history of racial bias in American urban policy and the state of many city-sponsored programs, fears about further exclusion of minorities from opportunities are well founded. As discussed above, gentrification and involuntary displacement can be disastrous for inner-city racial minority communities and, in many instances, the threat that gentrification poses is very real. That is why the "revitalizing" designation in the *Gautreaux* case is dangerous in that it assumes that a potentially unstable and temporarily integrated neighborhood will remain integrated, when in fact the neighborhood may already be experiencing gentrification and racial displacement.

However, it is a mistake to equate the terms "mixed income" and "gentrification," or to oppose any strategy for mixed-income development because of this association with gentrification. "Mixed income" is not a term that was created by developers as a smokescreen for gentrification, but is a real concept that, when applied carefully with a regional outlook, can be valuable for cities and areas of concentrated poverty. The term "concentrated poverty," another very real concept, has been abused by suburban jurisdictions, which have justified their opposition to 50-unit low-income developments by claiming that such developments would create "concentrated poverty." Clearly, this is a misapplication of the term, but it does not undermine its true meaning. Similarly, the fact that cities like Chicago have not augmented their mixed-income developments with the creation of adequate low-income housing choices in other neighborhoods does not undermine the potential value of mixed-income housing as a strategy for the elimination of concentrated poverty. *Regional*

Any discussion of affordable housing, gentrification, and concentrated poverty must be premised on the fact that concentrated poverty and gentrification are often *regionally driven phenomena* that cannot be solved or addressed at the neighborhood or even city level. Because educational, economic, social, and residential opportunities have been unequally distributed on a regional level in a way that profoundly affects racial minority communities, these disparities must likewise be addressed on a regional level with an emphasis on the needs of under-resourced racial minority communities. Solutions to problems like those in Chicago cannot be found by simply investing money on a neighborhood level to revitalize those communities from within. Rather, efforts must be made to bring resources into those areas that lack them and to more equitably distribute the burdens of poverty-stricken areas.

The goals for improving the lives of people living in concentrated poverty are generally agreed upon: People should be able to live in decent opportunity-based housing in stable communities, and people should have access to structures of opportunities. The choices of how to distribute low-income and public housing must be made based on notions of fairness. Such a program will both promote and constrain individual choices. People do not have access to structures of opportunity if there are not adequate resources in their neighborhoods. This suggests the need for mixed-income communities. Low-income people cannot move to different neighborhoods if affordable housing does not exist outside of their own neighborhood, or if they are unaware of other housing options, or if they are prevented from moving due to racial or class prejudice. This suggests the need for a variety of choices of affordable housing in different areas, and the careful oversight of development programs to prevent involuntary displacement. The solutions to all of these problems exist in understanding that the polarization of wealth, poverty, and opportunity is generated by regional sprawl patterns, and until we begin to address them as regional issues, they will remain unsolved.

## Conclusion

Neither gentrification nor continued concentrated poverty is an acceptable choice for the future of American metropolitan areas. Because gentrification results in the involuntary displacement of racial minority communities, it only exacerbates and reconfigures concentrated poverty. The dichotomy between gentrification and concentrated poverty is false, in that it frequently represents a "choice" between concentrated poverty in one neighborhood and concentrated poverty in another neighborhood. Metropolitan areas must adopt strategies for urban revitalization that include mixed-income housing, in-fill building, and, most importantly, federated regionalism in order to provide central-city racial minority residents with access to opportunity. We must make the implicit goal of linking housing explicit by pursuing opportunity-based housing throughout the region. Opportunity should not be understood narrowly, but defined to include the opportunity to effectively participate in public life as a citizen and to participate in culture and community.

This chapter should not be read as an argument against the importance of place. It is not enough to simply understand that place can be important; we must also understand *why* it is important. Cities are not clubs; there is something deeply wrong with consigning low-income people to resource-starved cites with high needs while denying these same low-income people access to rich cities with low needs. What we can imagine is often constrained by what we see as possible, and our structures and institutions have a strong impact on our vision of the possible. It is imperative that we not limit our options to gentrification or concentrated poverty. These options not only fail to represent choices, but they represent injustice.

We must pursue strategies that place opportunity-based housing in the central city as well as throughout the region, especially in the resource-rich sections of the region. In order to adopt these strategies, there must first be more clarification in the use of the term "gentrification" in order to separate the adverse effects it connotes for central-city racial minorities from other, potentially positive programs for revitalization. The use of the word "gentrification" to describe other types of urban revitalization efforts only confuses the issue, because it forces people to associate the adverse effects of gentrification, including the displacement of low-income racial minorities in favor of middle-class whites, with other terms like "revitalization" or "renewal." Furthermore, a more nuanced view of the differences in revitalization needed for rich, poor, and middle-class cities is necessary, along with a more sophisticated understanding of the dynamics and causes of gentrification as it operates differently in rich, poor, and middle-class cities. Matters of concern in a rich city may not be matters of concern in a poor city, and vice versa. Gentrification and revitalization operate differently in different kinds of regions, and there cannot be any catchall solution to either one by simply considering one type of city or region. The factors that Maureen Kennedy and Paul Leonard give for identifying gentrification potential and dynamics are useful, but policies must consider regional factors for individual cities. We must be willing to restructure the region so that we share both responsibility and risk and conceive of each other not simply as poor and rich, but as fellow citizens.

## NOTES

1. "A geographic entity designated by the federal Office of Management and Budget for use by federal statistical agencies. If an area meets the requirements to qualify as a metropolitan statistical area and has a population of 1 million or more, two or more PMSAs may be designated within it if they meet published statistical criteria and local opinion favors the designation. When PMSAs are designated within a MSA, the larger area of which they are components is designated a consolidated metropolitan statistical area (CMSA)" (U.S. Census Bureau 1999).

2. An entity "designated by the federal Office of Management and Budget for use by federal statistical agencies. These geographically based entities are a core area with a large population nucleus plus adjacent communities with a high degree of economic and social integration with the core" (U.S. Census Bureau 1999).

3. "A geographic entity designated by the federal Office of Management and Budget for use by federal statistical agencies. An area becomes a CMSA if it qualifies as a metropolitan statistical area (MSA), has a population of 1 million or more, and has component parts that qualify as primary metropolitan statistical areas, provided local opinion favors the designation" (U.S. Census Bureau 1999).

## REFERENCES

Boger, John Charles. 1993. "Race and the American City: The Kerner Commission in Retrospect—An Introduction." *North Carolina Law Review*, "Symposium on the Urban Crisis: The Kerner Commission Report Revisited," 71 (June): 1289–349. Citing *Report of the National Advisory Commission on Civil Disorders* (which is known as the Kerner Commission Report) (New York: Bantam Books, 1968), 12–13.

Brenzel, Barbara, and Harvey Kantor. 1993. "Urban Education and the Truly Disadvantaged: The Historical Roots of the Contemporary Crisis, 1945–1990." In *The Underclass Debate: Views from History*, edited by Michael Katz. Princeton, N.J.: Princeton University Press.

Conley, Dalton. 1999. *Being Black, Living in the Red*. Berkeley: University of California Press.

Denton, Nancy A., and Douglas Massey. 1993. *American Apartheid: Segregation and the Making of the Underclass*. Cambridge: Harvard University Press.

DeParle, Jason. 1996. "The Year That Housing Died: Slamming the Door." *New York Times* Magazine (October 20).

Ford, Richard Thompson. 1994. "The Boundaries of Race: Political Geography in Legal Analysis." *Harvard Law Review* 107 (June): 1841–921.

Galster, George C. 1998. *An Econometric Model of the Urban Opportunity Structure: Cumulative Causation among City Markets, Social Problems, and Underserved Areas*. Washington, D.C.: Fannie Mae Foundation.

Institute on Race and Poverty. 1999. *Concentrated Poverty: Causes, Effects, and Solutions*. Minneapolis: Institute on Race and Poverty.

Jackson, Kenneth T. 1985. *Crabgrass Frontier: The Suburbanization of America*. New York: Oxford University Press.

Jargowsky, Paul A. 1997. *Poverty and Place: Ghettos, Barrios, and the American City*. New York: Russell Sage Foundation.

Judd, Dennis, and Todd Swanstrom. 1994. *City Politics: Private Power and Public Policy*. New York: Harper Collins.

Kasarda, John D. 1985. "Urban Change and Minority Opportunities." In *The New Urban Reality*, edited by Paul Peterson. Washington, D.C.: Brookings Institution.

Kennedy, Maureen, and Paul Leonard. 2001. *Dealing with Neighborhood Change: A Primer on Gentrification and Policy Choices*. Washington, D.C.: Brookings Institution.

Massey, Douglas A. 1995. "Getting Away with Murder: Segregation and Violent Crime in Urban America." *University of Pennsylvania Law Review* 143 (5): 1203–32.

National Housing Law Project. 1996. "Housing Crisis Finally Makes Front-Page News." *Housing Law Bulletin* 26 (November).

Oliver, Melvin L., and Thomas M. Shapiro. 1995. *Black Wealth/White Wealth: A New Perspective on Racial Inequality*. London: Routledge.

Orfield, Myron. 1997. *Metropolitics: A Regional Agenda for Community and Stability.* Washington, D.C.: Brookings Institution.

Pierce, Neal R. 1993. *Citistates.* Washington, D.C.: Seven Locks Press.

powell, john a. 1996. "How Government Tax and Housing Policies Have Racially Segregated America." In *Taxing America,* edited by Karen B. Brown and Mary Louise Fellows. New York: New York University Press.

————. 1999a. "Race, Poverty, and Urban Sprawl: Access to Opportunities through Regional Strategies." *Forum for Social Economics* 28 (2): 1–20.

————. 1999b. "Achieving Racial Justice: What's Sprawl Got to Do with It?" *Poverty and Race* 8 (5).

Putnam, Robert D. 2000. *Bowling Alone: The Collapse and Revival of American Community.* New York: Simon and Schuster.

Roisman, Florence Wagman. 1995. "The Lessons of American Apartheid: The Necessity and Means of Promoting Residential Integration." *Iowa Law Review* 81 (2): 479–525.

Rusk, David. 1993. *Cities without Suburbs.* Washington, D.C.: Woodrow Wilson Center Press.

————. 1999. *Inside Game/Outside Game: Winning Strategies for Saving Urban America.* Washington, D.C.: Brookings Institution Press.

Schill, Michael H., and Susan M. Wachter. 1995. "The Spatial Bias of Federal Housing Law and Policy: Concentrated Poverty in Urban America." *University of Pennsylvania Law Review* 143 (5): 1285–342.

Smith, Matt. 1999. "Welcome Home." *San Francisco Weekly,* 18 August.

Stasell, Wendy L., and William P. Wilen. 2000. "Gautreaux and Chicago's Public Housing Crisis: The Conflict between Achieving Integration and Providing Decent Housing for Very Low-Income African Americans." *Clearinghouse Review* 34 (3).

U.S. Census Bureau. 1997. Small Area Poverty Estimates. http://socds.huduser.org/index.html.

————. 1999. Decennial Management Division Glossary. http://www.census.gov/dmd/www/glossary.html#M.

U.S. Department of Housing and Urban Development. 1990. State of the Cities Data Systems (demographic and economic data from the U.S. Census Bureau, 1990 Census, Summary Tape File 1, File 2, and File 3). http://socds.huduser.org/index.html.

————. 1997. State of the Cities Data Systems. County Business Patterns Spcial Data Extract (employment data from the U.S. Census Bureau, Standard Statistical Establishment List, for 1991–1997). http://socds.huduser.org/index.html.

————. 2000. State of the Cities Data Systems (demographic data from the U.S. Census Bureau, 2000 Census, Redistricting file). http://socds.huduser.org/index.html.

Vergara, Camilo Jose. 1997. *The New American Ghetto.* New Brunswick, N.J.: Rutgers University Press.

Weiher, Gregory R. 1991. *The Fractured Metropolis: Political Fragmentation and Metropolitan Segregation.* Albany, N.Y.: State University of New York Press.

Wilson, William Julius. 1997. *When Work Disappears: The World of the New Urban Poor.* New York: Alfred A. Knopf.

# 5

# Transportation, Land Use, and the Impacts of Sprawl on Poor Children and Families

Amy Helling

If urban sprawl imposes social costs on metropolitan area residents, some of these costs fall particularly heavily on low-income families and their children. Sprawl's most characteristic attributes—low residential density and extensive personal travel in vehicles—combine to specially restrict personal transportation and housing opportunities for poor families with children, although they are desired stepping stones to better lives for many American households. Exploring how these attributes of sprawl affect poor children and their families in comparison with the general population is made possible by the 1995–96 Nationwide Personal Transportation Survey, which provides data on both travel and residential density, as well as income and demographic information, for a national sample of households.

## Sprawl's Relationship to Density and Personal Travel

Low-density, sprawling development and high volumes of personal travel do not coexist by accident; they are the result of many individual households, equipped with convenient, inexpensive transportation and telecommunication, competing with one another for the living arrangements they most prefer. This competition may be somewhat facilitated or constrained by land use regulations. Sprawl around urban areas results from people balancing a desire for space against a desire for access to certain destinations, given that a limited supply of land is accessible to these destinations.[1] Since low-cost transportation expands the supply of accessible land in an urban area, it allows households to afford larger dwellings and/or lots in exchange for travelling greater distances away from established concentrations of desirable destinations, thus providing the impetus for low-density, sprawling development. When access was provided exclusively by walking and riding horses, land had to be very close to a destination to be accessible. Private automobiles, streets and highways engineered for higher speeds, and telecommunication have vastly increased the supply of land that is "accessible" in some sense,[2] making it possible for more households to act on their desires for more space.

As a result of people's widespread desire for access to similar things, like good job and shopping opportunities, space is more expensive in locations that are accessible to these things, all else being equal. If all households had the same economic resources and were otherwise free to make their own location choices, each household could buy or rent a dwelling with either more space or greater accessibility, but not both. However, households do not all have the same economic resources. Poor families act within the same system as others, trading off accessibility and space to try to meet their own needs and preferences, but with less to spend. This then provides the context for a discussion of the effects of sprawl on poor children and families. Though modern U.S. urban areas provide a variety of density and location options for those that have the financial means to choose, this chapter illustrates how housing and personal transportation options are restricted for low-income households with children.

## Sprawl and Children

Recent research emphasizes the importance of individuals' roles within households in explaining travel behavior, with children (age 5 through 15) having a more distinctive set of travel descriptors than any other household role (Al-Kazily, Barnes, and Coontz 1995). These differences have some obvious causes. The vast majority of children age 5 to 15 are not workers, whereas nationally two-thirds of all adults were in the labor force in 1990. Thus, most children younger than age 16 do not travel to work, during work, or in search of work. Children do, however, have destinations and trip purposes that are different from those of their parents, including day care, school, extracurricular activities, shopping, personal business, doctor and dentist appointments, church, recreation, and visits to family and friends. In addition, children must be accompanied if they are to travel by private motorized vehicle, as they are too young to obtain valid driver's licenses.

Critics of sprawl have speculated about its effects on children generally, suggesting, for example, that children who live in sprawling areas rely on being transported in vehicles, and thus are dependent on their parents, bored, and withdrawn, while teenage drivers are at great risk of automobile accidents (Duany, Plater-Zyberk, and Speck 2000). The only recent empirical study exclusively devoted to children's travel observed change over time, surveying parents and children age 7 to 15 in England in 1971 and 1990, and in Germany in 1990 (Hillman, Adams, and Whitelegg 1990). This study found that young British schoolchildren in 1990 were permitted far less independent mobility than British children in 1971. For example, though 80 percent of 7- and 8-year-old English children were allowed to go to school on their own in 1971, by 1990 only 9 percent were allowed to do this. This raised the average age at which British children were permitted to travel on their own to school and other destinations. Instead of travelling independently, children in 1990 were more often accompanied by an adult, frequently by car, and pursued more activities inside the home for the following reasons:

- widening car ownership and increasing motorized travel,
- more dispersed destinations, including greater school choice,
- a less extensive public transport system, which is also less used,
- greater comfort and opportunities for recreation at home (central heating, television, etc.),
- public policy that focuses primarily on increasing the speed, convenience, and safety of motorized travel, often reducing the convenience and safety of pedestrian and bicycle travel (which is how most children would travel on their own), and
- parents' fears of traffic, assault, and molestation, which causes them to limit independent mobility to later ages.

Hillman, Adams, and Whitelegg (1990) note five adverse consequences of these changes, including greater constraints on adult opportunities, higher costs to society (such as fuel), more traffic congestion, reduced opportunities for children's exercise and physical fitness, and more limited opportunities for children to develop their own independence.

## Different Issues for Poor Children

The most serious effects of sprawl on poor children are probably quite different. Poor families with children would likely live in sprawling development if they could afford it, as do most middle- and upper-income households. Extensive research has found that employment opportunities in metropolitan areas continue to disperse, leaving teenagers and adults disadvantaged by poor access to suburban jobs (Kain 1992; Kasarda 1990; Ihlanfeldt and Sjoquist 1990). A study of sprawl done for the Transportation Research Board (Burchell et al. 1998) concludes that there is evidence that suburbs are places where people can find opportunity and advance. "There is a 'rub-off' effect of place wherein success patterns can be communicated by residents to newcomers who specifically wish to improve their current economic and social positions" (105). Thus the fact that poor families and children are disproportionately concentrated in high-density portions of metropolitan areas is the most basic disadvantage of sprawl for poor children and families. Furthermore, employment is not the only type of trip destination that is dispersing. Sprawling suburbs contain many other opportunities for children and families as well, including good schools, shopping, medical care, and sports and recreational facilities.

Historically, reformers have been concerned with overcrowding, not with sprawl. This is understandable, as excessive density has destructive effects on social organization among animals and people (Gans 1991). Sprawling residential development spreads dwellings over larger areas, by definition providing each household with more space, and space has value. Lower densities permit families greater privacy, including the opportunity for private recreation. Private space also allows families more control,[3] something that is especially important to those who see themselves as having different values from those who live around them, a common situation in our diverse society. Families are also legitimately concerned about their children's safety, adding to the preference for privately controlled space. Children that live in high-density residential environments must either spend their time in the small space controlled by the family, or in a public space, exposed to others outside their household. A case study in a non-sprawling New York neighborhood showed that children's freedom of access to their neighborhood declined over the years, suggesting that keeping children inside the home is increasingly common, just as Hillman, Adams, and Whitelegg found to be the case in England and Germany (Gaster 1991). Many people around the world live in high-density areas, and there is no question that a high quality of life *can* be achieved in very dense residential areas when accompanied by high levels of communal responsibility and social control. However, public spaces (streets, sidewalks, parks) in many poor neighborhoods are sites of antisocial behavior of various kinds. Meanwhile, those who have ample private space because they live in low- and medium-density areas have fewer reasons to support publicly provided amenities and extra public safety precautions for those less fortunate.

For nearly a century in the United States, sprawl has been enabled by personal transportation for those who can afford it. Housing and transportation define economic position and quality of life for many Americans, and if sprawl affects how poor children and their families participate in this system, and whether they are able to make similar choices and secure similar opportunities, its impacts are significant. Thus, the consequences of sprawl for the poor children and families discussed here fall under two general headings: those relating to the housing families can afford, and those connected to the amount and nature of personal travel and accessibility.

## Survey Data

The empirical work for this chapter draws on the 1995 Nationwide Personal Transportation Survey (NPTS). The NPTS is a periodic federal survey used to inventory the daily personal travel of the civilian, non-institutionalized population of the United States. The most recent NPTS was conducted by telephone interviews with 42,033 households nationwide between May 1995 and July 1996. The data used here are from both the randomly selected, stratified national sample and from supplemental samples in several geographic areas. All of the calculations in the chapter have been appropriately weighted to expand the sample data to estimates for the U.S. population. The questionnaire contains both questions asked about each household[4] in the sample and person-level questions asked about each household member age 5 and older. Thus, the NPTS allows study only of the travel of children older than age 4. In this chapter, children are defined as 15 years old or younger, while adults are age 16 or older. This age cutoff is consistent with previous research on travel behavior and household roles, with federal labor statistics, and with states' general practice of granting full driver's license privileges no earlier than age 16. The data presented here come from two NPTS data files—the household file, containing general information about each household, and the travel day file. The travel day file contains information about all trips,[5] except trips made as an essential part of work, reported by each household during a 24-hour period beginning at 4:00 a.m. on a randomly assigned day of the week and ending at 3:59 a.m. the following day.

Because this chapter is concerned with impacts on "poor" children, it is necessary to define those households that were poor. Households with children under age 16 had lower incomes generally, as figure 5.1 indicates. The households with children considered "poor" in this paper are those reporting incomes of less than $10,000 per household member. Thus, the smallest such household would include one adult and one child under age 16, and have had an income of less than $20,000 in

Figure 5.1 *Cumulative Percentages of All Households and All Households with Children under 16, by Income*

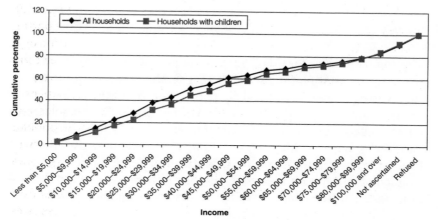

*Source:* Nationwide Personal Transportation Survey, 1995–1996.

1995–96. While this is not the official federal definition of poverty, it does include the households with the lowest incomes, as well as those with the lowest income per person. Low-per-capita-income households with children made up about 19.3 percent of all households, according to the NPTS, while households with children under age 16 of all income levels made up about 30 percent of all households.

## Housing Cost and Location

Inexpensive transportation opens the way to inexpensive and spacious housing, allowing households to choose more space and a higher quality of life at more remote residential locations than they could afford closer in. These households raise their quality of life through their own effort—time spent travelling—just as others do by fixing up inexpensive older houses in the city. Thus, for low-income families able to take advantage of the transportation system, the results of permissive land use policy and urban development that sprawls into exurban areas can be a broadened choice of home locations they can afford. Table 5.1 shows that the most affordable housing in metropolitan areas is concentrated in the lowest and very highest density areas. This shows that housing in sprawling suburbs and exurbs can be inexpensive. From these least expensive exurban sites, median housing unit values increase with density, except at the very highest densities, where low value units are also concentrated. Thus, for example, the proportion of housing units worth less than $50,000 in the very lowest density areas is more than twice (2.08 times) the proportion of all housing units in these areas. The proportion worth over $200,000, by contrast, is only 13 percent of the proportion of all housing units in the lowest density areas, while more than three times (3.05) the proportion of all housing units in the highest density areas.

Thus, the sprawl occasioned by increasingly convenient, inexpensive transportation would accommodate some low-income households, particularly on the more distant and less attractive fringes of metropolitan areas, and in pockets of high density (like trailer parks) in otherwise exurban areas. For, all else equal, smaller lots cost less than large ones, and land that is less accessible and has fewer amenities is cheaper.

Development controls play a role in preventing poor families from living in sprawling areas. When large lots, large minimum house sizes, and amenities like sidewalks are required by local zoning and subdivi-

Table 5.1  *Ratio of Actual to Expected Numbers of Households in MSAs,*
*by Median Value of Nearby Housing Units and Residential Density*

| Median unit value[a] | Density[b] (persons per square mile) | | | | | | | |
|---|---|---|---|---|---|---|---|---|
| | 0 to 100 | 100 to 500 | 500 to 1,000 | 1,000 to 2,000 | 2,000 to 4,000 | 4,000 to 10,000 | 10,000 to 25,000 | 25,000 to 100,000 |
| | Fewer than one HH per acre | | | 1 HH per acre | 2 HH per acre | 3–6 HH per acre | 7–15 HH per acre | More than 15 HH per acre |
| Up to $50,000 | 2.08 | 0.78 | 0.66 | 0.70 | 0.83 | 0.85 | 0.89 | 1.28 |
| $50,000–$69,999 | 1.69 | 1.28 | 0.99 | 0.85 | 0.86 | 0.88 | 0.54 | 0.31 |
| $70,000–$99,999 | 0.95 | 1.20 | 1.14 | 1.11 | 1.01 | 1.08 | 0.60 | 0.23 |
| $100,000–$149,999 | 0.52 | 1.03 | 1.14 | 1.21 | 1.20 | 1.03 | 1.02 | 0.71 |
| $150,000–$199,999 | 0.19 | 0.88 | 1.14 | 1.12 | 1.16 | 1.02 | 1.73 | 1.38 |
| $200,000–$1,000,000 | 0.13 | 0.60 | 0.88 | 0.98 | 0.98 | 1.16 | 1.84 | 3.05 |

*Source:* Nationwide Personal Transportation Survey, 1995–96.

*Notes:* Expected number determined by applying the share of all cases in each density category to the cases in each income category. Cases exclude those households (HH) for whom no density and/or income was reported. Shaded areas of the table include cells in which the ratio of actual to expected households was equal to or greater than 0.90. Ratios in **boldface** type are equal to or greater than 1.00. MSA = metropolitan statistical area.

[a] Median housing unit value is the 1990 median housing units value of the block group where the household was located, projected to 1995 by Claritas, Inc.

[b] The density variable is the 1990 density of the block group where the household was located, projected to 1995 by Claritas, Inc.

sion controls, and manufactured housing is prohibited by the same, this raises housing prices, and poor families are likely to be excluded. Similarly, when development constraints intended to reduce sprawl (like urban growth boundaries) limit the supply of housing, this too raises housing prices and tends to exclude poor families (Brueckner 1990). However, table 5.1 shows that these practices have not eliminated low-value housing in low-density areas. Nonetheless, low-income households are underrepresented for the most part at densities of less than three dwelling units per acre, as table 5.2 indicates.

Table 5.2 shows that there is a strong, but somewhat complex pattern of association between income and density. The lowest-income households are disproportionately concentrated in the highest-density areas. These are likely older and thus less expensive portions of central cities.

Table 5.2  *Ratio of Actual to Expected Numbers of Households in MSAs, by Income Levels and Residential Density*

| Household income | Density[a] (persons per square mile) | | | | | | | |
|---|---|---|---|---|---|---|---|---|
| | 0 to 100 | 100 to 500 | 500 to 1,000 | 1,000 to 2,000 | 2,000 to 4,000 | 4,000 to 10,000 | 10,000 to 25,000 | 25,000 to 100,000 |
| | *Fewer than one HH per acre* | | | *1 HH per acre* | *2 HH per acre* | *3–6 HH per acre* | *7–15 HH per acre* | *More than 15 HH per acre* |
| Less than $5,000 | 0.63 | 0.58 | 0.48 | 0.90 | 0.88 | 0.96 | **1.60** | **2.84** |
| $5,000–$9,999 | **1.15** | 0.83 | 0.64 | 0.74 | 0.89 | 0.97 | **1.40** | **2.09** |
| $10,000–$14,999 | 0.77 | 0.86 | 0.73 | 0.76 | 0.87 | **1.14** | **1.50** | **1.13** |
| $15,000–$19,999 | **1.33** | 0.91 | 0.79 | 0.80 | 0.92 | **1.02** | **1.31** | **1.11** |
| $20,000–$24,999 | **1.13** | 0.90 | 0.88 | 0.88 | 0.93 | **1.01** | **1.32** | **1.03** |
| $25,000–$29,999 | **1.20** | 0.93 | **1.09** | 0.82 | 0.93 | **1.08** | **1.01** | 0.93 |
| $30,000–$34,999 | **1.00** | 0.91 | **1.02** | 0.99 | 0.99 | **1.04** | 0.97 | **1.04** |
| $35,000–$39,999 | 0.95 | 0.95 | **1.09** | **1.02** | **1.03** | **1.02** | 0.94 | 0.89 |
| $40,000–$44,999 | **1.08** | 0.98 | 0.86 | **1.15** | **1.03** | **1.11** | 0.64 | 0.80 |
| $45,000–$49,999 | 0.87 | **1.18** | **1.07** | **1.03** | 0.98 | **1.03** | 0.89 | 0.70 |
| $50,000–$54,999 | **1.38** | **1.12** | 0.97 | **1.17** | **1.06** | 0.96 | 0.73 | 0.51 |
| $55,000–$59,999 | **1.08** | **1.17** | **1.00** | **1.15** | **1.10** | 0.97 | 0.65 | 0.75 |
| $60,000–$64,999 | **1.13** | **1.32** | **1.23** | **1.28** | **1.14** | 0.79 | 0.73 | 0.43 |
| $65,000–$69,999 | 0.87 | **1.32** | **1.14** | 0.97 | **1.09** | 0.95 | 0.78 | 0.71 |
| $70,000–$74,999 | 0.56 | **1.34** | **1.12** | 0.80 | **1.26** | 0.83 | **1.23** | 0.59 |
| $75,000–$79,999 | 0.84 | **1.00** | **1.30** | **1.29** | **1.09** | 0.98 | 0.56 | 0.83 |
| $80,000–$99,999 | 0.81 | **1.16** | **1.37** | **1.25** | **1.08** | 0.93 | 0.71 | 0.46 |
| $100,000 and over | 0.57 | **1.08** | **1.46** | **1.60** | **1.21** | 0.77 | 0.54 | 0.91 |

*Source:* Nationwide Personal Transportation Survey, 1995–96.

*Notes:* Expected number determined by applying the share of all cases in each density category to the cases in each income category. Cases exclude those households (HH) for whom no density and/or income was reported. Shaded areas of the table include cells in which the ratio of actual to expected households was equal to or greater than 0.90. Ratios in **boldface** type are equal to or greater than 1.00. MSA = metropolitan statistical area.

[a] The density variable is the 1990 density of the block group where the household was located, projected to 1995 by Claritas, Inc.

However, smaller concentrations also exist in the very least dense areas. The highest income households avoid these same areas, concentrating in low to medium density areas.

If the greatest concentration of inexpensive housing is in sprawling areas, why don't these areas also have the greatest concentrations of low-income households? First, crowding more people into less space saves money, so that poverty creates density. Second, as the next section shows, low-income households have different vehicle ownership and travel patterns. Low incomes make households less able than others to afford high-value housing, but also make them more dependent on transit and walking than those with more resources. While low- and medium-density portions of metropolitan areas in the recent past have offered a desirable combination of space and accessibility to those with cars and the income to operate them, the next section shows that personal transportation may be an important reason why poor children and their families do not live in sprawling areas.

## Personal Transportation and Accessibility

Real, disposable income rose faster than transportation costs between 1960 and the mid-1990s, allowing many American households either to increase their personal travel without economizing elsewhere or to reduce transportation's share of the household budget. For most people, therefore, the current transportation system offers a choice of destinations far greater than in the past, at a price they are willing and able to pay. But to take full advantage of the American transportation system requires money, and much of what American households spend for transportation is devoted to private vehicles.

The average size of a U.S. household in 1995 was 2.65 persons, and the number of vehicles per household was 1.78 (U.S. Department of Transportation 1998). After a household owns a vehicle for every driver, adding extra miles to obtain the benefits of living in a low-density area becomes convenient and inexpensive. However, the threshold level of expense this entails is too heavy for many low-income households. An average American household spent about $6,000 for personal transportation in 1995, when the median household income was $37,000. Purchasing, maintaining, and operating privately owned vehicles (POVs) accounted for approximately 93 percent of this total, and buying transportation services like air, transit, and taxi trips accounted for the remaining 7 percent (U.S. Department of Transportation 1999). Purchasing a vehicle requires either savings or good credit, or both. Yet vehicles, though useful, are poor investments; unlike houses, they lose rather than gain value over time. In addition, maintaining a vehicle, particularly an older vehicle, can also pose unexpected large expenses that also drain savings and credit reserves.

Thus, it is not surprising that poor families with children own fewer private vehicles. As table 5.3 shows, 12 percent of poor households who have children under age 16 do not own a private vehicle, while this is true for fewer than 6 percent of all households with children. Only about 56 percent of poor households with children under age 16 have multiple vehicles, while almost three-quarters of all households with children have more than one vehicle. Table 5.3 also shows that these differences are not because low-per-capita-income households with children are smaller. Over half of the low-per-capita-income households with children have four or more members, compared with 30 percent of households with children generally.

Private vehicles are key to taking advantage of the existing transportation system in the United States, whether or not one lives in a sprawling area, because an increasing number of destinations are in sprawling, low-density areas. Table 5.4 shows that over 86 percent of all trips are made in privately owned vehicles. Households with children under age 16 use the different transport modes in proportions very similar to the larger population. However, low-per-capita-income households with children travel less by private vehicle and more by public modes of transport, walking, and biking. This is even more pronounced among children under age 16, who are more than three times as likely to make a trip by public transport than the household population at large, and more than twice as likely to make a trip on foot or by bicycle. Children from households with low per capita incomes make the fewest trips by privately owned vehicles and the most trips by public transit, walking, and biking (table 5.4).

It is common to endorse greater use of transit in cities and applaud walking and biking to destinations, but there are logical reasons why those who can afford to travel by private vehicle generally do so. First, as noted above, as metropolitan areas spread out, an increasing number of destinations are accessible only by private vehicle. Second, private vehicles make marginal increases in personal travel inexpensive, allowing households to

Table 5.3  *Households with Privately Owned Vehicles, by Number of Vehicles and Household Size (percent)*

| | Household size | | | | Total |
|---|---|---|---|---|---|
| | *1* | *2* | *3* | *4 or more* | *Total* |
| | **All households** | | | | |
| **Vehicles** | | | | | |
| 0 | 5 | 2 | 1 | 1 | 8 |
| 1 | 17 | 8 | 3 | 4 | 32 |
| 2 | 2 | 18 | 7 | 13 | 40 |
| 3 | 0 | 4 | 4 | 5 | 14 |
| 4 or more | 0 | 1 | 1 | 3 | 5 |
| **Total** | **25** | **32** | **17** | **26** | **100** |
| | **Households with children under 16** | | | | |
| **Vehicles** | | | | | |
| 0 | — | 3 | 1 | 2 | 6 |
| 1 | — | 10 | 5 | 6 | 21 |
| 2 | — | 29 | 9 | 16 | 53 |
| 3 | — | 6 | 4 | 5 | 16 |
| 4 or more | — | 2 | 1 | 2 | 5 |
| **Total** | — | **50** | **20** | **30** | **100** |
| | **Low-per-capita-income households[a] with children under 16** | | | | |
| **Vehicles** | | | | | |
| 0 | — | 4 | 3 | 4 | 12 |
| 1 | — | 10 | 9 | 13 | 32 |
| 2 | — | 9 | 7 | 25 | 41 |
| 3 | — | 2 | 3 | 7 | 12 |
| 4 or more | — | 0 | 1 | 2 | 3 |
| **Total** | — | **25** | **24** | **51** | **100** |

*Source:* Nationwide Personal Transportation Survey, 1995–96.

*Note:* Percentages may not add to 100 due to rounding.

[a] Low-per-capita-income households are defined as those reporting incomes of less than $10,000 per person in 1995–96.

Table 5.4 *Trips Taken, by Mode of Travel (percent)*

| Travel mode | All household trips (%) | All trips by households with children under 16 (%) | All trips by low-per-capita-income households[a] with children under 16 (%) | All trips by children under 16 (%) | All trips by low-per-capita-income children under 16 (%) |
|---|---|---|---|---|---|
| Automobile | 58.2 | 57.0 | 54.6 | 41.2 | 42.3 |
| Van | 9.9 | 9.9 | 11.2 | 17.2 | 13.7 |
| Sport-utility vehicle | 5.9 | 6.5 | 3.8 | 5.1 | 3.4 |
| Pickup truck | 11.7 | 12.0 | 11.0 | 4.5 | 4.8 |
| Other truck | 0.6 | 0.7 | 0.6 | 0.1 | 0.1 |
| RV | 0.0 | 0.0 | 0.0 | 0.0 | 0.0 |
| Motorcycle | 0.1 | 0.1 | 0.1 | 0.0 | 0.0 |
| Other POV[b] | 0.1 | 0.1 | 0.0 | 0.0 | 0.0 |
| Bus | 1.2 | 1.3 | 2.1 | 1.8 | 2.2 |
| Amtrak | 0.0 | 0.0 | 0.0 | — | — |
| Commuter train | 0.2 | 0.2 | 0.2 | 0.0 | 0.0 |
| Streetcar | 0.0 | 0.0 | 0.0 | 0.0 | 0.0 |
| Subway | 0.4 | 0.5 | 0.5 | 0.2 | 0.2 |
| Airplane | 0.1 | 0.1 | 0.0 | 0.0 | 0.0 |
| Taxi | 0.2 | 0.2 | 0.2 | 0.2 | 0.2 |
| Bicycle | 0.9 | 0.8 | 1.5 | 3.1 | 3.5 |
| Walk | 5.4 | 5.2 | 6.9 | 9.9 | 11.2 |
| School bus | 1.7 | 1.6 | 2.8 | 10.1 | 10.9 |
| Other non-POV[b] | 0.3 | 0.3 | 0.2 | 0.1 | 0.0 |
| Not ascertained | 3.3 | 3.4 | 4.3 | 6.3 | 7.1 |
| Refused | 0.0 | 0.0 | 0.0 | 0.0 | 0.0 |
| **Total** | **100.0** | **100.0** | **100.0** | **100.0** | **100.0** |
| Total private vehicle trips | 86.5 | 86.3 | 81.3 | 68.1 | 64.3 |
| Total public transport trips | 3.8 | 3.9 | 5.8 | 12.3 | 13.5 |
| Total walk/bike trips | 6.3 | 6.0 | 8.4 | 13.0 | 14.7 |
| Unknown mode | 3.6 | 3.7 | 4.5 | 6.4 | 7.1 |
| **Total** | **100.0** | **100.0** | **100.0** | **100.0** | **100.0** |

*Source:* Nationwide Personal Transportation Survey, 1995–96.
*Note:* Percentages may not add to 100 due to rounding.
[a] Low-per-capita-income households are defined as those reporting incomes of less than $10,000 per person in 1995–96.
[b] POV = privately owned vehicle.

lengthen and add to their trips at only minor additional expense. Finally, trips in private vehicles are more comfortable and convenient than the same trips made by public transit, walking, or bicycles. The difference is partly speed. Table 5.5 shows the average speeds of all trips by the different modes. Travelling by most types of private vehicle is approximately ten times faster than walking, even though many of the trips in private vehicles are made in congested conditions. Trips by privately owned vehicles are made at speeds nearly twice as great as those by bus or subway on average, and the latter would be still slower if it included the time spent walking to the bus stop or station, or the waiting time.

Slower speeds mean the same trip takes much longer to complete, and thus has a higher opportunity cost. Paid work is the alternative with a well-known price tag, and the value of time spent travelling has generally been found to be proportional to a person's wage rate (Miller 1989). Therefore, low-wage workers lose less than persons with higher earning power

Table 5.5  *Average Travel Speed of All Trips Taken, by Mode*

| Travel mode | Avg. travel speed[a] (mph) |
| --- | --- |
| Automobile | 27 |
| Van | 28 |
| Sport-utility vehicle | 29 |
| Pickup truck | 30 |
| Other truck | 35 |
| RV | 36 |
| Motorcycle | 30 |
| Other privately owned vehicle | 24 |
| Bus | 15 |
| Amtrak | 38 |
| Commuter train | 28 |
| Streetcar | 8 |
| Subway | 17 |
| Airplane | 269 |
| Taxi | 19 |
| Bicycle | 7 |
| Walk | 3 |
| School bus | 17 |

*Source:* Nationwide Personal Transportation Survey, 1995–96.

[a] Average travel speed is calculated for each trip as the ratio of the length of the trip in minutes spent in travel divided by 60. Trips for which either of these variables was missing were omitted.

when they travel by slower modes, but their ability to work more hours, rather than spending them in travel, may be very important to the household. Thus, higher trip speeds are valued by everyone, but achieved less often by members of poor households.

One way to economize on the time a person or household devotes to travel, even when it means travel by slower modes, is to take shorter trips. Table 5.6 shows that walking and bicycle trips are most common on trips of under one mile, and transit trips on trips of one to five miles. The table also indicates that poor households with children clearly make a higher proportion of very short trips than do households with children gener-

Table 5.6  *Trips Taken, by Mode and Distance (percent)*

| | Distance (in miles) | | | | | | | |
|---|---|---|---|---|---|---|---|---|
| | Under 1 | 1 to 5 | 5 to 10 | 10 to 15 | 15 to 20 | 20 to 25 | 25 to 30 | Over 30 |
| **All trips (%)** | | | | | | | | |
| By POV[a] | 19.5 | 33.1 | 15.2 | 7.0 | 3.8 | 2.1 | 1.6 | 4.5 |
| By pub. trans. | 0.5 | 1.6 | 0.7 | 0.3 | 0.2 | 0.1 | 0.1 | 0.2 |
| By walk/bike | 5.6 | 0.7 | 0.0 | 0.0 | 0.0 | 0.0 | 0.0 | 0.0 |
| Unknown | 2.4 | 0.4 | 0.2 | 0.1 | 0.1 | 0.0 | 0.0 | 0.1 |
| **Total (100%)** | **28.0** | **35.8** | **16.1** | **7.4** | **4.0** | **2.2** | **1.6** | **4.8** |
| **All trips by households with children under 16 (%)** | | | | | | | | |
| By POV[a] | 14.1 | 32.0 | 15.1 | 7.2 | 3.9 | 2.1 | 1.7 | 10.2 |
| By pub. trans. | 0.5 | 1.6 | 0.7 | 0.3 | 0.1 | 0.1 | 0.1 | 0.6 |
| By walk/bike | 5.2 | 0.6 | 0.0 | 0.0 | 0.0 | 0.0 | 0.0 | 0.1 |
| Unknown | 0.3 | 0.5 | 0.2 | 0.1 | 0.1 | 0.0 | 0.0 | 2.5 |
| **Total (100%)** | **20.1** | **34.7** | **16.0** | **7.6** | **4.1** | **2.2** | **1.7** | **13.5** |
| **All trips by low-per-capita-income households[b] with children under 16 (%)** | | | | | | | | |
| By POV[a] | 20.6 | 31.4 | 13.0 | 6.2 | 3.3 | 1.9 | 1.4 | 4.1 |
| By pub. trans. | 0.9 | 2.5 | 1.1 | 0.4 | 0.1 | 0.1 | 0.1 | 0.2 |
| By walk/bike | 7.6 | 0.8 | 0.1 | 0.0 | 0.0 | 0.0 | 0.0 | 0.0 |
| Unknown | 3.2 | 0.6 | 0.1 | 0.1 | 0.1 | 0.0 | 0.0 | 0.0 |
| **Total (100%)** | **32.4** | **35.2** | **14.3** | **6.7** | **3.5** | **2.0** | **1.5** | **4.3** |

*Source:* Nationwide Personal Transportation Survey, 1995–96.

[a] POV = privately owned vehicle.

[b] Low-per-capita-income households are defined as those reporting incomes of less than $10,000 per person in 1995–96.

ally. Among all households with children, over 13 percent of the trips are over 30 miles long, and most of these are made by private vehicle. Only about 4 percent of poor households' trips are over 30 miles long.

Table 5.7 shows that people who live in sprawling areas make a greater proportion of long trips than do those who live in higher-density areas. There are many disadvantages to travelling long distances by transit, on foot, or by bicycle, especially for children. Long transit, walking, or bicycle trips often involve negotiating heavy traffic travelling at high speeds and are inconvenient for those carrying heavy or awkward items, like babies or groceries. Such trips sometimes involve inconvenient schedules and transfers, lack protection from weather, and commonly lack safe waiting places. Nonetheless, poor children living in low-density areas seem to make trips of all lengths in similar proportions to other children.

Travel time costs are especially great for households with children because children must be accompanied on many trips. Households that can afford to devote responsible adults' time to transporting children in private vehicles can provide their children more opportunities for education and enrichment without sacrificing their safety, while minimizing the time spent by the adult. Adults also bring children along on trips in order to supervise them while doing something else, reducing their own opportunity cost of travel. Adults in poor households who cannot make these trips by private vehicle face the choices of taking the child on a time-consuming trip on foot or by transit, not making the trip at all, or sending the child alone. As table 5.8 indicates, poor children are accompanied on about the same proportion of their trips as children in general.

Walking is particularly dangerous for children. Children between the ages of 5 and 15 made up 16 percent of the population in 1997, but accounted for 29 percent of pedestrian injuries (U.S. Department of Transportation 1999). Transit stops, too, pose danger, though more from crime, especially in poor areas. Poor children and families undoubtedly face greater exposure to these hazards as they walk and use transit more, but a measure of pedestrian exposure comparable to that calculated for passengers in vehicles does not yet exist[6] (Loukaitou-Sideris and Liggett 2000).

In spite of other differences, the purposes for which poor children make trips are very comparable to those of children generally, as table 5.9 indicates. Trips to school and church dominate, followed by trips for other social and recreational purposes. The latter, which are a slightly smaller share of the total for poor children, include trips to lessons,

Table 5.7 *Cumulative Percentage of Trips Taken, by Increasing Distance and Residential Density (percent)*

| Trip distance (in miles) | Residents of low-density areas[a] (%) | Residents of higher-density areas[b] (%) |
|---|---|---|
| **All trips** | | |
| 1 or less | 24.9 | 33.7 |
| 5 or less | 60.5 | 69.8 |
| 10 or less | 77.8 | 83.7 |
| 15 or less | 85.8 | 90.0 |
| 20 or less | 90.2 | 93.3 |
| 25 or less | 92.8 | 95.0 |
| 30 or less | 94.6 | 96.3 |
| **All trips** | **100.0** | **100.0** |
| | | |
| **Children's trips** | | |
| 1 or less | 34.0 | 46.2 |
| 5 or less | 70.4 | 80.8 |
| 10 or less | 86.1 | 90.5 |
| 15 or less | 91.9 | 95.1 |
| 20 or less | 94.8 | 96.6 |
| 25 or less | 96.0 | 97.3 |
| 30 or less | 96.6 | 97.7 |
| **All trips** | **100.0** | **100.0** |
| | | |
| **Low-per-capita-income[c] children's trips** | | |
| 1 or less | 36.8 | 47.6 |
| 5 or less | 70.3 | 82.9 |
| 10 or less | 85.9 | 91.3 |
| 15 or less | 91.4 | 95.5 |
| 20 or less | 94.3 | 97.2 |
| 25 or less | 95.4 | 98.0 |
| 30 or less | 96.2 | 98.3 |
| **All trips** | **100.0** | **100.0** |

*Source:* Nationwide Personal Transportation Survey, 1995–96.

[a] Low-density areas are defined as those areas with fewer than three households per acre.

[b] Higher-density areas are defined as those areas with three or more households per acre.

[c] Low-per-capita-income households are defined as those reporting incomes of less than $10,000 per person in 1995–96.

Table 5.8  *Children's Trips Taken, With or Without a Household Member (percent)*

|  | All children's trips (%) | Trips by children of low-per-capita-income households[a] (%) |
|---|---|---|
| Accompanied by a household member | 77.2 | 76.8 |
| Unaccompanied by a household member | 22.8 | 23.2 |

*Source:* Nationwide Personal Transportation Survey, 1995–96.

[a] Low-per-capita-income households are defined as those reporting incomes of less than $10,000 per person in 1995–96.

movies, sports practices, and other nonschool or church group activities, but exclude trips to visit friends and relatives, which are slightly more common for poor children.

Besides being the chief cause of sprawl, easy inexpensive transportation has the additional consequence of fostering more personal travel, including both more and longer vehicle trips. Vehicle miles of travel

Table 5.9  *Children's Trips Taken, by Purpose (percent)*

| Trip purpose | All children's trips (%) | Poor-per-capita children's trips (%) |
|---|---|---|
| To or from work | 0.7 | 0.6 |
| Work-related business | 0.1 | 0.1 |
| Shopping | 11.9 | 12.1 |
| Other family or personal business | 17.1 | 16.3 |
| School/church | 30.1 | 31.1 |
| Medical/dental | 0.8 | 0.7 |
| Vacation | 0.3 | 0.4 |
| Visit friends or relatives | 12.4 | 13.7 |
| Other social/recreational | 26.5 | 24.7 |
| Other | 0.2 | 0.2 |
| Not ascertained | — | — |
| **Total** | **100.0** | **100.0** |

*Source:* Nationwide Personal Transportation Survey, 1995–96.

(VMT) on urban streets and highways increased by 78 percent between 1980 and 1996 (U.S. Department of Transportation 1998). The extensive travel in vehicles that is characteristic of sprawling metropolitan areas has negative externalities that affect children, including air pollution, noise, and congestion. Low-density suburban residential areas are somewhat protected from air pollution and noise, but, as shown here, poor children are more likely to live in the densest portions of cities, including along transportation corridors, where transportation impacts are most concentrated. Such disadvantages make these locations more affordable as well as less desirable for residence.

## Conclusions

In summary, increasingly affordable personal travel by private vehicle has made it possible for jobs, residences, schools, and activities of all sorts to move away from established urban centers to more distant areas accessible only by car, where space is plentiful and cheap. There they sprawl, occupying more land than if travel were more limited and time-consuming, as in the past. While such dispersal is often criticized as unaesthetic and environmentally undesirable, it allows those who are able to travel extensively greater opportunities for economic advancement and consumption than ever before. However, taking full advantage of this transportation system requires an initial investment and subsequent monthly expenditures for one or more private vehicles, potentially consuming a substantial portion of a poor household's income. Low-per-capita-income households with children own fewer vehicles, travel more by public transit and walking, and take shorter trips than households generally. Therefore, they are less able to take advantage of the opportunities that lie in outlying portions of metropolitan areas where the vast majority travel by private vehicles.

### NOTES

1. The theory explaining the relationship between population density and travel behavior is based on observed empirical regularities that may be predicted with some certainty. Residential density is the dependent variable in the classic model of a monocentric urban area (Muth 1969) that has been generalized, elaborated, and built upon by

hundreds of scholarly articles. This model provided the theory to explain a striking fact; that without public intervention all urban areas concentrate many people on little land close to one or more "centers," of activity, and become predictably less and less dense with greater distance from these centers.

2. Accessibility preferences are not identical. Households have different destinations depending on where they work (if they do), where they shop and go to the doctor, where the children (if any) go to school, and where they go for recreation, as well as how frequently and urgently they need access to these destinations. However, there is substantial commonality. For example, measures of accessibility to employment by car have been shown to have a significant and predictable effect on residential density (Helling 1998).

3. Our political and legal system reflects the value of family control, allowing parents wide latitude in making decisions concerning their children, even when the majority does not agree with them.

4. In general, the NPTS uses the U.S. Census of Population and Housing concept of "household," meaning all those individuals who together occupy a single housing unit, rather than "family," meaning those who both live together and are related by birth, marriage or adoption. Median household income as measured by the NPTS, however, excludes the earnings of unrelated individuals.

5. A travel day trip is defined as any one-way travel from one address (place) to another by any means of transportation (e.g., private motor vehicle, public transportation, bicycle, or walking).

6. The rate of pedestrian injuries per mile traveled on foot is not known, preventing accurate comparison to injury rates in vehicles. However, 12 percent of all transportation fatalities in 1997 were pedestrians struck by motor vehicles, while 73 percent were occupants of cars and light trucks. Another 2 percent were pedalcyclists struck by motor vehicles. If levels of risk were the same, this would suggest that occupants of cars and light trucks covered only about six times as many miles as pedestrians, which is highly improbable.


REFERENCES

Al-Kazily, Joan, Carol Barnes, and Norman Coontz. 1995. *Household Structure and Travel Behavior*. Washington, D.C.: U.S. Department of Transportation, Federal Highway Administration.

Burchell, Robert W., Naveed A. Shad, David Listokin, Hillary Phillips, Anthony Downs, Samuel Seskin, Judy S. Davis, Terry Moore, David Helton, and Michelle Gall. 1998. *The Costs of Sprawl—Revisited*. Transit Cooperative Research Program Report 39. Washington, D.C.: National Academy Press.

Brueckner, Jan K. 1990. "Growth Controls and Land Values in an Open City." *Land Economics* 66 (3): 237–48.

Duany, Andres, Elizabeth Plater-Zyberk, and Jeff Speck. 2000. *Suburban Nation*. New York: North Point Press.

Gans, Herbert J. 1991. *People, Plans, and Policies: Essays on Poverty, Racism, and Other National Urban Problems*. New York: Columbia University Press.

Gaster, Sanford. 1991. "Urban Children's Access to Their Neighborhood: Changes over Three Generations." *Environment and Behavior* 23 (1): 70–85.

Helling, Amy. 1998. "Changing Intra-Metropolitan Accessibility in the U.S.: Evidence from Atlanta." *Progress in Planning* 49 (2): 55–107.

Hillman, Mayer, John Adams, and John Whitelegg. 1990. *One False Move: A Study of Children's Independent Mobility.* London: Policy Studies Institute.

Ihlanfeldt, Keith R., and David L. Sjoquist. 1990. "Job Accessibility and Racial Differences in Youth Unemployment Rates." *American Economic Review* 80 (1): 267–76.

Kain, John. 1992. "The Spatial Mismatch Hypothesis: Three Decades Later." *Housing Policy Debate* 3 (2): 371–459.

Kasarda, John D. 1990. "City Jobs and Residents on a Collision Course: The Urban Underclass Dilemma." *Economic Development Quarterly* 4 (4): 313–19.

Loukaitou-Sideris, Anastasia, and Robin Liggett. 2000. "On Bus-Stop Crime." *Access* 16 (Spring): 27–33.

Miller, T. R. 1989. "The Value of Travel Time and the Benefit of Time Saving: A Literature Synthesis and Recommendation on Values." Unpublished paper, prepared while author was a senior research associate at the Urban Institute.

Muth, Richard F. 1969. *Cities and Housing.* Chicago: University of Chicago Press.

U.S. Department of Transportation. Bureau of Transportation Statistics. 1998. *Transportation Statistics Annual Report 1998.* Washington, D.C.: U.S. Department of Transportation.

———. 1999. *Transportation Statistics Annual Report 1999.* Washington, D.C.: U.S. Department of Transportation.

U.S. Department of Transportation. Federal Highway Administration. 1995 NPTS data files. (Compact disk.)

6

# Encourage, Then Cope
## *Washington and the Sprawl Machine*

H. V. Savitch

## The Sprawl Machine

What has come to be known as sprawl cannot be attributed to any single cause, and certainly no single government by itself has brought it about. Rather, sprawl is an outcome of a complex array of factors that interact in innumerable ways. Technology, legal precepts, geography, the structure of local government, and pure politics have operated to bring about this peculiarly American invention. Federal policies have intersected with these tendencies—at times encouraging, if not staunchly pushing them, while at other times coping with them and trying to keep them from running wild. Washington does not operate in a vacuum and to understand what it has done, we should understand what it has acted upon.

First, advances in technology make sprawl possible. Centuries ago, human settlements were contained by limitations in transportation and communication. People clustered together because horses and carriages could not take them very far or very quickly. Human words and print could only be spread so far, and this, too, brought people closer together. Imagine how Paul Revere might have fared had he been forced to travel through endless stretches of suburbia instead of closely knit towns.

We now live in an era of rapid transportation and high technology. Automobiles and jet planes make long distance travel fast and relatively cheap. Telecommunications and the digital era make communication instant and easy. Some scholars claim that we no longer need highly dense surroundings and that cities are becoming obsolete. Presumably, we should be able to do everything from our computer terminals, even if we live in far away mountains and distant deserts. According to some futurists, technology has shrunk space and people should be able to live and work anywhere. Should face-to-face contact be necessary, we can occasionally hop on a plane or on the interstate. That is a disputable conclusion, but it has some resonance. Planners have argued that we can have community without propinquity; that we can build a highly interactive community without people being close to one another; and that living at great distances from one another is, in fact, quite desirable (Webber 1963; Gordon and Richardson 2000).

Second, the protection of private property is a sacred constitutional principle, and in some ways safeguards a right to sprawl. The roots of this value are largely historic and reflected in the constitutional precepts of limited government and personal liberty. Private property is one manifestation of those principles—so much so that two constitutional amendments were explicitly taken up with protecting private property. Indeed, some of the most quoted passages of *The Federalist Papers* deal with how limited government can protect private property. As Alexander Hamilton, John Jay, and James Madison tell it,

> The diversity in the faculties of men from which the rights of property originate is not less an insurmountable obstacle to a uniformity of interests. The protection of these faculties is the first object of government. From the protection of different and unequal faculties of acquiring property, the possession of different degrees and kinds of property immediately results, and from the influence of these sentiments and views of the respective proprietors, ensues a division of the society into different interests and parties (Hamilton, Jay, and Madison 1937, 55).

Third, an open frontier gave enormous tangibility to abstract legal principles by enabling people to travel across the continent and live wherever they chose. Not only did Americans have the right to be free and to be left alone, but geography gave them the capacity to realize that ambition. Americans could settle anywhere on the continent for religious or any other reason. Massachusetts for Puritans, Maryland for Roman Catholics, Utah for Mormons, and the deserts of Nevada for gamblers were just a few open space havens for nonconformists. Moreover, America's rough-hewn heroes were often cast as free-spirited cowboys who roamed across vast prairies or survived by steely courage as mountain trappers. Today's blue collar hero drives a ten-wheel tractor-trailer and races across an open landscape. While the lifestyle of truckers may be easier, their penchant for individualism and freedom is no less stringent.

Into this mix we introduce a fourth factor, namely the structure of local government. The United States contains a huge number of fragmented governments—over 85,000, with over 513,000 officials elected in townships, villages, small municipalities, and counties where power is very sharply and intensely lodged (U.S. Census Bureau 1997). These local governments are largely responsible for raising their own budgets, and do so by taxing residents and business. In a sample of 15 large cities, the average proportion of federal aid in 1996 was 6.2 percent, while the average state proportion was to 21.2 percent. This amounts to a total of just 27.4 percent of local budgets covered by intergovernmental aid, which is among the lowest for advanced industrial nations.[1] This low proportion of intergovernmental aid exposes localities to a competitive marketplace. To survive and prosper, localities must attract as many revenue raisers as possible, while minimizing revenue consumers. To do this, local governments may be forced to reduce land use controls, build more roadways, and provide infrastructure for sprawl.

No jurisdiction wants to embark upon growth restraint when it is competing with other jurisdictions for economic development. Localities compete by recruiting industry, by lowering taxes, by giving away land, and by permitting developers to build as they like. The rivalry for capital and jobs is fueled by aggressive advertising and the personal intervention of politicians. From the viewpoint of local economic development, we have embarked upon endless competition and what has come to be called "place wars" (Haider 1992). In New York and New Jersey, the competition for jobs and capital had become so fierce that the two states had to sign a "nonaggression pact" (Berg and Kantor 1996). No sooner had the pact been signed, than it was broken.

In the Midwest and South, localities enthusiastically build sports stadiums and construct factories. By and large, private investors determine placement and design. While some stadiums are built within urban cores, others cater to a "tailgating" clientele who seek large parking spaces so that fans can picnic out of their automobiles. Similarly, factories are built along spread patterns of linear rather than vertical design. In the West, water and sewerage is extended into deserts in order to accommodate development. Built out of the desert, both Las Vegas and Phoenix are among the country's fastest growing cities—made possible by an abundance of surrounding land.

Not surprisingly, house building follows the placement of industry and the infrastructure laid out to accommodate new capital. Typically, functions are separated by substantial spans. Residence is built apart from commerce and separated from commerce, schools, leisure, and other types of social activity. The contradictions are startling. While technology has shrunk time and distance, patterns of human settlement have expanded the time it takes to get from one place to another as well as the distance required for travel. People and buildings have thinned out across the American landscape.

Table 6.1 shows population densities for 20 of America's largest cities. Note that at the outset there are some bright spots. San Francisco and Miami gained population for the years indicated, and some cities like New York and Chicago showed gains over the most recent decade (not shown). Some very recent trends show an upsurge in downtown investment and settlement (Fannie Mae Foundation and Brookings Institution 2001). But on the whole, many older cities continued to lose residents and are rife with neighborhood abandonment.

These chronic patterns are reflected in decreasing central city densities. Most of the cities with thinning densities were older, industrial enclaves that lost industry and population. The localities include Philadelphia (down 28 percent), Detroit (down 37 percent), Cleveland (down 37 percent), and Washington, D.C. (down 24 percent). Over nearly three decades population dwindled in these cities, with large numbers of people moving into sparsely settled suburbs. These are obviously well-known trends and part of America's experience of deindustrialization and suburbanization.

The real story, however, can be found in growing sunbelt cities, some of whose densities have actually increased. Places like Houston (up 27 percent) and Phoenix (up 34 percent) were lightly settled in 1970. By the year 2000, sunbelt cities had increased their population by spreading people across greater distances, often annexing surrounding terrain. Today, these areas resemble expansive, functionally segregated suburbs rather than compact, mixed-use cities. In Houston, market-led development has been coupled with vigorous annexation of peripheral areas in order to preclude suburban competition. Houston's land area increased by 24 percent in less than three decades. That city acquired expansive authority to wield liberal annexation power or extend its borders by imposing extra territorial jurisdiction (ETJ). Today, Houston has a population density of 3,618 people per square mile, roughly half that of America's supposed paragon of sprawl, Los Angeles. Phoenix also increased its land area by 69 percent and exhibits even lower density than Houston at 3,146 people

Table 6.1 *Population and Densities in 20 Cities, 1970–2000*

| City | 1970 | | | 2000 | | | 1970–2000 | | |
|---|---|---|---|---|---|---|---|---|---|
| | Population | Area (in square miles) | Density (residents per sq. mile) | Population | Area (in square miles) | Density (residents per sq. mile)[a] | Population change (%) | Area change (%) | Density change (%) |
| New York | 7,894,862 | 299.7 | 26,343 | 8,008,278 | 308.9 | 25,925 | 1.44 | 3.07 | –1.58 |
| Los Angeles | 2,816,061 | 463.7 | 6,073 | 3,694,820 | 469.3 | 7,873 | 31.21 | 1.21 | 29.64 |
| Chicago | 3,366,957 | 222.6 | 15,126 | 2,896,016 | 227.2 | 12,747 | –13.99 | 2.07 | –15.73 |
| Houston | 1,232,802 | 433.9 | 2,841 | 1,953,631 | 539.9 | 3,619 | 58.47 | 24.43 | 27.36 |
| Philadelphia | 1,948,609 | 125.0 | 15,589 | 1,517,550 | 135.1 | 11,233 | –22.12 | 8.08 | –27.94 |
| Phoenix | 582,000 | 247.9 | 2,348 | 1,321,045 | 419.9 | 3,146 | 126.98 | 69.38 | 34.01 |
| San Diego | 696,769 | 316.9 | 2,199 | 1,223,400 | 324.0 | 3,776 | 75.58 | 2.24 | 71.73 |
| Dallas-Ft. Worth | 844,401 | 265.6 | 3,179 | 1,188,580 | 342.4 | 3,471 | 40.76 | 28.92 | 9.19 |
| Detroit | 1,511,482 | 138.0 | 10,953 | 951,270 | 138.7 | 6,858 | –37.06 | 0.51 | –37.38 |
| San Francisco[b] | 715,674 | 45.4 | 15,764 | 746,777 | 46.7 | 15,991 | 4.35 | 2.86 | 1.44 |
| Boston | 641,071 | 46.0 | 13,936 | 589,141 | 48.4 | 12,172 | –8.10 | 5.22 | –12.66 |
| Washington, D.C. | 756,510 | 61.4 | 12,321 | 572,059 | 61.4 | 9,317 | –24.38 | 0.00 | –24.38 |
| Seattle | 531,000 | 83.6 | 6,352 | 563,374 | 83.9 | 6,715 | 6.10 | 0.36 | 5.72 |
| Denver | 514,678 | 95.2 | 5,406 | 554,636 | 153.3 | 3,618 | 7.76 | 61.03 | –33.08 |
| Cleveland | 750,903 | 75.9 | 9,893 | 478,403 | 77.0 | 6,213 | –36.29 | 1.45 | –37.20 |
| Atlanta | 496,973 | 131.5 | 3,779 | 416,474 | 131.8 | 3,160 | –16.20 | 0.23 | –16.39 |
| Minneapolis-St. Paul[b] | 434,400 | 55.1 | 7,884 | 382,618 | 54.9 | 6,969 | –11.92 | –0.36 | –11.60 |
| Miami | 334,859 | 34.3 | 9,763 | 362,470 | 35.6 | 10,182 | 8.25 | 3.79 | 4.29 |
| St. Louis | 622,236 | 61.2 | 10,167 | 348,189 | 61.9 | 5,625 | –44.04 | 1.14 | –44.68 |
| Pittsburgh | 520,117 | 55.2 | 9,422 | 334,563 | 55.6 | 6,017 | –35.68 | 0.72 | –36.14 |

*Sources:* U.S. Census Bureau (1972, table 22; 1998, tables 20–22; 2000); State of the Cities Data Systems (2000).

[a] Densities are based on 1998 area data.

[b] Data are taken from U.S. Census Bureau (2000, table SU-99-1).

per square mile. Another rapidly growing city, Denver, expanded its land mass by an astounding 61 percent and lowered its density by an equally substantial 33 percent.

Elsewhere in the country, population has spread into unincorporated areas with little regard for land preservation, drainage, or traffic. In Cincinnati's suburbs, substantial growth occurs outside established municipalities and, in some counties, the rate of movement into unincorporated areas exceeds 50 percent (Kentucky State Data Center 1998). Other states like Michigan have lifted zoning and environmental regulations in distressed areas in order to encourage development.

Fifth and last, sprawl is not merely due to a confluence of abstract technological, market, social, or legal forces. Politics and the capacity of interest groups play an important role. Bankers, realtors, lawyers, developers, newspapers, organized labor, chambers of commerce, and innumerable actors drive sprawl machines. Bankers and realtors earn profits by supporting developers, while newspapers, business, and organized labor are anxious to build and sell as much as possible—activity is valued for its own sake no matter where the clientele is located.

Far from being a conspiracy, this confluence is better conceived of as multiple actions where shifting coalitions take turns at the sprawl machine. Norton Long (1958) sees this in its broadest perspective, as a series of individually calculated actions among actors in different sections of society (construction, banking, newspapers, politics, etc.). Other writers see the process as more purposeful and refer to those actors as "progrowth coalitions," "development regimes," or "growth machines" (Mollenkopf 1983; Logan and Molotch 1987; Stone and Sanders 1989; Stren 1996). Whatever the internal motivations, the tangible actions of people create sprawl, and they do it by driving the sprawl machine in different ways. Houston and the State of Texas combine liberal annexation, a huge land mass, and no zoning laws to facilitate low-density development. Los Angeles and the State of California allow new, small cities to incorporate and grow around central cities and into the western desert. In the Midwest, it is common for settlements to grow in helter-skelter fashion within unincorporated areas.

While the sprawl machine is a product of local and state action, it could not function with nearly the same capability were it not for federal intervention. Sprawl requires a larger cast of participants and coordinated support. More often than not, Washington has been an exuberant sponsor, though at times it has proceeded with greater caution.

## Washington's Hand

It is by now a "common sense," almost intuitive belief that federal poli-cies have encouraged sprawl. From the 1950s onward, a rash of literature has bemoaned Washington's role in destroying central cities and turning the country toward the suburbs (Anderson 1964; Gelfand 1975; Savitch 1979; Jackson 1985; Fishman 1987). The message of this literature was that federal programs raked inner cities with badly conceived urban renewal programs while feeding the suburbs with benefits for the middle class. Indirect assistance for mortgages, relief for taxation, and defense and highway, spending made suburbanization possible.

Indeed, the list of specific initiatives supporting this claim is quite lengthy. Reaching back to the 1930s, the Home Owners Loan Corporation and Federal Housing Authority (FHA) offered mortgage assistance to single-family buyers and began a residential surge toward urban periph-eries. By the time World War II was over, single-family housing assistance was also made possible by the GI Bill. These programs did nothing directly to build suburban housing, but instead accelerated the sprawl machine by insuring mortgages and helping to reduce interest rates. Before Washington's full-blown intervention, prospective buyers were required to put down one-third of the appraised value of a house before obtaining a mortgage. Home loans typically extended over 10 or perhaps 20 years.

Once undertaken, federal insurance simply eliminated the risk to lenders and not only made mortgages more abundant, but made them significantly cheaper and extended them over 30-year periods. More-over, postwar benefits helped write down loans to veterans, and this was eventually extended to modest-income buyers. Interest rates were grad-ually reduced, and by the 1950s were down to 5 percent. Houses could be bought with just a few thousand dollars in cash, and mortgage payments might very well equal the cost of renting an apartment. These policies paved the way for standardized housing construction. Much like auto-mobile production, suburban housing could be erected with assembly line and division-of-labor production. Farmland could be cheaply bought, subdivided, and superimposed with "Levittowns" spread across the landscape.

Through the 1930s, federal encouragement was a gradual process that was effectively halted during World War II, but resumed in an avalanche soon after. In 1933, FHA-supported mortgages amounted to just 93,000 single-family housing starts, but rose to nearly a half million by 1939.

Within decades after the war, more than 11 million families were assisted by FHA loans and another 22 million families were helped with FHA-supported property improvements (Jackson 1985).

Federal tax laws proved to be an even more powerful incentive for residential householders. Interest on mortgages could be deducted from the tax bill, and these payments often climbed to roughly half the cost of a house purchase. Meanwhile, no such advantages were accorded to renters living in apartment buildings. People discovered it was as cheap to buy as to rent shelter and quickly took advantage of the benefits. Since 1934, the proportion of families living in owner-occupied dwellings has risen from 44 to 67 percent (Jackson 1985; Siegel 1999). Home interest deductions have exacerbated the policy imbalances toward cities. Using 1997 as an example, the foregone taxes on these deductions (mostly benefiting suburbanites) were about four and a half times HUD's direct spending on housing subsidies (mostly benefiting city dwellers) (Pastor et al. 2000).[2]

There is no mistaking the popularity of tax benefits. Homeowners constitute a formidable political constituency and could prod politicians with measures for self-protection and taxpayer revolts. When President Jimmy Carter suggested a reduction in tax benefits for home mortgages, he found himself deluged with angry protestors and immediately retracted his hasty proposal. Since then, national politicians have steered clear of the issue. In fact, President Bill Clinton and Vice President Al Gore treated tax policies that encouraged sprawl very gingerly; on occasion they permitted transportation policies to induce more sprawl. They shied away from raising taxes on gasoline and took no stand on taxing high gas consuming vehicles. Meanwhile, tax laws permit deductions for parking spaces. Companies can offer up to $175 per month in tax-free parking for each employee, while mass transit benefits over $65 per month are counted as taxable income (Blumenauer 1998). In this country, a suburbanite driving a gas-consuming, high-polluting, sport-utility vehicle (SUV) enjoys subsidized parking, while most of the costs for rail transit are passed on to passengers.

Tax policies related to property may also have keyed up the urge to sprawl through the Taxpayer Relief Act of 1997. Under this law, individuals are permitted to exclude up to $250,000 ($500,000 for joint filers) of capital gain on the sale of a residence. In theory at least, the exclusion would yield large profits for lavish houses, and would encourage wealthier taxpayers to purchase larger homes on larger lots. Since the exclusion can be claimed every two years, prospective homeowners can move further into the countryside on larger spreads of land. The push toward exurbia is made all the more attractive by public subsidies for new sewer construction. By 1980, the federal government was absorbing 75 percent of sewer construction, up considerably from a previous 20-year period (Pastor et al. 2000). The irony is that while subsidies go toward the consumption of new land, the re-use of old land is actually penalized. Federal environmental requirements impose costs on city governments or potential purchasers to clean up "brownfields" (chemically contaminated land) before any development can be undertaken (see discussion below).

The defense and aerospace industries also tend to establish themselves in wide open spaces—especially through the sunbelt. Low-density states like Florida, California, and Texas have been heavy recipients of federal largesse to these industries. Some of the largest defense contractors were set up in southern California (Lockheed, Northrop) while a good many outlets have sprung up in Colorado (Hewlett Packard, Honeywell, United Technologies) (Markusen et al. 1991). Texas and Florida also house the National Aeronautics and Space Administration (NASA), the nation's space enterprise. Spending for aerospace and military purposes involve immense amounts of funding, and through the 1970s and 1980s constituted more than one-quarter of the national budget. Army and air bases are built in sparsely populated rural areas. Once established, they generate multiplier effects like commercial strips, low-density housing, artillery ranges, and airfields—all of which consume vast amounts of land for a variety of uses.

Not surprisingly, the combination of housing, mortgage, tax, and defense policies have a snowballing effect, creating strip-zoned commerce along the peripheries of residential subdivisions. The momentum generated by these policies has shaped land use patterns throughout the nation. Low-density "edge cities" have popped up around low-density housing subdivisions, replicating themselves across the nation.

Federal encouragement has not been unmitigated. Some measures have also been taken to dampen or temper sprawl. By the 1990s, the Department of Housing and Urban Development (HUD) could claim that 46 percent of home mortgages were made in central cities and 41 percent of loans were made in "underserved areas" (U.S. General Accounting Office [GAO] 1999, 11, 33). Substantial assistance was also given to needy populations through lending agencies like Fannie Mae, Ginnie Mae, and Freddie Mac. During the 1960s, familiar programs like public housing, rent supplements, and assistance to homebuyers effectively housed low- and moderate-income families within central cities. By the 1970s, vouchers were introduced, enabling less well off families to use federal subsidies to chose their housing (Savitch 1979).

Further, a host of measures were adopted by federal agencies prohibiting federal funds from being used to encourage "place wars" or attract industry from one locale to another. Newspapers chronicled stories of how one community used federal funds to lure investment and jobs from another community. Usually the raiding community was a sprawling suburb or exurb. Spurred on by these anecdotes, federal agencies are supposed to monitor localities to make sure that funds are not used to build infrastructure or provide benefits to relocating businesses. These measures pertain to a variety of federally supported programs, including aid for public works, grants for community development, funds for employment training, empowerment zones, and so on (GAO 1997).

At times, Washington has sought to act positively by placing its own resources within urban cores. In 1978, President Jimmy Carter issued an executive order that federal agencies give first consideration to locating in central areas. Nearly two decades later, President Bill Clinton reaffirmed the federal commitment to concentrated development by directing federal agencies to locate in central cities and historic districts. Indeed, Washington could recently claim that 45 percent of all federal buildings were located in central cities (GAO 1999, 15, 34).

President Bill Clinton and Vice President Al Gore also took steps to contain sprawl through an initiative called "Building Livable Communities" (Livable Communities 2000). This initiative consists of a series of proposals that would harness previous legislation, allocate funding, provide information, and generally encourage localities to combat sprawl. The centerpiece of the "Livable Communities" initiative allows localities to issue over $10 billion of tax credit bonds over five years. These bonds will be used to preserve open space, create or restore parks, clean up "brownfields," protect farmland and wetland, and improve water quality. Other parts of the initiative pull together funding for public transit from the Transportation Equity Act for the 21$^{st}$ Century (TEA-21). Over $6 billion will be used to get commuters out of private automobiles and into mass transit. Minor sections of the initiative are intended for brownfield clearance, and these provisions rely on funding from the Environmental Protection Agency (EPA) and HUD. While Livable Communities is a start, it works at the margins of sprawl. Funding is still weak and largely packaged from existing legislation, while bonds and grants target only snippets of land use practices, and almost all of its provisions are voluntary.

At first glance, the policies of encouraging and then tempering sprawl may appear contradictory, but these seemingly conflicting attitudes can be reconciled. Generally, policies with the greatest push and the highest cache *do* favor sprawl, while those with a dampening touch and marginal potency lean toward concentrated development. Consider, for example, the relative effects of mortgages for a rising middle class, tax benefits for affluent groups, and defense spending for giant industries. Compare these with housing assistance for struggling populations, marginal policies to prevent federal funding from being used to initiate "place wars," and weaker policies to clean up brownfields or locate federal buildings in central business or historic districts. Pro-sprawl policies are much more powerful and designed to energize pent-up economic forces and growth coalitions. Anti-sprawl policies are essentially reactions to aggressive development and are supposed to cope with some of its negative effects. Over the years, those negative effects have been substantial and are well known. While a white middle class spreads into the periphery, racial segregation and poverty have been concentrated within inner cities. By 1995, cities like Atlanta, Baltimore, Detroit, and Washington, D.C., were more than 60 percent African American. Also, by 1995, the poverty rate in all central cities rose to more than 20 percent (Katz 1998).

Put another way, policies designed to encourage sprawl are filled with the ability to produce wealth and animate production. These are particularly potent because they encompass jobs, and income and tax revenues, which everyone values. By contrast, policies used to cope with the effects of sprawl are intended to alleviate the pain of poverty and racial segregation. Poverty policies may be tolerated, but they are rarely valued. In a contest between growth and alleviation, growth will invariably win. Even environmental policies designed to deal with excessive waste, like brownfield clearance, often lose out to cheaper and faster development of new land. It is also cheaper to build anew on agricultural land than it is to clear and clean industrial terrain.

The operations of the marketplace coupled with federally subsidized infrastructure encourage developers to chose sprawl. Whatever its other virtues, America discards those things that are inconvenient. Citizens dispose of land much like they dispose of aluminum cans, cardboard cups, or used tires. Eventually the waste of it all builds to less tolerable levels, but this is a very slow process. The costs of sprawl are gradual and dispersed across a huge land mass, while the profits are immediate and substantial. By nature the federal government is sluggish and cumbersome. Given the conspicuous benefits, it is easy to see why national policies favor sprawl.

To be sure, these policies have a strong political component. In part, they are the outcome of bargaining among politicians representing different constituencies, and a measure of their relative power. Growth coalitions not only operate at the local level, but also in Washington. Home building, construction, mortgage banking, and labor interests lobby Congress and the executive branch to lubricate the sprawl machine with federal funds. Mayors, civil rights organizations, and environmental groups form a counter lobby, working to give needy populations a larger share of the "pie" or protect open space and watersheds. In part, federal policies are responses to larger trends. During the 1960s and early 1970s, the country was beset by the urge to grow and was faced with collective urban rioting. During the 1980s and early 1990s, the nation was simultaneously concerned with the need to "grow the economy" and worried about "global warming." Often the fight was between such organizations as the National Association of Home Builders and the Sierra Club, "free market" advocates and "managed growth" proponents, or advocates of private automobiles and those who favor mass transit. Intended or not, the effects are highly lopsided. Nothing so readily illustrates this as national highway policies.

## Paving the Way for the Sprawl Machine

Highways and automobiles make sprawl possible, probable, and desirable. The very character of highways means that transportation patterns can be fluid. Automobiles expand the uses for land, making settlement patterns more explosive—almost randomly apportioned by points along fluid highway corridors. To appreciate that argument, consider the multiple exits available along interstate corridors and the local roads onto which people can travel. Compare this situation with rail terminals, which are relatively fixed, and where settlement is clustered around set points, such as traditional cities, small villages, and new towns. In Europe, a national railway system makes compact development possible, and this is why France, Germany, Great Britain, and the Netherlands have been able to expand their suburbs without creating massive sprawl.

While Americans have always loved roads and highways, the romance blossomed with the adoption of the National Interstate and Defense Highway Act of 1956. The Act became an urgent priority for a number of reasons, not the least of which were industrial transition, market economics, and the possibility of another world war. President Dwight Eisenhower's recounting of the reasoning and inspiration behind the national highway system follows:

> The reasons for urgency were incontrovertible. . . . From coast to coast people were leaving the farms, and flocking to the cities. . . . And the rush carried people not only into the cities, but out into the areas just beyond them, creating great suburbs. With these movements and the burgeoning automobile population, the requirements for an efficient arterial network of roads, a true concrete and macadam lifeline, had become acute. . . . Our roads ought to be avenues for persons living in big cities threatened by aerial attack or natural disaster; but I knew that if such a crisis ever occurred, our obsolescent highways, too small for the flood of traffic of an entire city's population going one way, would turn into traps of death and destruction (Eisenhower 1963, 548).

The twin strands of economics and defense were further amplified by the president:

> The total pavement of the system would make a parking lot big enough to hold two-thirds of the automobiles in the United States. More than any single action by government this one would change the face of America. Its impact on the American economy—the jobs it would produce in manufacturing and construction, the rural areas it would open up was beyond calculation. And motorists by the millions would read a primary purpose in the signs that would sprout up alongside the pavements: "In the event of enemy attack this road will be closed" (Eisenhower 1963, 549).

While Eisenhower's belief that freeways could become avenues of escape in a nuclear war was egregiously naïve, the president's other remarks were prescient. Interstate highways did move the mass of Americans, they did "change the face of America" and because of congestion they even served as unintended "parking lots." The amounts of federal monies put into this "concrete and macadam lifeline" were astronomical and virtually unparalleled. In the past two decades alone, over a trillion dollars have been spent on highways ("Not Quite the Monster" 1999).

Figure 6.1 shows a line graph representing a recent 13-year period, and shows the relative amounts spent on highways versus mass transit. In order to better gauge the impact of this spending at the time of expenditure, the lines are calibrated to nominal dollars. Note that the nominal amounts spent on highways soared by more than 100 percent

Figure 6.1  *Federal Outlays on Highways and Mass Transit, 1982–1994*

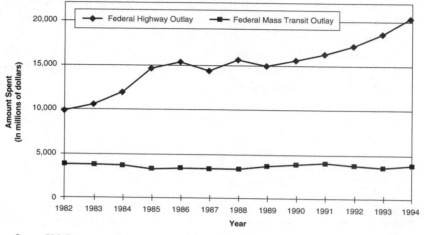

*Source:* U.S. Department of Transportation (1997a).

between 1982 and 1994.[3] The spread between highway and mass transit spending grew. In 1982, highways consumed at least 75 percent of total spending and, by 1994, this proportion had increased to 84 percent (U.S. Department of Transportation 1997a,b). Since that time, Congress passed (in 1998) a massive six-year $216 billion highway and mass transit law, which represents a 40 percent increase over previous spending. The measure has been hailed as the largest public works legislation in history. Again, in this new legislation, the proportional shares for highways versus mass transit are interesting. Highways absorb 80 percent of the bounty, while mass transit is left with 18 percent (2 percent is reserved for safety and miscellaneous purposes) (Clarke 1998).

Moreover, federal funding for interstate highways began far ahead of programs for mass transit, and from the onset was protected through the Highway Trust Fund. Even after the introduction of mass transit, highways enjoyed a looming advantage. Money for highway construction could be automatically tapped through user taxes with localities contributing just 10 percent of the cost, while Washington paid for 90 percent of the remainder. It took nearly two decades and a series of congressional brawls before cities could tap the Trust Fund for other transit purposes. Even then, cities choosing to substitute mass transit for highways received just 80 percent of matching funds from Washington (Savitch 1979). Highway defenders often argue that motorists and truckers pay their own way and are entitled to those funds, but this is not quite the case. A study by the U.S. Congressional Office of Technological Assessment (OTA) found that motorists "paid 62–72 percent of public expenditures for highway infrastructure," while government absorbed the rest. This does not include a host of indirect subsidies for the occurrence of personal injuries, opportunity costs for land use, pollution, and congestion (U.S. Congress 1995, 212–13).

Commensurate with these findings, federal actions have their consequences. Directly or indirectly, federally encouraged sprawl has increased both the trip length and travel time of commuters. Between 1969 and 1990, vehicle miles traveled for commuters soared by 74 percent while all types of vehicle miles traveled rose even higher—by 82 percent (U.S. Department of Transportation 1995). For most cities mean travel time has also increased. One study of more than 60 metropolitan areas showed that, in many instances, the average driver spent as much time in traffic each year as on vacation (Schrank and Lomax 1999).

Table 6.2 displays travel time in 20 American metropolitan areas over a 10-year period. The times shown are in minutes per trip. Overall, despite the billions of annual dollars invested in highways, both time and distance spent in automobiles have increased. In addition to longer distances, there is close to a 5 percent increase in travel time for these cities in just 10 years. Out of the 20 metropolitan areas, only two (New York and Pittsburgh) managed to decrease their commutation time. Two sunbelt metro areas (Los Angeles and San Diego) led the pack with double-digit rises. On the positive side, average travel time is still under 30 minutes. This still is within a reasonable range, though it should be considered against the costs of owning a private automobile and the costs transferred to the larger public.

A further examination of liabilities indicates that by 1997, the annual cost of driving an automobile for 15,000 miles came to nearly $8,000. This represents a 30 percent increase between 1990 and 1997 (American Automobile Manufacturers Association 1998). These costs rose in direct proportion to sprawl, so that gasoline consumption alone climbed by 58 percent as one moved from moderately dense inner suburbs to sparsely populated outer suburbs (U.S. Congress 1995, 213). Actual costs of congestion are more elusive and vary with area of the country.

Table 6.2  *Mean Travel Times in 20 Cities, 1980–1990*

| City | Time (in minutes) | | % Change 1980–1990 |
|------|------|------|------|
| | 1980 | 1990 | |
| New York | 33.1 | 31.1 | −6.04 |
| Los Angeles | 23.6 | 26.4 | 11.86 |
| Chicago | 26.3 | 28.1 | 6.84 |
| Houston | 25.9 | 26.1 | 0.77 |
| Philadelphia | 24.0 | 24.1 | 0.42 |
| Phoenix | 21.6 | 23.0 | 6.48 |
| San Diego | 19.5 | 22.2 | 13.85 |
| Dallas | 22.4 | 24.1 | 7.59 |
| Detroit | 22.5 | 23.4 | 4.00 |
| San Francisco | 23.9 | 25.6 | 7.11 |
| Boston | 23.4 | 24.2 | 3.42 |
| Washington, D.C. | 27.2 | 29.5 | 8.46 |
| Seattle | 22.8 | 24.3 | 6.58 |
| Denver | 22.0 | 22.4 | 1.82 |
| Cleveland | 21.6 | 22.0 | 1.85 |
| Atlanta | 24.9 | 26.0 | 4.42 |
| Minneapolis | 20.1 | 21.1 | 4.98 |
| Miami | 22.6 | 24.1 | 6.64 |
| St. Louis | 22.6 | 23.1 | 2.21 |
| Pittsburgh | 22.8 | 22.6 | −0.88 |
| **Average time—all cities** | **23.64** | **24.67** | **4.36** |

*Source:* U.S. Department of Transportation (1993), table 4–13.
*Note:* Mean travel times represent minutes traveled in a trip to work.

Table 6.3 shows these costs for 1991 through 1999. Congestion costs largely center on delay and fuel consumption. Note that over a five-year period, costs rose by nearly 40 percent. The most expensive metropolitan areas in which to operate an automobile are Washington, D.C., Seattle, and Denver. There does not appear to be a clear relationship between sprawl and the costs of congestion, and this is a complicated issue requiring extensive examination. Sprawled Los Angeles and Houston have somewhat higher congestion costs than compact Chicago and New York, though other results are mixed.

Automobiles and trucks are the major cause of air pollution and on this count the nation has managed to contain the worst tendencies.

Table 6.3  *Cost of Congestion in 20 Urban Areas, 1991–1999*

| City | Cost ($)[a] 1991 | 1993 | 1996 | 1999 | % Change 1991–1999 |
|---|---|---|---|---|---|
| New York | 390 | 460 | 570 | 595 | 52.56 |
| Los Angeles | 660 | 720 | 885 | 1,000 | 51.52 |
| Chicago | 310 | 390 | 510 | 570 | 83.87 |
| Houston | 600 | 680 | 785 | 850 | 41.67 |
| Philadelphia | 270 | 250 | 345 | 435 | 61.11 |
| Phoenix | 390 | 420 | 455 | 540 | 38.46 |
| San Diego | 300 | 310 | 470 | 675 | 125.00 |
| Dallas | 570 | 640 | 770 | 780 | 36.84 |
| Detroit | 400 | 600 | 840 | 700 | 75.00 |
| San Francisco | 760 | 790 | 835 | 760 | 0.00 |
| Boston | 510 | 550 | 720 | 715 | 40.20 |
| Washington, D.C. | 740 | 860 | 1,055 | 780 | 5.41 |
| Seattle | 660 | 740 | 915 | 930 | 40.91 |
| Denver | 390 | 470 | 630 | 760 | 94.87 |
| Cleveland | 120 | 200 | 305 | 350 | 191.67 |
| Atlanta | 530 | 640 | 855 | 915 | 72.64 |
| Minneapolis-St. Paul | 220 | 290 | 455 | 670 | 204.55 |
| Miami | 510 | 600 | 710 | 705 | 38.24 |
| St. Louis | 280 | 340 | 635 | 745 | 166.07 |
| Pittsburgh | 260 | 310 | 390 | 235 | −9.62 |
| **Average cost—all cities** | **543.05** | **612.65** | **756.55** | **685.5** | **70.55** |

*Sources:* Texas Transportation Institute (1996, 1998, 1999, 2001, table A-10).
[a] Cost of congestion is annual dollars per capita.

Nevertheless, the adverse impact is unmistakable. Figure 6.2 displays 20 of the largest metropolitan areas in terms of number of days with poor air quality in 1989 and 1998. In 1989, Los Angeles and San Diego led in the number of days with poor air quality. That record has been substantially improved since 1989, although sprawled cities still do worse than compact ones. Los Angeles, San Diego, Atlanta, and Houston fare worse than New York, Chicago, Boston, and Seattle. Nevertheless, the record is uneven and pollution may be due to other factors, such as topography, weather, and industrial uses.

Figure 6.2  *Air Quality in 20 Cities, 1989 and 1998*

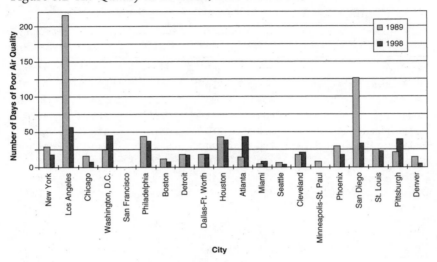

*Source:* U.S. Environmental Protection Agency (1998).

*Note:* The Air Quality Index (AQI) is measured for ground-level ozone, particulate matter, carbon monoxide, sulfur dioxide, and nitrogen dioxide. The AQI is normalized across pollutants so that an AQI value of 100 represents the level of health protection associated with the national health standard for each pollutant. The AQI has categories ranging from 0 ("Good") up to a value of 500 ("Hazardous"). An AQI value greater than 100 indicates that *at least* one criteria pollutant exceeded the level of the standard for that day. A value greater than 100 is designated to be "unhealthy for sensitive groups."

Finally, like other sprawl policies, the federal government has reacted to the negative effects of highway building. The earliest action occurred in 1991 with the passage of the Intermodal Surface Transportation and Efficiency Act (ISTEA). Under this legislation, localities were mandated to coordinate transportation, land use, and environmental planning in order to meet clean air standards. ISTEA put metropolitan planning organizations (MPOs) at the heart of this effort and provided them with funding. Areas failing to meet clean air requirements were threatened with sanctions, forcing delays in transportation funding. MPOs also sought to help localities develop alternatives to private reliance on automobiles. Since 1998, ISTEA has been replaced with the Transportation Equity Act for the 21st Century, or TEA-21. Like its predecessor, TEA-21 provides some funding for public transit and encourages localities to adopt stronger land use controls through MPOs. TEA-21 also tries to nudge localities toward "smart growth" by providing them with tools and techniques for mapping and envisioning new settlement.

Neither ISTEA nor TEA-21 have had much of an effect on sprawl. They may have put teeth in clean air legislation, explaining improved air quality across the country's metropolitan areas. By and large, the legislation alleviates the pain of sprawl rather than altering patterns of land use or transportation. Given the force and momentum of local sprawl machines, this could be expected and may be good politics. After all is said and done, to sprawl or not to sprawl may be more a matter of values than hard statistics.

## Conclusions

Whatever one might say about sprawl, it is not a spontaneous occurrence or a product of pure market forces. Washington interacted with and encouraged local sprawl machines with mortgage, housing, taxation, defense, and transportation policies. Some might cheer the federal role, and see it as a way of bringing more freedom, mobility, and prosperity to the American people (Bruegmann 1996). They might also see this as reconciling city and country living—bringing the countryside to an urban middle class. For the most part, they would be correct. But sprawl also has a downside. This includes a middle-class exodus from central cities, the rampancy of ugly brownfields, the ruination of green space, and the paving of America with endless and unsightly highways.

Much of the argument for and against sprawl depends upon these subjective factors and value judgments. Appropriately enough, decisions are made by elected legislatures and political executives. Inappropriately, however, decisions are heavily influenced by highly motivated and financially well-heeled growth coalitions who make up the sprawl machines. The sprawl machine in Washington has worked to no less a degree than those in localities. Since the 1950s, advocates have been enormously successful, managing to advance the most fundamental policies of money, taxation, and transportation. It is difficult to ascertain how much consumer demand for low-density development has been induced by Washington and how much might be due to other factors. One thing is sure: Federal action has contributed to making America a world exception by creating the first suburban nation.

## NOTES

1. European rates of intergovernmental aid range roughly from 40 percent in France to 60 percent in Great Britain and 80 percent in Italy. This does not include costs for education, firefighters, and police, which are often paid for by national government. The 15 American cities and their proportions of aid in 1970 and 1996 are contained in the table below.

*Intergovernmental Aid to 15 Cities: 1970 and 1996*

| | Revenues (in $ millions) | | | | |
|---|---|---|---|---|---|
| | *Federal* | *State* | *Total* | *% Federal* | *% State* |
| *City* | | | *1970* | | |
| New York | 158 | 2,878 | 7,655 | 2 | 37.59 |
| Los Angeles | 6 | 86 | 849 | 1 | 10.07 |
| Chicago | 91 | 58 | 731 | 12 | 7.98 |
| Houston | 4 | 1 | 166 | 2 | 0.66 |
| Philadelphia | 31 | 47 | 582 | 5 | 8.01 |
| Phoenix | 7 | 15 | 101 | 7 | 14.46 |
| San Diego | 2 | 16 | 126 | 1 | 12.38 |
| Dallas[a] | 3 | 2 | 169 | 2 | 1.12 |
| Detroit | 44 | 68 | 509 | 9 | 13.38 |
| San Francisco | 42 | 42 | 574 | 7 | 7.39 |
| Boston | 17 | 55 | 370 | 5 | 14.84 |
| Washington, D.C. | 247 | — | 718 | 34 | — |
| Seattle | 5 | 32 | 192 | 3 | 16.67 |
| Denver | 11 | 40 | 180 | 6 | 22.17 |
| Cleveland | 3 | 15 | 206 | 2 | 7.23 |
| **Average—all cities** | | | | **5.11** | **25.54** |
| | | | *1996* | | |
| New York | 1,895 | 14,414 | 49,292 | 3.84 | 29.24 |
| Los Angeles | 501 | 374 | 8,483 | 5.91 | 4.41 |
| Chicago | 349 | 797 | 5,036 | 6.93 | 15.83 |
| Houston | 88 | 30 | 2,327 | 3.78 | 1.29 |
| Philadelphia | 366 | 717 | 4,513 | 8.11 | 15.89 |
| Phoenix | 98 | 279 | 1,528 | 6.41 | 18.26 |
| San Diego | 170 | 99 | 1,716 | 9.91 | 5.77 |
| Dallas[a] | 63 | 22 | 1,628 | 3.87 | 1.35 |
| Detroit | 214 | 561 | 2,868 | 7.46 | 19.56 |
| San Francisco | 213 | 1,070 | 4,542 | 4.69 | 23.56 |

(Continued)

*Intergovernmental Aid to 15 Cities: 1970 and 1996 (Continued)*

| | Revenues (in $ millions) | | | | |
| | Federal | State | Total | % Federal | % State |
|---|---|---|---|---|---|
| City | | | 1996 | | |
| Boston | 50 | 855 | 2,296 | 2.18 | 37.24 |
| Washington, D.C. | 1,609 | — | 5,101 | 31.54 | — |
| Seattle | 30 | 95 | 1,358 | 2.21 | 7.00 |
| Denver | 29 | 314 | 1,612 | 1.80 | 19.48 |
| Cleveland | 84 | 85 | 898 | 9.35 | 9.47 |
| **Average—all cities** | | | | **6.18** | **21.15** |

*Sources:* U.S. Census Bureau (1972, table 670; 1999, table 530).

ᵃ Dallas represents city of Dallas only; Ft. Worth was listed separately.

2. This does not necessarily mean that single-family houses cannot be accommodated with moderately dense compact settlements, while also retaining the popularity of single-family houses. There is a difference between single-house sprawl and single houses built in towns, villages, or cities. Indeed, most American cities contain huge proportions of single-family housing that are clustered.

3. Even after adjusting for inflation, total expenditures rose by 30 percent over the same period.

## REFERENCES

Anderson, Martin. 1964. *The Federal Bulldozer: A Critical Analysis of Urban Renewal, 1949–1962*. Cambridge, Mass.: MIT Press.

American Automobile Manufacturers Association Inc. 1998. *Motor Vehicles Facts and Figures*. In U.S. Census Bureau, *Statistical Abstract of the United States, 1998*, table 1052. http://www.census.gov/statab/www. (Accessed May 2000.)

Berg, Bruce, and Paul Kantor. 1996. "New York: The Politics of Conflict and Avoidance." In *Regional Politics: America in a Post-City Age*, edited by H.V. Savitch and Ronald K. Vogel (25–45). Thousand Oaks, Calif.: Sage Publications.

Blumenauer, Earl. 1998. "The View from Capitol Hill." *Brookings Review* 16 (4, Fall): 16–17.

Bruegmann, Robert. 1996. "The American City: Urban Aberration or Glimpse of the Future?" In *Preparing for the Urban Future: Global Pressures and Local Forces*, edited by Michael A. Cohen, Blair A. Ruble, Joseph Tulchin, and Allison M. Garland (336–68). Baltimore, Md.: Johns Hopkins University Press.

Clarke, Elizabeth. 1998. "Congress Passes Historic Surface Transportation Bill." *Civil Engineering* (July): 104–105.

Cohen, Michael A., Blair A. Ruble, Joseph Tulchin, and Allison M. Garland, eds. 1996. *Preparing for the Urban Future: Global Pressures and Local Forces.* Baltimore, Md.: Johns Hopkins University Press.

Eisenhower, Dwight. 1963. *Mandate for Change.* New York: Doubleday.

Fannie Mae Foundation and The Brookings Institution. 2001. *Downtown Rebound.* Fannie Mae Foundation and The Brookings Institution Center on Urban and Metropolitan Policy Census Note (May).

Fishman, Robert. 1987. *Bourgeois Utopia: The Rise and Fall of Suburbia.* New York: Basic Books, Inc.

Gelfand, Mark. 1975. *A Nation of Cities.* New York: Oxford University Press.

Gordon, Peter, and Harry Richardson. 2000. "Defending Suburban Sprawl." *The Public Interest* Spring (139): 65–71.

Haider, Donald. 1992. "Place Wars: New Realities of the 1990's." *Economic Development Quarterly* 6 (2): 127–34.

Hamilton, Alexander, John Jay, and James Madison. 1937. *The Federalist Papers,* No. 10. New York: The Modern Library.

Jackson, Kenneth T. 1985. *Crabgrass Frontier: The Suburbanization of the United States.* New York: Oxford Press.

Katz, Bruce J. 1998. *Reviving Cities: Think Metropolitan.* Brookings Policy Brief #33. http://www.brook.edu/comm/PolicyBriefs/pb033/pb33.htm. (Accessed May 2000.)

Kentucky State Data Center. 1998. *Estimates of Area and Population.* Louisville, Ky.: Kentucky State Data Center.

Livable Communities. 2000. *Building Livable Communities.* Washington, D.C. June. http://www.livablecommunities.gov. (Accessed July 2000.)

Logan, John R., and Harvey L. Molotch. 1987. *Urban Fortunes: The Political Economy of Place.* Berkeley, Calif.: University of California Press.

Long, Norton E. 1958. "The Local Community As an Ecology of Games." *The American Journal of Sociology* 64 (3): 251–61.

Markusen, Ann, Scott Campbell, Peter Hall, and Sabrina Deitrich, eds. 1991. *The Rise of the Gunbelt: The Military Remapping of Industrial America.* New York: Oxford University Press.

Mollenkopf, John H. 1983. *The Contested City.* Princeton, N.J.: Princeton University Press.

"Not Quite the Monster They Call It." 1999. *The Economist,* 21 August, 24.

Pastor Jr., Manuel, Peter Dreier, J. Eugene Grigsby III, and Marta Lopez-Garza. 2000. *Regions That Work: How Cities and Suburbs Can Grow Together.* Minneapolis: University of Minnesota Press.

Savitch, H.V. 1979. *Urban Policy and the Exterior City: Federal, State and Corporate Impacts upon Major Cities.* New York: Pergamon Press.

Savitch, H.V., and Ronald K. Vogel, eds. 1996. *Regional Politics: America in a Post-City Age.* Thousand Oaks, Calif.: Sage Publications.

Schrank, David, and Tim Lomax. 1999. *The 1999 Annual Mobility Report.* College Station, Tex.: Texas Transportation Institute, Texas A&M University. http://mobility.tamu.edu. (Accessed May 2000.)

Siegel, Fred. 1999. "Is Regional Government the Answer?" *The Public Interest* Fall (137): 85–98.

State of the Cities Data Systems. 2000. "Historical Data from the 2000 Census." http://socds.huduser.org. (Accessed July 2000.)

Stone, Clarence N., and Heywood T. Sanders, eds. 1989. *The Politics of Urban Development.* Lawrence, Kans.: University Press of Kansas.

Stren, Richard. 1996. "The Studies of Cities: Popular Perceptions, Academic Disciplines, and Emerging Agendas." In *Preparing for the Urban Future: Global Pressures and Local Forces,* edited by Michael A. Cohen, Blair A. Ruble, Joseph Tulchin, and Allison M. Garland (392–420). Baltimore, Md.: Johns Hopkins University Press.

Texas Transportation Institute. 1996. *Roadway Congestion in Major Urban Areas.* In U.S. Census Bureau, *Statistical Abstract of the United States, 1996,* table 1009. http://www.census.gov/statab/www. (Accessed May 2000.)

———. 1998. *Roadway Congestion in Major Urban Areas.* In U.S. Census Bureau, *Statistical Abstract of the United States, 1998,* table 1040. http://www.census.gov/statab/www. (Accessed May 2000.)

———. 1999. *Roadway Congestion in Major Urban Areas.* In U.S. Census Bureau, *Statistical Abstract of the United States, 1999,* table 1040. http://www.census.gov/statab/www. (Accessed May 2000.)

———. 2001. "1999 Annual Individual Congestion Cost." In *2001 Urban Mobility Study.* College Station, Tex.: Texas Transportation Institute.

U.S. Census Bureau. 1972. *Statistical Abstract of the United States, 1972.* Washington, D.C.: U.S. Government Printing Office.

———. 1997. *1992 Census of Governments.* 1(2): V-VI. http://www.census.gov. (Accessed April 4, 2000.)

———. 1998. "Population of the 100 Largest Urban Places: 1970, 1980, 1990." http://www.census.gov/population/documentation/twps0027. (Accessed May 2000.)

———. 1999. *Statistical Abstract of the United States, 1999.* http://www.census.gov/statab/www. (Accessed May 2000.)

———. 2000. "Population Estimates for Cities with Populations of 100,000 and Greater." http://www.census.gov/population/estimates/metro-city. (Accessed May 2000.)

U.S. Congress. Office of Technology Assessment. 1995. *The Technological Reshaping of Metropolitan America.* OTA-ETI-643. Washington, D.C.: U.S. Government Printing Office. September.

U.S. Department of Transportation. Bureau of Transportation Statistics. 1997a. *Federal, State, and Local Transportation Financial Statistics, Fiscal Years 1982–1994.* Publ. No. BTS-97-E-02. http://www.bts.gov. (Accessed May 2000.)

———. 1997b. *Federal, State, and Local Transportation Financial Statistics, Fiscal Years 1977–1994.* Publ. No. BTS-97-E-01. http://www.bts.gov. (Accessed May 2000.)

U.S. Department of Transportation. Federal Highway Administration. 1993. *Journey-to-Work Trends in the United States and Its Major Metropolitan Areas, 1960–1990.* Publ. No. FHWA-PL-94-012. http://ntl.bts.gov/DOCS/473.html. (Accessed May 2000.)

———. 1995. *1995 Personal Transportation Survey.* Table 23. http://www.fhwa.dot.gov. (Accessed May 2000.)

———. Office of Policy Information. 1998. "Highway Statistics, 1998." Tables MT-1A, MT-2A, MT 2-B, HF-210. http://www.fhwa.dot.gov/ohim/hs. (Accessed May 2000.)

U.S. Environmental Protection Agency. 1998. *National Air Quality and Emissions Trends Report, 1998.* Washington, D.C.: U.S. Environmental Protection Agency.

U.S. General Accounting Office. 1997. *Economic Development Activities: Overview of Eight Federal Programs* (GAO). GAO Publ. No. RCED-97-193. http://www.gao.gov. (Accessed May 2000.)

————. 1999. *Community Development: Extent of Federal Influence on "Urban Sprawl" Is Unclear.* GAO Publ. No. RCED-99-87. http://www.gao.gov. (Accessed May 2000.)

Webber, Melvin M. 1963. "Order in Diversity: Community Without Propinquity." In *Cities and Space: The Future Use of Urban Land,* edited by Lowden Wingo (23–54). Baltimore, Md.: Johns Hopkins University Press.

# 7

# Suburban Expansion in Atlanta

## "The City without Limits" Faces Some

Charles Jaret

Compared with Atlanta, few other American communities have had citizens and leaders as conscious of and concerned about the image projected by their community. Both before and after newspaper editor Henry Grady's famous efforts to attract investment to the city in the 1880s, Atlantans have gone to great lengths trying to create a positive national and international reputation for social or cultural progress and an expanding economy. Much earlier, in 1837, engineer Stephen D. Long established Atlanta (then called "Terminus") as the end of a railroad line coming down from Chattanooga. In making a prediction about the community's prospects, he said this place would be "a good location for one tavern, a blacksmith shop, a grocery store, and nothing else" (Roth and Ambrose 1996, 1). Chafing under those meager expectations, it seems Atlantans have spent the past century and a half trying to show the world how wrong Stephen Long was. Boosterism and a strong desire for growth became well-established traditions among Atlanta's political and business influentials. They produced well-orchestrated public relations campaigns (e.g., "Forward Atlanta" I and II), vigorous efforts to bring international events to the city (e.g., Cotton States and International Exposition of 1895 and the 1996 Olympic Games), a fine-tuned growth machine (i.e., political leaders, developers, builders, real estate firms, financial lenders, and a zoning/legal structure that churns out a huge supply of homes to buy and apartment or office space to rent), and not-very-catchy slogans (e.g., "Atlanta: Come Celebrate Our Dream" and "Atlanta: Among the Trees Grows a City") intended to burn a positive impression of Atlanta into people's minds (White and Crimmins 1980; Rutheiser 1996).

By the mid-1980s, the most famous of these slogans, "Atlanta: The City Too Busy to Hate" (coined by Mayor William B. Hartsfield during the stormy era of civil rights conflicts), seemed quaint, outdated, and not wholly credible. Few people could say it with a straight face. In the 1990s, the local newspaper and the Atlanta Convention and Visitors Bureau held contests and hired consultants to produce fresh slogans for Atlanta. The one that caught on, though it had been created earlier, was "Atlanta: The City without Limits." It promoted and amplified the possibilities in Atlanta for spectacular entrepreneurial success (epitomized by Ted Turner taking a nearly bankrupt billboard advertising business and turning it into a global communications giant) and other "sky's the limit" achievements, like the "worst-to-first" turnaround by the Atlanta Braves from 1990 to 1991. Nowhere, however, did the phrase "Atlanta: The City without Limits" resonate more strongly than in the real estate, construction, and development industries. The slogan's allusion, for them, was to a metropolitan area that had no natural boundaries hemming in outward expansion—no coastline, no mountain range, no wide river or canyon, and no national park or other large preserved place that limited the extent or direction of new growth. Furthermore, neither national and regional economic conditions nor the state and local political-legal systems' land use policies placed many limits on the amount of new suburban subdivisions, condominium complexes, office parks, shopping malls, corporate campuses, and wide roads that could be built. The result was massive development and population growth, mainly in the outer suburbs and peripheral counties of metropolitan Atlanta. This population increase (38.9 percent from 1990 to 2000, with a net increase in population of 1,152,248) and the speed with which outlying land was built up and added to the metropolitan area prompted urban real estate development expert Christopher Leinberger to say, "Atlanta is probably the fastest-growing of any metropolitan area in the history of the world"[1] (Goldberg 1996, D-6).

By the late 1990s, however, it was clear that something had gone awry in at least three ways. For one thing, the image and reputation of Atlanta as a wonderful place to live was eroding, and no public relations campaign could stop it. Instead of being acclaimed for its quality of life,

Atlanta's image was tarnished by being labeled "the poster child" for a new social problem—suburban sprawl. A *New York Times* article called Atlanta "the epicenter of the nation's struggle with road congestion, air pollution and overdevelopment" (Firestone 1999, 1), and *Places Rated Almanac*, which ranks metropolitan areas' quality of life and in 1981 had rated Atlanta as "the best all around metro area," lowered Atlanta's rank to 7th and then down to 33rd in its 1997 and 2000 editions. Moreover, real estate consulting firms began advising clients that Atlanta was no longer at the top of the list of places in which they recommended investing. In discussing Atlanta, travel expert Arthur Frommer (1987) said it was "characterless and without charm, dull and excessively devoted to business and finance," and he criticized the destruction of older historic buildings downtown and the abandonment of city neighborhoods for the suburbs. Finally, Tom Wolfe chose Atlanta as the setting for his best-selling novel, *A Man in Full*, about some of the city's "heroes" who turn out to be excessive, pitifully overextended developers and financiers of sprawling office towers and malls—a tale that mocks and turns them into laughingstocks.

Next, despite the slogan's assertion that growth in Atlanta has had "no limits," it is obvious that recent growth certainly has been limited or restricted insofar as it has been very uneven development. While many "hot" areas have grown tremendously, other parts of the city and some suburban pockets have seen so few new people, construction, or other investment that you might think they were surrounded by an invisible mountain range. The favored quadrant of metropolitan Atlanta, running from the north-northwest to the north-northeast, received 75 percent of all the new jobs and 63 percent of the population growth between 1990 and 1997 (Brookings Institution 2000, 19). The outline of this uneven growth was created in earlier periods of development, and the recent round has reinforced it (though later in this chapter we examine efforts that try to counter the long-standing pattern of uneven development). In simplest terms, this uneven growth has four overlapping dimensions. First, a favored quarter on the north side of the city and suburbs has received the lion's share of new development, while much less has been done in the rest of the area, especially on the south side. Second, growth in the suburbs, in general, has outpaced by far the growth in the city of Atlanta. Third, investment in and the development of neighborhoods with fine amenities has been extensive in areas where whites live, but minimal in areas where blacks live, while Asian immigrants have established their own small-scale "growth machine" to push their development agenda. Fourth, within the city of Atlanta, development efforts in three nodes (downtown, Midtown, and Buckhead) have greatly exceeded development in all other parts of the city, especially the poorer neighborhoods.

Finally, "Atlanta: The City without Limits," actually has had some restraints put on it. The most serious and widely discussed limits were placed on it by an external source, the federal government, when in 1998 it suspended access to federal highway funds for road work in metropolitan Atlanta. This money is cut off until a regional transportation plan can be adopted that realistically promises to reduce air pollution to a level judged acceptable according to standards set forth in the Clean Air Act Amendments of 1990. Other temporary limits have been imposed on developers locally by county or municipal governments in the form of numerous moratoria on sewer hookups or building permits. Sewage facilities in some parts of metropolitan Atlanta just cannot handle the added load created by the size and rapidity of the population growth. Other anticipated limits are a water supply that may not be sufficient for Atlanta's projected population increases and other environmental problems that could lower the quality of life in the area (see Bullard, Johnson, and Torres 2000a; Brookings Institution 2000).

These then are the key sprawl-related issues that Atlanta is grappling with at present. The rest of this chapter examines these problems, first by fleshing out some of Atlanta's suburban history and showing the political-economic sources of its uneven development, then by discussing three specific policies designed to reduce sprawl around Atlanta—specifically the creation of the Georgia Regional Transportation Authority, green space legislation, and "smart growth" developments. The goal here is not a definitive history of suburbanization in Atlanta, but a balanced look at the past and present in order to understand the recent attention suburban sprawl has received and new proposals state and local groups are making with regard to such sprawl.

## Sprawling Atlanta: A Synopsis

Metropolitan Atlanta is expanding outward at a phenomenal rate, leaving the city and inner suburbs far behind. The city of Atlanta accounts for less than 3 percent of the land in the 20-county Atlanta metropolitan area defined by the U.S. Census Bureau, and has about 10 percent of the total metropolitan population, estimated at 4,112,198 in 2000. The city of Atlanta's population grew from 394,017 in 1990 to 416,474 in 2000, or by 5.7 percent, according to the Census Bureau. Despite this gain it is still far below its 1970 population of 495,000, and most of the decline is a result of people moving to the suburbs. In contrast, suburban growth has been explosive. The metropolitan area as a whole grew by almost 40 percent between 1990 and 2000. Gwinnett County, the fastest-growing county in the United States for much of the 1980s, added over 235,000 residents (66.7 percent) in the 1990s, while Cobb County added nearly 160,000 (35.8 percent). By the late 1990s, three other metropolitan area counties farther out from the city moved into the ranks of the nation's 10 fastest-growing counties: Forsyth (123 percent), Henry (103 percent), and Paulding (96.3 percent). This growth brings larger malls and retail outlets, traffic congestion, subdivisions of single-family homes, and loss of foliage and tree cover (Brookings Institution 2000; Bullard, Johnson, and Torres 1999, 2000b).

As a result, Atlanta is more suburban than most other U.S. metropolitan areas and is less densely settled than most. Contrary to some observers' claims (e.g., Tucker 1999), however, it does *not* have lower density than any other major metropolitan area. In fact, in 1990, population per square mile (553) in Atlanta's metropolitan statistical area was higher than in Denver (432), Seattle (468), Minneapolis-St. Paul (488), or New Orleans (537), and close to that of Dallas (571); during the 1990s, Atlanta's density went up, not down (Atlanta Regional Commission 1999). What is undeniable is that Atlanta's residents are increasingly dependent on automobiles, its roads are getting more crowded, its air pollution is getting worse, and its growth is very unevenly distributed, as illustrated by some often-cited facts. The average distance Atlantans drive each day, 35 miles, is more than any other place in the United States, and the average driver is burdened with 68 hours of traffic delays and 106 excess gallons of gas wasted each year (Brookings Institution 2000). Concerning uneven development, 70 percent of the new population growth that occurred in the 1990s in the 10-county metropolitan area defined by the Atlanta Regional Commission was located on the north side (Atlanta Regional Commission 1999).

Air pollution (mainly high amounts of ground level ozone due to heavy automobile use) has increased the suffering of people with asthma and other respiratory illnesses, though the places with the highest ozone and asthma levels are the densely settled parts of Fulton and DeKalb Counties, not the suburban fringe where most of the sprawl is occurring.

The problem involves other kinds of environmental destruction, too; between 1988 and 1998 Atlanta lost 190,000 acres of tree cover to make room for expanding suburban housing, roads, shopping centers, and other buildings (Bullard, Johnson, and Torres 1999). Public hearings sponsored by the Atlanta Sierra Club in Cobb County brought out many complaints about inadequate prevention of soil erosion on construction sites that causes dirt and other materials to run off into streams, killing fish and spoiling the Chattahoochee River and nearby streams.

Finally, sprawl is associated with some interrelated economic and social concerns. Among them are the high costs of constructing the new schools, libraries, parks, police and fire stations, or other public facilities in popular new suburbs (and under-utilization in unpopular areas), not to mention the divisive issue of who should bear the burden of paying for such facilities. Another concern results from increasing land costs and zoning laws that result in little or no moderate and low-cost housing being built in some suburban counties. Since many of the new jobs created in Atlanta are located in these counties, it is hard for lower-paid workers to live a convenient distance from their workplace, especially since there is little or no public transit in the outer suburbs. This not only hurts their employment opportunities, but also has become an issue for some employers who complain that they cannot find or keep workers due to lack of low-cost housing and public transportation in the area. Suburban expansion and dispersal may also widen the divisions within and between Atlanta's racial-ethnic groups, though evidence suggests that recent suburban sprawl here is not associated with increased residential segregation between whites and blacks and other racial categories (Jaret 2000). Critics blame weaknesses in the 1989 Georgia Planning Act, which requires little in the way of implementation of land use plans, and existing zoning ordinances, which, according to an Atlanta attorney who regularly represents developers, "cause us to segregate our land uses, which means we must get in our cars to go from office to shop to home and back again. They also promote cultural, racial and economic segregation" (Goldberg 1998, D-5).

Of course, many and perhaps most Atlantans do not perceive urban sprawl to be a problem. They put themselves deep into debt or commit themselves to long job commutes in order to live near or on the suburban edge, far away from what they feel are more serious problems (but even then, as events in suburban Rockdale County show, they do not always escape some of those problems).[2] As Mark Fitzgerald, executive director of the Atlanta Home Builders Association, says, "One man's 'sprawl' may be another's slice of heaven," and while he does not like sprawl—which he attributes to unnecessarily tight zoning laws—he also dislikes the idea of "a lot of new laws prescribing what type of development they can do" (Billips 2000, 80).

For others the lure of a larger home and big yard (and the accompanying tax breaks, status, and increased wealth from equity in a home appreciating in value), along with better schools and public services, lower taxes, less crime, and more space or privacy, create personal preferences that encourage sprawl. Developers and zoning officials are very adept at creating places that cater to these preferences, enabling sprawl to expand even into areas where some public opposition to suburban growth exists. To these individuals and other supporters of the existing suburban layout and way of life, proposals for higher-density, mixed-use communities that rely on public transportation sound threatening and are often dismissed as the ideas of "eco-cranks," "liberals," or "dictatorial" elitist social engineers (Wooten 2000; Wilson 2000). Clearly, those who would like to see a slowing or ending of urban sprawl and more "smart growth" have their work cut out for them.

## Atlanta's Suburban Expansion in Review

Suburban growth beyond downtown Atlanta began over a century ago with development of Midtown and Inman Park. This section summarizes this suburbanization from the past to the present eras and highlights the main forces behind it.

In the 1870s and 1880s, Richard Peters and George W. Adair were the entrepreneurs most responsible for creating residential options for Atlantans in areas beyond the core of the city (Klima 1982). Peters and Adair owned the trolley company in Atlanta as well as large tracts of undeveloped land. Adair's land was southwest, in West End, and Peters owned 405 acres on the northern periphery of downtown in what is now Midtown. They intentionally and shrewdly built the trolley lines directly to and through their land, enhancing its accessibility, and then sold off land parcels to people who could afford to move away from the increasingly congested and commercial sections of downtown. Peters was more successful at this than Adair; he grew very wealthy from the sale of his suburban land and the use of the trolley. He built his own mansion in this area and marketed the land in ways calculated to attract Atlanta's upper class. This started the pattern of uneven development resulting in the most affluent people living on the north side. A reporter asked Peters why he initially sold rather large parcels of land to the first rich purchasers at prices below what they could have afforded to pay. Peters said:

> It has made the rest of my property valuable. I have sold many an acre at $1,000 that is now worth $10,000. But if I hadn't sold a good many acres at that price, the town would have gone in another direction and none of my land would have been valuable. It has always been my policy to sell to good citizens on the best terms. I have never sold less than an acre at a time and have fought the small lot system steadily (Klima 1982, 76).

Peters' words, spoken in 1884, clearly show that the impetus for large-lot zoning, a desire to cater to the affluent consumer of residential space, and the ambition to direct the growth of the community toward one's own suburban land (thereby making it a more profitable commodity for sale) all have deep historical roots in Atlanta.

Another important site in Atlanta's early suburbanization is Inman Park, just over a mile from the center of downtown. Like Midtown and West End, it is now a city neighborhood, but was developed initially as a suburb for the social and economic elite. Its developer, Joel Hurt, was a real estate entrepreneur who conceived this community and built a trolley line between it and downtown to carry business owners, managers, and professionals to and from work as well as shoppers patronizing the downtown stores. Hurt tried to apply some design principles that Frederick Law Olmsted proposed earlier for suburban Riverside, outside Chicago. But, as historian Rick Beard (1982) shows, Hurt was not very successful in doing so, and for that and other reasons Inman Park did not live up to Hurt's dream as a successful upper-class suburb.

Inman Park is useful, however, in showing historical dynamics of suburban expansion in Atlanta. It illustrates the reality that suburbs are in competition with each other for residents and the powerful effects that federal and banks' home loan policies can have. Specifically, 10 to 20 years after Inman Park's initial development, two other prestigious new suburbs, Ansley Park and Druid Hills, began to attract actual and potential residents of Inman Park. Both Ansley Park (north of Midtown along Peachtree Street) and Druid Hills (east of Inman Park along Ponce de Leon Avenue) were farther from the downtown area. They were larger neighborhoods that had bigger lots, better landscaping, and more of the amenities desired by upper-class residents than Inman Park. By the

1920s, Inman Park was not attracting the more affluent homebuyers, and developers subdivided its open space for much smaller bungalow homes to sell to middle-income purchasers. Inman Park, like many areas, was relatively stagnant in the 1930s and 1940s. Furthermore, in the post–World War II era, Inman Park lost out in the competition for new residents and new construction compared with suburbs located farther out (e.g., Sandy Springs and suburban DeKalb County). Federal housing policies made guaranteed home mortgage loans available to new suburban areas but not to neighborhoods like Inman Park, and federal transportation policy subsidized highways to the more automobile-oriented suburbs farther out. Many large old Inman Park homes became the property of absentee landlords, were subdivided into small apartments for poor and transient renters, and became dilapidated. The community had no effective protective association (e.g., a neighborhood or civic association) and zoning changes destroyed the residential character of part of the neighborhood. A road was built through a park in the center of the neighborhood, banks "redlined" the area, and, by the late 1960s, it was one of the poorest white areas in the city.

Today we see many declining inner-ring suburbs across the country, but Inman Park's history shows that the processes that can weaken a suburb, even one that starts out as a high-status community, go back a long way. Ironically, things have changed greatly for Inman Park. From the 1970s to the present, it has been Atlanta's showcase gentrification area, and in many ways has reclaimed its short-lived original glory days. This rejuvenation process (Hiskey 1992; DeGiovanni 1984) is relevant to our concern—urban sprawl—mainly in one way. For a while in the late 1970s and early 1980s, when the success of gentrification in Inman Park and a few other in-town areas was becoming apparent, mortgage rates were high, and people were alarmed over the high cost of gasoline, some observers believed that a "back-to-the-city" movement was about to occur and that the booming development in Atlanta's outer suburbs would slow down. Clearly that did not happen; despite the gentrification of Inman Park and revitalization in other city neighborhoods, the pace of suburban sprawl actually increased in the 1980s and 1990s. Reasons for this will become apparent as we continue the historical narrative about suburbanization in Atlanta.

Ansley Park and Druid Hills were mentioned previously as Inman Park's competitor suburbs. Developed in the first two decades of the 20th century, each is important for understanding the larger picture of suburbanization. First, Ansley Park, like many early suburbs, is often thought of somewhat romantically as originating in the "use value" desire for a place that embodies the best of two worlds—city and countryside—enabling residents to be near and have access to the civilization and modern comforts of the city, but also have the pastoral beauty of nature in their yard and on their streets. However appealing that vision may have been back then or in marketing suburban communities (with names like Edenwilde or Laurel Brooke) today, it is crucial to realize one thing: sub-urban developers like Edwin P. Ansley (the developer of Ansley Park) and homebuyers have more than just use value in mind—they have their hearts set on profit and "exchange value." Simply stated, we would not have suburban expansion if large numbers of people did not see it to be in their financial interest to purchase land and build homes on the fringes of built-up areas. It is illuminating to see how clear Ansley was in appealing to people's desire for profit in his effort to interest people in his new suburb. An advertising brochure for Ansley Park, circa 1908, dis-played at the Atlanta Historical Center says:

> Do you realize that just nine years ago this was virgin forest? Nothing but woods. It is not difficult, is it, to look at this picture [brochure picture shows large homes under construction] and see at a glance that tremendous profits were made in the transformation. These profits, many as high as 100 to 300 percent . . . went to those who bought lots from Edwin P. Ansley. *You* are offered practically the same opportunity today. And the terms are far more attractive. GET BUSY! Catch opportunity before she slips away. Only 31 more lots remain. Every man who bought a lot . . . has made money—good money. Every man who has touched them has proven a Midas, they have made gold for him.

Many initial buyers of parcels in Ansley Park (and Inman Park) were speculators with no desire to live there themselves; they were merely waiting for the area to become popular so they could sell to someone else and make a profit. Here too, Ansley Park, which was the first Atlanta suburb specifically designed to accommodate automobile driving (with broader streets and traffic circles) surpassed Inman Park (Beard 1982). With the governor's mansion located in it (until 1967) and the Piedmont Driving Club, an exclusive upper-class institution, adjacent to it, Ansley Park maintained its prestigious status, though it did experience a decline in the 1960s that was soon turned around by the efforts of the remain-ing affluent and influential residents.

Druid Hills is an affluent suburb that developed in the first third of the 1900s on the eastern edge of the city, with portions extending into unincorporated DeKalb County. It was designed to be more than a set of houses that were expensive but good financial investments; Druid Hills' developers and homeowners tried to create a sense of community. Its parks and some other features were drawn up by Frederick Law Olmsted, and residents took seriously Olmsted's belief that suburban life should revolve around harmonious association and cooperation in a community characterized by close interaction and friendship among families. Druid Hills' social institutions cultivated this sense of community: many strong churches, a garden club, a large and powerful neighborhood association, and an old exclusive country club (which made it the forerunner of today's large suburban "golf communities" on the urban periphery). The result was a stable, sheltered, isolated, exceedingly private suburban community composed of well-to-do white families with a rich network of family and business relations (Ambrose 1982). To this day, Druid Hills has the strongest neighborhood association in Atlanta and it takes an extremely protective stance against any potential risk to property values, quality of life, or the historical ambience of the suburb. In recent land use controversies, the association's wealth and organizational skill have defeated plans by the state Department of Transportation, the Metropolitan Atlanta Rapid Transit Authority (MARTA), and a subsidiary of the Marriott International Hotel corporation. Thus, in several respects, Druid Hills' history epitomizes the upper-status residential suburban enclave.

The 1920s and 1930s were not periods of much new suburban growth in Atlanta. Most development in the 1920s focused on the downtown area, where several tall business buildings were constructed. However, two suburban developments in the 1920s should be noted. One was that trolley lines and residential growth moved north along Peachtree Street, beyond Buckhead, up to the Brookhaven area. There, at the end of the line, on one side of Peachtree Street, the transit company had very modest houses built for some of its workers; independent of that, on the other side of Peachtree, builders laid out a private golf and country club and an exclusive neighborhood with homes for much wealthier families. This early example of the suburban movement of people of modest means (streetcar workers) also illustrates a continuing tendency: despite sometimes living in close residential proximity, less affluent residents are not considered part of more affluent people's neighborhoods and are not integrated into their community life.

A second noteworthy suburban development in the 1920s was the creation of Avondale Estates, east of Decatur, by George F. Willis. Willis was a wealthy man with almost no real estate experience, but he had a strong desire to create "a model residential suburb, using international experts in civil engineering to make it the most remarkable in the country" (Avondale Estates Historical Society 1976, 2). He poured his fortune into creating a quite self-contained, small suburban municipality with fine amenities (e.g., its own parks, lakes, playgrounds, schools, and retail shops). It was probably Atlanta's first "themed community" (Gottdiener 1997), as all the stores and buildings on its few central blocks have an English Tudor design, much of the town's landscaping reflects British styles, and the town's name, Avondale Estates, as well as many of its street names (e.g., Exeter, Stratford, Sussex) convey an English motif. This and the fact that it has had a reputation for discouraging blacks and other outsiders "who have no business here" from entering, make it the forerunner of many of today's gated and themed neighborhoods in Atlanta's outlying suburbs. Due to the Great Depression, the 1930s saw little city or suburban growth (in fact, it brought numerous home foreclosures in Avondale Estates and other city and suburban areas); this was true nationally as well as in Atlanta.

World War II had important ramifications for Atlanta's modern suburban era. War production rapidly increased the population living in the city and outlying areas. Several large federal installations were built or expanded throughout the metropolitan area (e.g., Camp Gordon, on the suburban northeast; Fort McPherson, on the southwest; and the Atlanta General Depot [later Fort Gillem] in Clayton County, 15 miles from downtown) (Roth and Ambrose 1996). Factories were built or converted to make products for the war, and the largest of these, the Bell bomber facility, was located in Marietta, a suburban town in Cobb County. At its peak, Bell employed 30,000 workers, and the housing needs of workers at factories and military sites were enormous. This situation resulted in considerable new suburban housing that was small and inexpensive.

Meanwhile, in DeKalb County, directly east of the city of Atlanta, Scott Candler, county commissioner from 1939 to 1955, set up a system that would ultimately encourage more dispersed suburban settlement. Candler created the "urban county" concept, wherein DeKalb County would provide vital services to residents living in all unincorporated parts of the county (which, in DeKalb and most metropolitan Atlanta counties, is a large majority of the land area). Urban services that in many other places were provided by a city or municipal government only (e.g., garbage collection, water and sewage, police and fire protection, libraries) became, under Candler, available to residents and businesses even if they located themselves outside of DeKalb's existing suburban towns, such as Decatur, Avondale Estates, or Stone Mountain. Availability of these services encouraged the development of suburban homes and commercial sites in DeKalb's unincorporated areas, much of which had been dairy farms. The county population almost doubled during Candler's years in office, and from the 1940s through the 1960s, DeKalb became the primary area of suburban growth in the metropolitan area, with dispersed housing subdivisions, schools, and shopping centers springing up across most of the county. Other counties in metropolitan Atlanta borrowed Candler's innovation, which further encouraged the expansive development of subdivisions and malls outside existing towns.

The infrastructure and improvements made in DeKalb after Candler instituted the "urban county" service provision program for suburbanites were costly. Here, too, Candler was a local innovator; he sought and used money the federal government made available for construction or other projects (unlike many southern politicians, who denounced the federal government or certain of its agencies' programs and did not aggressively seek federal money). The desire for and success in obtaining federal funds demonstrated by Candler, Atlanta mayors, and officials in counties across the metropolitan area were vital components in the vast expansion of Atlanta's suburbs, especially with regard to the highway system. The Lochner Report, issued in 1946 by an outside traffic consultant, said that Atlanta needed a highway system to allow the growing number of suburbanites to drive into the city for work each day. Atlanta officials, as early as 1949, sought and obtained funds from federal and state government for highway construction and, with the start of the national interstate highway building project in 1956, more federal money was obtained. The result in Atlanta is a highway system that resembles the one proposed in the Lochner Report, but it has had a profoundly different impact than originally imagined. Rather than being a conduit for suburban access to the city of Atlanta, the highways have made outlying areas more accessible, and places near highway exits have become nodes of development (either low-density sprawl or high-density "edge cities") that appear farther and farther from the city.

Also in the post–World War II era, tensions and fears connected to racism resulted in decisions that extended the color line, increased residential separation of black and white Atlantans, and spurred suburban sprawl. African-American residential pockets existed on Atlanta's out-skirts beginning with the end of the Civil War, but by the early 20th cen-tury, the large black neighborhoods were close to the downtown core. Outward expansion into previously white areas occurred, producing conflict that the city tried to minimize by creating a zoning ordinance that dictated areas in which each race could reside. But in the 1920s, the color line was breeched along Ashby Street, on the west side, when black businessman Heman Perry's real estate enterprises built homes for middle-class blacks in the Washington Park area (White 1982). A period of resi-dential accommodation ensued, with city officials and the real estate industry acting to maintain and stabilize black and white areas. By the late 1940s and throughout the 1950s and 1960s, however, the pent-up demand for more housing for an overcrowded black community could no longer be restrained. Blacks began moving into what had been all-white neighborhoods on the west side. White residents opposed the entry of black neighbors, and city politicians and planners tried to manage the situation to minimize conflict and violence. They, along with organiza-tions like the West Side Mutual Development Committee, worked out "gentlemen's agreements" that defined new areas of black and white res-idence in western suburban areas. One tactic was for blacks or sympa-thetic whites to secretly purchase land out beyond existing white areas and then build homes for blacks on that land. Also, whites who agreed to give up their homes in one area, allowing it to "go black," were promised good terms on home loans for housing in suburban areas farther out from the city (Bayor 1996). In other areas, the arrival of blacks as neigh-bors resulted in the whites moving away, usually to more distant suburbs. The key point here is that whites' desire to avoid living with or near blacks has been a strong factor in promoting suburban expansion.

From the mid-1940s through the mid-1960s, when new suburban housing was built on the east side (mainly in DeKalb County), whites occupied the homes, and blacks were excluded. Federal Housing Admin-istration (FHA) guidelines, designed to protect property values, said that blacks were not eligible for federally guaranteed mortgage loans if they wanted to buy into a white neighborhood, and realtors' norms discour-aged racial integration in housing (Squires 1994). Besides those barriers, some early post–World War II suburban areas, like Forrest Hills, south-east of Decatur, put racially restrictive clauses in contracts for the homes, mandating that the property should be sold to a white person only. The Supreme Court ruled in 1948 (*Shelley v. Kraemer*) that these racially restrictive covenants are not enforceable in a court of law. Nevertheless, the anti-black sentiment remained strong and for many years blacks found themselves unwelcome in many of the newer suburban subdivisions of DeKalb. This changed by the early 1970s, when parts of south DeKalb experienced a severe case of blockbusting, racial steering, and foreclosures on homes low-income blacks had purchased through a HUD program. Whites quickly moved out of south DeKalb in the 1970s, often to more distant suburban areas. Here and elsewhere in Atlanta, a failure to accept black neighbors or the inability to maintain residential stability in integrated neighborhoods has fed the stream of people moving outward in Atlanta's sprawling metropolitan area.

Since the mid-1960s, suburban sprawl around Atlanta has resembled that of other large metropolitan areas, but in more extreme form. In a 1971 referendum, metropolitan area residents voted on whether or not to join the proposed MARTA public transit system (which would provide low-cost bus and train service); only Fulton and DeKalb approved it. This left the remaining suburban counties wholly dependent on automobiles for their transportation needs. Since the 1980s, the north side has seen the spread of ever more expensive and exclusive cul-de-sac suburban subdivisions and gated communities, larger and more extravagant malls, buyouts of old suburban, split-level residential areas that are replaced with post-modern office towers, and growth of the suburban "edge-city" complexes. Many of the large malls, office complexes, and hotels in the suburbs cluster in the north side's Cumberland-Galleria and Perimeter Center areas. Both surpass the downtown as retail centers and rival it as employment centers, especially for finance–insurance–real estate and some other white-collar services (Fujii and Hartshorn 1995).

Development of Cumberland-Galleria and Perimeter Center as suburban edge-city nodes was sparked in the early 1980s by the arrival of large projects created by national firms, like Trammel Crow and Gerald Hines, along with those of local developers like Tom Cousins. Heavy investment in Atlanta's northern suburbs by major national and international developers and investors added to the earlier pattern of uneven development. It started a new stage in Atlanta's suburban expansion and has strongly affected land prices and land uses, driving prices up and forcing residential use either to become more intensive or to move farther out. Cumberland-Galleria and Perimeter Center have become "suburban downtowns" and they dramatically affect the metropolitan area's economy and commuting patterns (Hartshorn and Muller 1989). Without a public governmental structure, local needs or problems are not addressed through normal political channels, and landowners, property managers, and planners in these edge cities invent private mechanisms of control over roads and space (though they are not accountable to the general public, at least not through the usual processes of representative democracy). The overall effect of Cumberland-Galleria and Perimeter Center on suburban sprawl is mixed, in that they have encouraged decentralization of the population and contributed to the dispersion of people to ever more distant northern suburbs, but they also have concentrated development into dense clusters that are beginning to form nodes and corridors of activity and residence that will be able to support mass public transit.

In the 1990s, Atlanta's suburban sprawl was widely defined as a public problem, though warning signs and some concern had appeared in the 1980s. Surprisingly, Tom Moreland, former commissioner of Georgia's Department of Transportation (which specializes in building highways), voiced alarm about unrestrained growth in the metropolitan region. In 1983, he briefly threatened to not build any more expressways in north Atlanta until "some brakes are applied to development." He said, "I'm getting sick and tired of building these highways to unclog traffic congestion and then seeing county officials approve all these developments which make traffic as bad or worse than before" (Murphy 1983, 68). The response was short-lived and an ineffective moratorium on development. An underlying problem causing sprawl was that county officials said they needed more revenue to provide services to people, so they must either raise taxes (politically unpopular hence usually avoided) or broaden the county's tax base by approving developers' projects and allowing more commercial and residential development. In cases where suburban county officials rejected growth projects, developers could sue them and often win approval because Georgia's laws generally affirm property owners' right to maximum gain from the use or sale of their land.

The 1990s' jobs and population boom in Atlanta brought new growth in the city and throughout the metropolitan area, with quite a bit occurring in counties so far away that they were not previously even considered part of metropolitan Atlanta. For example, in 1998, a developer who had speculatively purchased land years earlier in rural Jackson County got the county to approve construction of 1,000 homes and a golf course on his 1,143 acres. This development, called Mulberry Plantation, was rejected at first because the county's existing roads were too small for the anticipated traffic the development would bring. However, the head of the Georgia Department of Transportation intervened on behalf of the developer and arranged to have the state pay for the local road improvements; in addition, he offered an entrance/exit interchange providing access to Interstate 85. That arrangement made a profitable "go" for Mulberry Plantation's developer, and more residential and commercial projects in the same area are on the way (Bookman 1999). So the same land development "game" Richard Peters played in Midtown in the 1870s and 1880s is still being played today, only much farther out beyond Atlanta's city limits and with state funds subsidizing the development.

Finally, we must consider personal preferences and fears as another cause contributing to suburban sprawl. It is more than the simple desire for a nice large home and grounds and all that those things bring. As someone from suburban Marietta put it, "The truth is that people live outside the city to escape high taxes, poor public services, high crime and the lack of elbow room and breathing space" (Langley 1999). Commentator Bill Shipp (1999) asks who would want to live in a high-crime, high-tax city with bad schools when one could move farther out and feast on all the amenities there? A collective inability or unwillingness to resolve serious social problems creates a strong motive to move far away to places people think will not have those problems. While not everyone can afford to do that, many of those who can are doing so, and as Cobb and Gwinnett Counties get more expensive, people move farther out. Based on the standard that housing should cost no more than 30 percent of one's income, 60 percent of the people working in Cobb County cannot afford the average rent ($783 for a two-bedroom apartment). With new homes and resales in Cobb costing an average of $186,000 and $142,600, respectively, people who cannot afford them go to more distant areas, like the man who bought a house in Paulding County for $98,000 and said, "I drive an extra 10 miles and save myself $50,000" (Williams 2000, H1).

In sum, Atlanta currently has a large inner-suburban zone that many criticize for being too congested with traffic, too destructive to air and water quality, and too expensive for most ordinary people to live in. The response has been high levels of movement to and development of suburban areas like the northernmost parts of Fulton, Cobb, and Gwinnett, as well as Forsyth, Cherokee, Paulding, Henry, and Fayette Counties, which lie farther out and offer, at least for now, more reasonably priced homes, less traffic, and less air pollution, but bring more gasoline consumption and longer commutes to work, more land erosion and destruction of the natural habitat, and expensive investment in new schools, roads, services, and infrastructure.

## Two Exceptional Suburbs?

In the midst of this massive metropolitan peripheral expansion, two suburban places seem like exceptions—Decatur (just east of the city in DeKalb County) and Peachtree City (about 30 miles south of Atlanta in Fayette County). They show signs of possibly being alternatives to some problems facing the city and sprawling suburbs. A look at what has been done in these two communities provides a good lead into the next section, which examines three recent responses to urban sprawl in Atlanta.

Its boosters are now dubbing Decatur, a small suburban town older than the city of Atlanta, "the poster child for smart growth." Its small downtown, built around an old courthouse and village square, is thriving with small restaurants and shops flanked by government and commercial office buildings. This is a far cry from what people in the 1970s and 1980s thought the future held for Decatur. It looked then like Decatur would be decimated by a combination of middle-class white flight and the inconvenient disruption associated with construction of a MARTA train line right through the downtown area. Most of the old established businesses closed, property values were declining, and a sense of failure engulfed many residents. Town leaders were so desperate to improve the tax base that they drew up a plan that would clear out most of downtown Decatur, including the historic courthouse and village square, and turn it into a large shopping mall. Many of Decatur's remaining residents rallied against it and, in 1982, devised the "Town Center Plan" to revitalize the town. This plan stressed rehabilitation and renovation of old buildings. Stores and offices in them benefited from the excellent access the completed MARTA train line provided to downtown Decatur. The town was also helped by the growth that Emory University was experiencing (which, in turn, was largely due to huge financial contributions from the highly profitable Coca-Cola Company), since Emory began to rent a lot of office space in Decatur. Finally, Decatur's location in central DeKalb and its good access to downtown Atlanta via MARTA made its relatively low-priced housing very desirable to middle-class blacks and whites who were attracted rather than repelled by the prospect of a stable, racially integrated community.

Since the mid-1980s, Decatur has taken off on a cycle of small-scale development and gentrification that has made it a very popular place, with schools, housing, stores, and recreational venues in close proximity to each other. Today's Decatur retains and carefully protects its small town image. Community leaders no longer seem worried about the arrival of franchise fast food stores and "big box" chain stores, and are concerned about the side effects of "success"—rising rents that drive out small stores on the square and increased property values that make it hard for older poor residents, especially blacks, to remain in Decatur (Hill 2000).

Compared with Decatur, Peachtree City is a community of recent origin. It was created and incorporated in 1959 by Peter Knox and Joel Cowan, who purchased 15,500 acres of farmland in hopes of developing it into a "new town" like the "garden cities" built by Ebenezer Howard and his followers in England. In planning this community they were ahead of the short-lived "new town movement" that arose in the late 1960s, and in relying on private financing they got no funding or subsidies from the now-forgotten Urban Growth and New Community Development Act (Title VII of the 1970 Housing and Urban Development Act). Progress in building Peachtree City was slow and it almost failed, but by 1979 about 6,000 people lived there. From the start, its vision was to be a coherently planned, medium-sized mixed-use suburb that provides a variety of housing types and prices, employment opportunities, retail services, and social institutions (e.g., schools, churches, clubs, and voluntary organizations) while also giving residents abundant open green space. Presently about 33,000 people live in Peachtree City, and they are organized into four "villages" linked by roads and paths for bikes, walkers, and golf carts. Although some people work within the suburb, many work at Hartsfield Airport or other places; however, the residents' average commute to work takes 17 minutes, which is half the average commuting time for the rest of Atlanta's metropolitan area (Cowles 1999). A majority of the homes are on quarter- or half-acre lots, though some have more than an acre of land. Home prices range from the low $100,000s to over $1 million, a wider range than other suburbs with similar amenities (Brice 2000). Apartments are also included in the community, a feature not found in most other new Atlanta suburbs.

Critics of Peachtree City might say it is a classic example of "leapfrog development" and that it lacks public transportation and the density levels that appeal to "new urbanist" designers, so it is not a solution to suburban sprawl problems. Yet if one looks at land use and travel patterns or the price mix of housing, it is obvious that Peachtree City has avoided many of the problems that plague the fast-growing northside suburbs.

## Atlanta's Response to Sprawl: Three Proposals and Actions

People representing varied interests in Atlanta have made criticisms and suggestions on the subject of sprawl. Among these are organizations representing homebuilders and developers, other business interests, environmental groups, civic associations, urban planners, newspaper editors and writers, state and local politicians, and academic researchers. Three of the most significant responses to the problem are discussed and evaluated here. They represent proposals that are in the early action stage— first steps toward addressing the problem. The first is the newly created Georgia Regional Transportation Authority, next is a new state law that helps growing counties create and preserve green space, and the last consists of the application of "smart growth" ideas in several suburban and city development projects.

### *The Georgia Regional Transportation Authority*

Metropolitan Atlanta's loss of federal funds for road and highway construction in 1998 (estimated at $153 million a year) due to violations of clean air guidelines provided a palpable shock to political and business leaders locally and at the state level. This termination of money generated fears of stagnation and standstill in the metropolitan area, and was enough to make leaders realize that the existing regional planning authority, the Atlanta Regional Commission (ARC), was unable to control changes in the metropolitan area's transportation system or in its land use. Decisive action to resolve this issue became an important promise in Roy Barnes' campaign for governor, and soon after being elected he proposed and convinced the legislature to create a state "superagency"—the Georgia Regional Transportation Authority (GRTA)—with considerable power to use in addressing the problem. Some misconceptions have apparently arisen about GRTA; as one source says it has placed metropolitan Atlanta under "sprawl martial law" and "given the governor unusually strong powers to control growth" (Danielsen, Lang, and Fulton 1999, 514). This is an overstatement, as will be shown below.

The Georgia Regional Transportation Authority (GRTA) was created in mid-1999. It has a 15-member board of directors appointed by the governor and a small professional staff. Joel Cowan, a central figure in the development of suburban Peachtree City, is chairman of the board of directors, and Catherine Ross, a professor of city planning from Georgia Tech, is GRTA's executive director. Also appointed to the board were John Williams (chairman and CEO of Post Properties, which formerly built large, expensive suburban apartment complexes but now claims to specialize in mixed-use "new urbanism" communities) and John Sibley (president of the Georgia Conservancy and a seasoned figure in state and local politics). Appointees from the African-American community were Martin Luther King III (president of the Southern Christian Leadership Conference and a former member of the Fulton County Commission) and Shirley Franklin (a respected and influential public figure with extensive experience in city government and a member of the Atlanta Committee for the Olympic Games), though when they resigned in mid- and late April 2000, they were replaced by two less well known African Americans.[3] The GRTA board also includes other less prominent people who have varied backgrounds but cluster in banking, law, and ownership of medium-size businesses.

GRTA has authority over 13 counties (the 10 ARC counties plus Forsyth, Coweta, and Paulding) around Atlanta with air quality that violates federal pollution standards. Since GRTA's jurisdiction does not exactly align with Atlanta's metropolitan area boundaries as defined by ARC, the key regional planning agency, some administrative and political difficulties will be inevitable, and it cannot deal with sprawl occurring out beyond the 13 counties.

GRTA's first major action was to review the three-year transportation plan for metropolitan Atlanta recently submitted by ARC, and then decide whether or not to approve it. This plan, which designates how almost $2 billion will be spent on transportation projects (e.g., widening of existing roads, new roads, bridges, public transit, bike lanes, sidewalks, and HOV lanes) in metropolitan Atlanta over the next three years, is part of a larger 25-year regional transportation plan that ARC developed. The 25-year plan must contain realistic proposals and projections for a transportation system that will generate low levels of air pollutants and meet federal air quality standards, otherwise federal transportation funds will remain cut off. ARC claims that the new 25-year plan it approved and submitted in March 2000 does this successfully. It proposes $18 billion for new and expanded public transit systems and $500 million for new side-walks and bike paths, along with $11 billion for new or expanded roads.

However, opposition to ARC's transportation plan arose from two sources. First, several environmental groups in Atlanta, such as the Sierra Club with its "Challenge to Sprawl Campaign" and Georgians for Transportation Alternatives, dispute ARC's claim and say that the plan is still too road and highway oriented and does not do enough to improve air quality. Preliminary signs from two federal agencies indicated they were also critical of the plan (the 25-year plan ultimately must be approved by the Federal Transit Administration, the Federal Highway Administration, and the Environmental Protection Agency [EPA] before the transportation money now being withheld can be released to the Atlanta metropolitan area). Later, another group that opposed the ARC transportation plan spoke out against it in public. This group, the Republican Smart Growth Task Force, issued a written report that criticized the ARC plan. They claimed that ARC's plan will make Atlanta's transportation problems worse because it does not propose to build enough roads and highways to meet future needs and they defended *low* density land use as a solution to traffic congestion. The editorial boards of the *Journal* and the *Constitution* (despite being owned by the same company and often carrying identical news articles) joined the argument on opposite sides, with the *Journal's* Jim Wooten siding with the Republican Smart Growth Task Force position, and the *Constitution's* Jay Bookman defending ARC's transportation plan.

GRTA held public hearings on the three-year plan in early May 2000 and then postponed a decision on it until several questions and concerns raised in the hearings and in a lawsuit brought by environmental groups[4] could be answered. These issues centered on (a) the accuracy of data ARC used in making its projections of vehicle emissions (i.e., questions were raised about their estimates of average vehicle speeds and the mix of vehicles now on the roads because some of the data used were 10 years old); (b) the willingness of suburban counties to contribute local tax money to fund their share of road improvement and public transit expenses and to permit higher-density residential zoning in areas along transportation corridors; (c) the extent of input that African Americans had in the ARC plan and on the GRTA board (i.e., a group called the Metropolitan Atlanta Transportation Equity Coalition said that Atlanta's black community was not consulted by ARC and that the GRTA should not vote until Governor Barnes appointed replacements for two African Americans who resigned from the GRTA board in April 2000 [Simmons 2000c]).

At its June 14, 2000, meeting, the GRTA board unanimously approved the three-year ARC transportation plan. It also indicated its policy will be that if any county refuses to allow higher-density residential and business land use in certain transportation corridors or refuses to pay the local share of transportation improvements including public transit, then GRTA would withhold federal and state transportation money from the county. Earlier, federal authorities who had some misgivings about the transportation plan asked county commissioners to sign letters indicating their commitment to zoning density increases and to paying their share of the plan's costs, but most county leaders refused to do so (only Cherokee, Clayton, DeKalb, and Paulding Counties complied). So as an assurance to the federal authorities and to encourage them to approve the plan, the GRTA board issued its resolution threatening to deny funds to uncooperative counties (Simmons 2000b, d). The EPA then gave its approval to the motor vehicle emissions aspects of the transportation plan.

The U.S. Department of Transportation (DOT) still had to give its final approval to the transportation plan. On July 18, 2000, however, the 11th U.S. Circuit Court of Appeals stopped further action on the plan until it could hear the case in September 2000. The court's decision was in response to a lawsuit by the Southern Environmental Law Center, which sued the EPA in hopes of getting Atlanta's transportation plan modified to give higher priority to air quality, with more emphasis on public transit and other nonautomobile modes of transportation (Simmons 2000e). The court's ruling would delay approval of the larger 25-year plan and, more importantly for now, it would hold up the release of federal transportation money withheld since 1998.

It appeared that unless a deal or compromise could be struck, the situation would remain stalemated. Then, on July 26, DOT pulled a move designed to get around the circuit court's "hold" on approval of ARC's transportation plan. DOT approved a slightly different plan, one that on paper looks more stringent but probably is not. (The plan that the court halted action on claimed to be able to reduce nitrous oxide emissions from the current 264 tons a day to 224 tons by the year 2003; the transportation plan that the DOT approved promises to lower it to 214 tons per day by 2005 [McCosh 2000]). Since many county and business leaders want the flow of transportation funds to resume as soon as possible, they were happy about DOT's action. On the other hand, the environmental groups were angered by it since they believe that most of it is "road-building money" and a delay or halt in highway construction is beneficial for air quality. They agree with a *Constitution* editor, who earlier had written that a delay in releasing the money will slow down the pouring of "more sprawl-inducing asphalt in the countryside" and give more time to think up and mobilize support for needed alternative transportation solutions for the region ("GRTA Must Lead on Regional Plan" 2000, A14). During the second half of 2000, both sides negotiated for a regional transportation plan that met their needs and interests, and it appeared that they succeeded in producing one on which they could agree. But in early 2001, amid mutual distrust and charges of bad faith negotiating, the agreement fell through. The environmental groups were not satisfied that the new plan would effectively provide sufficient public transit alternatives to automobile-oriented road construction, and they filed lawsuits aimed at reversing the transportation plan's approval and halting the plan's highway projects that they oppose for air quality reasons. For most of 2001, the matter was tied up in litigation, though in June a judge ruled against a lawsuit seeking to cut off funds for road and highway construction.

At present (early November 2001), GRTA finds itself deep in controversy as it must consider ARC's proposal for a new three-year regional transportation improvement plan (for 2002–2004). While this plan gives a substantial percentage of money to public transit and high-occupancy vehicle lane construction, it also will fund many road-building projects that critics claim will increase pollution, sprawl, and automobile dependency. Most troubling is the plan's inclusion of $25 million for engineering and design work on a highway called the Northern Arc. Although Governor Barnes seems to be pushing for the construction of this new highway, environmental groups, many business leaders from the Metro Atlanta Chamber of Commerce, and local elected officials strongly oppose it, in part because it seems likely that it would stimulate even more unbalanced outward growth on the northern edge of metropolitan Atlanta. The looming battle over the Northern Arc will probably become GRTA's most visible real and symbolic challenge in its attempt to rein in urban sprawl.

GRTA's larger charge is to oversee all transportation and some related land use planning in the 13-county Atlanta region. In doing this, GRTA interacts with other official bodies and government agencies. As already noted, GRTA is above the Atlanta Regional Commission, and any transportation plans and related land use recommendations ARC makes are subject to GRTA's review, as are large residential and commercial projects deemed to have significant regional impact. GRTA will interact with the Georgia Department of Transportation, the agency responsible for building state roads and highways, and GRTA can veto their plans. Some observers think that getting the legislature to give GRTA that power over the state DOT was Governor Barnes' major political coupe in this matter.

In dealing with local governments (i.e., municipal and county officials), GRTA has considerable but not total power. This is where some dicey showdowns will occur. Local officials' decision to build a large development (residential, commercial, or industrial) can be vetoed by GRTA if the board thinks it creates excessive traffic or pollution problems. However, the local government can override GRTA's veto if it can obtain a three-fourths vote in favor of the project from its county commission or city council. GRTA, in turn, can deny federal funds and make the local jurisdiction bear the cost of the transportation system needed by the project in question. Board member John Williams urged GRTA to adopt the resolution stipulating that in order for counties to receive funds from the ARC three-year transportation plan, they must agree to accept public mass transit and adopt zoning for denser residential and commercial development. Even before the GRTA board adopted that policy, however, several officials from outlying suburban counties condemned it, arguing that it goes beyond the authority the legislature gave to GRTA. Jim Wooten, an *Atlanta Journal* editor, raised concerns about GRTA being anti-suburban and perhaps dictatorial. We can expect conflict and litigation on this matter.

Finally, GRTA will be in a strong position when it deals with county and local public transit authorities (e.g., MARTA, Cobb Community Transit [CCT], and the new bus systems Gwinnett County and Clayton County are now developing). Public transit trains now exist only in Fulton and DeKalb, but GRTA has the authority to extend existing rail lines into new areas, combine existing bus systems into a consolidated system, or build and operate a new mass transit system. GRTA acted quickly in announcing that it would start a public bus system in Clayton County, and in a July 2000 referendum residents there voted in favor of it by a 53 percent to 47 percent margin, prompting Clayton County commissioners to support the idea.

On May 17, 2000, federal highway administrators approved the data ARC used in its 25-year transportation plan. They also said they would release the federal transportation money now being withheld if metropolitan Atlanta county leaders gave written assurance of a commitment to (a) spend county money to pay the local portion of the costs of ARC's transportation plan and (b) change zoning laws to permit denser mixed-use developments. Eager for the federal money, many metropolitan county officials promised to spend local tax money to pay for the county's share of the transportation improvements (although Fulton County said it did not have the money and therefore could not make that promise). However, county officials suggested that changing zoning laws enough to satisfy federal agencies and ARC would be harder and could entail lawsuits, and in the end most counties did not give federal authorities the written assurances they wanted. GRTA's position was that it will not approve the ARC three-year spending plan for transportation improvements until the federal officials' concerns were satisfied (Simmons 2000a), and it lobbied hard to get federal approval.

Clearly, GRTA can affect patterns of development in Atlanta in a variety of ways. It is still too early to see how and where GRTA flexes these muscles in attempting to control or redirect growth in the metropolitan area. It will become enmeshed in political conflict and will make controversial decisions that affect people's fortunes. It will have a significant impact, but the idea that it will be able to stop urban sprawl in its tracks seems unrealistic.

## Preserving "Green Space"

In late February 2000, following another initiative by Governor Barnes, the state legislature passed a bill that addresses a common criticism of suburban expansion, namely the replacement of open land by so many roads, houses, stores, offices, and other buildings that little remains for trees, fields, or parkland. This action, called the Georgia Community Greenspace Initiative, creates a pool of $30 million that is available in 2001 to 40 rapidly growing counties around the state (including most counties in the Atlanta metropolitan area) to use to purchase land that will remain undeveloped and used for such things as parks, camping, boating, hiking, jogging and biking trails, agriculture, or forestry. The details of this plan were crafted in a way that produced bipartisan support and virtually no opposition, as it is attractive to people seeking use value and exchange value. In Governor Barnes's words, "Preserving green space is a sensible investment . . . in our quality of life, for our pocketbooks and for our children" (Pruitt 2000a, B5). Alluding to the use value benefits of the land set aside for green space, one legislator said, "This is really intended to be sort of a quiet area. Basically what we're trying to do is have areas where people can get away from the crowd noises of the city, get away from the hubbub." Another legislator, testifying to its exchange value benefits, said, "When you develop property and set aside green space and trees, it's an asset to your property. I get higher rents when I have extra buffers on my property" (Pruitt 2000b, A1). A local business columnist observed that "twenty years ago, tennis courts were the #1 amenity people wanted where they lived. Ten years ago, it was a golf course. Now it's walking trails and green ways" (Saporta 2000, D2). She then added the optimistic prediction that properties lying nearby the preserved green space will rise in value, so the counties that participate in the green space program also will be rewarded with increased tax revenues generated by the rising property values.

The details of this green space policy have interesting implications that need discussion. This analysis focuses on its voluntary nature, its funding level and source, and its possible effects on affordable housing. The way the policy works is that in order to receive any money, a rapidly growing county must formulate a plan that sets aside and permanently protects 20 percent of its total land area from development. These plans were to be submitted by December 2000 to a newly created Georgia Greenspace Commission, which then decided whether or not to approve each plan. If it is approved, the county receives a grant of money, which it then uses to begin purchasing and, if desired, creating the parkland or trails. This green space plan is wholly voluntary in that county officials can choose whether or not to create a plan and apply for the funds. To defuse potential opposition to the plan, Governor Barnes backed off an initial proposal that would have negatively sanctioned counties that did not plan to set aside and maintain 20 percent of their land in an undeveloped status. This disappointed some people who hoped that the state would push counties to set aside green space. In any event, the state plan is not the only option available; indeed, it is intended to encourage other voluntary green space initiatives at more local levels. So regardless of whether a county participates in this state-funded green space program, municipalities can, via their city councils and/or voters, choose to purchase land for green space using their own revenues or they may be part of a county plan and receive money from the state's green space grant to the county. Roswell, an old town in Atlanta's northern suburbs, has approved its own $30 million program for acquiring land for green space, and other local governments have also been acquiring undeveloped land allegedly for green space (Saporta 2000).

Georgia's Community Greenspace Initiative is funded annually, without a dedicated source, and the money comes from residential property taxes paid to the state by the rapidly growing counties. The governor said that in future years he will ask the state legislature for at least as much as was obtained for 2001 ($30 million), but nothing is guaranteed. Many green space advocates had hoped the plan would have included a secure source of tax revenue. Even some of the plan's supporters are critical of the amount of money involved. Wayne Hill, chairman of the Gwinnett County Commission, said that the amount his county is eligible for this year ($3 million) "could be spent in an hour on one little piece of land," and business reporter Maria Saporta (2000) notes that Georgia's initial foray into saving undeveloped land in rapidly growing metropolitan areas pales in comparison with the commitments made by New Jersey ($1.5 billion), Florida ($3 billion), and California ($4 billion).

It is hard to predict the impact of this green space plan. Some developers, property owners, and real estate interests may think setting aside 20 percent of a county's land is too much and might lobby the county officials against participating in it. In rapidly growing counties, however, supply-and-demand economics imply that setting aside 20 percent for green space would raise the value and cost of the remaining land. While property owners might be pleased with this outcome if they want to sell, it means higher land costs for residential developers, which is a disincentive for building inexpensive homes. If precautions are not taken to make it financially realistic to build low-cost housing in growing counties that set aside green space, the result will be continued "pricing out" of the less affluent. This means that much of the environmental benefits and use value of the green space would be unevenly distributed along socioeconomic lines. This is not idle speculation; some of the talk in favor of Roswell's purchase of land for green space was that doing so would prevent a developer from buying the land and building an apartment complex on it, presumably for less affluent renters.

## "Smart Growth" Development

No discussion of suburban sprawl can occur without mentioning the latest buzzwords—"smart growth." This loosely defined approach to

planning and development connotes denser, energy-efficient, environmentally friendly settlements that mix residential, office, retail, and institutional functions; development sites that use existing infrastructure and,
if possible, renovation of old buildings rather than new "leapfrog" development; layouts that promote walking or bicycling and have linkages to
public transit systems; and homes that have smaller yards but are close to
plenty of communal open space, such as public parks. These "smart
growth" ideas took longer to gain popularity in Georgia than they did in
several other states. Now, however, they are enthusiastically embraced
and promoted by several developers in Atlanta and by some county officials and neighborhood leaders. ARC has established a program, the "Livable Centers Initiative," to fund "smart growth" feasibility studies or to
implement these projects in a dozen areas, including West End, Peachtree
City, Sandy Springs, Chamblee, Canton, and Douglasville.

Projects and proposals aiming to use this approach are described later
in this section, but we should note that "smart growth," despite its current cachet, also has its opponents in Atlanta. Articles have been written
claiming that smart growth will have a harmful effect on continued economic development and will reduce the supply of affordable housing
for low-income people (Lawler 2001). A project called Vickery (Forsyth
County), designed by leading "new urbanist" architect Andres Duany
and proposed as "the smart growth model for metro Atlanta" had its
density level reduced and its lofts and affordable housing component
eliminated in a rezoning vote by the Forsyth County Commission. Some
of this opposition is rooted in an antidevelopment "no more growth"
mentality that has become popular among many suburban homeowner
associations. Speaking of his constituents, the mayor of Conyers (in suburban Rockdale County) said that for many of them "smart growth
equals pro growth, and that's not going to sell in our community. People
think we can just put a gate on I-20 and shut growth out." Similarly,
speaking for her suburban constituents, the commission chair for a
north suburban county noted that "most people in Cherokee County
today think smart growth will mean that they'll be packed in like sar-
dines" (McCosh 1999, E-8). County elections in August 1998 saw this
antigrowth movement defeat some Cherokee County commissioners
who were perceived as too favorable to developers and bring in new
ones, like Emily Lemcke (the new commission chairperson), who promised to curtail rampant development. Also, in recent Cobb County elections strong support by suburban homeowners associations brought

two "anti-sprawl" commissioners to office, and the trend toward electing "slow-growth" candidates continued and spread to other counties in 2000 (Gilpin 1999; Frankston 2000c).

Research on antigrowth movements elsewhere in the United States suggests that they usually are not too successful in holding back growth (Logan and Zhou 1989; Vogel and Swanson 1989; Warner and Molotch 1995). This will probably prove true in Atlanta, too. Even though at least two suburban developments that were presented as "smart growth" projects were rejected recently, zoning decisions made in response to those and other proposals show that the preference for low-density living centered on automobile travel between separated residential and commercial areas still runs strong and leaves the door open for much more of that type of development. One of those proposals was a small (26-acre) "live-work-play" project in Rockdale County near its border with Newton County. County commissioners rejected it on grounds that it is inconsistent with the county's comprehensive plan and also because the area lacks the infrastructure to support that sort of project, though existing land use zoning allows the developer to build an all-residential subdivision on that same parcel of land. The developer's attorney said, "We wanted to use the commercial facilities to keep traffic off Salem Road. Now, people will just have to go across town to do their shopping." This comment implies that the proposed mixed-use project would not have increased auto traffic congestion or produced much air pollution, but in denying it, the outcome for the county is likely to be single-family residential subdivision development that generates those adverse side effects. A spokesperson for GRTA indicated that it would not take a position on this specific site or project, indicating that there is "a right place and a wrong place for everything." But he described GRTA's position by saying that "people should have the option of living in places where they don't have to make as many trips in their cars—by being near either mass transit or their work, stores and parks," and added that GRTA would see it as a problem if county officials seemed unwilling to consider or approve any projects of that type (Nurse 2000, B3).

The second case is a much more ambitious suburban "smart growth" idea that was rejected in Cherokee County. The former planning department director led the county in creating an innovative land use plan that defined 13 "townships"—areas in which "smart growth" would occur, while outside the townships the land would retain its rural character. In the townships, each with its own architectural style, businesses and residences would be built close together. Sidewalks and biking and hiking trails would be built and much land would be left as open space. Although this plan, adopted in 1997, drew praise in some planning circles, most Cherokee County residents disliked it and were angry that they had not been involved in formulating it. Opposition came from landowners (some were from families that had farmed the land for generations and recognized that selling off to a developer could earn them a great deal of money, and others were owners who purchased the land as speculative investment) who fought against the county's attempt to control how they used and profited from their land. Additional opposition came from neighborhood associations that did not want to permit homes to be built on smaller-sized lots and did not want to allow stores to be built close to homes. They made the familiar "threat to property values" arguments. Sentiment against this "smart growth" plan was so intense that "township" became a dirty word in Cherokee County. With virtually no public support, the plan was repudiated by the new county commission and is all but dead (Bennett 1999).

Moreover, the Cherokee County Commission almost eliminated a key zoning classification, the "planned unit development" (PUD), that allows the building of mixed-use developments. Cherokee's PUD category (requiring at least 40 acres, with a mix of single-family and multi-family homes as well as some commercial space, and with 20 percent of the land as open green space) had been used to create communities like Lake Arrowhead, Towne Lake, and BridgeMill. But according to Cherokee County Commissioner J.J. Biello, who favored eliminating the PUD zoning category, "It is my quest to lower the density in this county. We have enough high-density to last a lifetime" (Frankston 2000a). But developers are clever and, as a countermove, they are trying to get some land lying in unincorporated Cherokee County to be annexed into a town (Canton) where local officials might be willing or eager to permit within their jurisdiction a denser development with "smart growth" features. In mid-June 2000, Cherokee County commissioners decided to place a 60-day moratorium on PUD developments and then revise the criteria for them, rather than drop them as a zoning category.

These cases suggest that efforts to restrict growth or to limit it to "smart growth" will be unsuccessful in many parts of metropolitan Atlanta and that sprawl will continue. For each tactic to stop or deal with sprawl, a counterresponse can be found.[5] Undoubtedly, the preferences of residents in outlying counties for no growth or low-density growth will collide with the calls for denser mixed-use development that GRTA and ARC are making. On May 10, 2000, the new executive director of ARC suggested giving suburban counties 18 months to adjust their land use and zoning regulations to bring them in line with proposals in ARC's transportation plan (specifically, to limit sprawl by clustering homes, shopping, and offices in newly defined mass transit corridors). Although ARC has no power to require county or local governments to do that, GRTA says it will back them up by withholding transportation money to those that do not comply (Bennett 2000). However, even if the counties in GRTA's jurisdiction do comply, there is nothing to prevent dispersed sprawl-type development from occurring in areas beyond GRTA's domain, like Bartow and Jackson Counties, and there are signs this is already happening (Bookman 1999).

Despite the above-mentioned challenges to and defeats of "smart growth" proposals in metropolitan Atlanta, this approach has some potential for success in alleviating problems of sprawl. Dan Reuter, a planner with ARC, thinks that "smart growth" is just starting to take hold across Atlanta and that the private sector is ahead of the public in trying to get zoning for these types of projects ("ARC: 'Smart Growth' Initiatives" 2000). This is true, though there are some exceptions, like Peachtree City and Decatur (discussed above), where it was embraced much earlier and where public officials were almost as involved as people from the private sector. As an indication of the private sector's current high interest in "smart growth," the Metro Atlanta Chamber of Commerce held a conference on April 24, 2000, called "The 2000 Smart Growth Employers Forum: Retrofitting and Maximizing Activity/ Employment Centers," and about 400 developers and business owners attended. In December 2000, the Urban Land Institute sponsored a well-attended, three-day "Partners for Smart Growth" conference in Atlanta. Despite these advances, however, some developers complain that some banks are still wary of lending for smart growth projects, and they face difficulties with zoning boards and neighborhood associations. Three developers whose projects illustrate the full range of sites in which smart growth is being applied in hopes of reducing suburban sprawl are highlighted below.

The first is Charles Ackerman, an Atlanta developer working with a development firm from Florida (Advantis) to create a 350-acre, mixed-use community called Manchester Pointe in College Park. This large project is notable because it is one of the few that are located on the south side of Atlanta and because it will attempt to revitalize an old "inner-ring" suburb that has been in decline for many years. College Park, a town on the south edge of the city of Atlanta, has been negatively affected by the expansion of nearby Hartsfield International Airport, white flight, business closings, and lack of new investment. Ackerman's project, built on empty land (partly due to an airport-related noise abatement buyout program), will contain single-family homes, a hotel, office and retail space, plus a golf course and other green space. The developers are keenly aware that in doing something to rejuvenate a suburb so near Atlanta's city limits they are going against the larger movement to the outer suburbs. They explained, "This is a rare opportunity. It's hard to find this large of an area to develop this close in. For the past 50 years the race has been to the next suburb. For the next 50 years, we believe the growth will be in the rebirth of urban areas" (Eckstein 2000, C3). This development is still in the planning stage and its success is uncertain, but it represents an important experiment and test in Atlanta's effort to redirect growth.

A developer who invokes "smart growth" principles in the distant suburbs is Steve Macauley. He is building the community of Ridenour on the northwest edge of the metropolitan area in Cobb County, near Kennesaw Mountain National Battlefield. It promises to be a sharp contrast to the tracts of single-family homes and regional malls surrounded by large parking lots that are so common in the outer suburbs. Ridenour is designed to have a village green and civic center at its core, along with offices and a range of stores, plus a mix of housing within a quarter-mile radius of the town center. The housing includes 350 apartments (which at the planned 21 units per acre give it the highest density in Cobb County), an assisted-living center, a day care facility, and 330 houses and condominiums (single-family homes are in the $250,000 to $450,000 range). Macauley believes the mix of different types of housing and price levels means that he is creating "a place where a schoolteacher can live in the same place as a bank president" (Netherton 1999, 40). Macauley is convinced that Ridenour will eventually be successful enough to create a strong market demand for similar places, but for now he still faces resistance from skeptical lenders at the banks and from homeowners and county officials afraid of higher-density living arrangements (Bookman 2000).

Finally, John Williams is a developer whose strong endorsement of "smart growth" policies has drawn national attention. In July 1999, he spoke to the U.S. Senate's Smart Growth Task Force advocating more residential options for people who want mixed-use, "live-work-walk" neighborhoods (Williams 1999). Future developments, he argues, "must be concentrated in areas where the infrastructure is already in place. Denser development would create transportation nodes—high-density employment centers—to be served by whatever mass transit system evolves" (Barry 1999a, 23). This represents a reversal in orientation for Williams. A *New York Times* article describes him and his company, Post Properties, as one of the reasons Atlanta became "a symbol of urban sprawl bursting out of control. Through the 1970s and 1980s, he turned thousands of acres of suburban forest into vast expanses of garden apartments. But today, Mr. Williams has become one of the nation's leading champions of renewed urbanism" (Tucker 2000, Section 3:1).

John Williams now speaks negatively of the suburbs and says he will create in-town neighborhoods that juxtapose retail, residential, office, and recreational facilities close together, but Post Parkside (on 10th St.) and Post Renaissance (near SciTrek) are merely expensive apartments with nice amenities close to downtown Atlanta. Williams' showcase project, Riverside by Post, is on a city-suburban boundary, the edge of the affluent north side of the city near the Chattahoochee River just across from suburban Cobb County. Designed by "new urbanist" architect Andres Duany, it is centered around a town square modeled after Princeton, New Jersey, and is bounded by a nine-story office building (housing Post Properties' corporate headquarters and other tenants) and a row of small stores and restaurants that have apartments (of varied sizes) above them. It aims to be a place that is friendly to walkers or bikers, and encourages people to come out and get to know each other. Most of its apartments (renting for $1,200 to $5,000) and offices are leased and it has a few homes, priced just under $1 million, for sale. Although the grounds are beautiful, one finds no playground, no day care or other features that would make it attractive to either families with children or to elderly people, and its link to public transportation is minimal. Yet Riverside by Post is hailed as a "new urbanist" success, and Williams is building places modeled after it in Denver, Phoenix, Dallas, Tampa, and Charlotte (Barry 1999b).

Of the three "smart growth" developers and projects discussed here, John Williams's Riverside and other communities are the farthest along and Post Properties is the most influential corporation. Aside from being its CEO, John Williams occupies other key positions: in January 1999 he became chair of the Metro Atlanta Chamber of Commerce, and in early 2000 he was appointed to the GRTA board of directors. He uses these positions to push for "smart growth" development by proposing that suburban counties must institute public transit and adopt denser zoning ordinances or face loss of federal transportation funds and by making Post Properties an active player in major "smart growth" development projects taking shape in the city of Atlanta.

Indeed, most "smart growth" projects in the next 10 years will be built in the city of Atlanta. The plan is to make parts of the city more attractive to affluent and middle-class residents and businesses in hopes of diminishing sprawl by diverting a substantial portion of the anticipated growth away from suburbia and into the city of Atlanta. Editors of the *Atlanta Constitution* strongly endorse and publicize the idea of "in-town living" and the "smart growth" projects that John Williams and others have planned for the city (Goldberg 2000), as do the downtown real estate interests. Southern Bell will consolidate 13,000 office jobs from suburban offices and relocate them at MARTA's major "transit-oriented developments" such as the Lindbergh City Center project, a 47-acre site intended to stimulate walking and public transit that will contain 5 million square feet of housing, offices, stores, and theaters.[6] In the next 10 years, other parts of the city will also see extensive, dense mixed-use redevelopment projects take shape. Atlanta is using Empowerment Zone and other federal funds, while the private sector is investing capital in a huge wave of building that includes converting old factories or warehouses to lofts and condominiums for residence and/or business. Public-private partnerships comprised of Atlanta Housing Authority officials and private developers are also dismantling large, public housing projects and making them into mixed-income communities and constructing new complexes that integrate office, hotel, entertainment, retail, and residential use. Besides Lindbergh City Center, other significant projects are the Atlantic Steel Mill conversion to mixed use, the Historic Westside Village project, Peachtree Portal/Centennial Hill (another transit-oriented development at the Civic Center MARTA train station), and a flurry of projects going on in Midtown. These are designed to attract or retain affluent and middle-class residents, assist business owners in the city, increase the fortunes of city property owners, and reduce Atlantans' reliance on automobiles. John Williams and his Post Properties are involved in providing the housing component for the Lindbergh City Center project, but when the economy weakened it pulled out of the

Atlantic Steel development and is now cautious about other plans for mixed-use office and residential projects in Midtown (like one adjacent to the new headquarters of the Atlanta Federal Reserve Bank).

As with GRTA, it is too early to evaluate "smart growth" projects' effects on Atlanta. At a minimum, they offer a useful option—yet another "lifestyle package" for people seeking an alternative to the common suburban pattern. Market surveys and demographic trends suggest that many more people in Atlanta today would choose to live in a "smart growth" community than was the case 20 years ago, and since most of these communities will be built "in town," the prospects for a "back to the city movement" are better now than back when that idea was first proposed. Nonetheless, a major reversal of the sprawl pattern is unlikely, given cost and preference factors. "Smart growth's" effect might be to slow sprawl down rather than to bring it to a halt. The lack of attention given to including a wide range of affordable housing in the "smart growth" and "new urbanism" developments is an important criticism. Although Atlanta has a few "co-housing" communities for people of modest means and an active network of affordable housing advocates, their concerns usually do not intersect with those of the major developers of "smart growth" projects. A possible forum for bringing these interests together might be the monthly "Sustainable Atlanta Roundtable" meetings, sponsored by Southface Energy Institute and other environmental groups, since it sometimes draws architects, urban planners, developers, and housing activists to its sessions.

## Conclusion

Atlanta's growth in the form of suburban expansion has a long history and a mix of causes. Making new places for people to live, work, and shop is a key element in the metropolitan region's economy. Charles Palmer recognized this when, in 1930, he said that "office buildings are to Atlanta what furniture is to Grand Rapids and automobiles are to Detroit" (Roth and Ambrose 1996, 94). By the 1960s, office parks were being built in Atlanta's suburbs and now tall glass office towers stand out there. But, of course, it is not just offices; suburban growth has put Atlanta at or near the top of the national list for new housing starts throughout the 1990s, and the purchase of the land and things needed to build and furnish these structures drives a big part of the metropolitan economy.

With so many people deriving economic benefit from this growth, even critics of sprawl wonder whether an end to unbridled growth would hurt Atlantans' financial security. As one of them says, "Yes, we need a healthy economy, since if you don't have money, you don't eat. But sooner or later, the land is sure to run out, unless the water goes first." So he recommends that "we wean ourselves off the easy money that development offers" and find something better than an economy based only on growth, but he does not suggest what that might be (Paulson 2000, A11). Others, more powerful and influential, have little interest in shutting down Atlanta's growth-based economy. Instead, they want to either relocate it (often to places where it works more to their advantage) or make its consequences less harmful. For them the question is, "How can cities and suburbs grow in population while avoiding the potentially devastating environmental and other consequences of asphalt-heavy sprawl or of poorly planned density?" Can we "tame sprawl" while still keeping current levels of homeownership, privacy, and reasonable auto use? (Goldberg 2000, G1). The three recent actions regarding sprawl discussed here—GRTA, the green space law, and "smart growth" projects—are clearly consistent with this latter approach. While they seem to be reforms that may not go far enough to solve the problem, each faces real obstacles or opposition, and the result will be an important test of how well the powers that be can institute change through legalistic and reform processes.

## NOTES

1. These population data are for the Metropolitan Statistical Area (MSA) as designated by the Census Bureau, which for Atlanta in the 1990s was a 20-county area. To put the size of its population increase in perspective, no other individual MSA had as large an increase in the 1990s as Atlanta's; it was surpassed only by the increase in the huge metropolitan regions of Los Angeles–Long Beach–Riverside, New York–Northern New Jersey–Long Island, and Dallas–Fort Worth (all CMSAs, in Census Bureau terms). Also, only one MSA that began the decade with at least one million residents had a larger percentage increase in population than Atlanta's 38.9 percent, and that was Phoenix (with a 45.3 percent increase).

2. In 1999, Heritage High School in Rockdale County was the scene of a sudden, deadly shooting attack in which one of its students killed several other people. That same year the community was also embarrassed by a large outbreak of sexually transmitted diseases among its teenagers, caused by a group of teens who were heavily involved in promiscuous sexual behavior and drug use (this situation was given national publicity

when it was featured on a *Frontline* documentary entitled "The Lost Children of Rockdale County").

3. In mid- and late April 2000, both African-American members of the GRTA board resigned in order to devote their energies elsewhere. Shirley Franklin entered an election campaign, ran as a candidate for mayor of Atlanta, and won the election in November 2001. Martin Luther King III is giving more attention to civil rights issues as head of the SCLC. Carolyn Williams and Andrella Baylis have replaced them on the GRTA board.

4. The lawsuit was filed by the Southern Environmental Law Center on behalf of four local groups: the Sierra Club, Georgians for Transportation Alternatives, the Southern Organizing Committee for Economic and Social Justice, and the Georgia Coalition for a People's Agenda. The suit charges that the ARC transportation plan is based on flawed data and that the EPA should not have extended metropolitan Atlanta's deadline for meeting acceptable vehicle emission standards from 1999 to 2003 (Seabrook 2000).

5. For instance, in late April 2000, Cherokee became the second county to adopt impact fees to cover some costs associated with the flood of newcomers it has received (Fulton County has one that is used in the rapidly growing northern part of the county). The Cherokee County fee adds $1,830 to the cost of a building permit for a new home, and has a sliding scale for businesses (e.g., $76 per 1,000 square feet for a miniwarehouse to $10,520 per 1,000 square feet for a fast-food restaurant). The fee pays capital expenses for county services like roads, public safety, libraries, and recreational facilities. Knowing Cherokee County was about to impose an impact fee, many developers avoided it by applying for building permits during the month before the impact fee was imposed. In March 2000, Cherokee County issued more building permits for homes than it did in any other month (a 119 percent increase over March of the previous year) and these had no impact fee attached to them (Frankston 2000b; Singleton 2000).

6. What is most controversial about the Lindbergh City Center project, however, is that it also includes provision for over 8,000 automobile parking spaces. Residents in two adjacent neighborhoods oppose the project and sued to prevent it (their lawsuit failed) because they feel that it will generate an intolerable amount of traffic through their streets.

# REFERENCES

Ambrose, Andrew M. 1982. "The Ties That Bind: Work and Family Patterns in the Oakdale Road Section of Druid Hills, 1910–1940." *Atlanta Historical Journal* 26 (2-3): 141–54.
"ARC: 'Smart Growth' Initiatives Taking Hold." 2000. *Atlanta Journal-Constitution,* 10 April, D1.
Atlanta Regional Commission (ARC). 1999. *1999 Population and Housing.* Atlanta: ARC.
Avondale Estates Historical Society. 1976. *Avondale Estates: The Early Years.* Atlanta: Avondale Estates Historical Society.
Barry, Tom. 1999a. "Atlanta's Changing Face: 21ˢᵗ Century Development." *Georgia Trend,* March, 22–23, 26–28.
———. 1999b. "A Hometown Statement." *Georgia Trend,* March, 24.

Bayor, Ronald H. 1996. *Race and the Shaping of Twentieth Century Atlanta*. Chapel Hill: University of North Carolina Press.

Beard, Rick. 1982. "From Suburb to Defended Neighborhood: The Evolution of Inman Park and Ansley Park, 1890–1980." *Atlanta Historical Journal* 26 (2-3): 113–40.

Bennett, D.L. 1999. "Smart Growth: Tensions High as Cherokee Weighs Zoning Plan." *Atlanta Journal-Constitution,* 8 November, A1, 6.

———. 2000. "Denser Suburban Growth Urged." *Atlanta Journal-Constitution,* 12 May, E1.

Billips, Mike. 2000. "Debate Rages: Just What Is Smart Growth?" *Georgia Trend,* March, 80.

Bookman, Jay. 1999. "Sprawling Plans Feed on DOT Willingness to Extend Exurbs." *Atlanta Journal-Constitution,* 18 January, F5.

———. 2000. "More Developers Junking Cookie-Cutter Formulas." *Atlanta Journal-Constitution,* 28 February, C8.

Brice, Leslie Everton. 2000. "Peachtree City." *Atlanta Journal-Constitution,* 19 March, HF8.

Brookings Institution. 2000. *Moving beyond Sprawl: The Challenge for Metropolitan Atlanta.* Washington, D.C.: Brookings Institution Center on Urban and Metropolitan Policy.

Bullard, Robert D., Glenn S. Johnson, and Angel O. Torres. 1999. "Atlanta Megasprawl." *Forum for Applied Research and Public Policy* 14 (3): 17–23.

———. 2000a. "Environmental Consequences of Sprawl." In *Sprawl Atlanta: Race, Politics, and Planning in Atlanta,* edited by Robert D. Bullard, Glenn S. Johnson, and Angel O. Torres (21–38). Washington, D.C.: Island Press.

———, eds. 2000b. *Sprawl Atlanta: Race, Politics, and Planning in Atlanta.* Washington, D.C.: Island Press.

Cowles, Anne. 1999. "Peachtree City Grows Smart." *Atlanta Journal-Constitution,* 20 September, B1, 3.

Danielsen, Karen A., Robert E. Lang, and William Fulton. 1999. "Retracting Suburbia: Smart Growth and the Future of Housing." *Housing Policy Debate* 1(3): 513–40.

DeGiovanni, Frank F. 1984. "An Examination of Selected Consequences of Revitalization in Six U.S. Cities." In *Gentrification, Displacement and Neighborhood Revitalization,* edited by J. John Palen and Bruce London (67–89). Albany: State University of New York Press.

Eckstein, Sandra. 2000. "Ackerman Ready to Develop College Park Mixed-Use Project." *Atlanta Journal-Constitution,* 28 February, C3.

Firestone, David. 1999. "Suburban Comforts Thwart Atlanta's Plans to Limit Sprawl." *New York Times,* 21 November, I1.

Frankston, Janet. 2000a. "Cherokee Commission May Kill Zoning Category." *Atlanta Journal-Constitution,* 29 March, B4.

———. 2000b. "Cherokee OKs Impact Fees on Its Newcomers." *Atlanta Journal-Constitution,* April 26, B1.

———. 2000c. "Slow Growth Is Catching On with Electorate." *Atlanta Journal-Constitution,* July 20, C1.

Frommer, Arthur. 1987. "Key to Atlanta's Future Lies in Its Past." *Atlanta Journal-Constitution,* 18 January, D1, 6.

Fujii, Tadashi, and Truman A. Hartshorn. 1995. "The Changing Metropolitan Structure of Atlanta, Georgia: Locations of Functions and Regional Structure in a Multinucleated Urban Area." *Urban Geography* 16: 680–707.

Gilpin, Francis X. 1999. "'Anti-Sprawl' Forces Get Victory in Cobb." *Atlanta Journal-Constitution*, 1 July, C3.

Goldberg, David. 1996. "Deadline Looming for Regional Plan." *Atlanta Journal-Constitution*, 29 December, D6.

———. 1998. "Trying to Get a Grip on the Sprawl." *Atlanta Journal-Constitution*, 12 July, D5.

———. 2000. "Accomplishing Growth without Sprawl." *Atlanta Journal-Constitution* 7 May, G1, 2.

Gottdiener, Mark. 1997. *The Theming of America*. Boulder, Colo.: Westview Press.

"GRTA Must Lead on Regional Plan." 2000. *Atlanta Journal-Constitution*, 22 March, A14.

Hartshorn, Truman A., and Peter O. Muller. 1989. "Suburban Downtowns and the Transformation of Atlanta's Business Landscape." *Urban Geography* 10: 375–95.

Hill, Karen. 2000. "Decatur: 'Poster Child for Smart Growth.'" *Atlanta Journal-Constitution*, 3 February, J3.

Hiskey, Michelle. 1992. "Historic Inman Park at a Crossroads." *Atlanta Journal-Constitution*, 12 April, D5.

Jaret, Charles. 2000. "Suburban Sprawl, Housing Opportunities, and Residential Segregation in Atlanta." Presented at the annual meeting of the Urban Affairs Association, Los Angeles, Calif., May 5.

Klima, Don L. 1982. "Breaking Out: Streetcars and Suburban Development, 1872–1900." *Atlanta Historical Journal* 26 (2-3): 67–82.

Langley, Tim. 1999. "Suburbanites Unfairly Demonized." *Atlanta Journal-Constitution*, 1 December, A22.

Lawler, Terry. 2001. "'Smart Growth' Creates Its Own Woes." *Atlanta Journal-Constitution*, 26 February, A9.

Logan, John R., and Min Zhou. 1989. "Do Suburban Growth Controls Control Growth?" *American Sociological Review* 54: 461–71.

McCosh, John. 1999. "'Smart Growth' Ideals Pitched to Local Leaders." *Atlanta Journal-Constitution*, 11 November, E8.

———. 2000. "Region Is 'One Step Closer' to Road Funds." *Atlanta Journal-Constitution*, 23 July, C1, 5.

Murphy, Harry. 1983. "The Dilemma of Suburban Sprawl." *Atlanta Magazine*, November, 68–69, 141–43.

Netherton, Martha. 1999. "A New Era Dawns for Developers." *Georgia Trend*, September, 39–42.

Nurse, Doug. 2000. "'Live-Work-Play' Plan Defeated in Rockdale." *Atlanta Journal-Constitution*, 12 April, B3.

Paulson, Paul B. 2000. "Sharing Blame for Sprawl." *Atlanta Journal-Constitution*, 8 January, A11.

Pruitt, Kathey. 2000a. "Barnes Asks Funding for Green Space." *Atlanta Journal-Constitution*, 2 February, B1, 5.

———. 2000b. "House OKs Green Space Protection." *Atlanta Journal-Constitution*, 1 March, A1.

Roth, Darlene R., and Andy Ambrose. 1996. *Metropolitan Frontiers: A Short History of Atlanta*. Atlanta: Longstreet Press.

Rutheiser, Charles. 1996. *Imagineering Atlanta.* New York: Verso.

Saporta, Maria. 2000. "Green-Space Investing Catching On in Georgia." *Atlanta Journal-Constitution,* 21 March, D2.

Seabrook, Charles. 2000. "Metro Air Plan Faces Roadblock." *Atlanta Journal-Constitution,* 29 April, E1.

Shipp, Bill. 1999. "Why We Have Sprawl." *Georgia Trend,* February, 86.

Simmons, Kelly. 2000a. "Green Light for Transit Aid?" *Atlanta Journal-Constitution,* 18 May, A1, 12.

———. 2000b. "GRTA Gets Tough with Counties." *Atlanta Journal-Constitution,* 15 June, A1, 18.

———. 2000c. "GRTA May Put Teeth in Road Plan." *Atlanta Journal-Constitution,* 2 May, F1.

———. 2000d. "GRTA OKs Three-Year Plan." *Atlanta Journal-Constitution,* 16 June, H3.

———. 2000e. "'Roadblockers' Aim for Clean Air." *Atlanta Journal-Constitution,* 22 July, A1, 9.

Singleton, Larry. 2000. "Cherokee Impact Fees Are Not Out of Line." *Atlanta Journal-Constitution,* 1 May, A10.

Squires, Gregory D. 1994. *Capital and Communities in Black and White.* Albany: State University of New York Press.

Tucker, Cynthia. 1999. "We're No. 1: When It Comes to Sprawl, Atlanta's World Class." *Atlanta Journal-Constitution,* 24 November, A16.

Tucker, Katheryn Hayes. 2000. "Saying Goodbye to the 'Burbs." *New York Times,* 5 March, Section 3: 1,15–16.

Vogel, Ronald, and Bert Swanson. 1989. "The Growth Machine Versus the Antigrowth Coalition: The Battle for Our Communities." *Urban Affairs Quarterly* 25: 63–85.

Warner, Kee, and Harvey Molotch. 1995. "Power to Build: How Development Persists Despite Local Limits." *Urban Affairs Review* 30: 378–406.

White, Dana F. 1982. "The Black Sides of Atlanta: A Geography of Expansion and Containment, 1870–1970." *Atlanta Historical Journal* 26 (2-3): 199–225.

White, Dana F., and Timothy J. Crimmins. 1980. "How Atlanta Grew: Cool Heads, Hot Air, and Hard Work." In *Urban Atlanta: Redefining the Role of the City,* edited by Andrew Marshall Hamer (25–44). Atlanta: Georgia State University College of Business Administration.

Williams, Clint. 2000. "Costly Cobb." *Atlanta Journal-Constitution,* 1 April, H1, 4.

Williams, John. 1999. "Alter Recipe for Growth." *Atlanta Journal-Constitution,* 11 August, A13.

Wilson, Jerry L. 2000. "Give Suburbs More Voice." *Atlanta Journal-Constitution,* 14 May, E4.

Wooten, Jim. 2000. "'High Priests' Direct GRTA Off Course." *Atlanta Journal-Constitution,* 14 May, E5.

# 8

# Planning a Sustainable City

## *The Promise and Performance of Portland's Urban Growth Boundary*

Carl Abbott

### The Moral Origins of Metropolitan Planning

On January 8, 1973, Governor Tom McCall unleashed the most quoted speech in Oregon political history (Walth 1994; MacColl 1995). Speaking to the state legislature in language that dripped with scorn, he called down judgment on scattershot land development. "There is a shameless threat to our environment and to the whole quality of life—the unfettered despoiling of the land," he admonished the lawmakers. He pointed an outraged finger at malefactors in the best style of Theodore Roosevelt. "Sagebrush subdivisions, coastal condomania, and the ravenous rampage of suburbia in the Willamette Valley all threaten to mock Oregon's status as the environmental model for the nation. . . . The interests of Oregon for today and in the future must be protected from grasping wastrels of the land."

Tom McCall's anathema on urban and rural sprawl introduced an unabashedly moral argument to the usually practical discussion of zoning, planning, and real estate development. The speech was a key step in the passage later in 1973 of Oregon Senate Bill (SB) 100, which established a statewide land use planning system that includes growth boundaries around towns and metropolitan areas. The program, which has survived numerous legal challenges and three statewide referenda, requires every Oregon city and county to prepare a comprehensive plan that responds to a set of statewide goals. The plans provide the legal support for zoning and other specific regulations, and the Land Conservation and Development Commission (LCDC) can require local governments to revise unsatisfactory plans. Oregon thus operates with a system of strong local planning carried on within enforceable state guidelines that express a vision of the public interest (see Knaap 1994; Knaap and Nelson 1992; Abbott and Howe 1993; MacColl 1995; Stroud and DeGrove 1980).

McCall's speech had practical relevance, but the words were also far more than a legislative proposal. In tone and substance, McCall invoked the judgmental stance of the Old Testament prophets. Here was no inevitable process of land conversion driven by an impersonal market. Like a latter day Amos or Jeremiah, McCall knew sinners when he saw them. His prophetic rhetoric targeted aberrant behavior ("condo*mania*") by miscreants ("grasping wastrels"). He indicted the sins of greed and sloth and gluttony. He invoked moral standards that should cause evil-doers to feel *shame* for their actions. And he called Oregonians to renew their covenant with their land.

The "grasping wastrels" speech is central to the foundation myth of modern Oregon. It came in the midst of a decade of extraordinary civic initiative around issues of environmental protection and urban growth. The legislature, which adopted SB 100 later in 1973, had already re-affirmed the right of public access to the state's Pacific Ocean beaches, passed a pioneering bottle deposit bill, and endorsed the idea of a Willamette River Greenway. McCall had turned the weak state Sanitary Commission into the Department of Environmental Quality and watched the culmination of efforts to save the Willamette River from city sewage and the effluent from paper mills and food processing plants (Walth 1994). Portlanders, meanwhile, were adopting an innovative Downtown Plan in 1972, creating the Office of Neighborhood Associations in 1974, rip-ping out one expressway to plant grass and trees in 1973, rejecting another freeway in 1975, and approving a regional government—Metro (in 1978)—with a directly elected council and executive (Abbott 1983).

In this environment of civic activism, McCall's argument resonated strongly with the distinctly moralistic aspects of Oregon political beliefs and culture (Abbott 1994a). Daniel Elazar (1972) categorized American states according to the dominance of traditional, individualistic, or moralistic political cultures. Moralistic communities "conceive of politics as a public activity centered on some notion of the public good and properly devoted to the advancement of the public interest. Good gov-ernment, then, is measured by the degree to which it promotes the public good" (1972, 96–97). Such a political culture places issues ahead of individuals and accepts that government can legitimately regulate private activities such as land development for the good of the commonwealth.

Both Elazar and Ira Sharkansky (1969) have placed Oregon firmly among the moralists. Anticipating Raymond Gastil's idea (1975) that cultural patterns are the product of "first effective settlement," Elazar traced Oregon's moralistic approach to the dominance of New Englanders in the leadership of Willamette Valley settlements. The initial political tone was presumably reinforced by the heavy reliance on northern tier states and northern Europe for new Oregonians in the later 19th century. Even in the second half of the 20th century, Oregon has been high in its number of Episcopalians and Congregationalists (Gaustad 1976).

A more detailed look at Oregon's first century as a state shows that its moralistic style contended with political individualists, including a long-lasting Republican party machine, well-placed practitioners of railroad and timber scams, and Portland city administrators who were simultaneously in the hip pockets of land developers and in bed with vice industries (MacColl 1979, 1988). The years between 1950 and 1970, however, saw the steady ascendancy of moralistic rhetoric and leaders who derived political positions from their understandings of the general public good. Richard Neuberger was a classic "Fair Dealer." Wayne Morse made an extraordinary switch from the Republican to the Democratic party over Dwight Eisenhower's energy giveaways and was one of the earliest opponents of the Vietnam War (Unruh 1992). Mark Hatfield based politically unpopular stands on issues such as the death penalty on his religious beliefs. And Tom McCall was known for his rousing calls for protection of the Oregon environment.

Elazar's categorization of postwar Oregon is supported by specific research findings. David Klingman and William Lammers (1984) calculated a state-by-state index of "general policy liberalism" based on levels of social service and welfare spending, antidiscrimination and consumer protection laws and programs, date of ratification of the Equal Rights Amendment, and overall policy innovation up to 1965.[1] Oregon ranked sixth in policy liberalism, behind New York, Massachusetts, New Jersey, California, and Connecticut, and just ahead of Wisconsin, Minnesota, Colorado, and Michigan. Studies of metropolitan quality of life also support the description of a "moralistic" commonwealth. Ben-Chieh Liu (1975) found that very high "livability" for Portland and Eugene was based in part on high ranks on indicators of civic involvement such as library circulation, newspaper readership, voting turnout, and educational investment and achievement. A review of livability studies by Nancy Chapman and Joan Starker (1987) noted Portland's participatory and issue-oriented politics. More targeted studies have found that Portland offers a civic environment that has been supportive of women's rights and economic and political opportunities (Starker and Abbott 1984; Sugarman and Straus 1988).

Beyond its consonance with the state's political style, the "grasping wastrels" speech drew much of its impact from an early image of Oregon's Willamette Valley as the unspoiled Eden at the end of the Transcontinental Trail. Americans in the early 19th century envisioned Oregon as a "fabled land of promise" where "nature without measure" could fulfill individual and national dreams (Ronda 1993, 121). In contrast to the arid plains, parched plateaus, and inhospitable mountains that lay between the Mississippi Valley and the Pacific shore, Oregon was a place of fertility and bounty that offered a fresh chance. Meriwether Lewis and William Clark described "a fertile and delightful country, shaded by thick groves of tall timber" with soil "rich and capable of any species of culture" (1965, vol. 2, 697–98). The common descriptor was "garden," with all its Edenic overtones. Theodore Winthrop captured the trope in 1862: "The sweet Arcadian valley of the Willamette, charming with meadow, park, and grove. In no older world where men have . . . recreated themselves for generations in taming the earth to orderly beauty, have they achieved a fairer garden than Nature's simple labor of love has made there" (quoted in Robbins 1997, 81).

In the late 20th century, the old imagery of arcadian Oregon reappeared not only in McCall's invocation of landscape but also in the vision of sustainable development. Oregon was the center of the environmentally sensitive Ecotopia envisioned by utopian novelist Ernest Callenbach (1975). Its western valleys lie at the heart of Cascadia, the "great green land on the northeast Pacific Rim" mapped by David McCloskey in 1988. McCloskey's evocative map pictures the northwest coast as a great exotic leaf, veined with delicate networks of streams and rivers such as the Columbia, the Willamette, and their tributaries. In McCloskey's vision and in the work of activist organizations such as Portland-based Ecotrust, provinces, states, and nations disappear under the imperative of the hydrologic cycle that endlessly links the Pacific Slope and the Pacific Ocean. To advocate sustainable urbanization and regional development is to attempt the reconciliation of city and country, temporary human action and eternal nature, past and future.

This context—love of landscape and political style both—goes far to explain why the Portland area Urban Growth Boundary or UGB, a specific planning tool mandated by SB 100, has acquired strong symbolic power, and why choices about the boundary's management are not only technical questions but also morally freighted policy decisions. Advocates of a loose and expanding growth boundary see the UGB as a blunt and sometimes counterproductive tool. Supporters of a tight and strong UGB believe not only that they are helping Portland to "grow smart," as current rhetoric would have it, but also that they are helping their fellow citizens "act right." The UGB, as the most prominent part of the state planning system, is more than a regulatory mechanism: The UGB is a symbol of a morally informed choice, an example to many (but not all) Oregonians of watchful, caring, rational stewardship.

## Legislation and Planning

Tom McCall, of course, did not "pass" SB 100 by himself. He worked diligently with legislators and lobbyists in a complex, multiyear process that stretched from initial efforts in the 1960s to the crafting of administration rules in 1974. The center of concern was the 100-mile-long Willamette Valley, which contains the state's richest farmland, its three largest cities of Portland, Salem, and Eugene, and 70 percent of its population. The blue barricade of the Coast Range rising on the west and the towering volcanic cones of the Cascades on the east remind residents that land is finite. The movement for state-mandated planning originated in efforts by Willamette Valley farmers to protect their livelihoods and communities from urban engulfment and scattershot subdivisions, with their disruptive effects on agricultural practices. As the effort moved through several legislative versions between 1970 and 1973, fear of California-style sprawl and the possibility of a minimegalopolis in the Eugene-Seattle corridor attracted Willamette Valley urbanites to the legislative coalition.

The first steps toward the idea of zoning for "exclusive farm use" in the early 1960s involved legislative action to set the tax rate on farm land by land rental values—in effect, by its productive capacity as farm land—rather than by comparative sales data, which might reflect the demand for suburban development. A conference on "The Willamette Valley—What Is Our Future in Land Use?" held early in 1967 spread awareness of urban pressures on Oregon's agricultural base. With key members drawn from the ranks of Oregon farmers, the Legislative Interim Committee on Agriculture responded by developing the proposal that became Senate Bill (SB) 10, Oregon's first mandatory planning legislation (Abbott and Howe 1993).

Adopted in 1969, SB 10 took the major step of requiring cities and counties to prepare comprehensive land use plans and zoning ordinances that met 10 broad goals. The deadline was December 31, 1971. However, the legislation failed to establish mechanisms or criteria for evaluating or coordinating local plans, allowing some counties to opt for pro forma compliance. McCall's successful re-election campaign in 1970 called for strengthening SB 10. At the same time, 55 percent of the state's voters supported the law in a referendum.

The Oregon legislature acted in 1973 on SB 100 to correct flaws in the 1969 law (SB 10). A state-sponsored report by landscape architect Lawrence Halprin (1972), *The Willamette Valley: Choices for the Future*, helped to set the stage in the fall of 1972. McCall's speech raised the curtain, while greatest credit for the passage of SB 100 went to Senator Hector Macpherson, a Linn County dairy farmer convinced of the need to fend off the suburbanization of the entire valley. Drawing on his experience on the Linn County Planning Commission, he articulated the importance of a statewide planning program in protecting and enhancing agricultural investment.[2] This served to dampen the demands of farmers to preserve property rights that would enable them to sell out to developers. When the dust of legislative skirmishing cleared, 49 out of 60 legislators from Willamette Valley districts voted in favor of SB 100. Only 9 of their 30 colleagues from coastal and eastern counties agreed.

Passage of the bill in May 1973 created a seven-member state Land Conservation and Development Commission (LCDC) whose task is to assure that local comprehensive land use plans—required under the new law—are compatible with statewide goals. Staff support for LCDC and the planning program comes from the Department of Land Conservation and Development (DLCD). As its first task, the new LCDC rewrote the state planning goals after dozens of workshops throughout the state (Stroud and DeGrove 1980).[3] The 10 goals of the 1969 legislation were made more clear and precise and 4 new goals were added. All 14 goals were adopted in December 1974. An additional goal on the Willamette River Greenway was added in December 1975 and 4 goals focusing on coastal zone issues were added in December 1976. The basic idea behind the program is that development is to be concentrated within urban growth boundaries (UGBs), which are established around incorporated cities. Outside of the UGBs are resource lands where land use policies are aimed at supporting the vitality of the agricultural and forest industries. Non–resource-related development is strictly limited in resource areas.[4]

The statewide goals have not been seriously challenged, in part because public participation in 1974 built a wide constituency of voters with a personal stake in the success of the program. Unsuccessful referendum challenges in 1976, 1978, and 1982 focused on questions of control and enforcement rather than content. The closest call, in 1982, involved a ballot measure to return final decisionmaking on land use plans to localities and retain statewide goals only as guidelines. Even the opponents of the LCDC system argued about *how* to plan, not whether to plan, leaving the goals themselves above the political battle as examples of right thinking. In the context of the early 1980s, when the "Sagebrush Rebellion" was mobilizing nearby states like Nevada and Utah around a radical individualist agenda, Oregon politics remained firmly centrist.

## The Urban Growth Boundary and Its Companions

The urban growth boundary for the Portland area is the keystone of metropolitan planning. The intent is to prevent sprawl by providing for "an orderly and efficient transition from rural to urban use." Within the UGB, the burden of proof rests on opponents of land development. Outside the boundary, the burden rests on developers to show that their land is easily supplied with necessary services, that it has little worth as open space or farmland, and that adequate land for the proposed development does not exist within the UGB. The formal language states:

> Urban growth boundaries shall be established to identify and separate urbanizable land from rural land. Establishment and change of the boundaries shall be based upon considerations of the following factors: (1) demonstrated need to accommodate long-range urban population growth requirements consistent with LCDC goals; (2) need for housing, employment opportunities, and livability; (3) orderly and economic provision for public facilities and services; (4) maximum efficiency of land uses within and on the fringe of the existing urban areas; (5) environmental, energy, economic and social consequences; (6) retention of agricultural land with Class I being the highest priority for retention and Class VI the lowest priority; and (7) compatibility of the proposed urban uses with nearby agricultural activities (Oregon Department of Land Conservation and Development 2001).

The UGB links older urban planning concerns to a newer environmentalism. The LCDC program rapidly evolved from a purely reactive effort to fend off erosion of the state's farm economy to a positive attempt to shape a particular urban form. Several goals have been of special importance for directing metropolitan growth. Goal 14 gains specific content from Goal 3 on the preservation of farmland, Goal 5 on the preservation of open space, Goal 10 on access to affordable housing, Goal 11 on the orderly development of public facilities and services, Goal 12 on transportation, and Goal 13 on energy-efficient land use (see note 4). Although very different in origins from Portland's *city* planning initiatives, the state program thus blended the interests and combined the votes of urbanists, agriculturalists, and environmental advocates in a way that has mirrored and supported the similar alliance at the metropolitan scale. The Oregon Farm Bureau, environmental activists, and Portland politicians have all remained strong supporters for more than 25 years.

Unlike most growth boundaries adopted by referendum or pushed through city councils by public pressure, the Portland UGB is a "Metro-GB" rather than a "MuniGB." The state gave responsibility for defining a single regional growth boundary to the Metropolitan Service District (Metro). As a result, the Portland UGB functions simultaneously for Portland and 24 suburban municipalities. Outlying metropolitan communities that are not part of the contiguous urbanized area have their own UGBs (as do all municipalities around the state). Metro adopted the UGB for the Portland area in 1979. Supposedly embracing a 20-year supply of developable land, the UGB embraced approximately 230,000 acres (360 square miles). Reliance on a single planning entity and UGB was possible in part because Portland is still a unicentric metropolis that displays the starfish pattern familiar from so many planning reports and growth projections of the 1950s and 1960s.

The UGB works in concert with Goal 10 (Toulan 1994), which essentially mandates a "fair share" housing policy by requiring that every jurisdiction within the UGB provide "appropriate types and amounts of land . . . necessary and suitable for housing that meets the housing needs of households of all income levels." In other words, suburbs are not allowed to use the techniques of exclusionary zoning to block apartment construction or to isolate themselves as islands of large-lot zoning. By limiting the speculative development of large, distant residential tracts, the LCDC system has tended to level the playing field for suburban development and discourage the emergence of suburban "super developers" with overwhelming political clout. In the Portland region, a hous-ing rule adopted by LCDC now requires that every jurisdiction zone at least half of its vacant residential land for attached single-family housing or apartments. In effect, the rule enacts a market-based version of a fair share program that hopes to reduce socioeconomic disparities between city and suburbs by manipulating density and urban form. However, the Oregon legislature in 1999 prohibited stronger fair share programs that might require inclusion of subsidized housing in new developments.

LCDC has also adopted a transportation rule that requires local juris-dictions in the Portland metropolitan area to plan land uses and facili-ties in such a way as to achieve a 10 percent *reduction* in vehicle miles traveled per capita over the next 20 years (Adler 1994). The rule flies in the face of the explosive nationwide growth of automobile mileage per capita. It requires a drastic rethinking of land use patterns and trans-portation investment to encourage mixed uses, higher densities, public transit, and pedestrians. It makes local land use planners and the Oregon Department of Transportation into allies at the same time that the fed-eral Intermodal Surface Transportation Enhancement Act is pushing highway builders to rethink their jobs.

Outside the specific framework of land use planning, the UGB func-tions in mutual support with efforts to develop strong public transit, con-serve older neighborhoods, and promote a multifunctional downtown. An urban growth boundary coupled with weak public transit, deterio-rating inner-city neighborhoods, and a declining downtown would be in deep trouble—hard to sell to residents and hard to enforce against the market forces of decentralization. Supporters of the LCDC system are fortunate that Portland's civic and business leadership devoted much effort in the 1970s and 1980s to exactly these concerns, which means that the UGB is a keystone in a very strong arch.

The City of Portland and key suburban cities shared a common trans-portation agenda during the late 1980s and 1990s. The coalition devel-oped around planning for a four-spoke light rail system after rejection of a radial freeway. Over the objections of weakly organized suburban man-ufacturers who prefer cross-suburb road improvements, the Portland area's civic leadership in the later 1980s decided that strong public tran-sit should be an axiom of regional development. The cities of Gresham, Milwaukie, Hillsboro, and Beaverton, along with Washington and Clackamas Counties, all recognized that light rail links to downtown Portland could offer strong development potential for secondary activity centers. With visions of Walnut Creek, California, and Bethesda, Maryland, glimmering in the future, leaders in these communities chose to pursue roles as outlying anchors on radial transportation lines rather than as beads on a beltway (Abbott 1997).[5]

The region's light rail system began with an east side line in 1986 and grew with an 18-mile, west side line, opened in 1998. A north-south line has been problematic, however. Voters in the three Oregon counties approved a line from Clackamas County through downtown Portland and across the Columbia River to Clark County, but rejection by Clark County voters forced the project back on the ballot. Despite the argument of *The Oregonian* that light rail is essential for "Oregon's environmentally wise anti-sprawl policy" ("Give Planners the Tools" 1991), voters statewide rejected a state contribution to an Oregon-only, north-south line in 1996, even in the face of attached "sweeteners" like highway projects around the state. Tri-county voters narrowly rejected a local financing package line in 1998. It is unclear whether the troubles of north-south light rail represent the first fracture of the city-suburb coalition or a combination of discrete factors: fallout from political infighting in Clackamas County, general anti-spending sentiment, downstate response to environmentally oriented ballot measures that could be read as antirural, second thoughts about the efficiency of rail transit investment—or all of the above. However, a spur line to the airport opened in September 2001 using money from the city, Tri-Met, airline fees, and a substantial private contribution from the Bechtel Corporation, which owns a large industrial park along the line. In addition, initial work on a scaled-down, six-mile North Portland line began in 2001 without requiring voter approval of new bonds or taxes.

The prosperity and livability of central Portland is a further support for the UGB. Since a period of economic crisis in the 1960s, city planning and public investment have attracted very substantial private investment to the central business district, whose employment total increased by 73 percent from 1970 to 1995. The business core and adjacent districts include nearly all of the major cultural and entertainment facilities for the metropolitan area—museums, universities, theaters, sports arenas, and a convention center. The commercial and civic core is immediately ringed by residential neighborhoods, many of them serving the upper middle class. There is thus a strong and politically savvy constituency of businesses and citizens who are committed to and invested in central-city living (Abbott 1994b, 1997; Abbott, Pagenstecher, and Parrott 1998; Garvin 1996).

## The UGB Debate

Although the Urban Growth Boundary was adopted in 1979, neither its effectiveness nor its political acceptability was tested until the 1990s. The national recession of the early 1980s persisted in Oregon several years after it ended in other parts of the country. Recovery began slowly in 1987, accelerated to a peak in 1996 and 1997, and remained strong into 2000. In turn, economic improvement and growing in-migration re-quired attention to the possible enlargement of the UGB. Since the late 1980s, Portlanders have therefore engaged in a prolonged and intelligent debate about metropolitan growth and form, a debate centered on the question of UGB expansion.

The first step came in 1988. Metro staff realized that there was no estab-lished process for amending the Portland area UGB, even though the state requires periodic review and anticipates incremental UGB expansion.[6] The reviving economy and fast-rising in-migration made the task more urgent. The agency, therefore, designed a classic planning process to cre-ate Regional Urban Growth Goals and Objectives (RUGGOs). Input at this stage came largely from opinion leaders, public officials, and interest groups. Metro adopted RUGGOs in 1991 that emphasized compact growth, mixed uses, improved transit, and strengthening of existing cen-ters (Metropolitan Service District 1995).

The second step was to develop a specific "Region 2040" plan for accommodating up to a million more residents in the four core counties over a 50-year span. The process was remarkable for the widening range of participation; large numbers of individual citizens joined elected offi-cials, growth management advocates, homebuilders, and commercial real estate interests. In 1994, for example, Metro received 17,000 responses to a mail-in questionnaire about regional planning issues. Half the respon-ses included additional write-in comments. The feedback strongly favored higher densities, smaller lots, and transit-oriented development.

The Metro Council adopted the "Region 2040 Growth Concept" in December 1994, outlining broad, spatially defined goals for accommo-dating anticipated growth over the next half century. The document matched the emerging belief among professional planners in the virtues of compact cities. The plan proposes to focus new jobs and housing on downtown Portland, urban and suburban centers, and transportation corridors; to identify rural reserves to remain permanently outside the UGB (including farmland, forestland, and prominent natural features);

and to adapt transportation improvements to the land use goals. The 2040 plan anticipates sharply increased population density in central Portland, in six regional growth centers, and along transit corridors.

Metro followed with a third step in October 1996 by adopting an Urban Growth Management Functional Plan. Providing detail within the 2040 framework, the 1996 plan allocates the half-million new residents and jobs anticipated by 2017 among jurisdictions *within* the UGB. Because of wide participation and discussion during previous years, the adoption was remarkably noncontroversial. The provisions of the plan include: (1) housing and job targets for each of the area's 24 cities and incorporated portions of three counties that will require higher overall densities; (2) requirements for minimum development densities for new housing averaging 80 percent of the zoned maximum; (3) exclusion of "big box" retailing from industrial zones; (4) minimum and maximum parking ratios for new development; (5) a requirement that Metro develop specific affordable housing goals; and (6) a provision for UGB expansion if enough communities demonstrate that the targets won't work. Critics argue that the plan actually involves substantial and unworkable increases from the density increases approved in the 2040 Growth Concept.

In turn, these goals are part of the comprehensive Regional Framework Plan that Metro adopted in December 1997 in accordance with a requirement in its home rule charter of 1992. Under that charter, local jurisdictions must modify their own zoning and land use regulations to implement "functional plans." In fact, a Metro Policy Advisory Committee (MPAC) of elected officials representing city, suburbs, and counties took the lead in sharing out the expected development. Created in the 1992 charter as a possible check on the Metro Council, MPAC instead became a forum in which political leaders agreed to match each other's efforts to absorb growth. The result was an agreement in 1996 on the number of new housing units and new jobs that each jurisdiction will try to accommodate. Among them, the three large suburbs of Gresham (population 90,000 in 2000), Hillsboro (population 70,000), and Beaverton (population 76,000) anticipate 45,000 new housing units, while Portland (population 529,000) anticipates 71,000 additional units. Indeed, several mayors and county commissioners on MPAC publicly urged the Metro Council to hang tough on growth management—a vivid demonstration of the strength of the city-suburb coalition around compact growth.

All of these carefully orchestrated steps provided the framework for deciding on the specific UGB expansion needs. The formal consideration process began in February 1995, after adoption of the 2040 Plan and November elections that brought a new Metro executive director, Mike Burton, and several new Metro Council members. Debate ranged around Burton's initial suggestion of a 4,000–9,000 acre expansion and the argument of Councilor Don Morissette, a successful homebuilder, that 10,000 acres was the minimum necessary addition. A year later, Burton had dropped to the low end of his estimate, while Morissette and Council allies continued to argue for 10,000 acres.

The original legislation and implementing rules assumed that UGBs would expand as a matter of course. Each UGB was viewed like a set of clothing that would be replaced by a larger size as its city or metropolitan area grew. The legislature in 1993 turned the expectation into a mandate, *requiring* that growth boundaries embrace a 20-year supply of residential land. The legislative requirement thus gave a central role to projections of population growth and land demand, making population forecasts and estimates of possible densities for new development into politically charged statements.

In this context, public discussion in the 1990s introduced the possibility of *freezing* the boundary for the indefinite future by slowing growth and/or requiring high development densities. More than 2,500 individuals testified on the UGB, many in favor of minimal or no expansion. Six hundred readers of *The Oregonian* responded to a detailed "growth game" survey in November 1995. Only 45 wanted to abolish the UGB in favor of an open market in suburban land, while 194 wanted to choke off population growth entirely, 277 wanted to accommodate growth within a frozen UGB, and 107 favored a slight enlargement. A number of business leaders and elected officials endorsed a tight or frozen UGB (Young 1995). An audience of civic leaders gave Portland Mayor Vera Katz a rousing round of applause in January 1996 when she vowed, "Your City Council is committed to the invisible line called the urban growth boundary. We will do our part to see that it does not have to expand" (Christ 1996).

In December 1998, the agency met a state deadline by bringing 3,500 acres inside the UGB and identifying 1,900 more acres to be included in the near future, in effect splitting the difference between Burton and Morissette. Metro estimated that the planned expansion would accommodate 23,000 houses and apartments and 14,000 jobs. The agency's projections also make it clear that further expansions are likely, for even at recommended densities, the region is expected to fall short of housing demand by at least 8,500 units without additional increments of "urbanizable" land, or land that is formally recognized as suitable for urban development.[7]

Although the UGB debate did not end with a decision to "freeze," the whole process was remarkable for actually changing ideas rather than hardening pre-established positions. What started as an effort to figure out how much to expand the UGB ended with a debate over how best to limit its expansion. The UGB has even attracted the attention of artists, surely a rarity for a land use regulation. Dancer and performance artist Linda K. Johnson set up camp for 36-hour stints at four different points on the UGB, living in a fence-like tent supplied with a TV set and Martha Stewart dishes and bedding. She quickly replaced her specialized choreography with straightforward chats with visitors, pulling opinions from yuppies, school kids, construction workers, and architects. Out of the resulting "suburban still life" came new, complex understandings of the way that the UGB has affected "every single solitary aspect of the way we live . . . traffic, education, taxes, our desires about housing and architecture." For Johnson—and for many other Portlanders—the growth boundary has become "a different viewfinder to see the city through" (Gragg 1999).

## The Urban Growth Boundary and a Sustainable Metropolis

We can roughly gauge the effect of outward growth on typical neighborhood character before and after LCDC by looking at census figures on the "urbanized area" within the Portland metropolitan area. The data in table 8.1 summarize three phases in postwar residential growth. Between 1950 and 1970—the first two decades of unimpeded automobile suburbanization—the area of urbanized land exploded while the average population density fell by a third. From 1970 to 1980, the subdivision frontier continued its rapid expansion but the decline in average density slowed markedly. Since then, perhaps reflecting the impacts of the new UGB, the area of developed land increased much more slowly and the downward trend in average residential density actually reversed. From 1980 to 1994, the metropolitan population increased by 25 percent, but the land devoted to urban uses increased only 16 percent.

Table 8.1  *Growth in the Portland-Vancouver Urbanized Area, 1950–1994*

| Year | Area (in sq. miles) | Population (per sq. mile) |
|---|---|---|
| 1950 | 114 | 4,517 |
| 1960 | 191 | 3,405 |
| 1970 | 267 | 3,092 |
| 1980 | 349 | 2,940 |
| 1990 | 388 | 3,021 |
| 1994 | 405 | 3,167 |

*Source:* U.S. Census and Metro.

The UGB quickly produced a dual land market (Knaap 1985; Nelson 1986). Land outside the boundary quickly lost most of its speculative value and prices dropped to levels congruent with agricultural uses. Land inside the boundary retained, or in some cases gained, speculative value.

A detailed analysis for the Department of Land Conservation and Development for 1985–89 found that 95 percent of new housing in the three core counties of the metropolitan area was built inside the UGB (ECO Northwest 1991). The new lots created by subdivision fell 34 percent below the allowed densities. However, the substantial proportion of apartments and attached dwellings meant that the overall density of new housing exceeded 6.23 units per acre, the figure assumed in defining the original boundary.

Data from the late 1990s suggest that the UGB is continuing to work. In 1994, the Portland area was building new housing at a density of five dwelling units per acre. By 1997 and 1998, the density of new development averaged eight dwellings per acre, actually exceeding the 2040 Plan target. Nearly half of all housing starts in the late 1990s involved multifamily or attached structures, up from 35 percent in 1992–95. The average new lot size in 1998 was 6,200 square feet, down from 12,800 square feet in 1978. Almost all the new housing outside the UGB was located in Clark County, Washington, a metropolitan county outside the Oregon regulatory system where traditional subdivisions of moderately priced houses were still available. Even here, however, new lot sizes fell in the 1990s and the median sales price of a single-family house had climbed by the year 2000 to 92 percent of the median price on the Oregon side of the Columbia River. A recent study using Landsat data found that each new resident in the Portland area leads to the urbanization of 120 square yards of land, compared with 480 square yards for the Washington State area (Hill 2000).

To evaluate the UGB in more detail, the categories that Scott Campbell (1996) defines as the components or vectors of sustainability are used here. As he points out, planners in various settings seek to move communities toward the three goals of environmental protection, economic development, and social equity. The goals of "green cities," "growing cities," and "just cities" remain in constant tension with each other as planners in different institutional and community settings usually emphasize one aim over the others. Seeing these goals as the points of a triangle, he argues that sustainable development lies at the triangle's center. "This center cannot be reached directly, but only approximately and indirectly, through a sustained period of confronting and resolving the triangle's conflicts" (Campbell 1996, 296).

## Green Cities

There is little argument that the UGB benefits the undeveloped landscape and natural systems. Environmental advocates take a strong interest in Portland's growth management. Their involvement links closely to the same sense of physical limits that influenced the origins of LCDC, for relatively little "urbanizable" land remains between the suburban frontier and edges of the Northwest forest to the east and west. Environmental groups have, therefore, been strong supporters of a compact metropolis, in spite of its bias toward urban social and cultural values.

The grudgingly expanding UGB restricts development of prime farmland in total, although it places strong pressure on the 13,000 acres of farmland inside the UGB. Berry and vegetable farms in the Columbia River flood plain east of the airport, for example, are rapidly converting to crops of slab-walled flex buildings for wholesaling and manufacturing, but comparable acreage on Sauvie Island, approximately the same distance from downtown, is firmly protected from suburban sprawl (Rusk 1999). In the words of Gresham Mayor Gussie McRobert, "I know it's motherhood and apple pie and the flag all wrapped up together, but the truth of the matter is, if the land is inside the urban growth boundary, it's supposed to grow houses" (Nokes 1994). Higher densities for new subdivisions and extensive construction of apartments and attached housing mean a net decrease in acres consumed.

A tight UGB that reduces disconnected land development facilitates the acquisition and preservation of open and natural spaces around the urbanized area. Such preservation can protect natural elements that have little market valuation, such as wildlife corridors. Voters in 1995 approved a $135.6 million bond issue for Metro to buy open and natural lands. Through April 2001, the agency had spent $53.6 million for 1,154 acres inside the UGB and $50.5 million for 5,756 acres outside. Several large acquisitions protect wildlife habitat that connects to the Coast Range or the Cascade foothills.

Compact growth presumably helps curtail growth in vehicle miles traveled per capita. Compactness means shorter trips, if not necessarily fewer trips. It makes the transportation rule feasible and lets local officials take it seriously. The presence of the UGB also offered a powerful argument against a proposed Westside Bypass that would have linked the southern and western arms of the Portland "starfish" by cutting through farm and forestland outside the boundary. Opponents argued that the bypass was a boundary-buster that would inevitably drag development in its wake.

Possible negatives include effects on drainage and runoff. Compact development may or may not reduce the amount of paved or impervious surface per new resident or dwelling unit. It will concentrate storm water runoff problems, but may reduce lawn fertilizer pollution.

Another negative is the reduction of open space within the UGB. Proposals to expand industrial uses onto undeveloped areas within the boundary (such as Port of Portland plans for a marine terminal expansion) may split environmentalists from compact growth advocates. Meanwhile, in-fill on vacant lots and blocks deprives older neighborhoods of informal open space. Where this sort of development is countered in turn by Portland's environmental overlay zone and stream buffers required by the Endangered Species Act, property owners face regulations piled on regulations. Indeed, a critic could argue that the result is "fixes to correct a fix," like the cycles and epicycles devised to save the Ptolemaic model of a terra-centric solar system.

## Growing Cities

There is no evidence that the simple presence of the UGB has inhibited economic development or undercut the prosperity of the Portland

region. Nonfarm employment in the six-county PMSA (primary metropolitan statistical area), as measured by the U.S. Bureau of Labor Statistics, grew by 272,000 jobs from January 1991 to December 2000, for a
total of 982,000 jobs. Unemployment for the metropolitan area ran at
just over 4 percent for the middle and late 1990s.[8]

Compact growth presumably encourages economic development by
keeping taxes low through reduced infrastructure costs, making more
dollars available for social services, education, and private consumption.
The accepted figure from national studies is a 20 percent reduction of
infrastructure costs over sprawling development (Downs 1999).

Although these gains could well be offset by higher industrial land
costs, there is not yet evidence of a problem, given the levels of job
increase. There are still opportunities—like that currently being pursued
by Bechtel Corporation east of the Portland airport—to build neotraditional industrial and office parks, rather than sprawling ones. In addition, livability may be a selling point for recruiting some businesses and
workers. The Portland mix of compactness and access to rural and
wilderness lands will not entice every footloose corporation and soft-
ware writer, but it certainly gives Portland a distinctive recruiting pitch
and competitive niche.

### Just Cities

In the mid-1990s, both Portlanders and urban specialists around the
United States discovered a housing affordability problem, and interested
journalists quickly brought the problem to national attention. Positive
write-ups of Portland's strong metropolitan governance and central city
vitality continued, but housing critics gleefully noted the negative consequences of the "Great Wall of Portland." Many analyses of Portland
have taken on a "yes . . . but" format that carefully balances praise with
sharp criticism of over-regulation. We find such stories not only in the
*Wall Street Journal,* which is ever vigilant to defend untrammeled markets, but also in such potentially sympathetic media as the *Washington
Post* (Claiborne 1997) and *Governing* (Ehrenhalt 1997).[9]

Portland in the middle and late 1990s *did* have a serious shortage of
single-family houses affordable to new households and working-class
families. In the aggregate, housing prices rose rapidly in the 1970s,
dropped during Oregon's prolonged recession in the early and middle
1980s, recovered in the late 1980s, and escalated rapidly in the 1990s. In

constant dollars, the median sale price of a single-family house in the Portland area increased by 50 percent from 1988 to 1995, passing the previous high achieved in 1979, according to Harvard's Joint Center for Housing Studies (1996). The price of undeveloped lots followed the same trajectory. In Washington County, for example, lot prices lagged the Consumer Price Index from 1985 to 1990, but then surged rapidly ahead. The median price of single-family houses is still below that in several other West Coast metropolitan areas. However, price increases have been especially troublesome because per capita income did not begin to increase until the mid-1990s, thus falling behind housing prices. Price increases have certainly pushed thousands of middle-priced houses out of the reach of lower-income households.

A tight housing market has also led to explosive price increases in previously undervalued neighborhoods. In the early 1990s, middle-class neighborhoods on the less fashionable east side of Portland closed much of the price gap with west side neighborhoods. By the mid-1990s, families and speculators were hunting for rapidly disappearing bargains in neglected working-class and racially mixed areas. A large community development corporation (CDC) that operates in inner southeast Portland (an area with many working-class and lower-middle-class neighborhoods) finds that houses in need of rehabilitation that could be acquired for $30,000 in the early 1990s now sell for $100,000 or more. The pattern was similar in modest and unfashionable neighborhoods elsewhere on the east side of the city. One retired grocery checker from northeast Portland commented to an *Oregonian* reporter, "That's the talk of the town, people coming over and buying up these houses. You look at all the people. They're not black. I thought you people were too scared to come over in this neighborhood" (Mayer 1996).

The most recent figures show at least a short-term cooling of the market for single-family housing. The median sales price in the Portland-Vancouver metro area increased by 4.6 percent in 1998, 6.7 percent in 1999, and 3.8 percent in 2000, rates lower than those found in San Francisco, Seattle, Denver, Phoenix, Boise, or Salt Lake City ("Indicators of Western U.S. Economy" 2000a). The affordability index of the National Association of Home Builders (NAHB) (based on the ratio of median sales price to median income for 191 metropolitan areas) had showed a steady loss of affordability from 1991, when Portland was the 112th least affordable market, to 1997, when Portland ranked as the 2nd least affordable market. In late 1999, the metro area had improved to 24th least affordable. The latter position, according to the NAHB, implied that a family with the median metropolitan income could afford 46 percent of the houses sold (Oliver 2000). In the fall of 1999, the *Oregonian* found a good supply of mid-market houses ($140,000 to $170,000) affordable to moderate-income families in all but a few subareas of the metropolitan area (Bjorhus 1999). It is also worth noting that researcher Chris Nelson has found that homeownership in recent years has increased faster in Portland than in Atlanta (Peirce 2000).

With a focus on single-family housing, advocates of growth management and proponents of free-range markets can agree on many facts but not the cause: Are rapid increases a direct result of the limitation of land supply, or are they a demand-driven speculative bubble? The Metropolitan Home Builders Association and market advocates cite the NAHB rankings and point to a tight UGB that artificially constricts land supply and drives up the price of undeveloped land. They also argue that Metro justifies its reluctance to approve substantial UGB with unrealistic expectations about possible densities. They believe that Metro assumes far greater changes in household behavior than are likely, given historic American housing preferences and consistent underbuilding within the UGB (Mildner, Dueker, and Rufolo 1996; Morissette 1996). With current population projections and development densities, a frozen UGB would create a 42,000 unit shortfall by 2017; even with development at recommended densities, there would be no place to put 8,600 needed units.

Critics of Metro's growth management assumptions point to examples of community resistance to higher densities. Several smaller suburbs, mostly residential and upper middle class, continue to favor large-lot, single-family development. Like their counterparts around the country, many residents of West Linn, Tigard, Milwaukie, and other south side suburbs fear both the local environmental costs and implied social diversification of the 2040 scheme. "Metro planners moan about the suburbs as if they were a disease," complains West Linn City Council member John Jackley (1996), "and do their best to plan us out of existence with their 'urban village' concepts, functional plans and density dictates" (also see O'Toole 1996). The mayor of Tigard complained that the plan precludes large-lot, upscale developments and other "lifestyle opportunities that Tigard has always had the opportunity to provide" ("Tigard Takes Issue," 1996). Similar sentiments in hilly postwar neighborhoods in the southwest quadrant of the city of Portland made a multiyear district planning process in the mid-1990s too politically dangerous to complete.

At a different point on the economic scale are a number of working-class neighborhoods in Portland that have parallel concerns about in-fill and redevelopment. These neighborhoods have struggled to maintain their viability in the face of suburbanization, institutional disinvestment, and sometimes-public neglect, even while middle-class Portland was thriving.[10] Residents fear that higher densities in the 2040 Plan "town centers" and along "main street" transit corridors will mean new low-income renters who will bring lower property values just as they have fought off urban decay—renters who will be "tucked neatly away . . . out of sight from the rest of Portland" (Gorman 2000). In fact, vacant lot in-fill, accessory apartments attached to single-family houses, and similar options will account for only a small fraction of Portland's planned addition of 71,000 dwelling units. A group of civic leaders recently suggested that the city back off from pushing such neighborhood in-fill because the political cost of decreasing support for city planning is not worth the incremental gain in density (City Club of Portland 1999).

In contrast, growth managers—and Metro in specific—think that the essential cause has been booming demand as Portland enjoys flush times and what may be a one-time influx of capital from a wave of California in-migrants in the early and middle 1990s. Rather than utilizing the NAHB rankings, they cite Urban Land Institute data that show price increases for residential building lots in Portland for 1990–95 to be in line with increases in numerous comparable cities from Albuquerque to Indianapolis to Charlotte (Burton 1996). Believers in a compact Portland also argue that expansion of the UGB would be a temporary fix at best, with most land freed by such an expansion being used for large-lot developments. Legislative action in 1999 that prohibited Metro from requiring the inclusion of affordable housing in new development supports that skepticism, especially given that the homebuilding industry strongly supported that action.

In the conventional demand-side explanation of housing inflation, rapid job growth attracts in-migrants who create a bull market by bidding on a supply of housing that grows more slowly than booming population. The real estate market can quickly take on the character of a speculative bubble in which price increases are supported by a boom psychology—investor reactions to each other and to recent price increases rather than to market fundamentals. A recent effort to model the Portland area housing market (Phillips and Goodstein 2000) utilized data from 37 metropolitan areas to estimate the effects of supply constraints, demand, and speculation on housing prices. The study concludes that Portland housing prices were playing catch-up during the early and middle 1990s and are probably nearing equilibrium with prices in comparable and competitive cities. The driving forces were the economic fundamentals of population, employment, and income growth combined with speculation. The study suggests that the UGB effect added at most $10,000 to housing prices—an important effect but one dwarfed by demand factors.

Often omitted from the discussion of housing costs is the behavior of the rental market. The UGB and the LCDC Housing Rule bias construction toward apartments. The current 50-50 split between single-family and multifamily units meets the needs of many small households. The large supply of new apartments also keeps rents relatively low. At the end of 1999, the average rent for a one-bedroom apartment in the Portland market was $746, less than the U.S. average of $858 and below other West Coast cities ("Indicators of Western U.S. Economy" 2000b). Average apartment rents increased only 33 percent during the 1990s, far less than the doubling of single-family house prices; adjusted for inflation, the comparative increases were 5 percent and 59 percent (Oliver 1999).

It is also important to note that rising prices for owner-occupied housing benefit existing homeowners at all economic levels. Maintaining a tight growth boundary tends to interrupt the classic trickle-down approach to affordable housing. Traditionally, we have assumed that the housing market operates like a big thrift shop. Upper-income families in search of newer and bigger houses will walk away from functional though somewhat worn neighborhoods and hand them down the economic ladder. This process has made some affordable housing available, but it has also tended to devalue working-class neighborhoods, except when aggregate demand is very high. Indeed, the trickle-down model has seriously undercut homeownership as a capital accumulation strategy for the working class (Edel, Sclar, and Luria 1984). With an inelastic UGB, the Portland area will be less likely to hand down cheap housing for new households, but also less likely to undermine the investments of many working-class and middle-class families.

A final equity issue is job access. We might expect that compactness would tend to maintain close-in jobs and support availability of public transit. Indeed, data for the early 1990s showed that 37 percent of new jobs were located on redevelopment or in-fill sites (Phillips and Goodstein 2000). Paul Lewis (1996) suggests that the jobs/housing imbalance is less severe in the Portland area than in the roughly comparable metropolis of Denver. Myron Orfield (1996) has found relatively less fiscal disparity between Portland and its suburbs than in other metropolitan areas. Differences in socioeconomic status between central-city residents and suburbanites are also relatively small (Abbott 1997).

## Markets, Morals, and Politics

The UGB is basically working as originally intended. It has created a dual land market and places major legal obstacles in the way of urban development on farmland and forestland. It increases the density of new development, as builders and homebuyers are unable to afford as much land per dwelling. It encourages in-fill, with 25 percent of new housing currently being constructed on in-fill or redevelopment sites. It has allowed Portland to absorb substantial increases in population and jobs with only a small increase in urbanized area, in sharp contrast to most American cities.

More problematic is the uncertain effect of the UGB on housing costs. Even factoring in reduced land consumption and lower infrastructure costs for each unit, the net effect is probably to increase housing prices. However, we are not certain of the magnitude of that effect in relation to the effects of booming demand and speculation. Nor do we know if the rapid price increases of the 1990s were a one-time adjustment or the start of a long-term trend.

The political reality is that the UGB is here to stay. Voters in Oregon have four times turned down efforts to abolish or weaken the state land use planning system. Voters in the Portland area have repeatedly chosen to retain Metro or to expand its authority and functions, of which regional growth management is one of the most prominent and controversial (Abbott and Abbott 1991). A prominent antigovernment activist with successful tax limitation campaigns under his belt, Bill Sizemore of Oregon Taxpayers United backed away from gathering signatures for anti-Metro ballot measures in both 1998 and 1999. Even market fundamentalists such as the Reason Public Policy Institute (Staley and Mildner 1999) argue for incrementally faster expansion, not abolition.

An ideological consensus about regional growth policy has therefore developed in parallel with the regional political coalition. The majority of *involved* citizens in Portland and the suburbs share a basic vision of a metropolis that above all else is "not Los Angeles" and "not Seattle." (Whether the Portland image of Los Angeles is accurate is another question.) They agree that the best way to avoid the gridlock and endless subdivisions that presumably characterize their West Coast neighbors is to support relatively compact land development within the constraints of the UGB.

The consensus is nourished by an array of "good planning" and environmental organizations that benefit from the high level of public awareness and approach growth management with a regional perspective. Supplementing locally oriented neighborhood and watershed groups are the Audubon Society, 1000 Friends of Oregon, Livable Oregon, STOP (Sensible Transportation Options for People), the Coalition for a Livable Future, and sometimes the Metropolitan Homebuilders Association. In the Portland style, these are pressure groups that speak to metropolitan concerns and utilize rational analysis and education to mobilize citizens around regulatory options to metropolitan sprawl.

Opponents phrase the issue as inefficient regulation versus efficient markets. Their arguments are pragmatic and grounded on market assumptions that have powerful sway at the opening of the 21st century. They correctly point out that a tightly patrolled UGB creates social costs as well as benefits and worry that regional plans do not adequately account for these costs. Many are uneasy with the "leftward" trend of opinion about regional planning, as described above, and growing political obstacles in the way of substantial UGB expansion (Staley and Mildner 1999).

Behind the competing assumptions are alternative analytical premises and different visions of the good city. Market arguments against UGBs (and light rail) are generic and theory based, asserting "this is how IT works." Such arguments have become more prominent as Portland has absorbed more outsiders without "Oregon" values.

Defenders of the "Portland way," in contrast, happily ignore the "marketist" *zeitgeist* in favor of particularity. They stress the importance of local circumstances and the special validity of place; they will deny, for example, that Portland would ever make the disastrous disinvestment in bus service that damaged Los Angeles in the 1990s. Remembering that households select a neighborhood as well as rent or buy a dwelling unit with each housing choice, UGB advocates can argue that compactness increases the value of the housing-neighborhood package by promoting more "real neighborhoods" along the neotraditional model. Those who argue for expansion might counter that a tight UGB reduces the value of the same package by making it more difficult to opt for "Green Acres."

Thus, the UGB is not only a planning tool, but also a symbol. Advocates of substantial and rapid expansion try to make the tight UGB a symbol of cultural elitism: To expand the boundary would be to recognize the legitimacy of the suburban lives that most Americans prefer, while freezing the boundary would impose the minority values of an environmentalist elite on the majority. Proponents of a constricting boundary see the specific land-planning choice as a symbol of community willingness to make hard choices for sustainability. Each side implicitly accuses the other of selfishness—of yuppie self-satisfaction and disregard for the poor, or heedless disregard of the consequences of personal gain.

In making symbolic claims, UGB advocates have enlisted moral rhetoric in ways that resonate strongly with American values as well as Oregon's political culture. It is fair to say that Portland frustrates market conservatives not only because they think the UGB is misguided and self-defeating, but also because its regional planning advocates have more effectively staked the claim to virtue. They have strong persuasive appeal because they have captured the classic conservative value of civil community, arguing that the UGB promotes the virtues of moderation (carefully planned growth) in contrast to the vice of greed, and the values of public interest against liberal individualism. They have enlisted William James, Herbert Croly, and the progressive tradition on behalf of the promise of metropolitan life. They also link the UGB to such well-seasoned and emotion-laden ideas as the moral benefits of family farm life and agriculture and the spiritual benefits of rural and backwoods landscapes—in effect drafting Thomas Jefferson and John Muir for the "smart growth" cause.

## NOTES

1. Examining the timing of adoption of 88 policies and programs, Jack Walker (1969) found that Oregon ranked eighth as an innovator among 48 states.

2. Hector Macpherson, interview by the author and Deborah Howe, 14 December 1992.

3. Arnold Cogan, interview by the author, 17 December 1992.

4. The 19 goals involve (1) Citizen Involvement; (2) Land Use Planning; (3) Agricultural Lands; (4) Forest Lands; (5) Open Spaces, Scenic and Historic Areas, and

Natural Resources; (6) Air, Water, and Land Resources Quality; (7) Areas Subject to Natural Disaster and Hazards; (8) Recreational Needs; (9) Economy of the State; (10) Housing; (11) Public Facilities and Service; (12) Transportation; (13) Energy Conservation;
(14) Urbanization; (15) Willamette River Greenway; (16) Estuarine Resources; (17) Coastal
Shorelands; (18) Beaches and Dunes; and (19) Ocean Resources.

5. In 1998, voters in Milwaukie, a largely residential community of 20,000,
recalled the members of their city council who supported light rail and its promise of
intensified development. A majority of that city's residents thus ally with other middle-
class residential suburbs in questioning the implications of the compact city model.

6. Ethan Seltzer, interview by the author, 4 April 1991.

7. In January 2000, the Oregon Court of Appeals rejected Metro's designation of
18,000 acres of "urban reserves," a designation of land onto which the UGB would eventually expand. The Court agreed with environmental and farm groups (1000 Friends of
Oregon and the Oregon Farm Bureau Federation) that Metro had incorrectly included
prime farmland in the reserves without fully considering alternatives. Metro and LCDC
will probably scrap the whole idea of urban reserves. Since the next UGB expansion was
to be into the urban reserves, however, Metro will probably need to restudy and rejustify
that expansion.

8. For 1994 through 2000, annual unemployment rates were 4.3, 3.7, 4.5, 4.3, 4.3,
4.5, and 3.9 percent, respectively.

9. There are actually two criticisms of Portland's growth pattern. In addition to
attacks on overregulation from the right, there are also attacks by such advocates of strong
design control as James Howard Kunstler and Andres Duany. These design-oriented critics point out that much of the area's actual suburban development of the 1980s and 1990s
looks like that throughout the United States. Their implication is that Portland has squan-
dered a chance to build a high-density, pedestrian-oriented metropolis by underregulat-
ing the subdivision layout and architecture.

10. This paragraph applies to much of North Portland/St. Johns and to low-
income areas in outer southeast Portland.

## REFERENCES

Abbott, Carl. 1983. *Portland: Planning, Politics, and Growth in a Twentieth Century City.*
Lincoln: University of Nebraska Press.
———. 1994a. "The Oregon Planning Style." In *Planning the Oregon Way: A Twenty-Year
Evaluation,* edited by Carl Abbott, Deborah Howe, and Sy Adler (205–26). Corvallis: Oregon State University Press.
———. 1994b. "Metropolitan Portland: Reputation and Reality." *Built Environment*
20 (1): 52–64.
———. 1997. "The Portland Region: Where Cities and Suburbs Talk to Each Other—
and Often Agree." *Housing Policy Debate* 8 (1): 11–51.
Abbott, Carl, and Margery Post Abbott. 1991. *Historical Development of the Metropolitan
Service District.* Portland, Ore.: Metropolitan Service District.

Abbott, Carl, and Deborah Howe. 1993. "The Politics of Land Use Law in Oregon: Senate Bill 100 Twenty Years After." *Oregon Historical Quarterly* 94 (1): 5–39.

Abbott, Carl, Gerhard Pagenstecher, and Britt Parrott. 1998. *From Downtown Plan to Central City Summit: Trends in Portland's Central City, 1970–1998.* Portland, Ore.: Association for Portland Progress.

Adler, Sy. 1994. "The Oregon Approach to Integrating Transportation and Land Use Planning." In *Planning the Oregon Way: A Twenty-Year Evaluation,* edited by Carl Abbott, Deborah Howe, and Sy Adler. Corvallis: Oregon State University Press.

Bjorhus, Jennifer. 1999. "Middle-Class Buyers Can Still Find a Way Home." *Oregonian,* 19 September.

Burton, Mike. 1996. Response to Mildner/Dueker/Rufolo report, "Impact of the Urban Growth Boundary on Metropolitan Housing Markets." Memorandum to Metro Council Growth Management Committee, May 21.

Callenbach, Ernest. 1975. *Ecotopia.* Berkeley, Calif.: Banyan Tree Press.

Campbell, Scott. 1996. "Green Cities, Growing Cities, Just Cities? Urban Planning and the Contradictions of Sustainable Development." *Journal of the American Planning Association* 62 (3): 296–312.

Chapman, Nancy, and Joan Starker. 1987. "Portland: The Most Livable City?" In *Portland's Changing Landscape,* edited by Larry Price (197–207). Portland, Ore.: Portland State University and Association of American Geographers.

Christ, Janet. 1996. "Katz Emphasizes Containment." *Oregonian,* 27 January.

City Club of Portland. 1999. *Increasing Density in Portland.* Portland, Ore.: City Club of Portland.

Claiborne, William. 1997. "Cracks in Portland's 'Great Wall': A Strict Model of Controlled Growth Begins to Budge." *Washington Post,* 29 September.

Downs, Anthony. 1999. "Some Realities about Sprawl and Urban Decline." *Housing Policy Debate* 10 (4): 955–74.

ECO Northwest. 1991. *Urban Growth Management Study: Case Studies Report.* Salem, Ore.: Department of Land Conservation and Development.

Edel, Matthew, Elliott Sclar, and Daniel Luria. 1984. *Shaky Palaces: Homeownership and Mobility in Boston's Suburbanization.* New York: Columbia University Press.

Ehrenhalt, Alan. 1997. "The Great Wall of Portland." *Governing* 10 (4): 20–24.

Elazar, Daniel. 1972. *American Federalism: A View from the States.* New York: Thomas Y. Crowell.

Garvin, Alexander. 1996. *The American City: What Works, What Doesn't.* New York: McGraw-Hill.

Gastil, Raymond. 1975. *Cultural Regions of the United States.* Seattle: University of Washington Press.

Gaustad, Edwin S. 1976. *Historical Atlas of Religion in America.* New York: Harper and Row.

"Give Planners the Tools." 1991. *Oregonian,* 1 October.

Gorman, Dan. 2000. "Two Groups Don't Work in St. Johns' Best Interests." *Oregonian,* 22 February, letter to the editor.

Gragg, Randy. 1999. "Linda K. Johnson: On Interpreting Urban Growth." *Oregonian,* 15 October.

Halprin, Lawrence. 1972. *The Willamette Valley: Choices for the Future.* San Francisco: Lawrence Halprin and Associates.

Harvard University Joint Center for Housing Studies. 1996. *The State of the Nation's Housing.* Cambridge, Mass.: Harvard University Joint Center for Housing Studies.

Hill, Richard. 2000. "A Satellite's View of Urban Sprawl." *Oregonian,* 8 March.

"Indicators of Western U.S. Economy." 2000a. *Oregonian,* 23 January.

"Indicators of Western U.S. Economy." 2000b. *Oregonian,* 13 February.

Jackley, John. 1996. "Endangered Species." *Oregonian,* 24 November.

Klingman, David, and William W. Lammers. 1984. "The 'General Policy Liberalism' Factor in American State Politics." *American Journal of Political Science* 28 (3): 598–610.

Knaap, Gerrit. 1985. "The Price Effects of an Urban Growth Boundary in Metropolitan Portland, Oregon." *Land Economics* 61 (1): 26–35.

———. 1994. "Land Use Politics in Oregon." In *Planning the Oregon Way: A Twenty-Year Evaluation,* edited by Carl Abbott, Deborah Howe, and Sy Adler (3–23). Corvallis: Oregon State University Press.

Knaap, Gerrit, and Arthur C. Nelson. 1992. *The Regulated Landscape: Lessons on State Land Use Planning from Oregon.* Cambridge, Mass.: Lincoln Institute of Land Policy.

Lewis, Meriwether, and William Clark. 1965. *History of the Expedition of Captains Lewis and Clark,* edited by Elliott Coues. New York: Dover.

Lewis, Paul. 1996. *Shaping Suburbia: How Political Institutions Organize Urban Development.* Pittsburgh: University of Pittsburgh Press.

Liu, Ben-Chieh. 1975. *Quality of Life Indicators in U.S. Metropolitan Areas, 1970: A Comprehensive Assessment.* Washington, D.C.: U.S. Environmental Protection Agency.

MacColl, E. Kimbark. 1979. *The Growth of a City: Power and Politics in Portland, Oregon, 1915–1950.* Portland, Ore.: Georgian Press.

———. 1988. *Merchants, Money, and Power: The Portland Establishment, 1843–1913.* Portland, Ore.: Georgian Press.

———. 1995. "The Battle to Control Land Use: Oregon's Unique Law of 1973." In *Politics in the Postwar American West,* edited by Richard Lowitt (203–20). Norman: University of Oklahoma Press.

Mayer, James. 1996. "Home Taxes Soar in North, Northeast." *Oregonian,* 20 October.

Metropolitan Service District. 1995. *Regional Growth Goals and Objectives.* Portland, Ore.: Metropolitan Service District.

Mildner, Gerard, Ken Dueker, and Anthony Rufolo. 1996. "Impact of the Urban Growth Boundary on Metropolitan Housing Markets." Portland, Ore.: Center for Urban Studies, Portland State University.

Morissette, Don. 1996. "Expanding Horizons: Managing the Future of Growth." Lake Oswego, Ore.: Don Morissette.

Nelson, Arthur C. 1986. "Using Land Markets to Evaluate Urban Containment Programs." *Journal of the American Planning Association* 52 (2): 156–71.

Nokes, R. Gregory. 1994. "Growing Houses." *Oregonian,* 27 November.

Oliver, Gordon. 1999. "Apartment Hunters Move In on Deals." *Oregonian,* 6 December.

———. 2000. "Portland Sees Gain in Affordable Housing." *Oregonian,* 25 January.

Oregon Department of Land Conservation and Development. 2001. *Oregon's Statewide Goals and Guidelines.* http://www.lcd.state.or.us/goalpdfs/goal14.pdf. (Accessed February 3, 2002).

Orfield, Myron. 1996. *Metropolitics.* Washington, D.C.: Brookings Institution and Lincoln Institute of Land Policy.

O'Toole, Randal. 1996. "Packing 'Em In." *Oregonian,* 15 November.

Peirce, Neal R. 2000. "Sprawl Ties with Crime as Community Concern." *Oregonian,* 5 March.

Phillips, Justin, and Eban Goodstein. 2000. "Growth Management and Housing Prices: The Case of Portland, Oregon." *Contemporary Economic Policy* 18 (3): 334–44.

Robbins, William. 1997. *Landscapes of Promise: The Oregon Story, 1800–1940.* Seattle: University of Washington Press.

Ronda, James. 1993. "Calculating Ouragon." *Oregon Historical Quarterly* 94 (2/3): 121–40.

Rusk, David. 1999. *Inside Game/Outside Game.* Washington, D.C.: Brookings Institution.

Sharkansky, Ira. 1969. "The Utility of Elazar's Political Culture." *Polity* 2 (1): 66–83.

Staley, Sam, and Gerard Mildner. 1999. "Urban Growth Boundaries and Housing Affordability." Los Angeles: Reason Public Policy Institute.

Starker, Joan, and Carl Abbott. 1984. "The Fourteen Best Cities for Single Women." *Ms* 13 (5): 129–32.

Stroud, Nancy, and John DeGrove. 1980. *Oregon's State Urban Strategy.* Washington, D.C.: National Academy of Public Administration.

Sugarman, David B., and Murray A. Straus. 1988. "Indicators of Gender Equality for American States and Regions." *Social Indicators Research* 20: 229–70.

"Tigard Takes Issue with Growth Blueprint." 1996. *Oregonian,* 3 September.

Toulan, Nohad. 1994. "Housing as a State Planning Goal." In *Planning the Oregon Way: A Twenty-Year Evaluation,* edited by Carl Abbott, Deborah Howe, and Sy Adler (91–120). Corvallis: Oregon State University Press.

Unruh, G. Q. 1992. "Republican Apostate: Senator Wayne L. Morse and His Quest for Independent Liberalism." *Pacific Northwest Quarterly* 82 (3): 82–91.

Walker, Jack. 1969. "Diffusion of Innovation among the American States." *American Political Science Review* 63 (3): 880–89.

Walth, Brent. 1994. *Fire at Eden's Gate: Tom McCall and the Oregon Story.* Portland: Oregon Historical Society.

Young, Bob. 1995. "Stunting Our Growth." *Willamette Week,* 28 June.

# 9

# Politics and Regionalism

Myron Orfield

I t is said that regional equity reform will never occur in metropolitan
regions because the suburbs are now in charge of American politics.
While many agree that the suburbs are in charge of American politics,
the description of metropolitan reform as a debate about cities versus
suburbs, and Democrats versus Republicans, is simply wrong. The suburbs are not a monolith—economically, racially, or politically. They are
as diverse among themselves as the nation.

There are at least four types of regional communities and three sorts
of suburbs in American regions. Among regional communities, there
are central cities, with high social needs (most often with a majority of
poor school district populations), and low per capita tax wealth. Next,
there are at-risk suburbs, which comprise about 40 percent of the population of large U.S. regions. These communities have relatively high
poverty in the school districts, are often changing racially, and have low
levels of local resources—about three-quarters of the property tax
wealth of the central cities they surround. Third, there are developing
"bedroom" cities and school districts (about 25 percent of large U.S. regions) that are growing rapidly in population, especially among school-
age children. However, these communities grow without a sufficient tax
base to support growing student populations, increasing traffic congestion, or accelerating groundwater pollution arising from large-scale septic sewer problems. Often they lose fiscal capacity as they grow.

Because these three types of regional communities have small tax bases, they have comparatively high tax rates and comparatively low spending. They also exhibit comparatively low median household incomes as compared with the high-tax-base suburbs discussed below (e.g., $25–$30,000 in central cities in 1990, $25–$40,000 in older suburbs, and $35–$50,000 in low-tax-base developing suburbs). Families with low incomes, as those who live in these communities, are much more sensitive to property tax increases.

Finally, the fourth type of regional community is the affluent job center. These places are dominated by expensive housing, and most often, commercial industrial property (Albert 1979).[1] Central to understanding the problem of metropolitan disparity, and the libertarian's assertion of the benefits of competition, is realizing that only those who can afford the expensive housing in these places, generally over $350,000, can truly choose these communities with the high tax base and affluent schools. In a very real sense, only those with significant means can choose to have all the benefits of a metropolitan association, and externalize many of the social and economic costs on the other, less fiscally strong communities. These affluent communities, with the region's highest median incomes, never amount to more than 10 to 15 percent of a region's population. A small subset of these communities consists of very high residential tax base communities. These places with even more expensive housing sometimes eschew commercial development.[2]

Moreover, contrary to what may be standard political beliefs, not all cities in America are Democratic and not all suburbs are Republican in their political affiliations. In the Philadelphia region, the Republicans are so dominant that they even control the white working-class parts of the city. In Pittsburgh, at the other end of the state, the Democrats control not only the city, but also virtually all the suburban seats. On the other side of the country, in San Francisco, almost all the suburbs are represented by Democrats, while in Los Angeles to the south, the white suburbs are virtually all represented by Republicans. In general, Democrats have built their base out of the central cities, moving to the older and low-tax-base suburbs. In addition, if they are very effective, the Democrats capture a few of the high-tax-base suburbs. Republicans do just the opposite, starting with the outer, high-tax-based suburbs and moving in toward the cities. In many states in the country, the balance of power rests in races in a few older or low-tax-capacity developing suburbs. In this sense, the stressed-out suburban communities become the pivotal point of American politics and the best hope of regional reform.

Regionalism, a broad term that includes the support of regional reforms in the area of land use planning, regional fiscal equity, and the structural reform of regional governance, is not about party or ideology. At first, as the debate begins, it is often about place and where a person or politician sits or lives in a region. Properly engaged, older and fully developed suburbs and suburbs developing without sufficient tax capacity are proregional, not out of altruism, but out of self-interest. In the end, regionalism is in everyone's best interest, and regions such as Minneapolis and Portland (Oregon) that have undertaken the challenge of regional reform are comparatively successful places.

This chapter will discuss three eras of regional legislative activity in Minnesota, two of significant advances and an intermediate one of retrenchment. Republicans led the first with bipartisan support, although there were controversial legislative battles. The last, again highly controversial, was led by Democrats with bipartisan solutions. The intermediate period was led by a regional consensus whose members concentrated on small issues and eschewed controversy. They believed the way to save regionalism from growing opposition in the high-tax-base suburbs and competing units of government was to slow its defeat. It was a period of significant retrenchment and near abolition of Minnesota's regional system.

## Types of Regionalists

### Progressive Regionalists

The first period of regional reform in the 1960s and 1970s was led by "good government" Rockefeller Republicans and reform Democrats—in a sense, the progressives that Richard Hofstader (1955) writes of in his *Age of Reform*. In addition, business people were involved during a time when local corporations felt a stake in the community. These progressives were interested in reforming waste planning and shaping a more cohesive, cost-effective, efficient, and equitable region. While they supported equity, it was with a hard-headed calculation of the costs of inequity and the destructive competition for development among municipalities in a region. It was not, at least in their minds, a class-warfare kind of equity. They were connected to a group of U.S. and state legislators who were more civically interested and capable than today's generation and who demanded real reform rather than "reinventing government." We had not yet come to the era of media savvy "infocrats" who tour the nation hawking their most recent book-cum-fad to make government a slimmer corporation through total quality management and Japanese production techniques.

It was also a time of the rise of the war on poverty, the community development movement, and a host of new programs and experiments that Anthony Downs, the Kerner Commission, David Rusk, Joe Persky, and more recently john powell and Nicolas Lehmen would call "ghetto enrichment," or place-based strategies. In some ways, progressive Republican regionalism was an elegant, direct, and limited government response to the growing sprawl and interlocal disparity in many regions of the country. Men like Minnesota Governor Harold LeVander, Oregon's moderate Republican Tom McCall, Governors William Milliken and George Romney of Michigan, and the great Republican mayor of Indianapolis, Richard Lugar, were embarking on a very important and far-sighted strategy. Had the country listened to them, the 1980s and 1990s might have been much different for the central cities and older suburbs.

The progressive Republican and reform Democrats in Minnesota created regional sewer, transit, and airport authorities and the Metropolitan Council, a regional government with weak supervisory powers over these increasingly significant entities.[3] It was the view of these progressives that the council must be elected and that no other type of government would be legitimate. They fought hard for this, but lost in a tie vote in 1967 in the Minnesota Senate. The bill would pass the Minnesota House again twice in the early 1970s and would not be brought forth again for serious debate until this author introduced the bill in 1993. The progressives also created a metropolitan land use planning framework and enacted Minnesota's famous tax-base sharing or fiscal disparities law in 1971. Each of these significant accomplishments was a struggle, yet these reformers were tough and unafraid of controversy.

Contrary to the saccharine song of more recent consensus-based regionalists, the passage of the original fiscal disparities act was a very tough fight. While its origin was the ethereal world of progressive idealism, its political managers were shrewd vote counters. They made sure that two-thirds of the Twin Cities would understand that the bill would lower their taxes and improve their schools and public services at the same time. Many of these politicians were the remnants of the populist forces that never came to terms with the progressives in the Age of Reform in the early 20th century. While the liberals were seeking community development programs and looking to enhance the least functional parts of the 1960s Great Society program, their cousins, the populists, did not hesitate to raise the class card of growing disparities and basic unfairness to blue-collar voters in the low-property-value suburbs. And they collected most of the votes. While this was not the method of the progressives, they were smart enough and worked hard enough to suspend their revulsion and pass a bill to create a tax-sharing system. The author of the bill was Charles R. Weaver Sr., a Republican from the low-tax-base city of Anoka, an older freestanding or satellite community of the Twin Cities. Weaver had heretofore been suspicious of the growing wave of metropolitanism; he was a blue-collar disbeliever in pinstriped, "goo-goo" regionalism. He believed its sewer and land-planning components threatened the ability of the low-tax-base northern suburbs to develop property wealth. In 1969, at the behest of the Citizens League—an impressive local citizens' group—he introduced the first fiscal disparities bill that would share part of the growth of the business property tax base throughout the Twin Cities metropolitan region. It passed the Minnesota House, but the Senate refused to take it up. In 1971, the bill was again brought forth and met with strenuous objection from the southern and western suburbs, which were beginning to build large commercial tax bases. Weaver was strenuously attacked and called a communist, a socialist, a fellow traveler, and every other name one can imagine. (Later, in the 1990s, when this author would carry these bills and was called by the same names, the reply was, "It is really nothing. They called Weaver that in the 1960s, when a charge of communism actually meant something.")

On March 31, 1971, the bill passed the House again, this time by 90 to 42—24 fewer votes than two years before, signifying the volatile climate surrounding the bill. It was supported by a coalition of central-city, poor suburban, and rural legislators, and opposed by rich suburban representatives and scattered rural reinforcements (Albert 1979). Because Charlie Weaver was a Republican, the Republicans from northern suburban low-tax-base areas, as well as metro Democrats, voted with him, as did many rural Republicans with whom Weaver had built personal relationships. However, Weaver never gained the support of his fellow Republicans from property-wealthy southern suburban areas. Under the bill, the two-thirds of the region that won a new tax base, Republicans and Democrats alike, supported Weaver; the one-third that did not, opposed him (Albert 1979).

In the Senate, where opponents sensed a strong chance of defeating the bill, representatives from the southern suburbs developing large commercial tax bases fought it violently. Jerry Minea, chairman of the legislative committee of the Dakota County Development Association, called the bill "community socialism" and said such bills "are like Robin Hood—they take from the progressive communities such as Dakota County and give to the so-called backward ones" (Ackerberg 1971, 14B). He continued, "We would be feeding our weaker communities with the product of the work of others . . . Why should those who wish to work be forced to share with those who won't or can't help themselves?" (Dornfeld 1971, 10A). Eagan Town Board Chairman John Klein stated, "The fiscal disparities law will destroy the state. The seven metro counties will lose potential, people will be unemployed and children will be sent outside their communities to go to school." Klein added, "It was all a plot for one large metropolitan government which is nothing more than creeping communism" (Carr 1971). Inver Grove Heights Mayor George Cameron denounced the proposal, asking, "How can metro government take 40 percent of what we have and give it to those who can't operate on 100 percent?" while repeating Cameron's assertion that the bill was "communistic" (Carr 1971).

Senator Howard Knutson of Dakota County believed the bill was good long-term policy for the region and became one of its authors. He was immediately denounced by Dakota County Commissioner Pat Scully who said, "[Knutson] is out to hurt the taxpayers of this county . . . and [doesn't] have the interests of this county at heart, that's for damn sure" (Becker 1971, 26A). There would never again be a prominent "loser" in favor of tax-base sharing.

The bill squeaked out of a special Senate fiscal disparities subcommittee of the Metropolitan Affairs Committee by a single vote. It was subsequently killed in a procedural motion on the Senate floor. During a special legislative session called that summer to solve a school-funding deadlock, the bill was brought up again and battled its way to the Senate floor, where it passed by a single vote after another bitter debate. Seventy-five percent of the suburban senators voted against the bill, and most of these senators spoke against it ("Tax-Base Pool Bill Advances" 1971). In many ways, because of the strong suburban opposition in the Senate, the rural senators had carried the day. The Senate bill was then sent back to the

House, where it passed on a final vote 83 to 39, losing another seven votes amid growing controversy.[4]

The cities of Burnsville, Bloomington, and Shakopee, thinking they would be losing tax base under the bill, brought suit against the bill almost immediately. One of the most vociferous opponents, Dakota County Commissioner Leo Murphy, declared that the fiscal disparities law was a threat to the free enterprise system. He said the thrust of the legislation is to "take from those who have and give to those who have not in a manner suggested by Karl Marx" (Rhodes 1974, 58). The bill was declared unconstitutional by the trial court, but that decision was overturned and the law upheld by the Minnesota Supreme Court in *Burnsville v. Onischuk (1976)*. The U.S. Supreme Court refused to hear the appeal. In February 1975, almost five years after it was passed, the fiscal disparities law finally went into effect. In 1981, the southern suburbs again challenged the constitutionality of the law in *McCutcheon v. Minnesota,* where the law was upheld by the Minnesota Tax Court. This would be the last legal challenge, but there never has been any acquiescence from the southern suburbs with high property wealth. Representatives and state senators from the southern and western suburbs have tried to repeal the statute in virtually every session for the last 25 years.

### Consensus-Based Regionalists

In the wake of the tough, progressive regionalists came the consensus-based regionalists. It has often been joked that they believed that the problems of the region could be solved if leaders from various parts of the region came together, preferably in the boardroom of a local bank, and all together hummed the word "regionalism." Much like the third generation in wealthy families or labor unions that long ago achieved very high salaries for their members, this group did not have the ability to create or the energy to organize for reform. Nor, unfortunately, did they even have the stomach to fight for the major regional reforms that the first generation had created. On top of this, business support for the regional activities of the Citizens League began to erode. This was due to the rise of national and multinational companies with rotating, frequently moving executives. These temporary chieftains, in a more competitive environment, were simply less interested in controversy and more interested in political action that affected the bottom line in the near term. Thus, by the 1980s, the regional perspective consisted of the chairmen of the

Citizens League, a half-dozen legislators who had survived or managed to comprehend in the most antiseptic way the planning significance of what had been accomplished, two or three executives of declining power, and the editorial board of the Minneapolis newspaper. There was no outreach or advocacy for regional reform, and suburbs, particularly the wealthy developing ones beginning to feel the potentiality of metropolitan regulation, rebelled.

In an age of governmental reform, the luminous progressive coalition, with a patina of business and media support, had defeated parochialism in close-fought battles in the Nixon 1970s. In the Reagan 1980s, as the Twin Cities region rapidly grew more like the rest of the nation—more racially and socially segregated, and fanned by an increasingly sensationalist television news media—the fundamental division between those "with" and those "without" hardened. As the blue-collar worker came home from a long drive from the white-collar center of employment, popped open a beer in his declining-value house in a racially changing suburb, and night after night watched three black men in three different stories committing crimes before the peppy weather girl came on, opponents of regionalism sensed its growing vulnerability. The wealthy suburbs hired high-priced lobbyists and prepared for a fight to dismantle "regional socialism." Toughness and organization in the regional debate shifted to the opponents. And the war that they were willing to fight to dismantle the system was based on such powerful appeals to preserve suburbs from the threats of city life, an issue central to American politics, that progressive forces had no plan with which to respond.

During this period, from 1980 to 1990, almost every legislative session from the time the consensus-based regionalists occupied the field witnessed the erosion of a significant metropolitan power or responsibility that had been put in place in the 1960s and 1970s. Sometimes the consensus-based regionalists would oppose these changes, but more frequently they would just let them happen, arguing that the cause was hopeless, the legislature was full of cretins, and/or the business community had let them down. It was as if the process of politics and reform had become too sordid, too controversial, and too filthy for participation by educated men in clean suits.

During this time, major projects that should have been supervised by the Metropolitan Council were removed from its authority—specifically, the construction of a downtown domed stadium, a new regional racetrack, and most significantly, the Mall of America, now a local landmark and architectural masterpiece, which by its sheer size had a thunderous effect on the retail market in the central cities and southern suburbs of Minneapolis-St. Paul. As local policymakers talked more and more to each other, the land use planning statute was severely damaged by an amendment that gave precedence to local zoning. A far-sighted council system of infrastructure pricing for sewer costs was overturned, creating a system where struggling central cities and older suburbs were forced to finance exclusive low-density growth at the periphery of cities. The regional affordable housing system was abandoned, and well-conceived regional density guidelines were shelved. The council was subjected to humiliating legislative scrutiny of its most minute budget processes and the Metropolitan Urban Service Area (MUSA) line, the region's growth boundary, was extended 78 times, adding over 20,000 acres to the already low-density urban service area, making the boundary almost meaningless. Moreover, as the consensus-based regionalists became a local laughing stock, developers of expensive housing and their lawyers obtained coveted seats on the council itself, all without any opposition. To the consensus-based regionalist, the greatest evil was not defeat, but controversy. When anyone disagreed with another, harsh words and gestures were squelched with a smiling compromise. Sometimes, they believed there should be a smiling compromise in advance of an angry word or gesture. Sadly, given their weak position, they were often forced to cede to the "reasonableness" of their opponents. As the hammer blows of the regional opponents from the high-tax-base suburb built a base of resentment in the blue-collar suburbs against the Metropolitan Council, the regional response to this crisis was almost ridiculously effete. Where the first generation would fight tough fights for land use planning, the consolidation of massive regional service, and tax equity, this group would propose a bus that looked like a trolley car to connect the state capital to downtown Saint Paul in order to build regional citizenship.

Illustrative of the consensus-based regionalists and their vision for the region was their move to save the regional transit system by devastating it. In 1967, the Twin Cities created a regional transit system with a tax base that encompassed seven regional counties and 187 cities. Thus, in the 1960s and 1970s, the region had one of the most financially broad-based transit systems in the nation. By 1998, its funding per capita was below average (Office of the Legislative Auditor 1998). This happened for several reasons. First, federal and state funding for transit declined. Second, the region committed itself to more highway building and a lower-density pattern of development than most other regions in the United States, making it difficult to make transit work on such a playing field. Third, the Citizens League and the consensus-based regionalists used their influence to both defeat the development of a fixed-rail transit service and to fragment and privatize the transit system. By the early 1980s, the most prosperous parts of the region—a large number of the southwestern developing suburbs and cities that benefited most by the development of a regional sewer and highway system—were allowed to "opt out" of funding the transit system that served the struggling core of the region.

During the 1980s, federal funds for the transit system declined significantly. In 1978, federal grants accounted for 20 percent of the Metropolitan Transit Commission (MTC)'s[5] funding source. Five years later, they accounted for only 9 percent. Similarly, state funds fell from 25 to 8 percent of MTC's budget. This meant that MTC had to rely increasingly on fares and regional property taxes to provide revenues. The portion of revenues provided by the regional transit property tax doubled from 21 to 41 percent between 1978 and 1983 (Metropolitan Council 1984, table 3.1).

Light rail transit (LRT) systems received strong backing from the core of the region and such suburban legislators as Republican Senator Phyllis McQuade of St. Louis Park. The measures would again and again come before the legislature, culminating in a $1.3 billion request from the former Regional Transit Board in 1991. In the 1980s, the Citizens League became decidedly hostile to LRT (Citizens League 1986, 1991; Kimball 1986; Beran 1986a, b; "Common Sense" 1986; Blake 1986). The League's then powerful influence in the business community and with the metropolitan newspapers' editorial boards would ultimately severely damage the potential for a rail system. In the meanwhile, the Metropolitan Council, now in thrall to developers, would allocate virtually all federal resources to its large highway building program.

Toward the end of the 1970s, the high-tax-base developing suburbs began to loudly complain that they were not getting back transit service equivalent to their payments into the system. It was true that most of the bus system was concentrated in the cities and older suburbs, where almost all the transit-dependent population lived. Further, the new high-tax-base suburbs were developing at such a low density, and without any significant clustering of jobs, that it was very difficult to make a transit system work there. The reverse-commute issue had not yet surfaced.

Services in the outer ring are considerably less cost-efficient than services provided for in the central city and inner ring. For instance, in the

Metropolitan Council's regional services study, fares for trips from 5 to 11 miles in 1983 covered 50 percent of the costs of operation, while fares for trips longer than 11 miles covered only one-third of these costs (Metropolitan Council 1984). According to the Metropolitan Council, the costliest addition to MTC's operating costs, which rose 203 percent between 1971 and 1981, was its service expansion into the suburbs (Citizens League 1986). These costly services to the developing outer ring were a new demand on the MTC's strained budget.

About this time, the Citizens League began to clamor for privatization and fragmentation of the transit system and supported the high-tax-base suburbs that wanted to opt out of funding for regional transit (Citizens League 1983, 1986; "MTCS's Fleet" 1982; Transportation 1983). Original legislation on the opt-out system was passed by the Minnesota legislature in 1981. The first community to opt out was Plymouth in late 1983. Since that time, 11 other communities have withdrawn from the system. A map highlighting these communities looks very similar to a map of the southwestern, high-tax-base developing suburbs.

The opt-out communities represent 15.8 percent of the metropolitan population[6] and could levy 18.3 percent of the available property tax revenues for transit in the region. They account for 6.7 percent of the fixed route service miles, but only 3 percent of the riders using either Metropolitan Council Transit Operations (MTCO)[7] or opt-out services in 1996.[8] The operating cost per ride on MTCO is $2.10; for the opt-outs, it is $5.70 (Office of the Legislative Auditor 1998).

By 1998, with a large mismatch between the location of jobs and people to fill them, the opt-outs nevertheless viewed their primary responsibility as bringing their white-collar workers from the developing suburbs into the central business district of Minneapolis. Between 1 and 12 percent of their ridership "reverse-commuted"; that is, riders from the city and older suburbs commuted to the jobs in the developing suburbs (Minnesota Valley Transit Authority 1998).[9] By 1998, the combined reverse-commute ridership of the opt-out communities was only 388 riders for a portion of the region where during the 1980s, 61 percent of the region's new jobs were created.[10] Faced with the pressure of industries lacking workers in the early 1990s, the opt-out communities came to the legislature several times to ask for special support for reverse commuting. Rather than touch their own enormous tax base, they considered support for reverse commuting a regional or statewide responsibility.

By 1991, the Metropolitan Council was on the verge of being abolished. A measure to abolish the council passed on the House floor and the governor said that it should either do something or face abolition. The consensus-based regionalists were so frustrated that they were not even talking to each other about the ignorant legislature; they were focusing on other important reforms to solve growing metropolitan problems, such as school vouchers.

## The Metropolitan Federalists

A new type of regionalist arose in the 1990s. This author was intimately involved in this and writes clearly as a part of this school. This group was not yet politically involved in the 1960s and 1970s; most members were just entering politics in the 1990s. During these years, the share of students in the Minneapolis and St. Paul public schools who were from poor and minority families increased from 32 percent to 55 percent. Concentrated segregated poverty had grown at the fourth fastest rate in the nation. By the early 1990s, the rising murder rate in Minneapolis would surpass the declining rate in New York City. Regional federalists were very concerned about the growing concentration of poverty in the central cities and deeply influenced by the work of Anthony Downs, David Rusk, and William Julius Wilson.

Regional federalists began to become very interested in the possibility of reforms at a metropolitan level, with fair housing of particular concern. They also began to question whether the sprawl at the edge of the city was undermining the stability at the core and whether the older suburbs adjacent to the city were having the same or even more serious problems. As lawyers, many began to realize, almost accidentally, that an amazing metropolitan structure had been put in place 20 years before— a metropolitan structure severely out of fashion and irrelevant in liberal circles. "What does land use planning in the suburbs have to do with us?" asked the central-city politicos. Regional federalists went to the Metropolitan Council and the Citizens League to discuss their growing concerns, but were rebuffed. "This is not what the Metropolitan Council is about," they said. "It is about land use planning and infrastructure, not about urban issues or poverty." The embattled staff of the council, hoping it would survive to service their pensions, would diplomatically try to encourage inaction. The mandarins of the national lecture circuit emphatically told the regional federalists that if they raised any of these hard or controversial issues, it would only hasten the ultimate decline of the council. "We must wait for a better time," they said. "It may not be in our lifetime." Thus, those that the metropolitan federalists had hoped to embrace as brothers did not even want to have lunch with them.

In addition to the concentration of poverty at the core, the federalists became interested in the subsidies and governmental actions supporting sprawl. They were inspired by the land use reforms of Oregon and the work of Tom McCall, Henry Richmond, and 1000 Friends of Oregon. They carefully read the infrastructure work of Robert Burchell at Rutgers, and became aesthetically attached to the New Urbanism and Peter Calthorpe, its proponent of metropolitan social equity and transit-oriented development.

This second thrust of regionalism would bring concentrated poverty and regional fair housing into an equity discussion that had been heretofore only involved with interlocal fiscal equity. In the process, the dormant strength of the civil rights movement and social gospel would begin to be reengaged on metropolitan playing fields. In only a few years' time, hundreds of churches would join the movement for regional reform and enter a series of struggles no less important or less controversial than the early civil rights bills.

The regional federalists would weld environmentalism and the strength of the environmental movement into what had previously been a sterile discussion of planning and efficiency. They would bring the force of the rapidly declining, blue-collar suburbs—angry places unattached to either political party—to a vigorous regional reform discussion in which these suburbs, land of the Reagan Democrats, used their political strength to advance regional reform and regional power. Blue-collar mayors, some with decidedly hostile views toward social and racial changes in their communities, would join forces with African-American political leaders, environmentalists, and bishops of the major regional churches to advance a regional agenda that involved fair housing, land use planning, tax equity, and an accountable, elected regional governance structure.

The regional federalists were not in favor of an all-powerful regional government, but like the delegates that assembled in 1787, were dedicated to a more sustainable compact between independent governments. They wanted more equity, more planning, and more rebuilding of old communities as opposed to just building new ones and letting the old ones decay. As the Articles of Confederation could not protect the individual states and their citizens from the external threat of war, the weak, consensus-based regional instrument could not protect the cities from the internal threats of core decline and sprawl. Regional federalists believed that these internal threats would threaten their survival and independence, and in this sense the ability to compete fairly in a sustainable metropolitan order, as much as external threats affected the early United States.

The regional federalists' most important coalition partners were perhaps the older, struggling, fully developed suburbs. Why did the older suburbs support this movement? Certainly the creation of such a coalition between the central cities and inner- and low-tax-base suburban communities is no mean feat. These middle-income (often working-class) suburbs, which have been a loose cannon politically since 1968, hold the balance of power on regional issues and arguably on most political issues in the United States. Our most distinguished political commentators have written about the central significance of this group in holding and maintaining a ruling political coalition (Dionne 1991; Greenberg 1995; Phillips 1969, 1990, 1993, 1994; Johnson 1994; Greider 1993; Edsall and Edsall 1991).

On these merits, these middle-income, blue-collar suburbs are the largest prospective winners in regional reform. To them, tax-base sharing means lower property taxes, better services, and in particular, better-funded schools. Regional housing policy means, over time, fewer units of affordable housing crowding their doorstep. Once understood, this combination is unbeatable. However, in the face of this coalition stand long-term, powerful resentments and distrust, based on class and race and fueled by every political campaign since Hubert Humphrey lost the White House in 1968—and Archie Bunker became a Republican.

In Minnesota, after two years of constant cajoling, courting, and constant repetition about the growing inequities among the suburbs, the middle-income, working-class blue-collar suburbs joined the central cities and created a political coalition of great political power in the legislature. In 1994, this coalition passed the Metropolitan Reorganization Act, which placed all regional sewer, transit, and land use planning under the operational authority of the Metropolitan Council of the Twin Cities. In doing so, it transformed the Metropolitan Council from a $40-million-per-year planning agency to a $600-million-per-year regional government operating regional sewers and transit, with supervisory authority over the major decisions of another $300-million-per-year agency that runs the regional airport.

That same year, in the Metropolitan Land Use Reform Act, metro-area farmers were insulated from public assessments that would have forced them to subdivide farmland for development. In both 1993 and

1994, the legislature passed sweeping fair housing bills (both vetoed), but in 1995 a weakened version was finally signed. In 1995, the legislature passed a bill that significantly increased the scale of the regional tax-sharing system. In 1996, a statewide land use planning framework was adopted, a regional brownfields fund was created, and the legislature passed (but the governor vetoed) a bill to elect the new powerful council. In 1998, the region flexed money for a new light rail line. In the process, the sewer funding mechanism was changed back to the Metropolitan Council and the Met Land Use Planning Act was given precedence over local zoning again. The council gained back its role in important regional decisions, such as airport planning, and the regional federalists were on the move again. They were, however, forced to spend too much time and energy undoing the failure of the consensus-based regionalists.

## The Future Struggle of Regionalism

In the end, regionalism is a struggle like all real reform—like the movement against municipal corruption, the fight against the trusts, the women's movement, the labor movement, the consumer movement, the environmental movement, and the civil rights movement. None of these things happened easily or at once. In every region of this nation, 30 to 40 percent of the people live in central cities, 25 to 30 percent in older declining suburbs, and 10 to 15 percent in low-tax-base developing suburbs. There is nothing these communities can do by themselves to counteract their basic problems. Moreover, the suburban areas represent the swing votes of American politics. Thus, in every region of the nation there is a coalition to be built to improve the lives of all its citizens and the future of the regional community. It will not be easy—it will involve real reform and thus sustained effort; however, it can and must be done.

## NOTES

   1. Christopher Leinberger and his colleagues at Robert Charles Lesser and Co. (RCL & Co.), one of the most successful real estate consulting firms in the country, have made a great deal of money locating for businesses the favored quarter in a given

metropolitan area. These quarters are developing suburban areas that have mastered the art of skimming off the cream of metropolitan growth, while accepting as few metropolitan responsibilities as possible. RCL & Co. looks for areas with concentrations of housing valued above $200,000, high-end regional malls, and the best freeway capacity. As these communities grow affluent and their tax base expands, their exclusive housing market actually causes their relatively small local social needs to decline.

2. This is based on analysis of the Portland (Oregon), Chicago, Philadelphia, Milwaukee, Pittsburgh, Cleveland, Seattle, San Francisco, Los Angeles, Atlanta, Miami, Baltimore, Minneapolis-Saint Paul, Detroit, and Grand Rapids regions by the Metropolitan Area Research Corporation.

3. The Met Council was created in 1967 with jurisdiction in the seven regional counties of Hennepin, Ramsey, Anoka, Scott, Carver, Dakota, and Washington. Its members are appointed by the governor and (until 1994) it had loose supervisory authority over separate regional transit, waste control, and airport agencies.

4. In 1995, the House fiscal disparities bill would pass 71 to 63 and the Senate bill, 36 to 30. By 1995, almost 40 percent of the suburban members supported the bill, a considerable increase from the 25 percent that did in 1970. Moreover, had the vote been taken before the new Gingrich Republicans had been seated, there is no doubt that more than half the suburbs would have supported it and it would have passed the House and Senate by a higher margin than it had 25 years before.

5. After the 1994 reorganization, the MTC would become Metropolitan Council Transit Operations (MCTO).

6. Communities opting out can levy up to 90 percent of their regional transit property tax for transit purposes. Currently, opt-out communities submit their plans and request for funds to the Metropolitan Council. The remaining property tax levy goes to fund transit for the metropolitan region. The legislature eliminated deadlines for applying to opt-out in 1988, due to the small number of communities that had opted out at that time. In 1996, opt-out communities were given the option to not go through the Metropolitan Council approval process. However, these communities are limited to levying only 88 percent of their regional transit property tax. Unlike the rest of the metropolitan region, which has funding from the federal and state level, the opt-out cities can only access their portion of the regional transit property tax.

According to the Metropolitan Council 1997 Unified Budget, the amount of total transit property taxes from the opt-outs still operating through the Metropolitan Council is $3.4 million. An additional $9.4 million is estimated from opt-outs choosing to levy their own funds. Together this accounts for an estimated 18.7 percent of the transit property tax collected by the MTC and 17.4 percent of the total Metropolitan Council transit funds. However, these numbers are not completely accurate since communities can levy only up to 90 percent of their regional property tax and most levy even less. The opt-outs collected an estimated $11,872,161 in regional transit property taxes in 1996. They levied $9.5 million, or 83 percent of the total revenues available.

7. After the 1994 reorganization, the Metropolitan Transit Commission (MTC) became a division of the Metropolitan Council and was named the Metropolitan Council Transit Operations (MTCO).

8. John Williams, Minnesota House Research, memorandum (by e-mail) regarding opt-outs to author, 30 March 1998.

9. See Minnesota Valley Transit Authority (1998) (the largest opt-out provider), chart on MVTA ridership by passenger type—indicating only 2 percent of ridership reverse commutes; and Williams, memo to author stating that MVTA reports 5 percent, Maple Grove Transit reports 1 percent, and Southwest Metro Transit reports 12 percent of its ridership are reverse commuters.

10. Williams, memo to author.

# REFERENCES

Ackerberg, Peter. 1971. "Not Understood, Fiscal Disparity Proposal Delayed." *Minneapolis Star Tribune*, 17 April, 14B.

Albert, Alan Dale. 1979. "Sharing Suburbia's Wealth: The Political Economy of Tax Base Sharing in the Twin Cities." Bachelor's thesis, Harvard University, Cambridge, Mass., March.

Becker, Betsy. 1971. "Tax Share Bill Draws Dakota Fire." *Saint Paul Pioneer Press*, 14 April, 26A.

Beran, George. 1986a. "Light Rail Transit Opposed." *Saint Paul Pioneer Press*, 21 November.

———. 1986b. "Rail Transit Runs Last in Report." *Saint Paul Pioneer Press*, 21 November.

Blake, Laurie. 1986. "Citizen's League Says Car-Pooling Is Transit Key." *Minneapolis Star Tribune*, 21 November, 1B.

Carr, Donnie. 1971. "South Area Officials Attack Fiscal Disparity, Metro Taxing Authority." *Saint Paul Dispatch*, 12 August.

Citizens League. 1983. "Statement to the Legislative Study Committee on Metropolitan Transit." Minneapolis, Minn.: Citizens League. December 15.

———. 1986. "New Destinations for Transit." Minneapolis, Minn.: Citizens League.

———. 1991. "Light Rail Transit: The Regional Transit Board's Proposal to the 1991 Minnesota Legislature." Minneapolis, Minn.: Citizens League.

"Common Sense vs. Transit Magic Carpets." 1986. *Minneapolis Star Tribune*, 22 November, Editorial (citing CL opposition).

Dionne, E. J. 1991. *Why Americans Hate Politics*. New York: Simon & Schuster.

Dornfeld, Steven. 1971. "Dakota County Officials Protest Tax-Sharing Plan for Metro Area." *Minneapolis Star Tribune*, 18 April, 10A.

Edsall, Thomas Byrne, with Mary D. Edsall. 1991. *Chain Reaction: The Impact of Race, Rights, and Taxes on American Politics*. New York: W. W. Norton.

Greenberg, Stanley. 1995. *Middle-Class Dreams: The Politics and Power of the New American Majority*. New York: Times Books.

Greider, William. 1993. *Who Will Tell the People? The Betrayal of American Democracy*. New York: Simon & Schuster.

Hofstader, Richard. 1955. *The Age of Reform: From Bryan to FDR*. New York: Knopf.

Johnson, Haynes. 1994. *Divided We Fall: Gambling with History in the Nineties*. New York: W. W. Norton.

Kimball, Joe. 1986. "Mixed Signals Make Light Rail Iffy Issue." *Minneapolis Star Tribune*, 21 November, 6B.

Metropolitan Council. 1984. *Regional Service and Finance Study—Report to the Legislative Study Commission on Metropolitan Transit*. St. Paul, Minn.: Metropolitan Council.

Minnesota Valley Transit Authority. 1998. "Testimony and Attachments to the State Advisory Committee on Local Government." Burnsville, Minn.: Minnesota Valley Transit Authority. January 22.

"MTCS's Fleet of Sinking Ships." 1982. *City Pages*, 13 October.

Office of the Legislative Auditor. 1998. *Transit Services: A Program Evaluation Report.* State of Minnesota, February.

Phillips, Kevin. 1969. *The Emerging Republican Majority.* New Rochelle, N.Y.: Arlington House.

———. 1990. *The Politics of Rich and Poor: Wealth and the American Electorate in the Reagan Aftermath.* New York: Random House.

———. 1993. *Boiling Point: Republicans, Democrats, and the Decline of Middle-Class Prosperity.* New York: Random House.

———. 1994. *Arrogant Capital: Washington, Wall Street, and the Frustration of American Politics.* Boston: Little, Brown.

Rhodes, Jack. 1974. "Dakota County Commissioners Seek Stay of Fiscal Disparities Law." *Saint Paul Dispatch,* 25 September, 58.

"Tax-Base Pool Bill Advances: Plan Designed for Cities Area." 1971. *Minneapolis Star Tribune,* 2 June, 1A.

*Transportation: The Road Ahead.* 1983. Transcript from a Transportation Conference for Local Citizens, September.

# 10

# Less Sprawl, Greater Equity?
## *The Potential for Revenue Sharing in the Chicago Region*

Wim Wiewel
Joseph Persky
Kimberly Schaffer

A s in most older U.S. cities, sprawl in the Chicago region is long-standing and endemic. Residents have been suburbanizing almost since the development of the city, and trends show no signs of significantly reversing in the near future. The consequences for the region remain substantial. For example, the continuing suburbanization of jobs raises serious equity issues: Both low-income and central-city residents bear more than their share of the costs of employment decon-centration. Collectively, municipal governments—even outer suburban ones—also lose out as jobs decentralize.

These inequities and public costs suggest a role for the public sector in addressing sprawl or its negative effects. One means by which municipal fiscal disparities have been addressed in some regions is through regional revenue sharing. This chapter considers various types of revenue-sharing programs; reviews current efforts in the Chicago region toward imple-menting revenue sharing; and looks at what effect a revenue-sharing pro-gram might have on sprawl, equity, and regional cooperation. Finally, the potential for what revenue sharing might be in the Chicago region is considered.

## Sprawl, Equity, and Regionalism in Chicago

Growth patterns in the Chicago six-county region over the past several decades clearly exhibit sprawl, or metropolitan deconcentration, as defined in this book. The City of Chicago lost 700,000 people between 1950 and 2000 as its share of regional population fell from 70 percent to 36 percent (U.S. Census Bureau 2001). Between 1972 and 1995, the city's share of regional jobs fell from 56 percent to 34 percent (Illinois Department of Employment Security 1999). From 1970 to 1990, the region's population increased by 4 percent and the number of households grew by 22 percent, while the amount of urbanized land used for housing increased by 46 percent (Metropolitan Planning Council 1995).[1]

Metropolitan deconcentration is about more than just land consumption, however. The dramatic suburbanization of the Chicago region can be further identified in terms of race and class—basically, the shifting of wealth and white households from the city and older suburbs to the newer, outer suburbs. In 2000, 37 percent of the city's population was black and 26 percent was Latino, as compared with the rest of the region's 9 percent black and 12 percent Latino population (U.S. Census Bureau 2001). Between 1970 and 1990, the median real income of city households fell by 3 percent in Chicago, while it rose 42 percent in suburban Lake County (Wiewel and Schaffer 2000). Over the same 20-year period, the percentage of blacks living in poverty in the city of Chicago increased from 25 percent to 33 percent (Wilson 1996). From 1980 to 1993, the real tax base per household declined in 26 suburbs, mostly those in southern Cook County, while the tax base increased by more than 48 percent in 77 suburbs, mostly those north and west of the city (Orfield 1996).[2]

When discussing fiscal equity in a region, we can frame the problem in ways that lead either to people-based or place-based solutions. At a people-based level, greater equity can be achieved by helping individual low-income households to increase their incomes and move out of poverty. This chapter, however, will focus on equity among places. At the municipal level, the idea of equity suggests that local governments be on even playing fields.

Fiscal equity does not require that all municipalities should be identical. Indeed, there is an extensive literature showing how places differentiate themselves in terms of service mix, job base, and tax levels (Schneider 1989; Peterson 1981). However, an equity approach does argue against unreasonable disparities in tax bases, tax rates, and the percentage of residents in poverty among municipalities. In other words, each community's fiscal ability should be able to cover its fiscal need.

The Chicago region falls far short of such a goal. Poor, especially minority poor, households tend to be segregated in areas with low tax capacity and resulting low services, while wealthier (and usually white) households are able to congregate in municipalities with low tax rates but a high level of services.

More politically fragmented than most regions, the Chicago Primary Metropolitan Statistical Area (PMSA) has 293 municipalities, while the average PMSA in the country boasts only 60 (Dye and McGuire 1999). More than 1,200 units of local government—counties, municipalities, school districts, library districts, and other special districts—have taxing authority.

A sense of regional cooperation plays an important role in addressing sprawl and fiscal equity issues. Regions around the United States are struggling to balance the parochial interests of local governments and other parties with the greater regional good. Moreover, in recent years, researchers have suggested that greater regional cooperation can lead to other benefits, primarily economic ones, for the metropolitan area. Levine's preliminary work finds that "the scope of regional planning has a generally positive effect on change in per-capita income, and a consistent positive effect on change in MSA income share" (2000). Foster (2000) finds that higher levels of regional capital (including civic, corporate, political, and structural factors) lead to better regional outcomes in economic performance, although not necessarily in measures of social equity.

With such goals in mind, observers have complained about Chicago's political fragmentation and general lack of regional purpose. Yet significant regionalism efforts have been under way for many years and should not be overlooked. First, several formal regional public agencies exist, such as the Regional Transportation Authority, the Metropolitan Water Reclamation District, the Northeastern Illinois Planning Commission, and the Chicago Area Transportation Study. Other organizations, too, have contributed to cooperation at a broader level, often dealing directly with sprawl and equity issues. In particular, Chicago is recognized for strong involvement by its corporate leaders and community activists. Groups that have made recent efforts include:

- *Corporate and civic leaders.* The Commercial Club of Chicago, a long-standing blue ribbon organization of Chicago's corporate

258 URBAN SPRAWL: CAUSES, CONSEQUENCES, & POLICY RESPONSES

elite, recently spawned the Chicago Metropolis 2020 organization with the purpose of working toward a range of regional goals. In addition, the Metropolitan Planning Council (MPC), a nonprofit, nonpartisan group of business and civic leaders, has established the Campaign for Sensible Growth.

- *Councils of governments* (COGs). The Chicago region includes nine councils of government, each representing municipalities from specific geographic parts of the region. These organizations work on projects such as subregional economic development, legislative lobbying, transportation planning, and joint purchasing (Lindstrom 1998).

  Since late 1997, mayors representing each of the COGs plus the mayor of the City of Chicago have been meeting quarterly to discuss issues of importance to the region's municipalities. Two main priorities of the Metropolitan Mayors Caucus are improving regional air quality and promoting balanced regional economic growth.

- *Faith-based organizations.* United Power, a 240-member coalition of religious congregations, unions, and nonprofit organizations, works to build city-suburban bonds with the purpose of addressing regional social problems, such as health care for the area's 800,000 uninsured residents and the lack of homeownership opportunities for low- and middle-income families (McClory 1999).

  The Metropolitan Alliance of Congregations (MAC) is another interfaith group active in community organizing. Founded in 1997, MAC has 150 member congregations representing Christian, Jewish, and Muslim faiths. MAC's community organizing work focuses on empowering social democracy around four key issues, including public education funding, the distribution of federal transportation funds, the fair distribution of private credit (especially mortgages), and the reduction of high property taxes.

## Why Sprawl? The Effects of Private Decisions and Local Policy

### The Case for Decentralization

With varying underlying objectives, the groups described above have worked for a reversal of sprawl or its accompanying effects, often with a call for greater regionalism. Others, however, have countered that the arguments against deconcentration are not so clear-cut.

First, it is important to remember that sprawl is not a recent phenomenon. The trend toward suburbanization in the Chicago region was well under way by the end of the 19th century, when wealthier families and some businesses were able to locate farther from the central city because of improvements to the transportation systems (Lindstrom 1999). In the 20th century, the rate of deconcentration in Chicago peaked between 1960 and 1970, during which time the urbanized area became 15 percent less dense. From 1980 to 1990, on the other hand, the region became only 5 percent less dense. Bruegmann points out that Chicago could be following trends seen in other U.S. regions (including Miami, Los Angeles, Portland, and Phoenix), where the rate of decentralization peaks, slows, and then reaches some point at which the trend reverses and the region begins to become more dense.[3]

Second, the continued preference of much of the population for low-density living should not be forgotten. A study by the Urban Transportation Center (1998) at the University of Illinois at Chicago finds that recent population decentralization is primarily due to increases in income that allow more people to purchase land and move outward as they choose. Certainly, state and federal policies have facilitated sprawl, but they did not cause it; a considerable amount of decentralization would have occurred anyway because of personal preferences and benefits (Wiewel and Schaffer 2000).

In a classic article questioning the merits of the anti-sprawl movement, Gordon and Richardson (1997) conclude that residents overwhelmingly prefer low-density housing. They argue that because the United States is not nearing a land or energy shortage and because smart growth advocates have not demonstrated conclusively that compact cities are more efficient or equitable, "attempting a *reversal* of existing urban development is neither feasible nor desirable"(103).

## Addressing the Efficiency and Equity Questions

As Gordon and Richardson (1997) point out, anti-sprawl groups have often invoked the inefficiency or inequity of sprawl in vague, unquantifiable statements. In an attempt to contribute to the efficiency and equity debates surrounding city versus suburban development, Persky and Wiewel (2000) modeled in detail the costs and benefits of alternative locations for hypothetical firms in the Chicago region. Specifically, they asked what efficiency and equity effects would follow from the decision to locate a new, 1,000-employee manufacturing plant either in the central city or on a suburban greenfield. The results are summarized below.

### EXTERNALITIES

Persky and Wiewel find that locating the plant at a greenfield site rather than a central city one imposes approximately $1.1 million more annually in negative externalities, borne by the region's residents. Chief among these externalities are highway congestion and spatial mismatch (the underutilization of city and inner-suburban low-skilled workers). The authors also consider accidents, air pollution, housing abandonment, and loss of open space.

### PUBLIC SECTOR COSTS

Manufacturing location decisions have important implications for public costs. A plant's location affects local government budgets and road construction. The largest local fiscal impact is residential development, as new households require expensive expansion of outer suburban services. In contrast, central-city services in deconcentrating cities like Chicago often have excess capacity. Second largest is the federal subsidy for home-ownership, which in this case implies substantial tax expenditures on outer suburban residents. In total, the authors estimate that a greenfield location for the hypothetical plant generates $1.5 million more in annual public costs than a central-city location.

### PRIVATE COSTS AND BENEFITS

In addition to public costs, the plant location will generate costs and benefits to the private sector. Persky and Wiewel look at costs and benefits to residents, land/structure owners, and businesses (including wage costs, land costs, business taxes, and construction costs). The authors find that some residents will benefit from a suburban location because their commute will be shorter and land prices are lower. Much of this gain is passed on to firms in the form of lower wage costs; wages, especially for women, are lower in the suburbs. For the case in question, this amounts to a net annual gain to suburban businesses of about $1.3 million. These savings represent half of the estimated private benefits of $2.6 million per year. The greatest part of these private gains is translated into profits for firms with a suburban location, although a portion may be passed along to consumers in reduced prices.

## The Distribution of Costs and Benefits

When the annual costs and benefits to all groups are summed, Persky and Wiewel find that they almost cancel each other out: $2.6 million in benefits and $2.7 million in costs. In other words, they find no overall efficiency gained by developing on the greenfield as opposed to in the city, or vice versa. While the private sector captures considerable benefits, these are fully offset by costs paid by governments or imposed as externalities on the public at large. The bulk of this burden (about 70 percent) falls on low- and middle-income households, and especially on those who are city residents. The same low- and middle-income households take home less than 10 percent of the private gains, while the other 90 percent is won by high-income households with income from stocks and business ownership.

## Local Governments: Individual Gains and Collective Losses

Obvious private benefits prompt firms to choose greenfield locations. However, local governments collectively would be better off with more centralized development as opposed to greenfield expansion. Why, then, do many suburban municipalities aggressively seek manufacturing development?

> One possibility is that suburban decisionmakers lack knowledge concerning likely impacts. Given the considerable energy now devoted to fiscal impact analysis this seems unlikely. A more convincing explanation of suburban behavior is that individual municipalities put no weight on fiscal costs imposed on their neighbors. When a suburb snags a new plant, it gains the substantial nonresidential surplus generated by that plant. Nevertheless, the fiscal burdens created by associated residential development are spread widely across nearby and distant communities. The lead suburb gains dramatically even if all suburbs as a whole gain little. Like businesses that focus only on their private profit, these municipalities ignore the broader consequences of their actions (Persky and Wiewel 2000, 108).

In short, current policies and the fragmented political system encourage governments to act in ways that benefit their municipality but are detrimental to the region as a whole, especially the lower-income public. This raises policy issues that can be addressed only at higher levels of government.

## Policy Responses to Address Sprawl and Inequity

As shown by Persky and Wiewel's hypothetical plant location, private firms have had powerful incentives to suburbanize in recent years. And as described, there is little economic reason for an individual suburban municipality to refuse new job growth. However, the costs that occur to local governments collectively and the inequity that results suggest a need for policies to address deconcentration. Ideally, the effects of sprawl would be addressed at the regional level. In some smaller regions, the county government encompasses enough of the region to make action at that level meaningful. However, in the six-county Chicago region, as in most metropolitan areas, no governing body with home rule authority covers the entire region. Therefore, as Rusk (1999) argues, the charge to change public policy falls to the state.

Nevertheless, while the state legislature is the primary place where regional legislation can be generated, this does not mean that strong regional legislation is actually enacted. In Illinois, as in many other home rule states, the notion that local governments will control their growth is primary. In general, state—as well as federal and local—governments take a laissez-faire approach to regional growth issues. However, policies that would counter sprawl are available to governments.

Regions seeking to offset metropolitan deconcentration and its negative effects have a wide choice of potential policy options to choose from. These include land use policies (urban growth boundaries, regional impact fees, limitations on infrastructure development, purchase of land development rights, and encouragement of central-city development and in-fill); housing policies (incentives for inclusionary zoning, encouragement of employer-assisted housing, and rental voucher use in the suburbs); transportation policies (gasoline taxes, congestion pricing, and proactive transit funding); and fiscal policies (equalization of school funding, reduced use of property taxes, and regional revenue sharing).

Each of these policies has certain strengths and weaknesses.[4] Several—like regional impact fees or urban growth boundaries—could have a significant impact on the amount of land consumed in a region, but would be nearly impossible to pass through the state legislature in the culture of home rule for municipalities. Other policies—like the purchase of open space—are more politically palatable, but promise only marginal effects on sprawl and equity.

Here we focus on one of these options for dealing with regional decentralization and inequity—revenue sharing. In general, revenue-sharing programs pool some amount of funding from the municipalities in a region and redistribute these funds according to a formula. Often, the redistribution formula is based on some measure of fiscal need. As will be discussed later, the implementation of revenue sharing would likely lead at best to a slight reduction in total land consumption, but it could create a shift in regional equity and foster other regional cooperation. The focus here on revenue sharing is not meant to indicate that this policy would necessarily be the most effective or only feasible option for dealing with sprawl and equity issues in the Chicago region. Certainly, depending on the program's design, revenue sharing could be either too extreme to be passed or too weak to be effective. However, there are enough examples of revenue sharing around the country and enough nascent action around the issue in Chicago that the potential for revenue sharing in the Chicago region warrants a further look.

The rest of this chapter will examine the potential for a regional revenue-sharing program to begin to address the region's fiscal disparities as well as other issues. The discussion will give examples of revenue sharing throughout the country, look at current revenue-sharing efforts already under way in the region, and then present an assessment of the potential of some kind of revenue-sharing program in Chicago. First, however, is an overview of the current tax situation in the Chicago region.

## Revenue Sharing As a Policy Response to Sprawl and Inequity

### Local Government Funding in Illinois

In Illinois, the main source of revenue for both municipalities and school districts is property taxes. These taxes are primarily collected from three types of properties: residential, commercial, and industrial. In the Chicago region, about 60 percent of an average property tax bill goes to support the school districts, 16 percent is allocated to the municipality where the property is located, 9 percent goes to the county, and the remaining 15 percent goes to various special districts or other taxing authorities. This system of local government and school funding that emphasizes property tax revenues has important consequences for the region.

At the local government level, for example, each municipality is free to set its own property tax rates. These rates reflect several factors, including the municipality's fiscal need, fiscal ability, and fiscal effort, or the extent to which it chooses to tap into its tax base. Because of these variables, property tax rates vary enormously throughout the six-county Chicago region.

Paradoxically, it is generally the least wealthy municipalities that have the highest tax rates. As a town's tax base starts to decay, municipal leaders have three basic choices: they can try to attract more development (increase their fiscal ability); they can raise taxes to provide a continuing level of services (increase their fiscal effort); or they can cut their level of services (meet less of the community's need). In many older municipalities, the realistic choices are usually between raising taxes or cutting services. Either of these cases provides the remaining residents and businesses with further incentives to move out, creating a self-reinforcing cycle of decline.

In Chicago, this scenario has generally played itself out in the older, inner-ring suburbs, especially those in southern Cook and Will Counties. The average municipal tax rate for all 269 municipalities in the region in 1997 was 1.35 percent of assessed value. However, the averages by county are strikingly different. While the average tax rate in McHenry County was 0.56 percent, the average rate in Cook County was 1.71 percent. Maywood, in western Cook County, had the highest 1997 municipal tax rate in the region at 5.49 percent. In other words, businesses and residents in Maywood pay an average of 5.49 percent of the assessed value of their property in taxes each year.[5]

On the other hand, 11 of the 269 municipalities have no municipal property taxes at all. In general, these municipalities have enough commercial development to make up their budgets solely from sales tax revenues. For example, the Village of Schaumburg, home of the regional shopping center Woodfield Mall, was as of 1997 able to generate more than $33 million per year, or $400 per resident, from a 0.5 percent sales tax it levies (Rodkin 1997). Further, the communities with no property taxes are also generally communities with low concentrations of poverty and therefore a lower level of fiscal need, so they do not need to collect as much in taxes as older municipalities do. These 11 municipalities are located in the northwest portion of the Chicago region; 5 of the 11 are located in Lake County. Figure 10.1 underscores the differences in tax rates by county.

The distinction between a residential tax base and a commercial/industrial tax base is also important. Generally, commercial and indus-

Figure 10.1 *Average Municipal Property Tax Rate in the Chicago Region, by County, 1997*

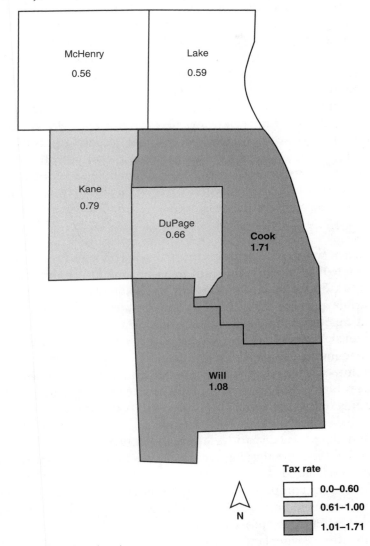

Source: Dye and McGuire (1999).

trial properties generate more in revenues than they require in services. On the other hand, taxes on residential properties, especially low-income ones, often do not cover the costs of services they require. This leads us back to the point raised in the last section—that communities in a region will often compete for commercial and industrial development, while discouraging low-income housing and other low-revenue land uses.

There is also mixed evidence on whether firms use tax rates as a factor in choosing a location. Dye, McGuire, and Merriman (1999) find little evidence that tax rates are a factor; of their four measures of economic activity, they find a clear tax effect for only one. McDonald and McMillen (1999), on the other hand, find that a Cook County location is a statistically significant deterrent to new businesses, probably because of higher property tax rates there.[6] This differential in tax rates could be an incentive for further job sprawl, reinforcing the cycle of decline.

## Revenue Sharing

The current system of local government funding presents two immediate problems to the Chicago region (and many regions throughout the country). First, some municipalities have a low fiscal ability and a high tax need, while others have a high fiscal ability and relatively low fiscal need. Second, because commercial and industrial development is more lucrative, municipalities find themselves competing for these development ratables, and municipalities with higher taxes are at a disadvantage.

Revenue-sharing programs have the potential to mitigate these and other problems. Programs are often designed with the intention of addressing one or more specific problems; in particular:

- To reduce fiscal disparities among municipalities.
- To help equalize funding gaps between a municipality's fiscal ability and its need to provide services.
- To reduce competition among municipalities in the region for commercial and industrial development, especially competition that results in the provision of expensive subsidies to firms.
- To promote wiser land use choices, since communities are under less pressure to accommodate high-revenue development. In other words, communities with sensitive lands that are more suited for parks or farmland would be under less pressure to develop their own commercial or industrial centers if they knew they would share in the benefits of a regional center.

- To reduce incentives for annexation, by providing municipalities with ways to increase their revenues without expanding their boundaries.
- To get municipalities thinking regionally, perhaps leading to cooperation in other areas (Orfield 1997, 84–85; Dustin 1994; Richman and Wilkinson 1993).

There are many ways to design a revenue-sharing program. Some communities pool property tax base; others share tax revenues. Some programs involve only one county; others share among the whole region. Regional taxes on sales or services can be a form of revenue sharing. Indeed, even traditional transfer programs from the state to inner cities are a sort of revenue sharing, since they involve a redistribution of funds.

Three examples from around the United States are summarized here: the Minneapolis-St. Paul fiscal disparities plan; the Montgomery County, Ohio, Economic Development/Government Equity program; and the Allegheny County, Pennsylvania, Regional Asset District.

## MINNEAPOLIS-ST. PAUL FISCAL DISPARITIES PLAN

The best-known case of revenue sharing and the only true example of tax-base sharing has been operating in Minneapolis-St. Paul since 1975. Under the fiscal disparities plan, each city must contribute to a regional fund 40 percent of the *growth* since 1971 in its commercial and industrial base. Revenue derived from a common tax on the pool is distributed to the municipalities based on population and tax capacity.

Because the program shares the growth in tax base, the regional pot gets larger each year. In 1975, the program redistributed just $19 million dollars, or 6 percent of the commercial/industrial tax base. By 1998, the regional pot had reached $410 million—about 30 percent of the regional commercial-industrial tax base, or $150 per capita. In 1998, 49 municipalities were net contributors and 137 were net recipients (Rusk 1999).

Certainly, the Minneapolis-St. Paul fiscal disparities plan has helped reduce fiscal inequality in the region. Orfield (1997, 87) estimates that the fiscal disparities plan has reduced tax base disparities among municipalities from approximately 50 to 1 to approximately 12 to 1. Among municipalities with populations greater than 9,000, commercial-industrial tax-base disparities are approximately 5 to 1, where they would be 18 to 1 without the revenue sharing.

However, the plan is not a panacea. As described, the program reduces disparities at the margins, but it has not eliminated them. Further, because the plan focuses exclusively on commercial and industrial properties, some communities that have expensive residential developments and no commercial-industrial growth can become net recipients, while communities with lower-income residents but substantial commercial and industrial growth can be net contributors. In general, however, tax dollars flow from the wealthy communities to the needier ones.

In recent years, the Minnesota state legislature, led by regional advocate and Democratic Farmer Labor Senator Myron Orfield, introduced two additional revenue-sharing plans for the region that would have addressed some of these concerns and made fiscal resources even more evenly distributed. Although neither bill was enacted, they illustrate possible variations on revenue sharing, while providing cursory insight into the political difficulties of passing such legislation.

- *Metropolitan Reinvestment Act/Housing Disparities Bill, 1994 session.* Modeled after the fiscal disparities plan, the Metropolitan Reinvestment Act of 1994 would have regionally pooled the tax base of homes worth more than $150,000 with the purpose of funding affordable housing and redevelopment. Even after dropping these spending restrictions, the bill's supporters faced a sure veto by the governor. Instead, they let it die in exchange for other votes on another bill.
- *Metro Fair Tax Base Act, 1995 session.* This act would have enlarged the fiscal disparities plan to redistribute $1 billion a year in revenues. With substantial concessions the bill passed, but was promptly vetoed by the governor in favor of a largely symbolic voluntary bill.

## MONTGOMERY COUNTY, OHIO, ECONOMIC DEVELOPMENT/
## GOVERNMENT EQUITY PROGRAM

The Montgomery County, Ohio, program differs from the Minneapolis-St. Paul fiscal disparities program in several significant ways: it is voluntary; it shares revenues, not tax base; it shares income tax revenue as well as revenue from all types of property classifications (not just commercial and industrial); and it involves one county instead of the entire region.

All but one of the county's cities, villages, and townships have signed on to the program, motivated by the county's tying a pool of $5 million a year of economic development grants to participation in the revenue-sharing program. The program is known as ED/GE (pronounced "edge"), for economic development and government equity. Under ED/GE, jurisdictions pool a percentage of the growth in their property and income tax revenues, which can be no more than 13 percent of their general fund. These funds, generally about $600,000 a year, are then redistributed in inverse proportion to the amount of growth in the jurisdictions.

The ED/GE program, initiated in 1989, at a time when federal cutbacks and changes in the local economy were hurting the region, grew out of a report from a county committee that included regional business leaders. As might be expected, the GE side of the program was finalized only after much debate, as the county sought to appease local officials while still creating an effective regional program. Among the compromises was the agreement to a sliding base year—one that would always be three years in the past. The sliding base year has kept the revenue pool from growing and leaves shared revenue at about $1 per capita, while the Minnesota fiscal disparities plan with its fixed base year shares approximately $150 per resident. Even more dramatic was a compromise that essentially negated the impact of revenue sharing by including a three-year settle-up provision: Every third year, any municipality that has made a net contribution in the last period receives economic development funding equal to their contribution, so all municipalities at least break even from the program. In essence, this provision makes the revenue-sharing portion of the program symbolic, as opposed to fiscally significant.[7]

However, Montgomery County Director of Community and Economic Development Ron Parker says the benefits of the program absolutely compensate for the marginal revenue sharing that occurs. Suburban municipalities have contributed to the construction of a new baseball stadium in Dayton, a new Port Authority, the downtown Dayton Riverscape project, a regional marketing effort, and the start-up of a new airline that will provide better regional service to the East Coast. Parker says that without a doubt, none of these collaborations would have occurred before the ED/GE program.

By several local accounts, the program has been a success. It has increased equity slightly and regional thinking considerably. In addition to the increased cooperation, the $5 million a year in economic development funds is credited with retaining or creating several thousand jobs in the county—Parker estimates 12,000. In all, 27 out of 31 municipalities chose to participate when the program started in 1991. By 1996, all but one of the jurisdictions had signed on, and the remaining municipality recently elected a new mayor who ran on a platform favoring ED/GE. The original ED/GE legislation, set to expire in 2000, was recently reauthorized for another 10 years.[8]

## ALLEGHENY COUNTY, PENNSYLVANIA, ALLEGHENY REGIONAL ASSET DISTRICT

Another well-known example of regional revenue sharing is the Allegheny Regional Asset District (ARAD) of Allegheny County, Pennsylvania. The county includes Pittsburgh and 129 suburban municipalities. Unlike the plans in Ohio and Minnesota, which are based on property and income taxes, ARAD pools sales tax revenues. Like the Montgomery County program, the program is not one that deals explicitly with revenue sharing, but which marries revenue sharing with another objective to address two issues at once, namely funding public cultural and recreational facilities as well as helping poorer municipalities.

The program is funded through an extra 1 percent sales tax on all goods to which the state sales tax normally applies. ARAD is best known as a funding mechanism for the region's assets—regional parks, libraries, museums, sports facilities, and other civic entities—which are enjoyed by residents of the entire county. Indeed, half of the revenues collected are allocated to such assets. The remaining half, however, is split between the county and the municipalities. The 25 percent allocated to the municipalities ($34.2 million in 1999) is distributed according to a formula that "provides special consideration to the poorest and most distressed."[9] The distress level is determined by comparing a municipality's tax rate with its tax revenues and favoring municipalities with higher rates and lower revenues. The 25 percent of the pot allocated to municipalities equals approximately $27 per person in the region; in total, then, the program generates more than $100 per capita (Allegheny Regional Asset District 1999).

The idea for the regional asset district was born in the late 1980s. While most of the region's cultural institutions were located in the City of Pittsburgh, the balance of users had shifted to the point where the majority came from outside the city. After exploring state and county options without success, the mayor of Pittsburgh worked out the concept of the regional asset district and combined it with the idea of revenue sharing.

The distribution part of the formula was developed with the explicit intention of lowering property taxes. In the first year, 1995, two-thirds of the funding given to municipalities had to be used to reduce local taxes. In subsequent years, 25 percent of the growth of the municipal pot has been limited to regional or municipal cooperation projects. The remaining 75 percent can be used to fund municipal infrastructure projects and other services (Allegheny Regional Asset District 1999).

Like the other plans described, the creation of ARAD as a special purpose unit of local government had to be authorized by the state legislature. Unlike the other revenue-sharing programs, however, municipalities do not have to give up revenues they already had—the special purpose district's sales tax created a new pool of funding. This aspect of the program may have helped to make its adoption less controversial.

The Regional Asset District has not escaped criticism. Some residents have called the tax an undeserved subsidy to the Pittsburgh Pirates, since the Pittsburgh Stadium Authority is one of the major recipients of funds. Some argued that the City of Pittsburgh never shared revenues with its surrounding suburbs when it was in its heyday, so there is no reason for those suburbs to assist the city now. Finally, others worried that the extra tax imposed on all goods sold from the county would make the region that much less competitive in the larger economy and encourage manufacturers to move out of the county.[10] However, a five-year review of the program found that growth in Allegheny County was essentially the same as or better than that in the surrounding counties.

In short, the asset district portion of the program has been generally successful, having achieved the legislature's original purpose. The revenue-sharing portion of the program has lowered property taxes and kept them lower since the program's inception. Both portions of the program increase regional equity: ARAD takes the burden of funding regional institutions off the city, and the second part distributes funds according to fiscal need.

## Revenue Sharing in the Chicago Region

While Chicago does not have a comprehensive, general revenue-sharing program like those described above, there *are* already some limited, specific examples of revenue sharing in the region:

- The Regional Transportation Authority (RTA) is the six-county umbrella organization for the mass transit operations in the city and suburbs. Since its reorganization in 1983, the authority's funding system may be described as a specific regional tax-sharing program (Summers 2000). Part of the RTA's funding comes from a local sales tax (1 percent in Cook County and .25 percent in the collar counties). A portion of the tax collected in suburban Cook County (but none of the tax collected in the collar counties) goes to fund the Chicago Transit Authority (DiJohn 1999).

- In northwest Cook County, Mayor Don Stephens needed support from neighboring municipalities to change a state law and allow construction of a casino in the Village of Rosemont. To gain this support, Stephens offered to share a portion of the casino revenues with these municipalities. Of the 5 percent of the total revenues that Rosemont would keep, the village proposed splitting 4 percent among the municipalities that agreed to support the plan. In all, 70 neighboring municipalities agreed to back the casino in exchange for a cut of the revenues. While the agreements remain in place, they have not yet taken effect because construction of the actual casino has been delayed.[11]
- A few municipalities in the region have established specific revenue-sharing agreements on a smaller scale. In Will County, the Villages of Bollingbrook and Romeoville agreed in the late 1980s to share evenly the property taxes from some of land along the I-55 commercial corridor. At the time of the agreement, the land was not yet developed or even annexed, but village officials wanted to ensure that the borders between the two towns remained firm as the area developed. Each municipality taxes the specified land that now lies within its borders at its own tax rate, and half of the total revenues collected on those properties is shared with the other. In practice, the agreement usually results in Bollingbrook, the larger of the two municipalities, sending a check to Romeoville.[12]

Despite these specific instances of fiscal cooperation, the region is not close to having a larger-scale, revenue-sharing program. On the other hand, a revenue-sharing program is not unimaginable in the Chicago region, and a surprisingly wide range of organizations have taken some first steps that could lead to the development of some type of program. Following are examples of efforts currently under way in Chicago that could result in the development of a regional revenue-sharing program.

## THE STATE LEGISLATORS

Because the Chicago region lacks a regional body with home rule powers, any regional revenue-sharing program would ultimately have to be authorized by the Illinois state legislature. To date, no actual revenue-sharing program has been considered by either house. However, the issue is at least on the radar screen of a few state legislators. In the Senate, Minority Caucus Whip Debbie Halvorson (D-Crete) appears the most committed to sparking interest in the revenue-sharing issue. (She became interested in the topic after discussions with Myron Orfield and the Metropolitan Alliance of Congregations [MAC].) In January 1999, Halvorson introduced a study bill to require that the Illinois Department of Revenue look at the distributional implications of a Twin Cities–type, tax-base revenue-sharing program for Cook County and its adjacent counties. The bill, which was not an actual proposal for revenue sharing, but called only for a study, became stuck in committee and never made it to the floor for a vote.

There has been no specific action on revenue sharing since the bill died in the Rules Committee in March of 1999, but Halvorson says she remains committed to the issue. She plans to reintroduce the study bill and to ask Governor George Ryan to appoint a task force that would look at the feasibility of revenue sharing.[13]

For Halvorson, revenue sharing is primarily an equity issue; as a senator from the south suburbs, she says she is acutely aware of how the municipalities with the highest tax need are the ones with the lowest resources. She says that while revenue sharing is not her number one issue, it is something she believes is crucial, and it does fit into her overall agenda. She stresses that serious discussion should begin sooner rather than later, since implementing a program would take a considerable amount of time.[14]

In the House, Representative Julie Hamos (D-Chicago) is also interested in revenue sharing, having worked as a consultant with Orfield and MAC before joining the legislature. Hamos's district includes part of Chicago and other suburban communities just north of Chicago, including some that would probably benefit from revenue sharing and others that could potentially be net contributors. So while Hamos is interested in equity issues as they affect her immediate district, she is also approaching revenue sharing from a regional interdependence standpoint, and believes that revenue sharing should be implemented for its benefit to the region as a whole. Certainly, this could be a politically risky move for her.

While Hamos would like to see a revenue-sharing program in place, she does not think the region is ready for a specific program proposal yet—she believes more education is needed among mayors, other legislators, and the general public. Hamos emphasizes that as in the Twin Cities, revenue sharing will never be an issue of complete consensus.[15] Instead, legislation must be passed by coalitions formed among the areas that would be net recipients.

Hamos says that if another legislator sponsored a revenue-sharing bill, she would work with him or her on its passage. For right now, though, she believes other regionalism equity programs—like targeted state funds—might be more politically feasible. Further, if the proposed program is expected to redistribute a relatively small amount of funds—say $25 million, Hamos says a state allocation to needier municipalities would have the same effect and be much less complicated, especially in a time of state budget surpluses.

Since any mandatory regional program would have to come out of state legislation, state legislators would have to be key actors in the push for regional revenue sharing. Currently, revenue sharing is not something in which most legislators have expressed an active interest. Senator Halvorson says this is not uncommon; however, most legislators will not latch on to a bill until it makes it out of committee.

### THE GRASSROOTS/FAITH-BASED ORGANIZATIONS

Poised to make sure that Illinois legislators take a more active interest in regional revenue sharing is the Metropolitan Alliance of Congregations. As noted above, MAC is a consortium of congregations and existing non-profit organizations that works to address issues of social justice in the Chicago region.

Since 1998, MAC has been working with Myron Orfield of Minnesota, holding meetings and discussing the need and potential for some type of revenue-sharing program in the Chicago region.[16] The organization has sponsored focus groups to educate residents about fiscal disparities and to gauge public support for some type of revenue-sharing program. MAC says support in the south suburbs has varied, with some political and religious leaders concerned that they need more immediate help than a revenue-sharing proposal could offer.

Early draft proposals from MAC have the region sharing 50 percent of the growth in the commercial, industrial, and high-end (probably over $200,000) residential tax base. However, even this ambitious scenario, which would share more of the region's growth than the Twin Cities plan does, would result in an initial regional pool of only $25 million. This relatively small amount equals about $3 per capita, although, like the Twin Cities program, it could be expected to grow over time if the base year is kept fixed.

The MacArthur Foundation has given MAC $300,000 over three years to pursue regionalism efforts. MAC's executive director, Mary Gonzales, says she plans to use a considerable amount of the award to hire a public relations firm to focus attention on the current fiscal disparities in the region and the potential benefits of tax-base sharing. "As they hear about the inequities in the region, the population will begin to say, 'That's ridiculous,' " Gonzales predicts.[17]

In short, MAC's primary goal is to fight for social justice, and its leaders see revenue sharing as one means to that end. Gonzales says MAC is prepared to see this fiscal disparity fight through to the end, whether it takes five, six, or more years. Although MAC is a fairly new organization, it has shown itself to be a powerful regional player,[18] and Gonzales's 25 years of organizing experience in the Chicago region—including engaging the public and pressuring legislators—will be an asset to the group's efforts.

### BUSINESS, CIVIC, AND PLANNING LEADERS

Other, more mainstream organizations are also interested in revenue sharing or some other type of regional fiscal reform, but as might be expected are taking a more cautious approach than MAC. As described, Chicago Metropolis 2020 is an organization representing the Chicagoland business community and was formed to implement the regional plan released by the Commercial Club of Chicago in March of 1999.[19] The plan, *Chicago Metropolis 2020: Preparing Metropolitan Chicago for the 21st Century,* deals with issues including land use and housing, transportation, governance, and education. Among other recommendations, it advocates the creation of a regional coordinating mechanism that would as part of its responsibilities coordinate a regional revenue-sharing program. This mechanism is envisioned as generating long-run, regional strategic plans providing financial incentives to encourage regional thinking among municipalities, determining access to sewer and wastewater systems, and receiving and distributing revenues to moderate disparities in fiscal and service quality among municipalities.

Yet, while there is a placeholder for revenue sharing in the organization's future agenda, spokesperson Theresa Mintle says it is not one of the items they are currently pursuing in depth.[20] Further, Metropolis 2020 is not working to establish a formal regional coordinating mechanism yet, mainly because there are "hotter" issues that members wish to address first. In addition, support for these items would be relatively hard to come by; the board of the Northeastern Illinois Planning Commission (NIPC), for example, explicitly does not support revenue sharing. (Of course, it is also in NIPC's interest to oppose the creation of the regional coordinating body that would absorb their planning functions.) Essentially, Metropolis 2020 is driven by what is politically feasible, and its members are careful to remain very sensitive to what is practical and realistic.

Another major organization's position on fiscal reform is important to note. Like the NIPC board, the Metropolitan Planning Council (MPC) specifically does not advocate the passage of a revenue-sharing program. While MPC takes the position that the system of local government funding is uneven and needs to be addressed, they do not advocate revenue sharing as a viable means of doing so.

First, MPC asserts that a revenue-sharing program—specifically a tax-base sharing program like that in Minnesota—would be too unpopular and too hard to market to much of the region. Along those lines, Scott Goldstein, vice president of policy and planning, says that a successful program would have to be generated locally, not one with the appearance of being forced on Chicago by advocates from another region. Moreover, Goldstein argues that simply shifting state development funding priorities toward needier areas without so blatantly identifying a group of municipal "losers" would be a better way to address the fiscal need in specific areas of the region.

MPC is also working on reform of school funding, which directly deals with property taxes since 60 percent of a typical property tax bill is for the school districts.[21] Certainly, such reform would also address fiscal disparities in the region, although it is unclear how much more popular these types of programs and reform would be.

As described, there is increasing discussion of equity issues among established civic and planning organizations in the Chicago region, but little direct action toward enacting a revenue-sharing program. The Commercial Club's inclusion of revenue sharing and the development of a regional coordinating mechanism in their recent regional plan is a big step forward, but for political reasons, action by Metropolis 2020 on either of these issues in the near future is unlikely. Other organizations, namely MPC, have started work on other programs that would address inequity in the region—essentially different means to a similar end.

## THE LOCAL GOVERNMENTS

As described, MPC does not support revenue sharing out of concern that any program would be too controversial among the municipalities.

Similarly, it is almost certain that state legislators would not vote for a program that did not have the support of local political leaders.

These local leaders—the mayors and village presidents of the region's 269 municipalities—have been talking and working with each other on issues dealing with regionalism, although not revenue sharing per se. A large part of this cooperation has come as a result of the Metropolitan Mayors Caucus, created as a forum for the municipal leaders to discuss issues that affect all parts of the region. One of the priorities of the caucus is the encouragement of balanced economic growth throughout the region, and to that end, the caucus has recently developed the Regional Economic Development Action Agenda.

While a revenue-sharing program would be one way of fostering this balanced growth, Caucus Coordinator Rita Athas[22] notes that support for a Twin Cities–style revenue sharing is not on the horizon among the region's mayors. First, mayors are not willing to give up part of their tax base or revenues. Further, communities have planned future budgets based on these expected revenues, and would not welcome being asked to rework these budgets. In addition, even among communities that would be net recipients, officials are reluctant to back a program that seems to imply a loss of local control.[23]

Nevertheless, Athas recognizes a major shift in attitude among the region's mayors from the time the caucus started in 1997. They do understand the need for regionalism, and there appears to be more enlightened self-interest and acknowledgment of the interdependence of the municipalities' economic well-being. Simply getting to know their fellow mayors has led to a greater sense of common purpose.[24]

So, if a revenue-sharing program in the tradition of the Twin Cities is not on the horizon, what options does the Mayors Caucus see for the region? As unlikely as it seems, Athas says that a new tax that creates and shares a new revenue source might be more popular than a program that cuts into municipalities' current budgets. Of course, a new tax would also raise issues of its own. Athas also suggested that directing state economic development resources to areas with greater need would also help equalize fiscal disparities while perhaps being less controversial.

In short, support among the region's mayors for regional fiscal reform is embryonic, and there is even less support for a revenue-sharing program. The mayors' understanding of regionalism, however, is greater than it was several years ago and much greater than anyone expected it to be at this point.

## The Public

The last crucial area of support for a regional revenue-sharing program is the general public. Orfield (1997) suggests that a majority of residents in a region should support a revenue-sharing program because a majority—between 60 percent and 85 percent—will benefit from it. However, just because people would benefit in one way from a program doesn't mean they will support it politically; translating that potential support into political support assumes a general knowledge of what revenue sharing is and how it could benefit them, and in some cases must involve overriding any concern about the autonomy of their municipality. There seems to be a perception among organizations and local leaders that residents are not aware of the fiscal disparities in the region, and if they are, they are not particularly interested in addressing them. However, a recent survey suggests residents may be more informed and willing to take action than is commonly assumed.

In 1999, the Survey Research Laboratory at the University of Illinois at Chicago surveyed 309 residents in the City of Chicago and the metropolitan region (consisting of the remainder of Cook County and the five collar counties) for their views on tax base sharing. Specifically, respondents were asked whether some of the tax funds generated from new industrial or commercial development should be shared with other municipalities and counties to provide more equitable service to all residents in the region, or whether the host municipality should keep all the new funds (table 10.1).[25]

Table 10.1 *Regional Attitudes toward Revenue Sharing (Responses to the question, "Should some of the tax funds generated from new industrial or commercial development be shared with other municipalities and counties?")*

| Responses | Respondents from Chicago | Respondents from Cook/Collar Counties | Combined Responses |
|---|---|---|---|
| Share revenue | 68% (82) | 62% (118) | 65% (200) |
| Keep revenue | 18% (22) | 32% (60) | 27% (82) |
| Don't know/refused | 13% (16) | 6% (11) | 9% (27) |
| Total | (120) | (189) | (309) |

*Source:* Illinois Omnibus Poll (1999).

*Notes:* Totals may not equal 100 percent due to rounding. Margin of error is +/− 5.7 percent.

In numbers that fit with Orfield's assessment that between 60 and 85 percent of the region's population should support regional tax base sharing, 65 percent of all respondents felt that some of the funds should be shared. Twenty-seven percent felt the original municipality should keep all of the revenue, and the remaining 9 percent did not know or refused to answer.

As might be expected, respondents from Chicago were more enthusiastic about revenue sharing than were their suburban counterparts, although a majority of both groups advocated sharing the funds. Sixty-eight percent of city respondents were in favor of tax base sharing. On the other hand, 62 percent of suburban residents favored revenue sharing, still a majority. Most of these suburban respondents lived in suburban Cook County, which is generally tax-poor. About 45 percent of the suburban respondents lived in the other, generally wealthier, collar counties.

It is also interesting to note that the "don't know/refused to answer" responses were much lower for this question than they were for others on the survey—9 percent here, as opposed to as much as 30 percent for some questions. Although it is commonly assumed that residents do not know what revenue sharing is, or would need to be educated or agitated into supporting it, these results suggest that residents are fairly well informed—and generally supportive—of the idea of revenue sharing.

## Likely Effect of Revenue Sharing on Sprawl, Equity, and Regionalism

### Effect of Revenue Sharing on Sprawl

This chapter has focused on the fiscal disparities among municipalities in the Chicago region. These disparities in part stem from the system of local government and school funding that primarily relies on locally set property taxes. One theoretical argument, as posited by Dye and McGuire (1999), supports the case that these uneven property taxes can facilitate metropolitan decentralization. The authors write: "If property taxes are a determining factor of business location decisions, and if property taxes are higher in the center of the metropolitan area relative to the urban fringe, and if population follows jobs, then differential property taxes will contribute to sprawl"(1).

One way to consider how much of an effect a revenue-sharing program would actually have on sprawl would be to assume that such a program, if enacted, would at best completely equalize property taxes in the region. Of course, it is almost certain that any program would not be completely equalizing. However, it makes sense to look at the complete counter-factual, since that will give us a sense of the maximum effect that a revenue-sharing program would have. If property taxes were equal throughout the region, how much of an effect would that have on sprawl? Our estimates, described in appendix 1, suggest that equalized property rates among the six counties would have resulted in 3.3 to 6.7 percent less land consumption over the past 25 years.

These estimates come from the assumption that to equalize taxes, tax rates in the five collar counties would increase by an average of 19 percent. This would have resulted in 86,000 fewer suburban workers, which would have translated into fewer acres of land used both for business and residential purposes. Even at the upper estimate, tax equalization would have resulted in a relatively small amount of land—12,900 acres or 20 square miles—remaining undeveloped over that 25-year period.

Although a revenue-sharing program may not greatly affect land consumption, its supporters contend revenue-sharing programs can have an effect on other land use decisions. According to Richman and Wilkinson (1993), one impetus for revenue sharing in the Twin Cities came from a land use planning issue. In the mid-1960s, a local municipality was set to build a power plant in an environmentally sensitive area because of the revenues such a plant would bring to the city. The state legislator for the area stated that he would have to support the plant's construction unless the municipality could somehow "receive some of the tax benefits from industry which locates elsewhere in the area." Similarly, a revenue-sharing program in New Jersey—the Hackensack Meadowlands District—was established with the intent of protecting environmentally sensitive lands from development (see Richman and Wilkinson 1993; Hackensack Meadowlands Development Commission 1999). Of course, a revenue-sharing program cannot be substituted for land use planning, but it does have the potential to bolster planning efforts by removing some of the fiscal incentives a municipality has for encouraging unsuitable but lucrative development.

## Effect of Revenue Sharing on Equity

Certainly, the main purpose in implementing a revenue-sharing program in the Chicago region would be to reduce the fiscal disparities among municipalities. The actual effects of such a program would depend on how it is designed. Of the programs reviewed, the Twin Cities tax-base sharing program distributes the most funding per capita and seems to have reduced fiscal disparities the most. According to a 1991 review of the program, communities with populations greater than 9,000 had a ratio between the highest and lowest tax bases per capita of 4 to 1 after revenue sharing, while without revenue sharing the difference would have been 22 to 1 (Richman and Wilkinson 1993).

It is also important to remember that the funds involved in the Twin Cities program have grown considerably since program inception; a similar program in Chicago with a fixed base year would also start small and grow over several decades. According to a scenario run by MAC, the early redistribution effect in the Chicago region would be about $25 million, or a relatively insignificant $3 per capita.

Finally, the distribution formula is also an important factor in determining how significantly disparities are reduced. Some regions find it is too politically difficult to design a program that considers fiscal need in the distribution of funds. In such cases, distribution formulas may be based solely on population, rather than a measure of need. It is also worth noting that there is evidence that in the Twin Cities, smaller municipalities benefit more from revenue sharing than do larger cities (Richman and Wilkinson 1993). This finding could have important consequences for the Chicago region, with its dominant central city and numerous municipalities with much lower populations.

It seems nearly impossible that any program considered would completely level the playing field between municipalities in the region. A program that considerably reduces inequities in the region could be imagined; however, such a program would probably be like the Twin Cities program in that it would need to grow over time, or would involve a type of revenue sharing unlike that seen in other regions.

## Effect of Revenue Sharing on Regionalism

Even if their effect on sprawl and equity is minimal, the Montgomery County, Ohio, and Allegheny County, Pennsylvania, examples illustrate that revenue-sharing programs can foster greater regional cooperation. Getting local political leaders cooperating on such a program can help them realize their interconnectedness and lead to a willingness to work together on other issues. On the other hand, passage of another type of revenue-sharing program (along the lines of the Twin Cities tax-base sharing program) is likely to create animosity between two groups of municipalities, as "winners" and "losers" are identified.

Although it could be a means to do so, advancing regional cooperation is certainly not a reason for local leaders to push for revenue sharing in Chicago. As described, there are existing venues, notably the Metropolitan Mayors Caucus, for local leaders to meet and work on common issues. The inordinate efforts required to pass a revenue-sharing program through the legislature would not be worth the additional cooperation that might be gained. In addition, the coalition building that would probably be necessary could even result in even greater factionalism within the region.

## Conclusions: The Potential for Revenue Sharing

The last few years have seen increasing debate in the Chicago region over whether sprawl and inequity need to be dealt with, and if so, how. As the Persky and Wiewel firm location model shows, there are genuine public costs associated with metropolitan decentralization, suggesting a role for the public sector in reducing either the occurrence of sprawl or the negative effects associated with sprawl. Numerous policy options for dealing with sprawl and inequity exist. One such policy, revenue sharing, attempts to reduce the fiscal disparities among municipalities and close the gap that exists between some municipalities' fiscal ability and their fiscal need. Revenue sharing was examined in more depth here because it appears to have been implemented effectively in other regions and because of the growing interest of some Chicago-based organizations in implementing some type of revenue-sharing program.

The examples from Minneapolis-St. Paul, Montgomery County, Ohio, and Allegheny County, Pennsylvania, illustrate three revenue-sharing programs. The Twin Cities' tax-base sharing program taxes a portion of a municipality's tax base at a common rate and shares these funds. The Montgomery County program is a voluntary one that uses economic development funds as an incentive for revenue sharing. The Allegheny County program levies a separate regional sales tax and then distributes a portion of the revenues according to a measure of need. In general, these programs appear to be regarded positively in their regions. However, the amount of revenues actually shared varies from almost nothing in Montgomery County (although economic development funds may be distributed with a more regional outlook) to approximately $150 per capita in the Twin Cities.

There are genuine reasons why the Chicago region might consider a revenue-sharing program—it could lead to better land use decisions or foster other types of regional cooperation. The primary reason to consider a revenue-sharing program, however, would be to reduce fiscal disparities among municipalities. There are two complementary but distinct lines of thought as to why these inequalities should be addressed. For some, the disparities should be reduced because doing so is fair. Others take the approach that municipalities in the region are interdependent, so it makes sense for the whole region to help municipalities with low fiscal capacities to meet their fiscal needs.

How effective would a revenue-sharing program in the Chicago region actually be at reducing sprawl and inequity and fostering more regional cooperation? We estimate that a revenue-sharing program would at most reduce land consumption by 3 to 6 percent if it completely equalized property taxes, which is unlikely. A program would also probably have a modest but noticeable effect on equity. This effect would largely depend on program design. As MAC estimates, a program modeled after the Twin Cities program would likely redistribute about $25 million at first. At $3 per person in the region, this would hardly rectify the region's inequities. However, as in the Twin Cities, the program would grow or could be expanded over time. In addition, other types of programs that involve more funds could of course be considered. Finally, a program could also lead to greater regional cooperation, but because other outlets for such cooperation already exist in the Chicago area, enacting a revenue-sharing program would be an unduly difficult means of doing so.

If the region is to consider a revenue-sharing program, the program should be designed based both on other regions' experiences and the local political climate. We do not attempt here to designate specifically how a revenue-sharing program for the Chicago region would best work. However, assuming current efforts to implement some type of program continue or expand, the following points might make passage more feasible and the program more effective. Although our primary focus is the Chicago region, the discussion might also serve as a starting point for other metropolitan regions dealing with similar inequities.

## Working Points for Revenue-Sharing Program Design

One of the main issues to be overcome is the idea of local autonomy. Although a revenue-sharing program with no restrictions on how funds are spent does not reduce local control (beyond the payment or receipts of some amount of funding), the perception that it would is strong. Probably the easiest and most effective means of overcoming such opposition is to make participation voluntary. Of course, on its own, a voluntary program would result in the participation of only municipalities that would be net recipients of shared funds. For this reason, participation would have to be tied to incentives that are greater than the actual and perceived costs. Thus, incentives would have to be substantial and would probably involve a considerable amount of state funds. In a less positive framework, the state could offer "sticks" instead of "carrots" by tying infrastructure or other state funding to program participation. On the other hand, if participation were not voluntary, the state could provide municipalities slated to be net contributors with various options: Instead of sending funds to the regional pool, they could perhaps build additional units of affordable housing, or otherwise make a contribution to equity in the region.

Other issues will also need to be decided as proposed revenue-sharing legislation is written. Notably, MAC leaders are considering framing the issue around school funding equalization. The pros and cons of such an angle will need to be considered. Also, as mentioned above, there is some evidence that smaller cities in the Twin Cities' region benefit more than do larger cities. In 1991, for example, Minneapolis made a net contribution of $19 million to the regional pool, yet the city had a relatively higher number of citizens requiring social services than other cities, some of which were net recipients (Richman and Wilkinson 1993). It does seem likely that Chicago, with its recent growth in commercial and industrial properties, could be a net contributor under a similar tax-base sharing program. This would have political consequences and ignore the need that still exists, at least in parts of the city. Any program design should consider carefully the role that the City of Chicago would play.

Although no fiscal reform will pass easily, it would be worthwhile for advocates to consider whether other programs might reach similar ends with less political battle than revenue sharing would. Chicago groups like the Metropolitan Planning Council are discussing some suggestions for other types of fiscal reform. Implementing a policy to shift allocation of state economic development funds to municipalities with the greatest need would also begin to address regional fiscal disparities, probably with less political contention. Alternatively, as in Allegheny County, the region could impose some type of regionwide tax that could be used to fund something specific like the region's cultural facilities. Further, the same redistribution results could be achieved by shifting school and local revenue reliance from property taxes to state income taxes. There is something to be said for actually changing the problematic policy (i.e., reliance on local property taxes) rather than simply layering these policies with corrective programs (i.e., revenue sharing).

No matter how fiscal disparities begin to be addressed, one strength evident in the Chicago region is that there are several organizations dealing with these issues. As we have seen, the Metropolitan Alliance of Congregations is willing to do battle; this in turn is likely to make it easier for the more cautious, mainstream organizations like Metropolis 2020 and the Metropolitan Planning Council to garner support as specific proposals make headway. Moreover, these organizations are, of course, constructing their own approaches to dealing with regional inequities. Foster's work (2000) provides preliminary evidence that this type of civic and corporate capital might give the region a leg up in addressing regional issues. Further, as the Illinois Omnibus Poll (1999) results indicate, the public may be more aware of the inequities that exist and more willing to do something about the issues than local politicians and groups would give them credit. Finally, whichever type of program goes forward, its proponents might consider pushing for a statewide equity program, as opposed to one that covers only the Chicago region. There would be several benefits to this approach. First, there are genuine reasons for addressing equity at higher levels of government than the regional level.[26] As Summers (2000) writes,

> The social welfare and redistributive arguments for sharing the burden of central-city poverty lead to replacing responsibility with higher levels of government, not with suburban neighbors. Costs of concentrated poverty are substantial, but they are the social responsibility of all citizens in the country, not only those living in close proximity (190).

If the main goal of such a program is reducing inequity, there seems no reason not to do so throughout the state. In addition, if leaders decide to push for an Allegheny County–type program (levying an additional tax to redistribute based on need), it would also perhaps make more sense to enact a new tax statewide, so that the Chicago region—already growing at a slower rate than all other regions in the state (Persky et al. 2000)—would not be burdened with even higher rates than the rest of the state. Enacting tax reform by emphasizing income taxes over property taxes would also be better done at the state level, both for fairness and administrative purposes.

Certainly, there will not be a revenue-sharing program in effect in the Chicago region or the state of Illinois anytime soon; passing an effective program through the state legislature would be a political challenge that could consume much of the decade. If and when a program is implemented, it is likely that once all the compromises were made, the program would not have huge redistributional effects. But legislators and other proponents can work now to pass as effective a program as possible that would increase equity, and then if necessary work to expand it later. Because of the political difficulties that would be involved in working out program specifics, that program may or may not be a type of revenue sharing. A reorganization of state funding priorities may be just as effective and less difficult to adopt and administer. However, the climate in the Chicago region appears to be better than in the recent past for enacting some type of program that would address equity issues among municipalities.

## Appendix 1

*How much of an effect would equalized property taxes have on sprawl?*

We assume that the long-run elasticity of business activity to effective property tax is −0.5. This figure is lower than intrametropolitan tax studies reported in Bartik (1991) for two reasons: (1) A recent study by Dye et al. (1999) suggests lower figures for Chicago, and (2) higher figures in Bartik reflect a single municipality changing its tax rates while all others stay constant; but here the bulk of these outer suburbs will raise their rates together, hence the lower figure suggested by "inter-metropolitan studies" reported in Bartik seems more reasonable.

To equalize effective tax rate on assessed property (assuming no change in the current Cook County classification system), effective tax rates in the five collar counties (DuPage, Kane, Lake, McHenry, and Will) would increase by 19 percent on average (U.S. Census Bureau 1992). Hence, in the end, business activity would be down by −0.5 * 19% = −9.5%, as compared with what it would otherwise have been.

What does this mean over the last 25 years? We estimate that direct land consumption averages about .05 acres per suburban worker. Over the last 25 years, total employment rose by about 908,000 workers in the collar counties. Hence, if the property tax had been equalized in this period, one would have expected 86,000 fewer workers in the collar counties and hence direct land consumption would have been less by 4,300 fewer acres. To this is added another 4,300 acres for residential uses. This gives 8,600 acres that are multiplied by 1.5 to account for public uses, such as highways, parks, and the like, to generate a final estimate of 12,900 acres or about 20 square miles.

Compare this with the total of 300 square miles of urbanized area in these counties as of 1990 and the result is about 6.7 percent less developed land had total equalization been in effect over the last 25 years. We suspect this is an overestimate, since if much of the employment had stayed in the metropolitan area, locating in the closer-in suburbs, many of the new employees would still have chosen peripheral locations for housing. Thus, our best estimate might be about 3.3 percent less land absorption in these counties.

## NOTES

Thanks to Diane McCarthy at the Institute of Government and Public Affairs at UIC for assistance in analyzing tax data for Illinois municipalities, and to Bonnie Lindstrom, UIC research professor, who wrote the question that appeared on the Illinois Omnibus Poll.

1. While regionally the trend is still toward decentralization, it should be noted that the City of Chicago saw a modest gain in the 2000 Census, the first upswing in 50 years. Likewise, the city gained a few thousand jobs each year during the late 1990s (Illinois Department of Employment Security 1999).

2. The 1993 average tax base per household was $121,007 and ranged from $23,616 in Robbins on the south side to more than $2 million in northwest municipalities with considerable business development but few households. Interestingly, while the City of Chicago's tax base was below average at $83,884 per household, it grew by 50 percent in the period, thanks to a considerable amount of downtown development (Orfield 1996).

3. Robert Bruegmann, professor of art history, University of Illinois at Chicago, e-mail correspondence with Kimberly Schaffer, 2 February 2000.

4. A large body of literature is developing that describes and evaluates these and other policy options. Wiewel and Schaffer (2000), for example, evaluate 22 public policies that would either slow deconcentration or reduce its negative effects. This evaluation is based on each policy's likely effectiveness on land consumption, impact on equity, political feasibility, effort to administer, and secondary effects. Other policy descriptions and evaluations may be found in Rusk (1999), Porter (1996), and Nelson and Duncan (1995).

5. The taxable property value is the equalized assessed value, which in Illinois is, on average, one-third of market value. These data are from the Illinois Department of

Revenue and were compiled and analyzed with assistance from Diane McCarthy of UIC's Institute for Government and Public Affairs (Dye and McGuire 1999).

6. In general, property tax rates are higher in Cook County than in the collar counties (Lake, DuPage, Kane, McHenry, and Will). In addition, unlike the collar counties, Cook County uses a property classification system that taxes commercial and industrial properties at a higher rate than residential development. These factors combine to make the average commercial and industrial property tax rates in Cook County at least double the rates in any of the collar counties (McDonald and McMillen 1999).

7. Ron Parker, director of community and economic development for Montgomery County (Ohio), telephone interview with Kimberly Schaffer, 26 April 2000.

8. Parker, interview.

9. David Donahoe, executive director of the Allegheny Regional Asset District, telephone interview with Kimberly Schaffer, 25 April 2000.

10. Donahoe, telephone interview.

11. John Hochstettler, finance officer for the Village of Rosemont, telephone interview with Kimberly Schaffer, 12 June 2000.

12. Kirk Openchowski, director of finance for the Village of Bollingbrook, telephone interview with Kimberly Schaffer, 7 June 2000.

13. Debbie Halvorson, Illinois senator, telephone interview with Kimberly Schaffer, 26 April 2000.

14. Specifically, Halvorson says she would like to see a revenue-sharing program in place before a third airport would be built. In another contentious policy debate, the region is looking at ways to expand its air traffic capacity. One of the solutions calls for building a third airport in southern Will County, where it would be a much-needed economic stimulus for the southern suburbs. However, if built in the Village of Peotone (in southern Will County), as is currently proposed, that municipality would reap most of the tax benefits.

15. Julie Hamos, Illinois representative, telephone interview with Kimberly Schaffer, 14 May 2000.

16. While MAC leaders understand that there are many revenue-sharing models, their focus has been on how the Twin Cities model would transfer here, since it is well known and generally effective.

17. Mary Gonzales, executive director, Metropolitan Alliance of Congregations, interview with Kimberly Schaffer, 17 May 2000.

18. MAC has implemented a program to provide $1 billion in loans for a housing program.

19. The Commercial Club has a long history of civic involvement in Chicago and is well known for its planning tradition. At the turn of the 19th century, the club commissioned Daniel Burnham to create the still-famous 1909 Plan for Chicago, which laid out the city's lakefront parks and other elements that remain today.

20. Theresa Mintle, program director for Metropolis 2020, telephone interview with Kimberly Schaffer, 21 March 2000.

21. Scott Goldstein, vice president for policy and planning, Metropolitan Planning Council, telephone interview with Kimberly Schaffer, 17 May 2000.

22. Rita Athas, director of regional programs for the City of Chicago, telephone interview with Kimberly Schaffer, 10 May 2000.

23. This fear of loss of local control may be more a perception problem than anything else. As Hamos points out, one of the strengths of revenue-sharing programs is that there is no loss of local control; money changes hands, but unless the program is designed with specific spending requirements, recipient communities are free to spend the funds as they choose.

24. Athas, telephone interview.

25. The question in full reads as follows: "As you know, new industrial and commercial development generates tax dollars for local governments—the city or town where the development is located. The greater Chicago area has hundreds of municipalities and counties that provide service to all residents—many of whom live in one place and work in another. If a new industrial or commercial development opens and generates new tax funds, should **some** of those funds be **shared** with other municipalities and counties in order to provide more equitable service to **all** residents in the region or should the one municipality keep **all** the funds?" The margin of error for the question is plus or minus 5.7 percent.

26. This would assume action for reasons of "fairness" as opposed to regional competitiveness.

# REFERENCES

Allegheny Regional Asset District. 1999. http://trfn.clpgh.org/Government/Arad. (Accessed March 25, 2000.)

Bartik, Timothy J. 1991. *Who Benefits from State and Local Economic Development Policies?* Kalamazoo, Mich.: W. E. Upjohn Institute for Employment Research.

DiJohn, Joseph. 1999. "Transportation in the Chicago Metropolitan Region Since 1970." Great Cities Institute Working Paper. Chicago: University of Illinois at Chicago.

Dustin, Jack L. 1994. *Cooperative Communities—Competitive Communities: The Role of Interlocal Tax Revenue Sharing.* Urban Policy Monograph Series on Regional Competitiveness and Cooperation. Cleveland, Ohio: The Northeast Ohio Inter-Institutional Urban Research Consortium.

Dye, Richard F., and Therese J. McGuire. 1999. "Property Taxes, Schools, and Sprawl." Great Cities Institute Working Paper. Chicago: University of Illinois at Chicago.

Dye, Richard F., Therese J. McGuire, and David F. Merriman. 1999. "The Impact of Property Taxes and Property Tax Classification on Business Activity in the Chicago Metropolitan Area." Report prepared for the Lincoln Institute of Land Policy, Cambridge, Mass.

Foster, Kathryn A. 2000. "Regional Capital." In *Urban-Suburban Interdependencies,* edited by Rosalind Greenstein and Wim Wiewel. Cambridge, Mass.: Lincoln Institute of Land Policy.

Gordon, Peter, and Harry W. Richardson. 1997. "Are Compact Cities a Desirable Planning Goal?" *Journal of the American Planning Association* 63 (Winter, 1): 95–106.

Hackensack Meadowlands Development Commission. 1999. "HMDC: What Is HMDC—Tax Sharing Made Simple." http://www.hmdc.state.nj.us/taxshare.html. (Accessed September 1999.)

Illinois Department of Employment Security. 1999. "Where Workers Work in the Chicago Metro Area—Summary Report: 1972–1997." http://lmi.ides.state.il.us/wwwork/intro.htm.

Illinois General Assembly. 2000. State of Illinois 91st General Assembly Legislation. Senate Bill 93. http://www.legis.state.il.us.

Illinois Omnibus Poll. 1999. Revenue sharing question written by Bonnie Lindstrom. Chicago: University of Illinois at Chicago, Survey Research Laboratory.

Johnson, Elmer W. 1999. Chicago Metropolis 2020: Preparing Metropolitan Chicago for the 21st Century. Chicago: The Commercial Club of Chicago.

Levine, Joyce N. 2000. "Is There a Link between Regional Planning and Economic Growth?" College of Urban and Public Affairs Working Paper 66. New Orleans, La.: University of New Orleans.

Lindstrom, Bonnie. 1998. "Regional Cooperation and Sustainable Growth: Nine Councils of Government in Northeastern Illinois." Journal of Urban Affairs 20(3): 327–42.

———. 1999. "Public Works and Land Use Policies: The Importance of Public Infrastructure in Chicago's Metropolitan Development, 1830–1970." Great Cities Institute Working Paper. Chicago: University of Illinois at Chicago.

McClory, Robert. 1999. "Reviving the Energy for Action and Justice." National Catholic Reporter, 15 January, 3–4.

McDonald, John F., and Daniel P. McMillen. 1999. "Employment Subcenters and Subsequent Real Estate Development in Suburban Chicago." Great Cities Institute Working Paper. Chicago: University of Illinois at Chicago.

Metropolitan Planning Council. 1995. "Creating a Regional Community: The Case for Metropolitan Cooperation." Chicago: Metropolitan Planning Council.

Nelson, Arthur C., and James P. Duncan. 1995. Growth Management Principles and Practices. Chicago: APA Planners Press.

Northeastern Illinois Planning Commission. 1999. "Census Bureau Releases Updated Income and Poverty Estimates for Illinois and Northeastern Illinois Counties." http://www.nipc.cog.il.us/pov95nei.htm. (Accessed February 12, 1999.)

Orfield, Myron. 1996. Chicago Regional Report. Minneapolis, Minn.: Metropolitan Area Program.

———. 1997. Metropolitics: A Regional Agenda for Community and Stability. Washington, D.C.: Brookings Institution Press and The Lincoln Institute of Land Policy.

Persky, Joseph, and Wim Wiewel. 2000. When Corporations Leave Town: The Costs and Benefits of Metropolitan Job Sprawl. Detroit, Mich.: Wayne State University Press.

Persky, Joseph, Bill Howard, Cedric Williams, Haydar Kurban, Kimberly Schaffer, and Bill Lester. 2000. Illinois Jobs—Recent Industrial Growth and Future Prospects. Chicago: Center for Urban Economic Development, University of Illinois at Chicago.

Peterson, Paul E. 1981. City Limits. Chicago: University of Chicago Press.

Porter, Douglas R. 1996. Profiles in Growth Management. Washington, D.C.: The Urban Land Institute.

Richman, Roger S., and M. H. Wilkinson. 1993. "Interlocal Revenue Sharing: Practice and Potential." Issues and Options 1(1).

Rodkin, Dennis. 1997. "How Do Your Taxes Compare?" *Chicago Magazine.* http://www.
    chicagomag.com/chicagomag/Text/features/taxes/1997.htm. (Accessed September
    1999.)
Rusk, David. 1999. *Inside Game/Outside Game: Winning Strategies for Saving Urban
    America.* Washington, D.C.: Brookings Institution Press.
Schneider, Mark. 1989. *The Competitive City—The Political Economy of Suburbia.* Pitts-
    burgh: University of Pittsburgh Press.
Summers, Anita A. 2000. "Regionalization Efforts between Big Cities and Their Sub-
    urbs: Rhetoric and Reality." In *Urban-Suburban Interdependencies,* edited by Ros-
    alind Greenstein and Wim Wiewel. Cambridge, Mass.: Lincoln Institute of Land
    Policy.
Urban Transportation Center. 1998. *Highways and Urban Decentralization.* Chicago:
    University of Illinois at Chicago.
U.S. Census Bureau. 1992. *Census of Population and Housing, 1990: Public Use Microdata
    Sample U.S. Technical Documentation.* Washington, D.C.: U.S. Census Bureau.
————. 2001. *Census of Population and Housing, 2000.* Washington, D.C.: U.S. Census
    Bureau.
Wiewel, Wim. 2000. *Summary Findings of the Chicago Metropolitan Case Study.* Chicago:
    University of Illinois at Chicago.
Wiewel, Wim, and Kimberly Schaffer. 2000. *Chicago Metropolitan Case Study: Policy Rec-
    ommendations.* Chicago: University of Illinois at Chicago.
Wilson, William J. 1996. *When Work Disappears: The World of the New Urban Poor.* New
    York: Alfred A. Knopf.

# 11

# Maryland's "Smart Growth"
## Using Incentives to Combat Sprawl

James R. Cohen

In 1996, Maryland Governor Parris N. Glendening declared his commitment to create and secure passage of a comprehensive package of legislation that would enhance the state's capacity to direct new growth and to revitalize older, developed areas. Faced with the projection of a million new Maryland residents by the year 2015—a 20 percent increase—the governor realized that prevailing state and local planning, capital spending, and regulatory practices were insufficient to prevent suburban sprawl and the decline of aging cities and inner suburbs. A prime example of the problem is the Baltimore region: while Baltimore City lost over 84,000 residents between 1990 and 2000, the Baltimore region's population outside the City increased by nearly 256,000 over the same period.[1] The emerging package of legislation was given the name "Smart Growth," and even before implementation, the Maryland program earned immediate recognition as a bold, creative approach to growth management. The director of a land use institute in Michigan called the Maryland Smart Growth program "the most promising new tool for managing growth in a generation" (Goodman 1998), and in October 2000 the program was named as one of 10 winners in the annual "Innovations in American Government" program sponsored by the Ford Foundation and Harvard's John F. Kennedy School of Government.

Maryland Smart Growth encompasses a number of state laws and programs passed by the Maryland legislature beginning in 1997. Smart Growth has three major objectives:

- "to save our most valuable remaining natural resources before they are forever lost";
- "to support existing communities and neighborhoods by targeting state resources to support development in areas where the infrastructure is already in place or planned to support it"; and
- "to save taxpayers millions of dollars in the unnecessary cost of building the infrastructure required to support sprawl" (Maryland Office of Planning 2000a).

At the heart of Maryland Smart Growth are the following five core initiatives:

1. The **1997 Smart Growth Areas Act,** which directs state funding into already developed areas and areas planned for growth. With certain exceptions, only areas designated as "Smart Growth Areas" or "Priority Funding Areas" may qualify for state funds for transportation, housing, economic development, and environmental projects. The act's intent is to discourage sprawl by denying state subsidies that would promote sprawl, and to promote development and revitalization in cities and inner suburbs.
2. The **1997 Rural Legacy Act,** which established a grant program enabling local governments and private land trusts to purchase easements and development rights in "Rural Legacy Areas." The program's intent is to protect regions with agricultural, forestry, natural, and cultural resources that, if conserved, could promote resource-based economies, provide greenbelts around developed areas, and maintain the character of rural communities.
3. The **Brownfields Voluntary Cleanup and Revitalization Incentive Programs,** which attempt to stimulate the reuse of contaminated properties by relieving current owners from retroactive liability, offering loans and grants for site cleanup, and providing a 50 percent tax break on the increased assessment resulting from property improvements.
4. An updated **Job Creation Tax Credit Program,** originally established in 1996, which encourages businesses to expand or relocate

in Maryland by providing tax credits for each new, full-time job a qualified business creates.

5. The **Live Near Your Work Program,** which creates incentives for employees to buy homes near their workplaces. State grants match contributions by businesses and local governments that assist employees with house purchases. The program goals are to stabilize targeted neighborhoods by promoting homeownership, and to reduce employees' commuting time.

In addition to the five core programs, there are a number of other state programs and policies that complement the Smart Growth objectives. For example, it is state policy "that the emphasis of funding for public school construction projects shall be to target the rehabilitation of existing schools to ensure that facilities in established neighborhoods are of equal quality to new schools" (*Annotated Code of Maryland,* Section 5-7B-07). Also, state agencies are to "give priority to central business districts, downtown cores, empowerment zones and revitalization areas when funding infrastructure projects or locating new facilities" (Executive Order 01—1.1998.04).

Maryland's key Smart Growth Initiatives are intended to address some of the consequences of uneven development outlined by Gregory Squires in chapter 1. Maryland's cities and inner suburbs, which house most of the state's low-income and minority population, are favored for state infrastructure spending and the targeting of job-creation tax credits. The Live Near Your Work program can entice workers to buy houses in downtown rather than in suburban locations, thereby contributing to city revitalization. Brownfields cleanup and incentive programs can stimulate the reuse of contaminated, vacant, and underused industrial sites, which are concentrated in cities and inner suburbs. The brownfields programs can thereby generate needed economic activity and employment in areas negatively impacted by deindustrialization and the suburbanization of manufacturing employment. The state's new policy of targeting public school construction funds for the renovation of existing schools can result in the physical upgrading of previously neglected, inner-city schools. The Rural Legacy program can reduce sprawl by preserving rural resource lands and, in the process, provide compensation (equity) to rural landowners who voluntarily forgo development options on their lands.

This chapter will analyze the degree to which Maryland's Smart Growth Initiatives are not only preventing sprawl, but also addressing the goal of city and inner-suburb revitalization in a way that benefits low- and moderate-income households. The analysis will begin with a review of the historical context of these initiatives in order to provide a better understanding of the program's overall design in relation to prior state land use legislation. The overview will indicate that, prior to the Smart Growth Initiatives, Maryland's growth management legislation was almost exclusively concerned with land preservation and Chesapeake Bay protection, rather than urban revitalization. The chapter will then focus on each of the main Smart Growth programs and policies in turn, pointing out their potential in terms of sprawl prevention *and* urban revitalization. While the programs have not been in place long enough to evaluate long-term program outcomes, observations will be made from program design and currently available data.

## The Historical Context of Maryland Smart Growth

### Factors Shaping Maryland Anti-Sprawl Policies

Eleven states currently conduct comprehensive growth management programs (Porter 1999). Each program reflects that state's distinctive political traditions, geography, growth patterns, economic base, and environmental problems (Diamond and Noonan 1996, 104). In Maryland, anti-sprawl programs are primarily shaped by three main factors: a widespread public desire to preserve the health of the Chesapeake Bay, a strong resistance to state intervention in local land use planning, and political tension between urbanized and less-populated jurisdictions.

Maryland's 1997 Smart Growth Initiatives were preceded by a series of state land use laws enacted to conserve open space and to help protect and restore the ecology of the Chesapeake Bay, North America's largest and most productive estuary. Table 11.1 provides a summary of key environmental laws in Maryland.

### The Year 2020 Panel

The Chesapeake Bay is 195 miles long and from 4 to 30 miles wide, bordered on either side by tidewater Maryland and Virginia. The bay's watershed covers an enormous 64,000-square-mile area—encompassing parts of the states of Maryland, Virginia, New York, Pennsylvania, Delaware, West Virginia, and Pennsylvania (Horton and Eichbaum 1991).

Table 11.1 *Major Land Use and Environmental Legislation in Maryland since 1969*

| Year | Legislation/Program | Purpose |
|------|---------------------|---------|
| 1969 | Program Open Space | Earmarks funds from state's real estate transfer tax to purchase open space for parks and natural resources areas. |
| 1970 | Tidal Wetlands Act | Requires permit from state for alteration of tidal wetlands; requires mitigation of any wetland loss. |
| 1975 | MD Agricultural Land Preservation Foundation | Allows rural landowners to create districts within which a state foundation may buy conservation easements to preserve productive agricultural land and woodlands. |
| 1982 | Stormwater Management Act | Requires on-site treatment of stormwater on new development sites to prevent nonpoint source pollution. |
| 1984 | Critical Area Act | Places restrictions on land use activities within a zone measured 1,000 ft. from the Chesapeake Bay and its major tributaries. |
| 1989 | Nontidal Wetlands Act | Requires permit from state for alteration of nontidal wetland; requires minimum 25 ft. buffer from outer edge of wetland; requires mitigation for any nontidal wetland loss. |
| 1991 | Forest Conservation Act | Requires developers to replace some of forest cleared for building; requires tree planting on development sites that have few or no trees; applies to parcels >40,000 sq. ft. |
| 1992 | Economic Growth, Resource Protection and Planning Act | Described herein. |
| 1997 | Smart Growth Initiatives | Described herein. |
| 2001 | GreenPrint Program | Uses state appropriations, over five years, to preserve a network of the state's most valuable ecological lands through targeted acquisitions and easements. |

Alarm over a sobering U.S. Environmental Protection Agency (EPA) report on the declining health of the Bay (EPA 1983) led to several federal and state initiatives to restore the Bay, including some of the Maryland measures listed in table 11.1. In 1987, Maryland, Virginia, Pennsylvania, the District of Columbia, and the EPA signed a Chesapeake Bay agreement. One of the measures included in the agreement was the appointment of The 2020 Commission (hereinafter referred to as "the 2020 panel"), a panel of experts who were charged with producing a report by December 1988 on growth management regulations, environmental programs, and infrastructure requirements necessary to protect the Bay, while still accommodating projected population growth in the Bay region through the year 2020. In its subsequent report, the panel expressed concern over the increasingly resource-consumptive and polluting nature of population growth in the region. The panel noted that "more than any other single development factor, we are more concerned about low density sprawl. . . . The low density alternative produces environmental effects and infrastructure demands that are more expensive to remedy" and stated that it was "dismayed by the lack of growth management and planning, particularly on a state and regional level" (The 2020 Commission 1988, 2). The panel then presented the following six visions created to guide policymakers in the region, and outlined an action plan each:

1. development is concentrated in suitable areas;
2. sensitive areas are protected;
3. in rural areas, growth is directed to existing population centers and resource areas are protected;
4. stewardship of the Chesapeake Bay and the land is a universal ethic;
5. conservation of resources, including a reduction in resource consumption, is practiced; and
6. funding mechanisms are addressed to achieve these visions.

## The 1992 Economic Development, Resource Protection and Planning Act

In 1989, several months after the 2020 report was published, then-Maryland Governor William Donald Schaefer appointed the Governor's Commission on Growth in the Chesapeake Bay Region. Referred to by the name of its chair, former Maryland Congressman Michael Barnes, the Barnes Commission was directed to review the findings of the 2020 panel, determine their application to Maryland, and identify growth issues the state should address by the year 2020.

The Barnes Commission eventually proposed legislation to create a growth management system in Maryland that would have dramatically increased state regulatory authority over local land use planning. Unveiled in November of 1990, the Maryland Growth and Chesapeake Bay Protection Act of 1991 would have required local governments to divide land in their jurisdictions into four categories. These categories, based on criteria specified in the legislation, are developed areas, growth areas, sensitive areas, and rural and resource areas. Also specified were permitted densities and performance standards within growth, developed and rural resource areas. In rural and resource areas, for example, the proposed act would have limited density to one unit per 20 acres. Each local government would have to inventory environmentally sensitive areas and develop protection programs following state criteria. The state would have approval authority over local planning programs, which would then be valid for three years. The state would have certified local compliance after review of performance, and could have withheld funds for development activities in cases of noncompliance.

Response to the Barnes Commission bill was overwhelmingly negative. Environmental organizations provided the bill with its only support, while bankers, homebuilders, farmers, foresters, county and municipal officials all vehemently opposed it. The opposition denounced the proposed bill for weakening local government control over land use and for failing to acknowledge the state's regional and geographic diversity. The 1991 bill was never reported out of committee.

Opponents of the Barnes Commission proposals worked with a joint committee of 10 state delegates and 10 state senators to craft an alternative bill that passed in the 1992 legislative session. The Maryland Economic Growth, Resource Protection and Planning Act of 1992 (hereafter referred to as the 1992 Planning Act) requires local governments to incorporate the six visions—plus a new vision encouraging economic growth and streamlining regulatory mechanisms—into their comprehensive plans. The plans must contain sensitive area elements, although each jurisdiction may define and determine the level of protection for each of the four categories of sensitive areas contained in the failed 1991 bill (steep slopes, streams and their buffers, the 100-year floodplain, and habitats of endangered species). Once the plan with the new sensitive-areas element is adopted, the jurisdiction's zoning and subdivisions must be made consistent with the plan. Local planning commissions must review and, if necessary, amend their plans every six years. Jurisdictions had until January of 1997 to update their comprehensive plans to incorporate the visions and the new element.

The 1992 Planning Act does not provide the state with the expansive responsibilities for growth management that were contained in the 2020 Panel report nor the Barnes Commission's proposed 1991 legislation. Under the 1992 act, the state does not prepare a state plan. In contrast to the 2020 Panel's recommendations, the state does not map sensitive areas, adopt criteria for buffer zone widths based on the resource needing protection, or establish and enforce minimum standards for site development, construction, and maintenance to minimize environmental impacts. As stated in the 1992 act's preamble, most of the discretion in growth management and sensitive area protection is left to local governments.

The Maryland Department of Planning (MDP)[2] provides staff support to the Economic Growth, Resource Protection and Planning Committee (established by the Planning Act) and provides written commentary on all sensitive area elements prepared by local government. Local governments must consider MDP's critical commentary, but there is no requirement that the state's recommendations be included in the final plan.

Since enactment of the Planning Act, MDP has produced a score of publications under a "Managing Maryland's Growth: Models and Guidelines" series. These well-designed and clearly written publications are intended to assist local governments in preparing their plans and implementing programs to address growth management goals. Examples of titles include, "Achieving 'Consistency' under the Planning Act of 1992," "Preparing a Sensitive Areas Element for the Comprehensive Plan," and "Interjurisdictional Coordination for Comprehensive Planning." Similar publications have been created and distributed since 1997 to assist local governments in implementing the Smart Growth Initiatives.

As mentioned above, the Planning Act established a 17-member, Economic Growth, Resource Protection and Planning Commission (hereafter referred to as the "Growth Commission") to advise the governor on progress in achieving the visions and the growth policies. One of the issues is "progress in providing affordable housing." Although there were no requirements in the Planning Act for local provision of affordable housing, a companion bill did grant local governments the discretion to implement various kinds of affordable housing programs. The Growth

Commission has also been given some advisory roles under the Smart Growth Initiatives.

## Origins of the Smart Growth Initiatives

In its 1996 annual report, Maryland's Growth Commission (1996, 4–6) outlined four major strengths of the 1992 Planning Act. The commission found that the act (a) "preserves local land use authority"; (b) "allows flexibility to reflect unique local conditions"; (c) "focuses state and local activities on directed growth in a consistent manner" (since the act requires that local regulations and state and local capital spending be consistent with the local comprehensive plan, and that regulatory streamlining and flexibility facilitate economic growth in suitable areas); and (d) "measures progress and is open to future action" (since the act provides for an annual reporting process to the governor and General Assembly and requires that the act be evaluated by the year 2002).

However, the 1992 act has its limitations. The Growth Commission's 1996 annual report asserted that the act did not adequately define what "concentrated" or "suitable areas" meant in vision 1 ("development is concentrated in suitable areas"), nor clarify what "rural resources" meant in vision 3. Similarly, a case study of local government response to the 1992 act (Cohen and McAbee-Cummings 1998) found insufficient county government reporting on the extent to which new growth has been consistent with vision 1. Some counties that did report on the location of new growth indicated it was mostly occurring (in terms of acreage developed) outside of county-designated growth areas. The study also found "protection" of rural resources needed clarification, since some jurisdictions considered agricultural land "protection" to include zoning of one unit per three acres—an ineffective farmland preservation technique.

Widespread concerns that the 1992 Planning Act and other measures could not adequately direct growth and revitalize older neighborhoods led Governor Glendening, in 1996, to implement a "we listened, you recommended" campaign to solicit ideas from interested citizen and stakeholder groups on how to better manage growth. According to MDP's Ron Young, who spearheaded the campaign, the governor was interested in a strategy that was:

- incentive based,
- would not intrude on local land use authority,

- could be implemented immediately,
- would not require creation of a new bureaucracy, and
- would mainly rely on reprioritization of existing spending rather than new spending.[3]

Meetings and forums were held in all of Maryland's 23 counties and Baltimore City. Over 100 legislative and administrative suggestions were submitted to the governor by the end of the year (Maryland Office of Planning 1998, 7). The outcome of this effort was the set of five initiatives listed at the beginning of this chapter, each of which is analyzed below.

## Analysis of the Smart Growth Initiatives

### Smart Growth and Priority Funding Areas

The centerpiece of Maryland's Smart Growth Initiatives is the Smart Growth Areas Act, which constrains the state from subsidizing low-density development. In effect, the act is a means of clarifying and further implementing some of the visions contained in the 1992 Planning Act (especially visions 1, 3, and 6, see page 298). In promoting smart growth, Governor Glendening asserted that restricting and targeting state funding is the most efficient and effective use of taxpayer money, by avoiding the higher taxes that would be necessary to fund infrastructure for sprawl development. "Every new classroom costs $90,000. Every mile of new sewer line costs roughly $200,000. And every single-lane mile of new road costs at least $4 million."[4]

Under the Smart Growth Areas Act, state permitting or funding of infrastructure and other facilities for new development projects is only allowed in "Priority Funding Areas" (PFAs). PFAs automatically include (a) municipalities; (b) areas designated by the Department of Housing and Community Development (DHCD) for revitalization; (c) an enterprise zone as designated under the state or by the federal government; and (d) areas of the state located between Interstate 495 and Washington, D.C., or between Interstate 695 and Baltimore City.

In addition, county governments have the option of identifying PFAs not included in the above designations. Among the areas that qualify for county PFA designation are (a) a community existing prior to 1997 that is located within a locally designated growth area, served by a public/

community sewer *or* water system, and has an allowed, average residential density of ≥ 2.0 units per acre; (b) an area outside the developed portion of an existing community, if the area has a permitted, average build-out density of ≥ 3.5 units/acre; and (c) a currently undeveloped area that is within a county-designated growth area, is scheduled for public water and sewer service, and has a permitted residential density of ≥ 3.5 units per acre.

The MDP provided county governments with guidelines for determining residential density and for the appropriate sizing of county-designated PFAs. Once they had completed their designations, the counties provided the MDP with maps and other information showing the precise location of the PFAs. MDP staff then reviewed each county's proposed PFAs to determine its consistency with water and sewer facilities and plans, the residential density thresholds specified in the legislation, and the jurisdiction's projected population growth. The final maps become the basis for state agency funding of development-related projects.

The Smart Growth Areas Act bolstered Maryland's reputation as a leader in state growth management. As Porter (1999) observes, of the 11 states with comprehensive growth management legislation, only Maryland's 1997 law explicitly mandates that state funds for growth-inducing projects be limited to designated growth areas. However, unlike the state growth management programs in Oregon and Florida, Maryland does not have final approval authority over local comprehensive plans. Unlike Vermont, Maryland does not have regional boards that can reject, or substantially modify, a development that has regional impacts, nor does it have a transportation super-agency, as does Georgia, that can reject a proposed development project.[5] Instead, the act relies on state fiscal incentives. However, there are three main aspects of the law and its implementation that, critics believe, may limit its effectiveness in controlling sprawl and stimulating revitalization of cities and inner suburbs.

First, the law does not prevent sprawl that is privately and/or local-government funded. As reported by Montgomery (2000a), Wal-Mart is constructing stores in Worcester and Kent Counties that are outside those jurisdictions' PFAs as well as the growth areas identified in their comprehensive plan updates mandated by the 1992 Planning Act. In Kent County, the proposed store is on an island within view of the Chesapeake Bay Bridge. The store would require a state-funded expansion of the local water treatment plant, but the expansion cannot be canceled because it also serves development located inside the county's PFA. In Worcester County, Wal-Mart obtained building approval from the local government by promising to build a service road to the store site. Governor Glendening, who opposed both projects, admitted: "I have directed every single agency that no state resources should be used in any way to make any of those projects work. But the reality is smart growth has some built-in limitations" (Montgomery 2000a).

Second, there are concerns about the definitions of PFAs. Some critics contend that the density requirements are too low. The minimum density thresholds are the result of political compromise rather than concrete analysis of density and service efficiency. Early drafts of the legislation called for minimum PFA densities of five units per acre, but the threshold was reduced in the final version.[6] A smart growth advocacy organization, 1000 Friends of Maryland (1999) pointed out that in many counties, developments often fail to meet zoning-permitted densities. Since state funding of infrastructure is based on actual *and* permitted densities, state spending in some PFAs may not be as cost-efficient as hoped, nor as effective in discouraging sprawl.

In addition to questionable thresholds, the PFA criteria are nearly exclusively focused on density at the expense of other considerations. As noted by 1000 Friends of Maryland: "Smart Growth does little to address the quality of development—efficient use of land, mixed-use environments, minimized auto dependency, housing choices to provide socioeconomic diversity . . . nor does it address projects with regional impact" (1999, 8).

While these criticisms of the PFA density provisions are well-founded, they should be put in the context of the failed 1991 legislation that would have allowed the state to assert greater control, via performance standards, over local land use planning. It is highly unlikely that a bill with more expansive conditional requirements would have passed the legislature. Instead, a jurisdiction committed to smart growth principles could establish more mixed-use, socioeconomically diverse, and less auto-dependent areas by creative utilization of other Smart Growth Initiatives along with other state and federal programs.

A third issue related to PFA designation is that consistent implementation of the Smart Growth Areas Act is greatly dependent upon the commitment of future governors and state agency directors. For example, in November 1999, Governor Glendening selected a vacant building complex in downtown Hagerstown as the location for the University of

Maryland's new Washington County Center. One of the two alternative locations, favored by the University's chancellor, was a greenfield site that would have required extensive infrastructure construction and precluded an opportune boost of downtown Hagerstown's revitalization efforts. A governor less committed to smart growth principles could have selected the greenfield location.

The act does allow for state-subsidized development outside of PFAs under certain conditions. Some decisions on whether to fund a growth-related project that is *not* within a PFA are made by the state Board of Public Works (BPW), a three-person entity consisting of the governor, the state comptroller, and state treasurer. Whether or not decisions on exemptions are consistent with the intentions of the Smart Growth legislation greatly depends on the growth-management orientation of the BPW. The act also lists certain situations in which the state may provide funding for a growth-related project not in a PFA *without* receiving approval from the BPW. One such exception is for "a growth-related project related to a commercial or industrial activity which, due to its operational or physical characteristics, shall be located away from other development, including . . . an industry that is proximate to . . . a railroad facility, a transit facility, or a major highway interchange." One critic observes that since the law provides no definition of "proximate," state agencies could approve projects that generate "the very kind of outward sprawl development that the Smart Growth Areas Act was designed to limit" (Porter 1999, 5).

While interpretation of some guidelines is at the discretion of the BPW and state agency officials, the law has some potential checks and balances. When a funding request is made to the BPW for a growth-related project that is *not* within a PFA, the BPW *may* request an advisory opinion from the State Growth Commission. If requested by a member of the public, the commission will hold a public meeting to obtain information relevant to the advisory opinion. However, the BPW determines whether there will be a Growth Commission review, and thereby the option for a public meeting.

In summary, the Smart Growth Areas Act does not command local governments to focus development in PFAs. Unlike Oregon, Maryland does not require jurisdictions to create urban growth boundaries, outside of which development is severely restricted. Instead, the PFA program is incentive based. It is too early to tell the degree to which the program will produce more compact and cost-efficient development patterns.

## Rural Legacy Program

The Rural Legacy Program, created by the legislature in 1997 and amended in 2000, provides funds to local governments and land trusts to purchase land, easements, and transferable development rights from willing sellers in designated receiving areas. Proponents of the program cite multiple goals for the Rural Legacy Program, including preserving wildlife habitat; reducing pollution runoff into streams and the Chesapeake Bay by protecting greenbelts, forest land, and open spaces surrounding populated areas; supporting the state's resource-based industries (farming, forestry, outdoor recreation, and tourism) from sprawl development; reducing public infrastructure costs of sprawl; and preserving a so-called "sense of place" in the countryside (Maryland Department of Natural Resources [DNR] 2000). From FY (fiscal year) 1998 through FY 2002, between $70 million and $140 million will be committed to preserve from 50,000 to 75,000 acres of farm, forest, and open space land. The funds will be generated through a combination of Maryland Program Open Space dollars (table 11.1) and general obligation bonds from Maryland's capital budget (DNR 2000).

A year 2000 amendment to the legislation allows development rights purchased from landowners in rural legacy areas to be transferred (resold) to developers, but the developers may only use those rights in PFAs. Fifty percent of the proceeds from transfer of development rights (TDR) sales are to be used by the local government for capital projects in the county or municipality in which the TDRs originated. If the TDR-receiving area is within a municipality, then the proceeds go the municipality. The other half of the monies received from TDR sales are returned to the Rural Legacy Program, but the program must use those funds for conservation purposes (including funding of land acquisition or easement purchase) in the county in which the TDR sales occurred.

To participate in the Rural Legacy Program, partnerships of local governments, land trusts, and landowners submit competitive applications to the state. Applications are reviewed by the Rural Legacy Board, consisting of the secretaries of agriculture, DNR, and MDP. Following its review, the board makes recommendations on projects and funding levels to the Board of Public Works, which makes final selections (Natural Resources Article, Sec. 5-9A-01–05). In FY 2000, there were 25 applications requesting a total of $90 million.[7] The BPW approved 19 of the applications and $25 million in funding. Some of the winning entries involved multijurisdictional collaboration, such as the partnerships among Washington, Montgomery, and Frederick Counties, and between Baltimore and Harford Counties.

The act outlines criteria that the Rural Legacy Board is to use in reviewing applications. One criterion is the significance of the agricultural, forestry, and natural resource land proposed for protection. Among the factors to be examined by the Rural Legacy Board in relation to this criterion include the degree to which the proposed fee or easement purchases will protect contiguous blocks of land, and the nature, size, and importance of the land area. Additional evaluative criteria include the degree to which the resources and character of the proposed area are threatened by development, the significance of any historic sites or archaeological sites in the area, and the economic value of the resource-based industries or services proposed for protection. The legislation also instructs the Rural Legacy Board to examine the degree to which existing planning, zoning, and growth management policies of the sponsoring jurisdictions are contributing to land conservation.

Two of the above-mentioned criteria used by the Rural Legacy Board to review proposals appear contradictory. On the one hand, the board is to consider the degree to which land in the proposed rural legacy area is threatened by development. On the other hand, the board examines the extent to which the sponsor applicants are using their planning and zoning powers to support land conservation. A major reason why natural resource land in a jurisdiction is being threatened by sprawl is because the jurisdiction has ineffectual land preservation policies and programs. For example, Charles and Howard Counties each use three-acre zoning in rural areas, a policy that is inadequate as a farmland preservation tool. If land regulations in those jurisdictions remain unchanged, then the success of the Rural Legacy Program would be compromised (Kreitner and Young 1998).[8] However, excluding such jurisdictions from the Rural Legacy Program would jeopardize any chances of preserving remaining valuable resource lands.

The above-described dilemma becomes a social equity issue when taxpayer money is used to preserve rural lands where there are adjacent, nonparticipating, vacant parcels zoned for three-acre lots. In effect, the state would be subsidizing the creation of permanent open space for future homeowners who can afford a three-acre lot. The Rural Legacy Board has responded to this situation as well as it can, given the constraints on state interference with local government land use policy.

Sponsors awarded grants must sign a contract with the Rural Legacy Board that outlines performance standards for strengthening their rural land conservation policies. The sponsors are urged to create more stringent rural zoning and introduce or expand TDR and Purchase of Development Rights (PDR) programs. The sponsors' required annual reports to the board must include a section that describes improvements (or lack thereof) to their rural land preservation. The lack of progress in strengthening support for land regulation can be the basis for denial of continuing funds for the sponsor's program.

## Brownfields Incentives

Cities and inner suburbs contain unutilized or abandoned properties that are contaminated, or are perceived to be contaminated, due to prior industrial uses. Many of these so-called "brownfield" sites are already served by water and sewer systems, and could be cleaned to a level suitable for commercial and industrial uses. However, largely because of uncertainty over liability, commercial and industrial developers have usually shunned brownfield sites in favor of "greenfields." Developing on greenfields leads to loss of farms and open space, requires taxpayer expenses for construction of new roads and utilities, and denies older areas of opportunities for reinvestment, revitalization, and new employment.

The Maryland brownfields initiatives attempt to overcome some of the negative perceptions (and reality) of the potential for brownfield reuse that was generated by the federal Comprehensive Environmental Response, Compensation and Liability Act (CERCLA) of 1980. The "superfund" program, focused on the country's most severely polluted properties, imposed liability for cleanup expenses on current owners, many of whom were not involved in the discharge of pollutants on their properties. The program involved enormous cleanup expenses and unpredictability in terms of what constituted "clean" and how long such cleanup would take (Bartsch and Collaton 1996). The federal government gave grants to states for preliminary assessments. The worst sites were placed on the federal National Priorities List (NPL); sites that were somewhat less contaminated were placed on the each state's superfund list. Maryland has 21 sites on the NPL list and 400 state superfund sites. The Maryland legislation also intends to address many of these factors for contaminated sites that are not on either list.

Maryland's brownfields programs include a Voluntary Cleanup Program (VCP), administered by the Maryland Department of the Environment (MDE), and a Brownfield Revitalization Incentive Program (BRIP) within the Department of Business and Economic Development (DBED). These programs are designed to encourage the investigation of eligible properties with known or perceived contamination, protect public health and the environment where cleanup projects are either being performed or need to be performed, accelerate the cleanup of eligible properties, and provide predictability and finality to the cleanup of eligible properties.

Under the VCP, eligible participants include "inculpable" and "responsible" persons. An inculpable person is a prospective buyer who has not caused or contributed to the contamination on the property. A responsible person is an owner or lender of a subject property who has "not knowingly or willfully violated any law or regulation" concerning the discharge of controlled hazardous substances on the property (*Annotated Code of Maryland,* Subtitle 5, Section 7-501). The legislation differentiates between a "responsible" person and a "person responsible for the discharge"; the latter is not eligible for the VCP program.

To participate in the VCP, eligible participants submit an application that includes Phase I and II environmental site assessments,[9] all known information about potential sources and areas of contamination on the site, a summary description of a proposed voluntary cleanup strategy that incorporates cleanup criteria established under the legislation, and an application fee to pay for MDE oversight costs.

Upon receipt of an application, MDE has 60 days to determine if the applicant is eligible and, if so, whether any cleanup is required. If the agency determines that no cleanup is necessary, it issues a written statement that there are no further requirements related to the investigation of hazardous wastes on the property. If MDE determines that a cleanup is required, the applicant must provide the department with a "response action plan," which includes an outline and schedule of all work necessary to achieve the health-related outcome criteria listed in the legislation.

MDE has 120 days following receipt of a proposed action plan to review the plan and all public comments, and to notify the applicant if the plan has been approved or rejected. If MDE is convinced that the proposed actions will produce outcomes that will protect public health and the environment, it provides the applicant with an approval letter that states no further actions will be required other than those contained in the plan.

If a response action plan is implemented to MDE's satisfaction, the department issues the participant a certificate of completion, thereby releasing the applicant from further liability to the state for the contamination identified and treated through the voluntary cleanup process. Under a memorandum of understanding between MDE and Region III of the EPA, sites that have successfully participated in the Maryland program will be considered by the EPA to be of "no federal interest."

The 1997 Smart Growth legislation also established a Brownfields Revitalization Incentive Program (BRIP) within the Maryland Department of Business and Economic Development (DBED), which provides grants and low-interest loans. As originally implemented, the funds were available only to "inculpable" persons who had received MDE approval for their VCP response action plans, and therefore could only be used for cleanup, not assessments. As a result of amendments in 2000, "inculpable" persons may receive DBED financial assistance for both environmental assessments and for cleanup, and "responsible" persons may obtain assistance, but only for assessments.

Included in the BRIP are property tax abatements for site owners who have completed MDE-approved cleanups, as long as the property is located in a taxing jurisdiction that chooses to participate. For each of the five years immediately following completion of a voluntary cleanup of a site, the participating jurisdiction must grant a property tax credit to the site that is equal to 50 percent of the property tax attributable to the increase since the last pre-cleanup assessment. In addition, over the same five-year period, the jurisdiction must contribute to the Brownfields Incentive Fund an amount equal to 30 percent of the property tax attributable to the increased assessment. If it chooses, a jurisdiction may grant a property tax credit of up to an additional 20 percent of the remaining property tax attributable to the assessment increase.

Participation in the VCP program is slowly increasing, partly as a result of legislative revisions making "responsible" persons eligible for environmental assessments. According to MDE's Smart Growth coordinator, as of mid-May 2000, there were 58 VCP sites encompassing over 1,300 acres.[10] Cleanup on 27 properties had been completed; 24 of them had been given a "no further requirements" (i.e., no cleanup required) classification from MDE, while 3 properties had been given certificates of completion. However, participation in BRIP has been very slow to materialize. About $1.3 million was originally made available in the Brownfields Incentive Fund. As of May 2000, only one VCP participant had received funding for cleanup. In addition, only two firms had been approved for the tax credits.

According to a DBED official, firms have been slow to use the program due to lingering perceptions about liability.[11] However, in May 2000, partly due to publicity about the state's brownfields programs, MDE reported that nine additional firms were working with the department on financial assistance arrangements. Low participation in the tax credit program has been attributed to the original requirement that a participating jurisdiction had to pass legislation authorizing the abatements. By November 1999, only seven jurisdictions had approved such legislation. Revisions to the law in 2000 removed that requirement. Now, participating jurisdictions must provide DBED with an annually updated list of potential brownfield sites, ranked in order of priority for redevelopment. It remains to be seen whether this revision will result in more tax credit use.

In a study conducted before implementation of the 1997 Smart Growth Initiatives, Howland (2000) examined the land market in the Canton industrial area of southeast Baltimore. She divided her 480 study parcels into three categories—"known to be contaminated," "possibly contaminated," and "known to be clean"—and then tracked the market outcome of each of the 68 parcels that were for sale between September 1995 and November 1996. Howland found an active market for industrial land, a market in which actual or possible contamination was not a deterrent to sales. Sellers were dropping their prices to compensate for known and unpredictable future cleanup expenses—brownfield sites sold for an average of 55 percent of the per-acre price of clean sites. High price and small parcel size were found to be more important factors than contamination in explaining why some parcels were not purchased.

A research agenda for examining the effectiveness of the brownfields initiatives would include analysis of trends in brownfields resale and utilization prior to and after implementation of the initiative. A follow-up of Howland's study, examining the Canton industrial area land market *after* implementation of the Smart Growth Initiatives, could indicate whether the state's brownfields programs are having an impact. Howland suggests that the brownfields initiatives would benefit sellers of contaminated properties because they can raise their asking prices due to the decreased risk to buyers. Sellers also benefit because the legislation protects third-party lenders from future liability, which means that buyers have more access to capital. Howland found that prior to Smart

Growth implementation, all the purchasers in the study area utilized their own savings to acquire and redevelop the sites, limiting demand to investors with deep pockets.

Analysis also needs to be made of VCP sites in terms of the numbers of jobs created, payrolls, median wages, workers' places of residence (to see if city and inner-suburb residents are benefiting from brownfields reutilization), and increases in property value and tax revenues. Opportunities for creating employment for low- and moderate-income residents in Maryland's brownfields assessment and cleanup need to be explored; EPA has been funding national pilot demonstration programs in several communities that have such job creation as an objective (Goode et al. 1999).

While Maryland has a smaller industrial base than most states, the level of state money for assessment and cleanup is very low. Maryland's BRIP fund has $1.3 million. In contrast, in November 1998, Michigan voters approved a bond issue designating $335 million for environmental response activities for brownfields redevelopment and for acute public health and environmental problems. Ninety projects, totaling over $47 million in response activities, were proposed for FY 99 (Michigan Department of Environmental Quality 2000). Maryland's slow pace in using the relatively low BRIP fund suggests that additional funding is not justified until demand for the VCP program increases. A stronger marketing campaign might boost participation in the VCP program and create demand for more financial assistance.

## Job Creation Tax Credits

The fifth Smart Growth Initiative in 1997 was the modification of Maryland's Job Creation Tax Credit (JCTC) program. As originally passed in 1996, the JCTC program required a participating business to declare its intent to use the credit prior to hiring and to create 60 new, full-time jobs paying salaries at least 1.5 times the federal minimum wage. In 1997, the state reduced job creation minimums to 25 in Smart Growth and PFAs; increased incentives in state enterprise zones, federal empowerment zones, and state-designated revitalization areas; and increased the basic credit of $1,000 per employee to $1,500 in the designated areas (*Annotated Code of Maryland,* Article 83A, 5-1101–5-1103).

The JCTC law limits eligibility to specific industries. Among the eligible industries are manufacturing; biotechnology; research development or testing; computer programming, data processing, or other computer-related services; transportation; and communications. Retail establishments are not on the list of eligible firms, and the act specifically excludes professional sports franchises and gaming facilities. Entertainment, recreation, cultural, and tourism-related businesses are eligible for the JCTC only if they are located within a state-designated revitalization area, and only if the facility generates a minimum of 1,000 new full-time-equivalent jobs in a 24-month period. Business services firms are eligible only if they are located in PFAs.

In several respects, the JCTC program addresses social equity concerns by minimizing potential exploitation of workers. A job qualifies only if it is a net, new position in Maryland—a firm cannot simply transfer a position from one of its facilities in one part of the state to another facility, nor count a position that was created through a contractual arrangement that replaced an employee in another firm. The position must be full-time (at least 35 hours per week), and be retained for a three-year period after the year the credit is granted. The tax credit can be recaptured by the state if, during any of the three years of the retention period, the number of qualified positions declines more than 5 percent below the average number of qualified positions claimed during the year on which the tax credit was computed. In such cases, the amount of the credit repayment is calculated in a manner that reflects the percentage reduction in the number of qualified employees. The state can recapture the tax credit in its entirety if, during the three-year retention period, the average number of qualified positions falls below the applicable minimum threshold that was needed to qualify for the credit. However, if the 5 percent threshold is exceeded (or the minimum threshold is unmet) because of a labor action, fire, or other cause beyond the employer's control, the retention period may be extended by a corresponding time period. The amount of a firm's tax credit is not allowed to exceed $1 million per year. However, unused credits may be carried forward for up to five years following the first year in which the credit was claimed.

The JCTC Act reflects both a person- and a place-based policy. The person-based aspect of the program is embodied in the worker retention requirements for employer access to the tax credits. The place-based aspect is reflected in the preference given to PFAs, designated revitalization neighborhoods, and other target areas that benefit from the increased economic activity. However, the act contains no residency requirement for qualified employees, so there is no necessary connection between a firm's location in a designated revitalization area and job opportunities for the area's residents.

According to a DBED official, as of June 30, 1999, DBED had received 123 applications from qualified firms, which proposed to generate 28,062 jobs.[12] Although the minimum qualifying annual salary under the JCTC program would be approximately $13,000 per year, the 123 applications projected an average annual salary of $39,696.

Only in existence five years, there are several questions about the JCTC that need to be researched. Are the thresholds favoring location in Smart Growth–targeted neighborhoods actually resulting in business development and job creation within those areas? Within Smart Growth–targeted neighborhoods, are the types of businesses and jobs created using tax credits, and average salaries paid, different from those in other areas in which the program is utilized? To what extent are residents of targeted neighborhoods being hired? Are any of the participating firms also involved in the Live Near Your Work Program? Would firms have located in the target areas without the tax credits? At the time of this writing, it was too early in program implementation to answer any of these questions. One DBED manager stated that it may be 2004 before there is sufficient data to begin analyzing the program.[13]

## Live Near Your Work Program

The Live Near Your Work (LNYW) program provides incentives for employees to purchase homes near their workplaces. The two main goals of the program are urban revitalization (by increasing homeownership in targeted neighborhoods) and the environmental and social benefits produced by reductions in worker commuting time and distances. Local governments apply to the Maryland Department of Housing and Community Development (DHCD) to have certain neighborhoods designated for revitalization. Once designated, the program involves participation of approved employers, their employees, the local government, and DHCD. The employers set eligibility requirements, promote the program to their workers, and provide at least $1,000 to assist participating employees with down payment and closing costs. The employee contributes at least $1,000 toward the home purchase in the LNYW designated area. The local government administers and promotes the program, and also provides $1,000 to each participating employee. DHCD publicizes the pro-

gram across the state, provides technical assistance to governments'
LNYW programs, and provides grants to local governments for funding
the $1,000 to each participating employee (DHCD 2000a).

The LNYW legislation does not include income restrictions for
employee eligibility. In fact, according to the LNYW program director,
income restrictions were removed from the draft legislation under the
premise that targeted neighborhoods would benefit from an influx of
higher-income workers.[14] Furthermore, the LNYW law gives discretion
to local governments and employers to define what "near" means. There
are no clear mileage criteria in order to allow for local variation in commuting distance and time. The legislation only states that the home purchased by the employee should have "a reasonable relationship to the
location of the employer." By the end of February 2000, 267 homeowners had purchased their homes through the LNYW program.[15] At that
time, 49 employers in seven Maryland jurisdictions were participating in
the LNYW program (DHCD 2000a).

Information on the characteristics of homebuyers participating in the
LNYW program is derived from surveys completed by the first 175 LNYW
homebuyers at or shortly after settlement (DHCD 2000a). The surveyed
homebuyers worked for 20 different employers, with over 83 percent of
the respondents working in Baltimore City. The following are some of the
survey highlights:

- About 80 percent (or 134 households) were first-time homebuyers,
  and nearly 40 percent indicated that they would not have purchased their homes without the LNYW incentive.
- About two-thirds of the homebuyers had annual incomes of
  $50,000 or less, while 31 percent of the buyers earned $30,000 or
  less. The estimated median household income for Baltimore City
  was $35,200 in 1998 (Maryland Office of Planning 2000b). It is safe
  to estimate, therefore, that at least a third of the LNYW homebuyers earned less than the city's median income.
- More than 46 percent of the buyers paid $70,000 or less for their
  new homes, while 28 percent paid more than $100,000. In 1999,
  the median price for a house sold in Baltimore City was $68,000
  (MRIS 2000), so nearly half of the LNYW purchasers paid the city's
  median sales price.
- Slightly over 30 percent of the buyers had children of school age or
  younger. By way of comparison, this is slightly lower than the 1990

census finding that 33.7 percent of all Baltimore City households had children.

- Adjusting for multiple modes of travel, the number of LNYW homebuyers walking or taking public transportation (bus, metro, or shuttle) to work increased from 49 to 73, a 49.0 percent increase. The number of homebuyers driving to work decreased from 101 to 61, a 39.6 percent decrease.
- The number of LNYW buyers who had work commutes of 10 minutes or less went from 54, before purchase, to 100 after purchase.

The LNYW program is targeted to "designated neighborhoods," which are mixed-use areas in need of revitalization. However, it is too early to determine whether the program is addressing its revitalization goal. A researcher studying the impact of the program on a given neighborhood would have to examine the change in homeownership rates over time and attempt to correlate these changing rates with indicators of public safety, school quality, and other quality-of-life measures.

The participant survey results do suggest that the program is addressing its goal of reducing work commute time for participating homeowners. However, it is not known whether these new owners have been able to reduce travel times for nonwork trips. Additional research would be needed to determine if, and the degree to which, total automobile usage has declined among LNYW participants.

## Summary: Is "Smart Growth" Smart Enough?

Maryland's Smart Growth Initiatives build on the planning framework established by the 1992 Planning Act by providing programmatic responses to several of the visions. The program is based on the principle that preventing sprawl involves much more than preventing or discouraging development on greenfield sites: resources and programs are directed to cities and inner suburbs in order to enhance the ability of those areas to retain and attract residents and commerce.

Maryland's Smart Growth program is an innovative response to the consequences of uneven development. Whether or not it will be a successful response will depend on four major factors:

1. adequate funding for the infrastructure needed to serve growth in targeted growth areas;

2. the provision of sufficient incentives to convince households and the private sector to make personal and business decisions that are consistent with Smart Growth principles;
3. sustained public sector support for Smart Growth Initiatives; and
4. the creation and utilization of benchmarks and indicators that will enable citizens and state and local governments to assess how Smart Growth is functioning.

First, Smart Growth will only be successful if there is adequate state and local funding for the current and future infrastructure and service needs in the PFAs. A 1998 MDP survey of county capital spending and infrastructure needs found that, over the next six years, there would be a funding gap of $9.0 billion between recent rates of capital spending and reported infrastructure needs (MDP 1999). Over a 20-year period, the study found a $41 billion funding gap for local governments and state agencies. In response, in 1999 the Growth Commission recommended the creation of a Smart Growth Infrastructure Development fund to help fill the gap, with first priority given for local projects that encouraged the revitalization of, and in-migration to, formerly distressed areas, and those addressing existing infrastructure deficiencies within PFAs. Unless such funding assistance is provided, more residential development will occur in locations outside of PFAs, with developer-subsidized infrastructure. Jurisdictions will be further tempted to use "fiscal zoning"—regulations that ensure that only high tax ratables will be constructed in order to have sufficient funding for services and infrastructure (Fulton 1993). Such regulations reduce opportunities for affordable housing creation.

Second, since the Smart Growth Initiatives are incentive oriented rather than command-and-control based, citizens and business persons need to be informed about these initiatives. Publicity of the Job Creation Tax Credit, Live Near Your Work, and Brownfields Initiatives needs to include testimonials from homeowners, employees, and business people who have benefited from them. Furthermore, it is possible that additional incentives will be needed to revitalize Maryland's cities and inner suburbs. For example, current Smart Growth programs may be insufficient to attract middle-class family households to Baltimore City. Unless great improvements are made in school quality and public safety—which Maryland is attempting to address with programs other than the Smart Growth Initiatives—only certain types of individuals and households will be attracted to the city (e.g., single, young adults, empty-nesters).

Even for those households, additional incentives may be needed. In its 1999 report, the Growth Commission suggested that attracting residents to downtown cores and designated neighborhoods could be enhanced by a 10-year property tax abatement for home purchases and relaxation of income restrictions for state mortgage funding (Economic Growth, Resource Protection and Planning Commission 1999b).

Governor Glendening has initiated additional legislation to augment the five core Smart Growth programs. In the Spring of 2000, the legislature passed Senate Bill 207, which streamlines the maze of local building codes by creating a single Maryland Building Rehabilitation Code. The new code is intended to make it easier and less expensive for developers to reuse existing buildings. Evidence from New Jersey, where a similar code became effective in 1998, is that annual private, rehabilitation investment increased by more than 60 percent in Newark, Paterson, Elizabeth, and Trenton (Montgomery 2000b).

Also in Spring 2000, the legislature passed House Bill 285, which directs the Maryland Department of Planning to draft model land use codes and guidelines for in-fill development and "smart neighborhood development," the latter defined as "comprehensively planned, compact, mixed-use development within a Priority Funding Area that integrates residential, commercial, open space and public uses." The model codes and guidelines can help local governments revise their zoning and subdivision regulations, since traditional, Euclidean zoning precludes "smart neighborhood development." Code revisions can reduce rehabilitation costs and regulatory delays, thereby providing incentives for in-fill developers.

Three additional Glendening proposals that can assist in PFA revitalization were passed by the Maryland legislature in 2001:

- the Neighborhood Parks and Playgrounds Program, which will offer a total of $11 million in competitive grants during FY 2002 to enable existing communities to establish or renovate parks and playgrounds;
- the Community Legacy Program, which will offer $10 million in competitive grants during FY 2002 to help existing communities plan and implement revitalization projects; and
- a number of transit proposals, which will invest over $500 million through FY 2008 in upgrading mass transit infrastructure and service.

Third, the success of Smart Growth in spurring city and inner-suburb revitalization will depend on continued state and local government support for, and creative use of, its various programs. The profile of the Smart Growth Areas Act, herein, pointed out why support of future governors and state agency officials is critical. Local government entrepreneurship in program use is also important. Available programs include not only the five core initiatives and new measures discussed in this chapter, but a range of already existing and recently established state housing, transportation, economic development, land conservation, and public safety programs.[16]

Some local governments in Maryland are not yet converted to Smart Growth principles. Dana Jones, executive director of the Southern Maryland Tri-County Community Action Agency, Inc., describes a "Smart Growth backlash" in southern Maryland jurisdictions that is impeding efforts to construct low-income housing and defeating the purpose of the 1997 initiatives.[17] Under Smart Growth, state subsidies for affordable housing construction and rehabilitation are limited to PFAs, including designated town centers in rural areas. Some jurisdictions are concerned that increased densities accompanying Smart Growth, combined with a concentration of low-income housing in the town centers, will depress property values. As a result, says Jones, Charles County has established a minimum house size of 1,650 square feet, while Calvert County cut allowable densities in some development districts by one-half. Charles County had granted nonprofit developers a waiver in impact fees, but removed the waiver when Smart Growth was implemented.

Of course, local officials pass such regulations in response to their constituents' perceptions of the impact of new growth. Voters in Dunkirk, a town center in Calvert County, changed the composition of their town council in recent elections in order to guarantee that the town center would not develop water and sewer service. As a result, the new shopping center in Dunkirk is on a septic system. Jones concludes that the state did not adequately acknowledge the impact that Smart Growth might have in convincing less populated (but rapidly growing) counties to undercut compact development patterns.

Fourth, while the Smart Growth program has received much favorable national publicity, very little is known about its effectiveness. Neither benchmarks nor indicators were established with the 1997 legislation, and the programs have not been in place for a time sufficient to evaluate their impacts. The indicators were still in their formulation stage in

November 2001. A Maryland Department of Planning December 2000 draft indicator list groups indicators under the goals of "reduce sprawl," "support and revitalize older cities and towns," "save taxpayers from the high cost of infrastructure needed to support sprawl," "permanently preserve the state's best rural resources," and "protect our fragile environment." Examples included in the "reduce sprawl" category are such indicators as the ratio of the number of new residential units inside PFAs to the total number of new residential units, and the ratio of average lot sizes inside PFAs to average lot size outside PFAs. Draft indicators for the "support and revitalize older towns and cities" include the assessed value of properties in revitalization areas and change in net migration rate. Many of the state-level indicators are proposed to be disaggregated by jurisdiction, enabling citizens and local governments to compare their progress with the statewide trends, and better informing local planning and policymaking.

For citizens and analysts concerned with the consequences of uneven development, MDP's December 2000 draft indicator list is not as encouraging as a draft produced a few months earlier. Some of the earlier proposed measures, such as those related to housing affordability, would help to discern improvement in city neighborhood conditions that are not merely the result of gentrification. For example, two of the earlier proposed indicators were "percent of households below median income that spend less than 30 percent on housing and utilities," and "percent of low- and moderate-income households that spend more than 50 percent of their income on housing and housing-related expenses." If such indicators are not included in the state's final version, they will undoubtedly be tracked by other organizations.

Indicators will eventually show trends in growth patterns since a given benchmark year. What the indicators will not automatically show is whether the Smart Growth programs have been successful. Since there were no quantified growth or revitalization goals included in the original legislation, nor contained in MDP's proposed indicator report, the adequacy of Smart Growth will have to be determined by public discussion of the revealed trends.

However, Governor Glendening has not waited for a formal indicator report before adding some muscle to the state's Smart Growth Initiatives. Concerned by recent cases of local government approval of sprawl development and of citizen opposition to "smart" projects, the governor announced at a May 30, 2001, press conference that he was going to encourage state officials to invoke a little-used 1974 law that empowers the Maryland Department of Planning to intervene in local zoning decisions (Leduc and Huslin 2001). While the State Land Use Act does not enable the MDP to overrule local zoning and planning decisions, it does allow the department to lobby for and against projects, as well as to file lawsuits to contest local zoning decisions. Although the governor said that MDP would limit its intervention to high-profile, precedent-setting cases, the announcement heralds what could be a new phase in Maryland's experiment in incentive-based growth management.

## NOTES

1. 1990 data for jurisdictions in the Baltimore region are from the Maryland Office of Planning Web site (2000b). Year 2000 population totals for jurisdictions in the Baltimore region are from the U.S. Census Bureau Web site (2001).

2. Formerly the Maryland Office of Planning. In May 2000, Governor Glendening signed an administration-sponsored bill (SB204) that elevated the Office of Planning to its former status as a cabinet-level department. The office was renamed the Maryland Department of Planning, effective July 1, 2000.

3. Ron Young, personal communication with the author, 16 May 2000.

4. Remarks made by Maryland Governor Parris Glendening at the National Issues Forum on Forging Metropolitan Solutions to Urban and Regional Problems, Brookings Institution, May 28, 1997 (as quoted in Benfield, Raimi, and Chen 1999).

5. For a review of Oregon's growth management system, see Knaap and Nelson (1992); for a summary of Vermont's Act 250, see DeGrove (1984); and for a description of Georgia's Regional Transportation Authority, see Firestone (1999).

6. Jim Noonan, MDP, personal communication with the author, 10 March 2000.

7. Dan Rosen, MDP, personal communication with the author, 17 May 2000.

8. In reference to the Rural Legacy Program in Charles County, Kreitner and Young state: "With just a few scattered easements, little financial commitment for easements and unprotective zoning, it is only the lack of high development pressure that can [prevent] farm land being fragmented in ways that would damage the State's investment in viable farms" (1998, 2).

9. Phase I assessments involve a visual inspection of the property and an examination of documents that would shed light on its environmental condition. Phase II assessments involve testing of soil samples, groundwater and surface water, and sediment. Phase II assessments for the VCP must follow principles established by the American Society for Testing and Materials.

10. Shari Wilson, personal communication with the author, 19 May 2000.

11. Steve Lynch, personal communication with the author, 15 May 2000.

12. Jerry Wade, personal communication with the author, 10 May 2000.

13. Employers have up to 24 months to hire the threshold number of employees, so it could be three years before they would claim the tax credit. The job retention period includes three years subsequent to the year the credit is claimed. Wade, personal communication.

14. John Papagni, DHCD, personal communication with the author, 16 March 2000.

15. Papagni, personal communication with the author, 3 May 2000.

16. The Maryland Office of Planning (1998) profiles the five core Smart Growth programs along with 38 other state programs that may be accessed by local governments to pursue Smart Growth objectives.

17. Dana Jones, personal communication with the author, 15 May 2000.

# REFERENCES

Bartsch, Charles. 1996. "Paying for Our Industrial Past." *Commentary* (winter): 14–23.

Bartsch, Charles, and Elizabeth Collaton. 1996. *Coming Clean for Economic Development.* Washington, D.C.: Northeast-Midwest Institute.

Benfield, F. Kaid, Matthew D. Raimi, and Donald D. T. Chen. 1999. *Once There Were Greenfields.* New York: Natural Resources Defense Council.

Cohen, James R., and Amy McAbee-Cummings. 1998. "A Case-Study Evaluation of Local Government Response to the Maryland Economic Development, Resource Protection and Planning Act of 1992." Paper presented at the annual conference of the Association of Collegiate Schools of Planning, Pasadena, Calif., Nov. 5–8.

DeGrove, John M. 1984. *Land, Growth and Politics.* Washington, D.C.: American Planning Association.

DHCD. *See* Maryland Department of Housing and Community Development.

Diamond, Henry L., and Patrick F. Noonan. 1996. *Land Use in America.* Washington, D.C.: Island Press.

DNR. *See* Maryland Department of Natural Resources.

Economic Growth, Resource Protection and Planning Commission. 1996. *1996 Report. Volume I: Recommendations and Report.* Baltimore, Md.: Maryland Office of Planning. December.

———. 1999a. Subcommittee on the Environment and Economic Development. *Making Smart Growth Work: Meeting Public Facility Needs in Growth Areas.* Baltimore, Md.: Economic Growth, Resource Protection and Planning Commission. October.

———. 1999b. "Urban Revitalization Proposal." Baltimore, Md.: Economic Growth, Resource Protection and Planning Commission. September 23.

EPA. *See* U.S. Environmental Protection Agency.

Firestone, David. 1999. "Georgia Setting Up Tough Anti-Sprawl Agency." *New York Times,* 25 March, A18.

Fulton, William. 1993. "Sliced on the Cutting Edge: Growth Management and Growth Control in California." In *Growth Management: The Planning Challenge of the 1990's,* edited by Jay M. Stein (113–26). Newbury Park, Calif.: Sage Publications.

Goode, Ann E., Elizabeth Collaton, Charles Bartsch, Philip Strother, Bennett Gray, and Edith Pepper. 1999. *Guide to Federal Brownfield Programs.* Washington, D.C.: Northeast-Midwest Institute.

Goodman, Peter S. 1998. "Glendening vs. Suburban Sprawl." *Washington Post,* 6 October, B1.

Horton, Tom, and William M. Eichbaum. 1991. *Turning the Tide.* Washington, D.C.: Island Press.

Howland, Marie. 2000. "The Impact of Contamination on the Canton/Southeast Baltimore Land Market." *Journal of the American Planning Association* 66 (4): 411–20.

Knaap, Gerrit, and Arthur C. Nelson. 1992. *The Regulated Landscape.* Cambridge, Mass.: Lincoln Institute of Land Policy.

Kreitner, Ron, and Ron Young. 1998. "The Importance of Planning and Zoning Context for Protecting State Investment in Rural Legacy Easements." Memo to Rural Legacy Board and Advisory Committee. October 1.

Leduc, Daniel, and Anita Huslin. 2001. "In the War on Sprawl, Md. Aims at Zoning." *Washington Post,* 30 May, B1.

Maryland Department of Housing and Community Development Web site. 2000a. http://www.dhcd.state.md.us/revit/lnyw.htm. (Accessed May 11, 2000.)

———. 2000b. http://www.dhcd.state.md.us. (Accessed May 10, 2000.)

Maryland Department of the Environment. 1999. "Voluntary Cleanup Program Update." Briefing for the Environment Subcommittee of the Senate Economic and Environmental Affairs Committee. Baltimore, Md.: Maryland Department of the Environment. October 28.

Maryland Department of Natural Resources (DNR) Web site. 2000. http:/www.dnr.state.md.us/rurallegacy.html. (Accessed May 18, 2000.)

Maryland Department of Planning (MDP). *See* Maryland Office of Planning.

Maryland Office of Planning. 1998. *Smart Growth and Neighborhood Conservation Initiatives.* Publication 98-05. Baltimore, Md.: Maryland Office of Planning. February.

———. 1999. *1998 Infrastructure Needs Survey—Part One: Report to the Governor and General Assembly.* Publication 99-4. Baltimore, Md.: Maryland Office of Planning.

———. Web site. 2000a. http://www.mdp.state.md.us/MSDC/index.html.

———. Web site. 2000b. http://www.op.state.md.us/MCDC/index.html. (Accessed May 18, 2000.)

Metropolitan Regional Information Systems, Inc. (MRIS). 2000. *Year End Real Estate Trend Indicators.* Rockville, Md.: MRIS. February 16.

Michigan Department of Environmental Quality Web site. 2000. http://www.deq.state.mi.us/erd/brownfields/bf2.html. (Accessed May 15, 2000.)

Montgomery, Lori. 2000a. "Maryland Land-Use Weapon Backfires." *Washington Post,* 14 May, C5.

———. 2000b. " 'Smart Code' Targets Crumbling Buildings." *Washington Post,* 24 April, B1.

MRIS. *See* Metropolitan Regional Information Systems, Inc.

1000 Friends of Maryland. 1999. *Maryland's Next Steps: Making Smart Growth Smarter.* "Technical Appendix A: Analysis of Submittals of County-Designated Smart Growth Areas." Baltimore, Md.: Chesapeake Bay Foundation. October.

Porter, Douglas R. 1999. "Will 'Smart Growth' Produce Smart Growth?" *The Abell Report* 12 (1, January): 1–8.

The 2020 Commission. 1988. *Population Growth and Development in the Chesapeake Bay Watershed to the Year 2020.* The Report of the Year 2020 Panel to the Chesapeake Bay Program Executive Council. Annapolis, Md.: Chesapeake Bay Program. December.

Starnes, Earl M. 1993. "Sub-State Frameworks for Growth Management: Florida and Georgia." In *Growth Management: The Planning Challenge of the 1990's,* edited by Jay M. Stein (76–95). Newbury Park, Calif.: Sage Publications.

U.S. Census Bureau Web site. 2001. http://quickfacts.census.gov/qfd/states/24/24510.html. (Accessed March 4, 2001.)

U.S. Environmental Protection Agency. 1983. *Chesapeake Bay: A Profile of Environmental Change.* Washington, D.C.: EPA.

# 12

# Equity and the Future Politics of Growth

Jeffrey R. Henig

What is the power of an idea? The notion that the growth of metropolitan areas calls for new modes of collective decisionmaking—methods better able to encompass the complex interrelationships between cities and their surrounding jurisdictions—is nothing new. Appeals to rationalize the structure of metropolitan government were common enough in the mid-20th century that Charles Adrian (1961) coined the term "metropology" to characterize them. This "first wave" of study of metropolitan areas reverberated in academic hallways, but the abstract appeal of the idea—of cities and suburbs working together—typically did not translate into votes when it counted, in state legislatures or public referenda. This chapter considers whether a similar fate awaits the second wave of metropolitan reform.

There are some reasons to be hopeful. The contemporary wave of metropolitan reform, represented well by the chapters in this volume, is more than a rehash of old ideas. Most important from the standpoint of political feasibility, the themes of the second wave reformers add up to a program that is more politically astute. While they share with their intellectual predecessors a vision of a unified metropolitan region, these reformers are not as willing to rely on the power of ideas to win the day. Their formulations link the rational-planning themes of the earlier reformers to other issues, like environmentalism and equity, and build a case that suburban and even rural residents may share a common cause with declining central cities. In this manner, they redefine the problems of urban sprawl in ways that expand the potential constituency for change beyond the narrow elite that has historically found metropolitan solutions compelling as rational and modern responses to central cities' needs.

But the political challenge faced by contemporary metropolitan reformers has grown in some ways as well. For those who hope to address urban sprawl in a manner that promotes greater equity, the political challenges have both an internal and an external component. The internal component involves maintaining a coalition that is not only broad, but also focused and sustainable. Yet these objectives can work in conflicting directions. In emphasizing the need to expand the breadth of the coalition supporting some sort of metropolitan-wide solutions, reformers have tactically downplayed latent tensions within their own ranks. In particular, suburban interests attracted by pro-environmental and anti-growth themes may prove to be unreliable allies for those truly committed to meeting the needs of inner-city minorities and the poor.

The external political challenge arises from the fact that the loose coalition of those who oppose metropolitan solutions has been changing as well. It arguably is a better armed and more intensely motivated force than when it blunted the first wave of reform efforts half a century ago— better armed because it has adopted a more sophisticated and potent intellectual rationale. The early reformers pitted their well-developed theories about why metropolitan solutions were more rational against a base of resistance that was grounded more in concrete interests, allegiance to local loyalties, and pragmatic suspicion of change. While theoretically less sophisticated, this rationale for opposition to metropolitan solutions found a sympathetic audience among the community actors upon whom political feasibility depended and was sufficient to stymie calls for metropolitan institutions in the mid-20th century. Today's opponents of metropolitan solutions are not limited to appeals to what Greer (1962) referred to as "folk rationality"; they can draw on an intellectual rationale for the status quo that has just as fine an academic pedigree as that employed by their counterparts. Public choice theories provide credence to a more traditional and instinctive American localism with the sophisticated argument that smaller jurisdictions are more efficient, responsive, and conducive to personal freedom.

Also raising the bar for metropolitan reform is the fact that the multiple jurisdictions fragmenting metropolitan areas have had time to grow longer political roots. Both the first and the second waves of metropolitan reformers have underestimated the resilience of existing institutions because they have failed to appreciate how institutions reconfigure political interests in ways that replenish and strengthen themselves over time. The evolving spatial distributions of poverty and wealth (Jargowsky, chapter 3) and race (powell, chapter 4) are more than an undesirable consequence of fragmentation and sprawl—they have the power to alter the objective interests of key actors in ways that make the opposition more animated and more embedded and, therefore, make political prospects for reform even more problematic.

The general thrust of this analysis may deflate the belief some hold that the current regime of metropolitan fragmentation is ripe to fall in the face of a revitalized reform ideal. The political challenge is more daunting than they anticipate. If headway is to be made, it is important to loosen the hold of the reigning form of institutionalized decentralization, which overemphatically favors personal mobility and segregation as the alternative to collectively tackling the problems of inequality and sprawl. The chapter concludes with a suggestion for a political strategy that uses the power of institutions to change institutions.

## Lessons from the First Generation of Metropolitan Reform

Concern about the unchecked growth and fragmentation of the American metropolis was in the air for much of the 20th century,[1] but reached its apogee during the 1960s. Savitch and Vogel (1996, 1) observe that the "scholarly critique" of metropolitan fragmentation "was given official credence by a series of government reports" later in the decade. Nor was this solely or particularly an American notion. Keating (1995) notes similar themes in Great Britain and continental Europe at much the same time, a reflection, he suggests, of "a spirit of optimism about the potential of government to solve social and economic problems" that helped to put large-scale organization and planning "in fashion" (132).

Mid-20th century calls for metropolitan governance did not go unheeded, but their footprint was small. There were a few noteworthy city-county consolidations—for example, Nashville-Davidson (1962), Jacksonville-Duval (1967), and Indianapolis-Marion Counties (1969). More common, however, was the pattern of continued growth and fragmentation, described well in the preceding chapters of this volume. Roughly 80 percent of the 110 consolidation proposals on public referenda were defeated between 1921 and 1989 (Harrigan and Vogel 2000, 352).

These earlier "first-wave" calls for metropolitan solutions rested heavily on a particular vision of reason and the power of rational ideas to lead to restructured institutions. First-wave reformers implicitly believed that metropolitan fragmentation was a passing phase, one that depended on such outmoded institutions and parochial loyalties that it would inevitably be dropped, like so many baby teeth, as the nation matured. But the ideas of that day—which associated metropolitan solutions with efficiencies of scale, coordination, planning, and consistency—proved puny and effete in the *realpolitik* of state and local decisionmaking.

The existing institutional boundaries that carved metropolitan areas into small and competing fiefdoms have shown that they are quite resistant to change. The creation of these fragmenting boundaries may or may not have been arbitrary or idiosyncratic in their origin (powell, in this volume, strongly suggests that racial exclusion was typically and not accidentally behind the phenomenon). Regardless, once institutionalized they behaved like institutions: they shaped behavior more than they were shaped by behavior. Material interests as well as more gut-level loyalties gave these jurisdictions a powerful constituency. Even those who could appreciate the power of the ideas behind proposals for metropolitan-oriented reforms were often quite unwilling to try putting those ideas into practice.

The chapters in this book renew the call to deal with metropolitan problems on a metropolitan scale. Has anything changed that should make us confident, or even hopeful, that the reformulated vision will carry the day?


## Redefining the Problem and Broadening the Scope of Conflict

Baumgartner and Jones (1993) have shown that new problem definitions can reshuffle the deck of political power within a given policy subsystem, rather quickly unseating elite interests that have stymied efforts at non-incremental change. The "second wave" of calls for metropolitan solutions incorporates at least three elements not found in the earlier iteration, and it is possible that these new elements hold the key to greater political feasibility.

Two of the elements characterizing the second wave have the potential to *add new interests* to the pro-reform coalition. These involve heightened emphasis on the themes of environmentalism and social equity. The earlier wave of reforms relied heavily on the abstract appeal of efficiency and rational planning. The result was that their proposals were fated to "nearly always be[ing] greeted by an enormous citizen yawn" (Adrian 1967, 454). Adrian blamed the "efficiency and economy fallacy"—the assumption that the average citizen cared as deeply about efficiency and prudent spending as did the upper-middle-class community leaders—for seducing metropolitan reformers into misgauging the latent constituency for their proposals. The second wave introduces environmentalism and social equity as motivating values, each of which has mobilized constituencies of its own.

While some first-wave reformers touched on important themes about pollution, congestion, and the loss of open space, environmentalism as a powerful political movement did not come into its own until the 1970s (Dunlap and Mertig 1992). Cieslewicz (chapter 2) lays out a stark tale of the multiple and interlocking environmental costs attributable to unchecked metropolitan development. His accounting of shrinking open space, increased fuel consumption, congestion, and water and air pollution was foreshadowed by others writing four or five decades before. While the basic themes are not novel, his contemporary telling differs from the earlier iterations in at least four senses. First, the passage of time allows him to tally costs *already registered,* whereas mid-20th century visionaries were primarily *projecting* costs based on nascent trends. Second, the science of environmentalism has identified some new threats—notably global warming and the loss of biodiversity—that are more systemic, less reversible, and affect a much larger proportion of the citizenry. Third, there already exists an informed and readily mobilizable audience, primed to hear and respond to appeals of this kind. Finally, as suggested in the Jaret, Abbott, and Cohen chapters (7, 8, and 11, respectively), there are working models that appear to provide proof that unchecked development is not inevitable and that governmental intervention, properly structured, need not translate into over-regulation that chokes off healthy investment and economic vitality. More so than before, the focus on sprawl as a source of pollution, congestion, waste, and environmental degradation may allow the metropolitan reform movement to tap into a new reservoir of support that will prove to be politically decisive.

While in some senses a subset of the broader environmentalism theme, the incorporation of the specific issue of traffic congestion into the pro-reform agenda has political consequences of its own. Whereas environmentalism carries broader political connotations that can rankle conservatives wary of governmental regulation, traffic congestion is a universal grievance that can link Republican and Democrat, city dweller and suburbanite, left and right in a common cause.

Like environmentalism, the pursuit of equity as an alternative to the racial and economic inequalities that characterize so much of the American landscape also matured as a political movement after the initial metropolitan reform wave. Equity concerns thread their way through most of the chapters in this book, but they get their most focused treatment from Jargowsky, powell, Helling, and Wiewel, Persky, and Schaffer (chapters 3, 4, 5, and 10, respectively). Altogether these chapters tell us much about the cause, perpetuation, and consequences of sprawl. The notion that metropolitan sprawl contributes to racial and economic concentration is not a new one. Jargowsky's contribution is partly to describe this more precisely and to establish that this trend was not a historic artifact of an earlier era that we have "grown" out of. More significant, though, is his argument that concentrated poverty is not simply an unintended and peripheral by-product of outward growth, but in fact the two phenomena are intricately intertwined. powell emphasizes the role of race in structuring both local and national policies; his effort to demonstrate that concentration of poverty and gentrification are not opposites but two sides of a single coin has the potential to reformulate contemporary debate. Wiewel, Persky, and Schaffer highlight the way that—once initially in place—fragmentation and interjurisdictional competition create very powerful incentives for local governments to pursue "beggar-thy-neighbor" policies that raise parochial interests over those of the broader region. And Helling, by linking sprawl, transportation, and families, provides a clear bridge between some of the infrastructure concerns that occupied first-wave reformers and the equity concerns that are more prominent today. This general redefinition of urban sprawl as the source of concentrated poverty, the severing of social networks for upward mobility, a job-housing mismatch, and gross disparities in local tax capacities has the potential to bring unions, civil rights organizations, and others—motivated more by a vision of social justice than the earlier appeal to reason, order, and efficiency—into the metropolitan reform movement.

The concept that the contemporary emphasis on environmentalism, congestion, and equity might alter the political feasibility of the anti-sprawl agenda is consistent with Schattschneider's (1960) ideas—movements that are outgunned by their direct competitors can sometimes shift the balance of power by expanding the scope of the conflict and enlisting powerful third parties to their cause. The final new element in the second wave of the metropolitan reform movement has less to do with adding themes to attract previously neutral parties than it does with *converting the opposition.* As Squires notes in chapter 1, "Many of the apparent winners of the process of sprawl and uneven development are starting to experience severe costs." This raises the possibility that inner-ring suburban residents who are beginning to face problems of aging infrastructure, crime, and so on; businesses concerned about excessive commuting time for workers; and suburban employers that cannot fill jobs despite abundant underemployed labor in the central cities might begin to embrace metropolitan reform as their own issue.

Myron Orfield (1997 and this book) is among the leaders of a small group of scholars that have been building the case that residents and leaders in inner suburbs and declining rural areas should reconsider their traditional resistance to pro-metropolitan solutions. Along with Rusk (1993), Ledebur and Barnes (1993), and Savitch et al. (1993), Orfield challenges the zero-sum framing that leads suburbanites to compete with central cities in a "beggar-thy-neighbor" strategy to attract residents and businesses that generate excess tax revenue, while excluding undesirable land uses and newcomers likely to demand more in public services than they will pay into the public coffers. The others just mentioned have emphasized the extent to which a metropolitan area's economic and social health tends to be greater when its central city is vital and when the disparities between city and suburb are not too sharp. Orfield's particular contribution has been to bring that macro argument down to a finer level of detail and to link it to a more explicitly political strategy for coalition building in state legislatures. Rather than simply arguing that suburbs *in general* do better when their central cities do well, Orfield uses available data at the neighborhood and census tract level to demonstrate that *particular* areas share problems that span jurisdictional boundaries. Relying heavily on detailed maps to make that point, Orfield feels he has been able to change legislators' minds and votes on key issues related to tax sharing and other metropolitan strategies in Minnesota.

This last component to the new metropolitanism hinges on the analytic distinction between objective and subjective interests. Noncity residents and politicians recoil from regional solutions because they (mistakenly, it is argued) assume that they will absorb uncompensated costs. If this is so, then more and better information is the solution. Appeals to environmentalism and equity add new values into the mix. Appeals to economic self-interest speak to the values that have traditionally driven a wedge between city and suburb, but suggest that those economic interests have heretofore been misunderstood.

Taken together, these elements of the new metropolitanism add up to a more politically sophisticated assault on the forces of fragmentation than was mounted during the last century—partly because they carry a stronger normative punch. Like appeals to rational planning and consistency, arguments oriented around environmentalism and equity count to some extent on the belief that citizens and leaders will *do the right thing*. But appeals to saving the planet and social justice are more likely to stir hearts and minds. Probably more important, though, is the fact that these new elements better link abstract norms and reasons to an understanding of interest-group politics. In the interaction among ideas, interests, and institutions, second-wave reform appeals present an implicit theory about how ideas, in the form of new problem definitions, can shift the balance of interest-group politics in a way that makes it possible to reform otherwise well-defended institutions.

While more self-conscious than their predecessors about the need to construct a broad-based coalition to add support to their ideas, however, contemporary proponents of metropolitan solutions to urban problems may yet be too naïve about the political obstacles they face. A metropolitan reform coalition oriented around environmentalism, equity, and common interests between cities and their suburbs will almost certainly be broader than one oriented around rational planning and economies of scale. But "broader" is not the same as more powerful, and "more powerful" is not the same as "powerful enough." While the new reform movement has been broadening its appeal, the challenges it faces have not been static. The internal and external political obstacles to enacting serious reforms have also become greater in the intervening years. While a new problem definition may be broadening the coalition, the disparate motivations of the fellow travelers make for a fragile bond. Moreover, like their predecessors, the second wave of metropolitan reform thinkers may be underestimating the power of institutions to shape and channel interests in ways that reinforce deep cleavages involving race and class.

## Why New Ways of Looking at the Issue May Not Suffice

The first wave of metropolitan reform pitted a strong idea against institutional inertia and resistant interests. The idea lost. The reformulated metropolitan reform argument uses ideas to mobilize interests, resulting in a more potent combination. However, the prospects for political victories also depend upon the power and institutional advantages possessed by those that oppose change. Opposition to specific metropolitan and anti-sprawl measures can come from disparate corners, as Squires notes in chapter 1. Some resistance comes from those with a direct and material stake in fighting specific proposals, for example, those who know or suspect that ameliorative measures might translate into higher local taxes or weakened local regulatory power and thereby threaten their advantaged lifestyle. In other cases, the reluctance may be more visceral than rational, rooted in racial and class suspicions that make those currently buffered reluctant to link fates with central-city populations, regardless of material consequences. In still other cases, resistance may be rooted in adherence to ideas and theories that defend fragmentation and localism as the cornerstones of democracy, free markets, and individual enterprise.

Neither material self-interest nor exclusionary norms provide a generally acceptable public rationale for resistance to metropolitan reforms intended to promote equity and constrain urban sprawl. Rather, they appeal to the ideals of markets and local democracy. At the same time that metropolitan reform proponents have been reframing their position in order to attract a broader array of allies, the coalition against them has become more sophisticated through the elaboration of its own, powerful set of ideas. Furthermore, it also has become more ingrained, because the institutions of metropolitan fragmentation have, over time and cumulatively, reconfigured interests in ways that further buttress them.

### Countertheories

Although there were contemporary criticisms of the first wave of metropolitan reform from within the academic community, it was not really until the 1970s that a more fully elaborated intellectual critique began to coalesce. This public choice critique was rooted in the language and concepts of microeconomics. Rather than speculate about a broadly shared set of interests in a well-organized and planned metropolitan area, public choice theorists argued that analysts should work from the starting point of individuals and their more immediate concerns. The best way to ensure that individual interests are maximized, they reasoned, is to allow them to pursue those interests within market-like institutions. And the best way to make metropolitan area governments exhibit market-like responsiveness is to have multiple small jurisdictions competing (like firms) for citizen-customers.

The public choice response to metropolitanism focused first on undermining the conventional wisdom that bigger governments would provide economies of scale. Influential economists like Friedman (1962), Stigler (1962), and Buchanan and Tullock (1962) laid out the initial theoretical challenge to the presumption that smaller governments would have higher unit costs. By the early 1970s, these arguments had been fleshed out into a full-scale rebuttal of the metropolitan "consolidationist" view, complete with empirical support (notably Bish and Ostrom 1973).

According to public choice theory, smaller units of government would be more efficient for several reasons. First, in order to be attractive to potential residents and businesses, multiple governments would be forced to compete to keep costs (and taxes) low. This competition would minimize traditional sources of inefficiency—such as waste, corruption, and obsolete techniques—that raise the unit price of service "X." Public choice theorists also argued that there was also another kind of inefficiency, which revolves around providing more of "X" than some citizens really want (or at least want at the going price). A second way that smaller jurisdictions would be more efficient, then, would evolve out of their greater ability to put together packages of services appealing to subsets of the population that shared a particular preference hierarchy. A community comprising many elderly residents, for example, would be less likely to "overproduce" schools and ball fields. Finally, since economies of scale were neither consistent across all local services nor over time, they argued, smaller units of government would have greater flexibility and freedom to engage in formal and informal cooperative arrangements to fit the scale of the solution to the specific task at hand.

The empirical base developed by public choice analysts included studies looking at the unit costs of and citizen satisfaction with various municipal services, such as garbage collection, policing, and the like. Studies demonstrated clear threshold effects in the "optimal" size of the service delivering unit; beyond a certain city size threshold, for example, marginal increases in population were associated with growing unit costs. Ostrom and Parks (1973), for example, used national data to analyze policing expenditures, crime, and citizen satisfaction with police services. They found that crime was higher in large jurisdictions, satisfaction was higher in smaller jurisdictions, and that metropolitan areas with a higher density of separate local jurisdictions had lower per capita costs, holding service levels equal.[2]

A second important empirical component of the developing public choice perspective involved the systematic chronicling of examples of formal and informal intergovernmental compacts and intergovernmental contracting for services. Since "diversity in the nature of public goods and services means that different kinds of services are produced efficiently by different-sized jurisdictions" (Bish and Ostrom 1973, 59–60), there can be no one city size that is ideal for maximizing economies of scale. Public choice theory pointed in the direction, then, of a more fluid system in which small jurisdictions would either join together or contract with a larger jurisdiction in order to selectively take advantage of economies of scale when and where they existed. By highlighting working examples, public choice advocates built the case that this was a practical solution as well as a theoretical one. Much was made, for example, of the "Lakewood Plan," which had become popular in California. Lakewood was a small jurisdiction that incorporated specifically to avoid being annexed by the larger and more urban Long Beach. Rather than build its own service delivery bureaucracy, Lakewood contracted with other jurisdictions to provide its residents with such services as police, animal control, and street maintenance. The model caught on quickly (Bish and Ostrom 1973, 60; Miller 1981, ch. 1).

Because the first-wave metropolitan reformers placed so great an emphasis on efficiency, the public choice argument that "smaller" was (or at least could be) more efficient was a critical first line of assault. Perhaps more significant in the long run, however, was a second line of criticism that focused less on economic efficiency than on political responsiveness. Many metropolitan reformers had promoted the notion that the consolidation of governmental authority into larger and more comprehensive units would make it more feasible for citizens to hold government accountable. Public choice theory employed the market analogy to stand that reasoning on its head. Charles Tiebout (1956), in a classic and extremely influential article, emphasized the extent to which metropolitan fragmentation provided individuals with the potential to "vote with one's feet." Those dissatisfied with the mix, quality, or cost of local services always are free to relocate to a more compatible jurisdiction, but the information, mobility, and opportunity costs of doing so are much less when there are many small and nearby units of government from which to choose.

Linking small jurisdictions to both efficiency and responsiveness offered a powerful challenge to the metropolitan reform idea. This left equity issues off the table,[3] but that was not considered a major lapse as the nation moved out of the War on Poverty era and toward the Reagan revolution. The public choice perspective, a nascent and peripheral intellectual movement in the mid-20th century, became by the 1980s well established in academia and public policy circles, raising the hurdles that the contemporary metropolitan reform movement must now face if it is to move from idea into political practice.

## The Resilience of Institutions

During the first wave of metropolitan reformism and again today, those who are convinced of the ultimate benefit of dealing with challenges on a metropolitan scale have often been perplexed by the resilience of the more localistic jurisdictions. Reasonably enough, they think of institutions as human creations, organizational tools through which we structure our relationships so as to better confront shared problems and pursue collective goals. As problems change and goals shift, this reasoning implies institutions must change, too, or be discarded for newer organizational forms that better match the times. As the problems confronting cities and suburbs have become broader in scope and more interlocking, the smaller, more intimate jurisdictions that emerged in earlier times appear to some to be residual appendages, lacking a contemporary societal function and therefore primed for extinction.

It is quite true that institutions can whither and die when they get disconnected from the social and political arteries that nourish them. A powerful example of this is the collapse of the Soviet Union. In that collapse we witnessed the stunning self-destruction of an institutional arrangement that had seemed powerful and well defended—literally armed against challengers both inside and outside the state.

But institutions do not inevitably age in place. Those who view the fragmented arrangements of today's metropolitan areas as artifacts of an earlier period misunderstand the real power of institutions not just to hold on, but to "hardwire" themselves into the social environment. Such institutions become part of the supporting infrastructure of a wide range of contemporary activities, continually generating new interests dependent upon those institutions and willing to rally to their defense. Consider the footpath between two villages that becomes a horse path, then becomes a paved street, and finally becomes part of an interstate highway. Laying down the initial markers can alter future development in ways that reinforce and replenish, rather than displace, what came before.

Most of the contributions to this book strike a fairly optimistic note about the prospects for change. While recognizing that there are political obstacles, they reject the notion that sprawl is ordained by either natural law or market forces. The requisite policies may be tough to put into place, but there are feasible policies that can make a difference. Abbott (chapter 8), for example, while acknowledging some fraying of the constituency behind Portland's Urban Growth Boundary, concludes that the "political reality is that UGB is here to stay."

A few of the contributors raise yellow flags of caution, however. After discussing a number of promising growth-control initiatives in the Atlanta region, for example, Jaret (chapter 7) concludes that "efforts to restrict growth or to limit it to 'smart growth' will be unsuccessful in many parts of metropolitan Atlanta and that sprawl will continue." Similarly, Cohen (chapter 11) notes a "smart growth backlash," in parts of Maryland. Wiewel, Persky, and Schaffer report a growing willingness of various Chicago-area interests to *discuss* regional equity issues, but "little direct action" to address them. Orfield's account (chapter 9) is aggressively optimistic in one sense—he sees the demographic configuration of metropolitan areas universally moving in a direction conducive to metropolitan reform coalition-building—but his tale of the near dismantling of regionalism under the "consensus-based regionalists" ultimately displays the fragility of regional coalitions and their reforms. Even the pessimists within the pro-reform movement typically presume that the problem is getting a reform into law in the first place; Orfield's account reveals that, once in place, metropolitan institutions remain vulnerable.

Lying behind this more gloomy assessment of reform prospects are at least two ideas about the residual power of the existing institutional framework of fragmentation. One has to do with "exit"—the option to pick up and leave an undesirable situation—as an alternative to governmental action. The other has to do with federalism as a platform for political mobilization in the United States. Exit and the politics of federalism may represent the most serious challenges to the metropolitan reform agenda. First-wave reformers had considerable support among upper-class elites who valued the goals of planning and efficiency. However, both exit and the politics of federalism systematically advantage interests that are relatively mobile and relatively wealthy. This means that pivotal political elites that supported earlier reform efforts may now line up on the opposite side of the battle.

Jaret, writing about Georgia, observes that "a collective inability or unwillingness to resolve social problems creates a strong motive to move far away to places people think will not have those problems" (chapter 7). As explained by Albert O. Hirschman (1970), the option to exit from an undesirable situation serves as an alternative to the need to try to change conditions directly through collective action. In a wide array of settings— the relationship between a shopper and a local supermarket, the relationship between a resident and a local jurisdiction, and the relationship between a nation and an alliance—individual exit and collective "voice" present alternative paths for rationally pursuing goals. Significantly, as Hirschman pointed out, the more viable one strategy becomes, the less attractive the other becomes. Since exercising political voice, in particular, requires a certain degree of practice and skill, "the presence of the exit alternative can therefore tend to *atrophy the development of the art of voice*" (italics in original) (Hirschman 1970, 43).

Whether or not that was its initial raison d'être, a powerful consequence of metropolitan jurisdictional fragmentation has been its systemic boost to the attractiveness of mobility as a means of improving one's condition. Hirschman's analysis suggests the possibility that the institutionalization of fragmentation may function as more than a static arena within which citizens and politicians rationally pursue their interests. It may also act directly to make some kinds of political action less rational. Particularly for businesses and middle- and upper-class residents, the appeal of the exit alternative grows as the problems concentrated in the central city become more intractable. Jargowsky, Helling, and others in this book have alluded extensively to the social consequences of concentrated poverty, but there are also distinct conse-quences for politics and government. The combination of ease of exit for advantaged interests and spatial concentration of difficult problems may be contributing to a general privatization of American life—a broad loss of confidence in the likelihood that collective action can solve people's problems. The result is a self-perpetuating downward cycle in which ready access to the exit option discourages collective action, in turn mak-ing personal exit relatively easy and more effective. At the same time, because they must be hyperattentive to the threat of exit by residents and businesses that pay more in taxes than they consume in public expenditure, cities are simply unable to wrestle with issues involving redistribution from the advantaged to the needy (Peterson 1981). Calls for equity-responsive metropolitan reform ultimately depend upon a belief in governmental capacity. In an era of privatization, the prospects are grim.

In addition to the exit option, a second way in which fragmentation may have become increasingly "hardwired" into the institutional envi-ronment involves the ways in which federalism structures how political actors *think of* as well as *act upon* their interests. Both metropolitan reformers and their public choice critics have tended to think of interests as "givens" and judge institutions by their effectiveness in realizing those interests. Their disagreements arise out of how they conceptualize those interests. Metropolitan reformers tend to think in terms of broadly shared, objectively defined interests; public choice theorists think in terms of personal, subjective preferences. For metropolitan reformers, federalism is seen as an institutional arrangement for organizing the administration of policy to pursue those broad, shared interests, with the assumption that larger and more comprehensive governance arrangements are generally better. For public choice theorists, federalism is seen as an institutional arrangement for aggregating those individual preferences, with the assumption that smaller units are generally better. However, fed-eralism is not just a vehicle for aggregating or pursuing interests; it is also an integral part of the process through which interests come to be shaped and mobilized. In this sense, the existing arrangements of local govern-ments continually re-create the conditions for their continuation.

The "new institutionalism" within political science recognizes that "governmental agencies are not neutral instruments. They are carriers of culture, missions, values, and identities" (March and Olsen 1989, 113–14). In a practical sense, citizens and elected leaders often look through the prism of federalism as they try to think through what their political interests might be. Citizens who hear that a particular policy will benefit or hurt their local jurisdiction typically react as if that benefit or cost automatically gets transferred to them. Elected officials who do not place representation of their jurisdiction as a top priority—for example, by supporting a regional transportation initiative that is seen primarily to benefit other jurisdictions—risk being seen as traitors by their constituents, even though many of these constituents might personally benefit or later even move on to one of the more favored jurisdictions. In the United States, moreover, deference to localism has the status of what March and Olsen (1989, 111) refer to as *constitutional principles:* "those aspects of a polity that are generally viewed as not subject to routine political determination through various forms of majority rule." While traditional democratic theory "assumes that elected leaders may design or choose the institutional forms so that they contribute to the achievement of political goals in the most effective and efficient manner," when constitutional principles are involved, institutional reforms can be "seen as challenging elements of the core system of meaning, belief, interpretation, status, power, and alliances in politics." Change in this context "requires something closer to consensus than do other kinds of political actions" (March and Olsen, 111–12).

Finally, the existing institutions of metropolitan governance are resilient because federalism is a basic building block of political mobilization in the United States. Both formal political authority and many of the informal elements that sustain civic life (e.g., political parties, community foundations, and local chambers of commerce) are built around jurisdictional boundaries. When individuals and groups organize to act collectively in the United States, it is most often on a spatially defined basis and very often that spatial unit is more or less coterminous with existing local government boundaries. Interests that align with local boundaries, as a result, tend to be more readily mobilizable. Those that are dispersed or cut across boundaries are more likely to be disorganized or inchoate.

## Racial and Economic Exclusion As an Animating Force

Institutions of localism create new interests at odds with metropolitan solutions, but they also amplify the potency of long-standing cleavages. While the ideal of racial and economic *equity* has many subscribers when framed in abstract terms, there is no denying the sad fact that pursuit of racial and economic *exclusion* has been, in actuality, a powerful driving force (Massey and Denton 1993). Demographic patterns discussed throughout this book show that poverty and race are now intertwined with issues of metropolitan organization and policy in ways that are more complex and consequential than was the case in the earlier era of metropolitan reform. Racial fears and suspicions have played a uniquely powerful role in structuring political attitudes in the United States. So has reluctance of citizens to bear the fiscal burden of supporting services for the poor or to have their children exposed to the culture of poverty that low-income communities are presumed to harbor. But whether and how those attitudes animate the key debates on the policy agenda depends on contextual factors that shift over time. The increasing identification of cities and suburbs as institutional bases of governmental authority that have been more or less "captured" by differing racial and economic constituencies exacerbates both the internal and external political challenges confronting metropolitan reform.

There are ramifications both for the internal challenge of coalition maintenance and the external challenge of "besting" competing interests. Internally, race and class differences are loose threads that, if tugged upon, can potentially pull apart what is a looser alliance than many would like to believe. It is well and good to support good planning, integrated transportation networks, environmental protection, comprehensive and coordinated structures for governance, racial and economic equity, and integrated living, but what happens when these various goals come into conflict with one another at critical decision points? While the environmental movement itself is potent, many of the individuals and groups who subscribe to its ideals are pulled in different directions when it comes to the equity aspects of metropolitan reform. Suburban environmentalists rally to the call to reduce traffic congestion and pollution in their particular communities, but normally resist proposals to reallocate opportunities by, for example, working to deconcentrate inner-city poor or adopting new regional finance mechanisms that would redistribute tax revenues from suburb to city. As often as not, the environmental agenda has contributed to central-city problems by rationalizing exclusionary suburban land use patterns (Frieden 1979). At the same time, the interests that stand to directly benefit from an equity-oriented metropolitan reform agenda are those groups that have historically been among the most difficult to mobilize and that have relatively few resources to bring to the battle when they do mobilize.

Even if it is true that inner suburbanites have a growing objective interest in subscribing to the metropolitan reform agenda, as Orfield (chapter 9) and others have argued, the evidence to date in most communities seems to suggest that old fears, stereotypes, localist loyalties, and other subjective forces make most inner suburbanites resistant to this "conversion." There is a lesson to be learned here from the long-standing (and still unfulfilled) Marxist prediction that white and black blue-collar workers will recognize their shared class interest and emerge as a united political force: those most closely linked by economic circumstance are just as likely to see themselves as natural competitors as natural allies.

Proponents of metropolitan reform as an antidote to sprawl have side-stepped difficult questions related to race and class differences as a means of holding together their new and more disparate coalition. However, the result may be a paper-thin coalition that is too fragile to adopt an agenda that would confront the sources of inequality in more than a symbolic, "feel-good" crusade. Or, even worse from the standpoint of equity, failure to acknowledge internal cross-pressures may leave the movement vulnerable to co-optation by whichever subsets are more fully mobilized and well resourced. The result could be a new metropolitan reform movement that draws legitimacy and added clout from its appearance as a diverse and equity-oriented coalition while pursuing anti-sprawl measures that have the primary effect of raising financial and regulatory barriers to affordable housing in the suburbs, ironically exacerbating the concentration of poverty and racial segregation that purportedly were the target.

Externally, race and class antagonisms complicate the metropolitan reform agenda by injecting fervor into some of the resistance beyond what would be stimulated by abstract debates about governmental structure, urban planning, land use regulation, or the proper balance within federalism. Ideas about markets and individual mobility provide the intellectual rationale for opposition. Institutions of localism provide the barrier walls that give opponents a structural advantage. But reluctance to share fates with the less advantaged is probably what gives the opposing coalition much of its populist zeal.

## A Positive Agenda? Using Institutions to Change Institutions

The new framing of metropolitan issues in terms of environmentalism, equity, and inner-suburban self-interest has the potential to expand the pro-reform coalition. But the elaboration of a public choice critique of metropolitanism, combined with the institutional resilience embedded in the exit option and federalism as a shaper of ideas and a platform for collective action, means that the obstacles have grown as well. The political routing of the pro-reform movement during most of the last century points to a fairly pessimistic conclusion about the prospects for 21st century success.

Others who have considered the political prospects for metropolitan reform also have reached bleak conclusions. Anthony Downs (1994) is painfully blunt: A single metropolitan-wide government "has absolutely no political support from either suburban or city residents or officials; hence it will never happen in most metropolitan areas." A recent report from the National Academy of Sciences concludes that "the politics of bringing into being even the weakened forms of metropolitan government appear to be nearly insurmountable" (Altschuler et al. 1999, 107). Significantly, these authors emphasize that regional reforms designed to reduce inequities may be especially problematic. Where obstacles to regionalism have successfully been overcome, it has most often been around issues of physical infrastructure, planning, or economic development.

This reality need not—and should not—mean that those concerned about the negative consequences of sprawl should simply concede, but it probably does mean that tactics need to be reconsidered. Some things are unlikely to suffice. The first-wave failures taught that it is not enough to rely on the power of the argument alone. Ideas can be powerful, but when they are stacked up against entrenched interests and institutions, they typically come up short. The second-wave effort to expand the scope of conflict by redefining the issue has some potential to add interests to the pro-reform coalition, but that, too, is unlikely to suffice. Not only has the opposing camp been strengthened in the interim, but the particular interests attracted by the reformulated arguments are likely to be either politically weak or of uncertain reliability.

The most promising tactic may be to shift from directly challenging existing institutions to finding ways to exploit and redirect the power of institutions to define interests. There are at least four broad strategies for engaging in such "institutional jujitsu." The particular actions that each of these strategies would entail are not new or radical within the metropolitan reform debate, but this particular way of conceptualizing the broad tactic is somewhat innovative and provides a unifying rationale to what have otherwise been presented as disjointed, incremental initiatives.

The first tactic involves using the authoritative power of higher levels of government to mandate or systematically encourage local reforms. The national and state governments have the capacity to address the problems associated with unchecked metropolitan sprawl. The states have the greater constitutional leverage and perhaps the greater direct incentive, leaving some prominent analysts like David Rusk (1993) convinced that they are the linchpins for any successful initiatives. States have the direct legal authority to restructure metropolitan government. Our national government lacks that authority, but it does have the capacity to create strong incentives for local governments to cooperate, and it has exploited that capacity at times to a greater extent than it does today (Henig, Brunori, and Ebert 1996). The problem at both levels has been political will. Suburban and rural coalitions are potent resisters at the state level. Savitch (chapter 6) chronicles both federal action and inaction, and shows that, sometimes unintentionally and sometimes with intention, the national government has weighed in as heavily on the side of sprawl as on the other end of the scale.

The "so-so" record of top-down efforts to impose metropolitanism does not mean that efforts along those lines should be abandoned. Indeed, the record may not be as weak as most accounts suggest. State and national government efforts to directly challenge jurisdictional fragmentation have been scattered and weak, but state and national efforts to address the equity *consequences* of metropolitan fragmentation and sprawl have been more impressive. These include such redistributory, compensatory, and countercyclical forms of intergovernmental grants as Community Development Block Grants, Empowerment Zones, and Title 1 of the Education and Elementary Education Act. Enacting and sustaining programs that narrow the revenue gap between city and suburb remain tough political battles to win, but they are more "winnable" when they do not directly challenge the existing institutional framework. And precisely because the exit option is more attenuated when the unit of effective governance is larger, states and the federal government *are* politically less constrained than local and metropolitan jurisdictions in undertaking redistributory initiatives (Peterson 1995).

A second form of institutional jujitsu involves using the authoritative power of the judicial system. The courts are institutionally designed to be less responsive to political tides, and as a result they are sometimes freer than elected leaders to challenge the structure of metropolitan governance. Probably the most direct judicial challenge to the existing arrangements has been the efforts by the New Jersey Supreme Court, through the Mount Laurel decisions and their aftermath, to open up the suburbs to their fair share of affordable housing. Charles Haar (1996), a fierce proponent of judicial leadership on this issue, believes that elected leaders, precisely because they are responsive to majoritarian sentiments, are incapable of tackling exclusionary zoning. He rejects the view that shared objective interests make the inner suburbs viable coalition partners for central-city interests. "Even if residents of suburban communities were aware of the true costs of exclusion, to themselves as well as to the residents of inner cities," he writes, "a collective action paradox prevents the formation of a coalition for effective remedies that could express itself through legislative or executive actions." His description of that paradox parallels, in key respects, the analysis presented in chapter 10. Haar writes:

> Since the public service costs of low-income housing are immediately felt in the locality, while its potential benefits—say, of availability of workers for the industries sought by those local governments—are not confined to the site, each locality has the incentive to wait for another to address the lack of affordable housing. Under the existing legal structure of local boundaries, no town can be certain that it can capture the benefits if it undertakes the expense; but it is clear that each one can benefit in the short term by shunting to its neighbor the obligation to house low-income populations (1996, 179).

In Haar's view, only a nonmajoritarian institution like the courts has the capacity to take the leadership in structurally addressing the equity dimensions of metropolitan sprawl.

Ultimately, of course, a court cannot outrun political sentiment forever. Courts depend upon the legislative and executive branches to implement their rulings; they also depend on them for their budgets and, often, their personnel. But courts *do* have institutional leverage. Just as local jurisdictions have gained power, authority, and a certain degree of political invulnerability over the years because they are broadly accepted and because the fortunes of various powerful interests are now intertwined with them, so it is the case with the courts. Moreover, the courts carry a legitimacy that enables them, on occasion, to serve as moral leaders in a way that leads other groups to reconceptualize their interests. The conservative leanings of the current U.S. Supreme Court make it an unlikely leader on the issue of metropolitan reform. However, in a number of areas (e.g., school finance and anti-tobacco lawsuits), the state courts are proving to be productive venues for groups that have failed to surmount hurdles in the conventional political battlefield. Proponents of metropolitan equity may want to take that into account.

A third tactic involves shifting authority over certain kinds of decisions to already existing units of government that operate on a metropolitan or state scale. This is the approach settled on by the National Academy of Science's Committee on Improving the Future of U.S. Cities through Improved Metropolitan Area Governance. Noting the political obstacles to direct challenges to metropolitan fragmentation, that group draws a useful distinction between restructuring *government* versus restructuring *governance.* Many of the goals of the metropolitan reformers can be met, they argue (Altshuler et al. 1999) without altering the existing system of "nested local governments," which is not only firmly entrenched, but which also offers many advantages that metropolitan reformers sometimes overlook. If new metropolitan entities are not likely to emerge, "then we find most appropriate the use and expansion of existing metropolitan forums and agencies, such as councils of governments, metropolitan planning organizations, regional special-purpose authorities, and public-private alliances on the metropolitan level" (129). As with the national government, states, and courts, these units have the considerable advantages of already existing, of controlling resources, and of having established constituencies and allies. And, as with those other units, there is a prospect that the institutional platform can become a node for gradually aggregating a more potent coalition. "It is possible that, over time, one or more of these will organically emerge into an institution that has the ability to make decisions for the entire region in several functional areas" (Altshuler et al. 1999, 129).

Finally, a fourth strategy involves "seeding" the ideas and interests of metropolitanism by opportunistically creating new institutions that initially have minor consequences, and are therefore politically unobjectionable, but which are designed to develop into more substantial enterprises over time. The histories of those cases in which new metropolitan units *have* successfully been launched are revealing in several respects. First, the initiation often has depended on a certain alignment of political stars, what Kingdon (1995) refers to as an "open window of opportunity." Metropolitanism fares best under historically contingent conditions: when regions are younger and growing, when the economy is strong, and when state and local politics leave room for entrepreneurs to build coalitions across party lines. Second, when funding is linked to sources that expand with population and economic growth (e.g., incremental property tax revenues, and mass transit fares and tolls), the resistance by existing jurisdictions may be lessened, while the long-term funding potential might be great. Third, it is easier to establish single-issue special districts than multipurpose entities (Burns 1994). This is partly because the process is less visible, but also because some multijurisdictional functions (e.g., transit, sports authorities, and parks and planning) can be highly popular with either or both the general public and business interests.

Gradually expanding the number of government units that subsume multiple jurisdictions may be a double-edged sword. Pursued willy-nilly, it has the potential to aggravate fragmentation and make the existing jurisdictional enterprises even more bewildering. But special districts, even when they focus on a single issue or service, do have the effect of objectively altering the extent to which citizens' direct material interests are aligned with local municipal boundaries. Regional financing for regional services can be structured so that local jurisdictions genuinely receive some benefit from economic growth within their neighbors' boundary. The key here is that the change is objective and material and does not rely upon appeals to some abstract and disembodied idea of regional identity. Even this is not likely to erase the sense of competition over growth, but it can attenuate it to some degree. Over the long run, loyalties to parochial jurisdictions may be tamed a bit as citizens slowly come to see regional institutions as important to their quality of life.

First-wave metropolitan reformers were politically naïve and overly optimistic. Second-wave reformers seem to have a politically more sophisticated approach. In their eagerness to convince others that their vision is feasible, though, they sometimes get diverted down the path of optimistic pronouncements, even when they realize that the obstacles are severe. But a "can do" spirit is more effective as a spark for mobilization than as a fuel for sustained momentum. The combination of entrenched institutions and a well-developed rationale for their sustenance means that metropolitan reformers should anticipate the need for a long assault, and plan their political tactics accordingly. An appreciation of the capacity of institutions to shape interests makes the prospects for broad reform initially bleaker, but it also provides the inkling of an institutionally augmented strategy for reform.

## NOTES

The author wishes to acknowledge the helpful commentary that Greg Squires and Hal Wolman provided in response to an earlier draft.

1. Greer, in 1962, noted that recommendations for metropolitan government at that time were "by no means new ideas" (1962, 121) and traced academic concern back at least to McKenzie (1933). Wood (1958, 79) notes that "in the 1940s and 1950s, a whole series of proposals blossomed forth" to tame suburban fragmentation, and that "finding 'solutions' to the metropolitan problem took on aspects of an academic crusade" (80).

2. For a fuller and more up-to-date review of the empirical literature dealing with the question of the optimal jurisdictional size, see Dowding, John, and Biggs (1994) and Altshuler et al. (1999, 65–66).

3. Bish and Ostrom (1973, 22) excused their decision to put aside equity issues by noting that the "criterion of fairness or equity is difficult to formulate in a way that can be used to measure comparative performance." Others (e.g., Rich 1977) worried about this, and sought to address the matter by presuming that a market-oriented competition among multiple jurisdictions could be coupled with a much more aggressive redistributory taxing and financing regime by states and the federal government. Miller (1981) highlights inequity as the major Achilles' heel of the Lakewood Plan.

## REFERENCES

Adrian, Charles R. 1961. "Metropology: Folklore and Field Research." *Public Administration Review* 21 (2, Summer): 148–53.

———. 1967. "Public Attitudes and Metropolitan Decision Making." In *Politics in the Metropolis*, edited by Thomas R. Dye and Brett W. Hawkins (454–71). Columbus, Ohio: Charles E. Merrill Publishing.

Altshuler, Alan, William Morrill, Harold Wolman, and Faith Mitchell, eds. 1999. Committee on Improving the Future of U.S. Cities through Improved Metropolitan Area Governance. *Governance and Opportunity in Metropolitan America.* Washington, D.C.: National Academy Press.

Baumgartner, Frank R., and Bryan D. Jones. 1993. *Agendas and Instability in American Politics.* Chicago: University of Chicago Press.

Bish, Robert L., and Vincent Ostrom. 1973. *Understanding Urban Government: Metropolitan Reform Reconsidered.* Washington, D.C.: American Enterprise Institute.

Buchanan, James M., and Gordon Tullock. 1962. *The Calculus of Consent.* Ann Arbor: University of Michigan Press.

Burns, Nancy. 1994. *The Formation of American Local Governments: Private Values in Public Institutions.* New York: Oxford University Press.

Dowding, Keith, Peter John, and Stephen Biggs. 1994. "Tiebout: A Survey of the Empirical Literature." *Urban Studies* 31 (4/5): 767–97.

Downs, Anthony. 1994. *New Visions for Metropolitan America.* Washington, D.C.: Brookings Institution.

Dunlap, Riley E., and Angela G. Mertig. 1992. *American Environmentalism: The U.S. Environmental Movement, 1970–1990.* New York: Taylor and Francis.

Frieden, Bernard J. 1979. *The Environmental Protection Hustle.* Cambridge, Mass.: MIT Press.

Friedman, Milton. 1962. *Capitalism and Freedom.* Chicago: University of Chicago Press.

Greer, Scott. 1962. *Governing the Metropolis.* New York: John Wiley and Sons, Inc.

Haar, Charles M. 1996. *Suburbs under Siege: Race, Space, and Audacious Judges.* Princeton, N.J.: Princeton University Press.

Harrigan, John H., and Ronald K. Vogel. 2000. *Political Change in the Metropolis,* 6th ed. New York: Longman.

Henig, Jeffrey, David Brunori, and Mark Ebert. 1996. "Washington, D.C.: Cautious and Constrained Cooperation." In *Regional Politics: America in a Post-City Age,* edited by H. V. Savitch and Ronald K. Vogel (101–29). Thousand Oaks, Calif.: Sage Publications.

Hirschman, Albert O. 1970. *Exit Voice and Loyalty: Responses to Decline in Firms, Organizations, and States.* Cambridge, Mass.: Harvard University Press.

Keating, Michael. 1995. "Size, Efficiency and Democracy: Consolidation, Fragmentation and Public Choice." In *Theories of Urban Politics,* edited by David Judge, Gerry Stoker, and Harold Wolman (117–34). Thousand Oaks, Calif.: Sage Publications.

Kingdon, John W. 1995. *Agendas, Alternatives and Public Policies,* 2nd ed. Boston: Addison-Wesley.

Ledebur, Larry C., and William R. Barnes. 1993. *"All In It Together": Cities, Suburbs, and Local Economic Regions.* Washington, D.C.: National League of Cities.

March, James G., and Johan P. Olsen. 1989. *Rediscovering Institutions: The Organizational Basis of Politics.* New York: The Free Press.

Massey, Douglas S., and Nancy A. Denton. 1993. *American Apartheid: Segregation and the Making of the Underclass.* Cambridge, Mass.: Harvard University Press.

McKenzie, Roderick D. 1933. "The Rise of Metropolitan Communities." In *Recent Social Trends in the United States,* edited by President's Research Committee on Social Trends. New York: McGraw-Hill.

Miller, Gary J. 1981. *Cities by Contract: The Politics of Municipal Incorporation.* Cambridge, Mass.: MIT Press.

Orfield, Myron. 1997. *Metropolitics: A Regional Agenda for Community and Stability.* Washington, D.C.: Brookings Institution.

Ostrom, Elinor, and Roger B. Parks. 1973. "Suburban Police Departments: Too Many and Too Small?" In *The Urbanization of the Suburbs: Urban Affairs Annual Reviews,* vol. 7, edited by Louis H. Masotti and Jeffrey K. Hadden (367–402). Beverly Hills, Calif.: Sage Publications.

Peterson, Paul E. 1981. *City Limits.* Chicago: University of Chicago Press.

———. 1995. *The Price of Federalism.* Washington, D.C.: Brookings Institution.

Rich, Richard C. 1977. "Equity and Institutional Design in Urban Service Delivery." *Urban Affairs Quarterly* 12 (March): 383–410.

Rusk, David. 1993. *Cities without Suburbs.* Washington, D.C.: Woodrow Wilson Center Press.

Savitch, H. V., David Collins, Daniel Sanders, and John P. Markham. 1993. "Ties That Bind: Central Cities, Suburbs, and the New Metropolitan Region." *Economic Development Quarterly* 7 (4): 341–57.

Savitch, H. V., and Ronald K. Vogel. 1996. "Introduction: Regional Patterns in a Post-City Era," in *Regional Politics: America in a Post-City Age,* edited by H. V. Savitch and Ronald K. Vogel (1–24). Thousand Oaks, Calif.: Sage Publications.

Schattschneider, Elmer E. 1960. *The Semi-Sovereign People.* New York: Holt, Rinehart and Winston.

Stigler, George J. 1962. "The Tenable Range of Functions of Local Government." In *Private Wants and Public Needs,* edited by Edmund S. Phelps. New York: W. W. Norton.

Tiebout, Charles. 1956. "A Pure Theory of Local Expenditures." *Journal of Political Economy* 64 (5): 416–24.

Wood, Robert C. 1958. *Suburbia: Its People and Their Politics.* Boston: Houghton Mifflin.

# About the Editor

**Gregory D. Squires** is a professor and chair of the Department of Sociology at George Washington University. Currently he is a member of the board of directors of the Woodstock Institute and the advisory board of the John Marshall Law School Fair Housing Legal Support Center in Chicago. He has served as a consultant and expert witness for fair housing groups and civil rights organizations around the country and as a member of the Consumer Advisory Council of the Federal Reserve Board. Dr. Squires has written for several academic journals and general interest publications, including *Social Science Quarterly, Urban Affairs Review*, the *Journal of Urban Affairs*, the *New York Times*, and the *Washington Post*. His recent books include *Capital and Communities in Black and White* (State University of New York Press, 1994), *Insurance Redlining* (Urban Institute Press, 1997), and (with Sally O'Connor) *Color and Money* (State University of New York Press, 2001).

# About the Contributors

**Carl Abbott** is a professor of urban studies and planning at Portland State University. He is the author of a number of books on the development of American cities, including *The Metropolitan Frontier: Cities in the Modern American West* (University of Arizona Press, 1993), *Political Terrain: Washington, D.C., from Tidewater Town to Global Metropolis* (University of North Carolina Press, 1999), and *Greater Portland: Urban Life and Landscape in the Pacific Northwest* (University of Pennsylvania Press, 2001).

**David J. Cieslewicz** is cofounder and has served as executive director of 1000 Friends of Wisconsin since the organization's inception in 1997. He has worked as the government relations director for the Wisconsin chapter of The Nature Conservancy, staffed the Wisconsin Assembly Natural Resources Committee, served on the board of directors of Wisconsin's Environmental Decade (the state's largest environmental group), and served two terms on the Dane County Board of Supervisors, where he specialized in environmental and land use issues.

**James R. Cohen** is currently director of graduate studies in the Urban Studies and Planning Program at the University of Maryland. He conducts research and teaches in the areas of growth management and land use planning.

ABOUT THE CONTRIBUTORS

**Amy Helling** is an associate professor in the Department of Public Administration and Urban Studies at Georgia State University's Andrew Young School of Policy Studies. Before joining the Georgia State faculty, she practiced planning in both the public and private sectors for 16 years. Her research interests include the role of planning and policy in the spatial and economic development of metropolitan regions, public infrastructure planning and policy, and public involvement in planning and policy-making processes. Dr. Helling has also studied women's and children's travel, accessibility's effect on travel and urban form, and the consequences of work-related telecommunication for personal travel and location. Her articles have been published in numerous journals, and she serves on the editorial board of *Economic Development Quarterly*.

**Jeffrey R. Henig** is a professor and chair of the Department of Political Science and director of the Center for Washington Area Studies at George Washington University. His research over the years has focused on the boundary between private action and public action in addressing social problems. He is the author or coauthor of six books, including *Public Policy and Federalism* (St. Martin's Press, 1985) and *The Color of School Reform: Race, Politics and the Challenge of Urban Education* (Princeton University Press, 1999), which the Urban Politics Section of the American Political Science Association named the best book written on urban politics in 1999.

**Charles Jaret** is a professor in the Department of Sociology at Georgia State University. His research interests include urban sociology, race and ethnic relations, and immigration, with particular focus on urban growth and sprawl, racial income equality, racial-ethnic identity, and attitudes toward immigrants. Among his recent publications are *Contemporary Racial and Ethnic Relations* (HarperCollins, 1995) and "Troubled by Newcomers: Anti-Immigrant Attitudes and Actions during Two Eras of Mass Immigration to the United States" (*Journal of American Ethnic History*, 1999).

**Paul A. Jargowsky** is associate professor of political economy at the University of Texas at Dallas. His current areas of research include racial and economic segregation, the impacts of economic and spatial inequality, and the causes and consequences of exclusionary suburban development patterns. He has been involved in policy development at both the state and federal levels and has served as a consultant and expert witness in fair housing and school desegregation litigation. Dr. Jargowsky was a visiting scholar at the U.S. Department of Health and Human Services in 1993, where he helped design the simulation model used for welfare reform planning. In 1986, he was the project director for the New York State Task Force on Poverty and Welfare Reform. His book, *Poverty and Place: Ghettos, Barrios, and the American City* (Russell Sage Foundation, 1997), was named the "Best Book in Urban Affairs Published in 1997 or 1998" by the Urban Affairs Association.

**Myron Orfield** teaches at the University of Minnesota Law School and was elected to the Minnesota House of Representatives in 1990. He is the author of *Metropolitics: A Regional Agenda for Community and Stability* (Brookings Institution and Lincoln Institute of Land Policy, 1997).

**Joseph Persky** is professor of economics at the University of Illinois at Chicago. He is coauthor (with Wim Wiewel) of the recent book *When Corporations Leave Town: The Costs and Benefits of Metropolitan Job Sprawl* (Wayne State University Press, 2000).

**john powell** is the founder and executive director of the Institute on Race and Poverty, established in 1993. He is also professor of law at the University of Minnesota Law School, and was formerly the national legal director for the American Civil Liberties Union. He has written extensively on the intersections of race and poverty and how they affect U.S. society. Professor powell speaks throughout the country on related issues, including the benefits of regionalism, urban problems associated with sprawl, the negative effects of concentrated poverty, and issues associated with welfare reform.

**H. V. Savitch** is professor of urban and public affairs and director of the MPA program at the University of Louisville. His articles have appeared in numerous journals, and he has authored three books on various aspects of urban affairs, including decentralization, regionalism, national urban policy, and comparative urban development. His book *Post Industrial Cities* (Princeton University Press, 1989) was nominated for the best volume on urban politics by the American Political Science Association. In addition, he was coeditor of *Big Cities in Transition* (Sage Publications, 1991), *Regional Politics* (Sage, 1996), *Urban Democracy* (Leske and Budrich, 2000), and *Globalization and Local Democracy* (Palgrave, 2002). Dr. Savitch is currently working on a book dealing with how cities cope with industrial change and formulate economic strategies. He previously worked for David Dinkins, former mayor of New York City, and served as a consultant to the U.S. Mayors' Urban Summit.

**Kimberly Schaffer** is a candidate for the master's degree in urban planning and policy at the University of Illinois at Chicago. She collaborated with Wim Wiewel and Joseph Persky on the "Chicago Metropolitan Case Study," an analysis for the Brookings Institution of the effect of state and federal policies on regional sprawl.

**Wim Wiewel** is dean of the College of Business Administration at the University of Illinois at Chicago, and professor of urban planning and policy and of managerial studies. Previously he served as dean of the university's College of Urban Planning and Public Affairs. His recent publications include *Regional Interdependencies* (Lincoln Institute of Land Policy, 2000), with Rosaline Greenstein; *When Corporations Leave Town: The Costs and Benefits of Metropolitan Job Sprawl* (Wayne State University Press, 2000), with Joseph Persky; and *Sprawl, Chicago-Style: The Role of Public Programs and Policies* (E. M. Sharpe, 2002), with Joseph Persky.

# Index

358    INDEX